ISBN 978-0-282-38249-0
PIBN 10849020

1 MONTH OF
FREE
READING

at
www.ForgottenBooks.com

By purchasing this book you are eligible for one month membership to ForgottenBooks.com, giving you unlimited access to our entire collection of over 1,000,000 titles via our web site and mobile apps.

To claim your free month visit:
www.forgottenbooks.com/free849020

English
Français
Deutsche
Italiano
Español
Português

www.forgottenbooks.com

Mythology Photography **Fiction**
Fishing Christianity **Art** Cooking
Essays Buddhism Freemasonry
Medicine **Biology** Music **Ancient
Egypt** Evolution Carpentry Physics
Dance Geology **Mathematics** Fitness
Shakespeare **Folklore** Yoga Marketing
Confidence Immortality Biographies
Poetry **Psychology** Witchcraft
Electronics Chemistry History **Law**
Accounting **Philosophy** Anthropology
Alchemy Drama Quantum Mechanics
Atheism Sexual Health **Ancient History**
Entrepreneurship Languages Sport
Paleontology Needlework Islam
Metaphysics Investment Archaeology
Parenting Statistics Criminology
Motivational

Harper's Stereotype Edition.

VIEW

OF

ANCIENT AND MODERN

EGYPT;

WITH

AN OUTLINE OF ITS NATURAL HISTORY

BY THE
REV. MICHAEL RUSSELL, LL.D bp. of Glas
& Galloway

WITH A MAP AND ENGRAVINGS.

NEW-YORK:

PUBLISHED BY HARPER & BROTHERS,

NO. 82 CLIFF-STREET.

1842.

ADVERTISEMENT

THE American publishers of this volume, while they acknowledge the general accuracy of the author's statements, and the clearness and interest ing nature of the information he has laboriously collected from so many sources, feel themselves obliged to enter their protest against the disparaging and, in their opinion, unjust remarks with which it is interspersed, reflecting upon the scientific Frenchmen who accompanied Napoleon's expedition to Egypt: the reverend author has not, in their judgment, done justice either to the efforts of those gentlemen, or to their success. It may be true that much was not accomplished which might have been expected from the magnitude and completeness of their preparations and appointments; but it is to be remembered that their time to investigate and explore was too often lamentably abridged, by the necessity under which they laboured of accompanying the rapid movements of the army: and no unprejudiced man will or can deny that the results of their exertions were highly important, and very honourable to themselves, when fairly estimated with a reasonable consideration for the difficulties and embarrassments with which they had to contend.

NEW-YORK, *August*, 1831.

414220

PREFACE.

THE object of this volume is to present to the reader, in a condensed form, an account of all that is known respecting Egypt, both in its ancient and in its modern state. The history alone of such a country could not fail to be highly interesting to every one who has any curiosity to mark the progress of the human race in civilization and learning, and more especially the beginnings of society at that earliest period to which the writings of uninspired annalists carry back the mind of the contemplative student. It has indeed been our main endeavour to represent the genius and astonishing acquirements of the old Egyptians through the medium of the great works of architecture, statuary, and sculpture, which are still to-be found on the banks of the Nile. In this part of our undertaking we have spared no pains to illustrate the descriptions of the Grecian, Roman, and Arabian historians, by a reference to the actual condition of that singular country in our own times ; attempting by these means to supply to the reader of Herodotus, Diodorus Siculus, Strabo, Pliny, and Abdolatiph, a light reflected from the ruins of those splendid monuments which they were the first to make known to the great body of their less-informed contemporaries.

However dark may be the cloud which still hangs over the more ancient portion of Egyptian history, it is much less obscure than it was thirty years ago. The united exertions of travellers abroad, and of learned men at home, since the beginning of the present century, have contributed not a little towards removing the perplexity which was wont to beset the historian and chronologer at the very threshold of their inquiries. The labours of Dr. Young and of M. Champollion have opened up a path by which, there is great reason to hope, the research of modern authors will be enabled to penetrate into those remote ages which preceded the Persian conquest, and which it has too long been the fashion to consign to mysticism and fable. Without permitting ourselves to yield to an undue confidence in regard to the discoveries which are said to have been made since the comparatively recent period when the language of hieroglyphics was supplied with a key, we may nevertheless cherish the expectation that the light which has been already thrown on the dynasties of the ancient kings of Egypt will increase hereafter into a much greater degree of brightness. It was not the least pleasant part of our task to trace the steps of that arduous investigation which finally led to the knowledge of Phonetic hieroglyphics: one of the most valuable additions made to literature in modern times.

The reader will find that we have not neglected any source of information in respect to the learning and science of the Egyptians, and more especially as these are in any way connected with the mechanical labours, the arts, or the political government which distinguished the first ages of their history. It was our intention to have included an account of Nubia and Abyssinia in the narrative now submitted to the public; but we soon discovered that the interesting notices which are daily reaching this kingdom relative to the improvements introduced by Mohammed Ali, the present viceroy of Egypt, and the important changes which he still appears to meditate, would necessarily prevent the accomplishment of so extended a plan. Hence it has been determined to reserve a full and methodical description of those vast countries for a future volume of the Library.

In collecting materials for the history of modern Egypt, we placed the greatest reliance on the works of such writers as had lived some time in the country, and had thereby an opportunity not only of marking the progress of events under the extraordinary man who for more than twenty years has directed the government, but also of comparing the actual condition of the inhabitants with the oppression and barbarism from which they have gradually emerged. In this point of view the successive communications of Mr. Salt are extremely valuable; as are also several notices which have been received in this country through the medium of France. Among these last a distinguished place is due to the "Histoire de la Régénération de l'Egypte," written in the form of letters by Jules Planat, a staff-officer in the service of the pasha.

The reader may be surprised, that in describing the manners and customs of the modern Egyptians, we have not taken any notice of a volume by the late Mr. Burckhardt on this very subject. Suffice

it to observe that the work in question is simply a
collection of Arabic proverbs, which illustrate the
sentiments of the people rather than their customs
or manners, and was therefore altogether unsuitable
for the purpose which we had in view.

It is not necessary to remark that the chapter on
Natural History is meant entirely for popular use,
and has no claims to scientific precision either in
the description or arrangement. Besides, as the
sixteenth volume of this Library contains a full
view of the Geology and Animal Kingdom of Africa, contributed by two able writers, we have in-
tentionally limited our survey to such objects as
are peculiar to the Egyptian valley and to the
rocky barrier by which it is bounded.

EDINBURGH, *April,* 1830.

CONTENTS.

B

CHAPTER IV.

MECHANICAL LABOURS OF THE ANCIENT EGYPTIANS.

CHAPTER V.

THE LITERATURE AND SCIENCE OF THE ANCIENT EGYPTIANS.

CHAPTER VI.

REMAINS OF ANCIENT ART IN VARIOUS PARTS OF EGYPT.

CHAPTER VII.

THE CIVIL HISTORY OF MODERN EGYPT.

CHAPTER VIII.

THE ACTUAL STATE OF EGYPT UNDER THE GOVERNMENT OF MOHAMMED ALI.

CHAPTER IX.

THE OASES, ANCIENT BERENICE, AND DESERT OF THE THEBAID.

CHAPTER X.

MANNERS AND CUSTOMS OF THE EGYPTIANS.

CHAPTER XI.

THE NATURAL HISTORY OF EGYPT.

ENGRAVINGS.

A VIEW

OF

ANCIENT AND MODERN EGYPT, &c

CHAPTER I.

Introduction.

Importance of Egyptian Antiquities—Egypt an old Country in the Infant Age of Greece—Thebes famous in the Days of Homer—Learning and Science of Europe derived from Egypt through Phenicia and Greece—Inquiry into the Source of Egyptian Learning and Civilization—The early Improvement of Nubia and Abyssinia—Resemblance between the Religion, the Symbols, and Architecture of India and of Egypt—Anecdote of the Sepoys in the British Army—Remarks on the Temples in both Countries—A similar Resemblance between the Egyptians and Chinese—All primitive Tribes derived their Knowledge from the same Source—Institution of Castes in Egypt and India—Statements of Herodotus and Diodorus on that Subject—Probability that Civilization and the Arts descended the Nile—Contrast between their advanced Knowledge and their debased Worship—Reflection on the Importance attached to the durable Nature of Architectural Monuments.

In many respects Egypt has long appeared to the scholar, the antiquary, and the philosopher the most interesting country on the face of the earth. Relatively to the various tribes who, at successive eras, have founded states westward of the Black Sea and the Syrian Desert, it has been universally regarded as the cradle of science, as well as the first seat of regular government; and hence we find that even the polished nations of modern Europe are accustomed to ascribe the rudiments of their literature and arts to the ingenious people who, at a period beyond the records of civil history, occupied the banks of the Nile.

B 2

It is, no doubt, extremely difficult to construct, out of the scanty materials which have reached our times, a chain of narrative so complete and satisfactory as to connect, without the absence of some essential links, the present with the past, and to enable us to derive an explanation of what we see from a competent knowledge of what we are told has been. Between the immediate successors of Menes, twenty centuries before the Christian era, and the delegated rule which now directs the affairs of Egypt, there is a wide gulf, through which neither the boldest archæologist has yet been able to establish a path, nor the eye of history to direct its vision. It requires even a great effort of imagination to combine the ideas of that magnificence and power which must have distinguished the epoch when Thebes was built, and the splendid monuments of her kings were erected, with the facts which meet the view of the traveller in our own days, amid the desolations of Karnac and the ruins of Luxor.

The land of the Pharaohs, in truth, was an old country in the infant age of Greece. The earliest writers of Europe described its grandeur as having already reached its consummation, and even as beginning to pass away; while the philosophers and historians who crossed the Mediterranean in search of knowledge were astonished at the proofs of an antiquity which surpassed all their notions of recorded time, and at the tokens of a wisdom, genius, and opulence of which they could hardly hope that their countrymen would believe the description. In the days of Homer the capital of the Thebaid, with its hundred gates and its vast population, was a subject of wonder and of the most exalted panegyric,—an effect which we should at once attribute to the exaggeration of the poet, were it not that the remains which, even after the lapse of three thousand years, continue to resist the injuries of the atmosphere and of barbarism, bear evidence to a still greater magnificence than is recorded in the pages of the Odyssey. While the nations which at present make the greatest figure in the world, and influence most deeply the condition of human nature, had not yet passed through the first stage of social life, the inhabitants of Thebes and of Memphis had made a vast progress in civilization, and were even found gratifying a learned curiosity by inquiries into the constitution of the universe, and into the laws which regulate the movements of the heavenly bodies. Nor was it only the learning and mythological doctrines which characterized the brightest periods of Greece and Rome that were borrowed from the Egyptians. On the contrary, we can trace to the same source those more valuable sciences which exercised the talents of the most ancient and renowned among European sages. Pythagoras submitted to study the elements of mathematics in the schools of the priests; while Hecatæus and Herodotus collected the materials of history among the same class of men, who had carefully preserved the knowledge of former generations.

The Greeks, it has been frequently remarked, were the only nation in Europe who had any pretensions to antiquity. But the wisest even among that ambitious people considered themselves as of yesterday compared to the Egyptians. Plato confessed that his countrymen had no memorial of any event beyond a thousand, or at most two thousand years before his own time ; whereas, in the days of Moses, the wisdom of Egypt had already become proverbial, and that, too, among the Syrian tribes who bordered upon the original seats of primeval knowledge. Phenicia, which appears to have set the first example of commercial intercourse to the rude colonies on the northern shores of the great sea, proved the medium through which the learning, the laws, and the religion of the Nile were conveyed to the ancestors of those brave and ingenious nations who have since associated an imperishable fame with the memory of Athens and Lacedemon. The names of Cadmus, Cecrops, and Danaus continue to represent those missions or voluntary migrations which, at a remote period, transported from Africa to Europe the treasures of oriental wisdom.

It has long been an object of inquiry among scholars to discover the channel through which civilization, science, and an acquaintance with the liberal arts first reached the valley which is watered by the Nile. Without analyzing the numerous hypotheses which have been successively formed and abandoned, or repeating the various conjectures which have, age after age, amused the ingenuity of the learned, we shall state, at once, as the most probable of the opinions that have been entertained on this subject, that the stream of knowledge accompanied the progress of commerce along

he banks of those great rivers which fall into the Persian
Gulf, and thence along the coast of Arabia to the shores of
the Red Sea.   There is the best reason to believe that those
passes or lateral defiles which connect the sea just named
with the river of Egypt witnessed the earliest migration of
colonists from Asia ; who, in the pursuits of commerce, or
in search of more fertile lands, or of mountains enriched
with gold, found their way into Nubia and Abyssinia.
Meantime, it is probable, a similar current set eastward
across the mouths of the Indus, carrying arts and institu
tions of a corresponding character into the countries which
stretch from that river to the great peninsula of Hindoostan.

The most obvious confirmation of the opinion now stated
may be drawn from the striking resemblance which is known
to subsist between the usages, the superstitions, the arts,
and the mythology. of the ancient inhabitants of Western
India, and those of the first settlers on the Upper Nile.
The temples of Nubia, for example, exhibit the same features, whether as to the style of architecture or the form of
worship which must have been practised in them, with the
similar buildings which have been recently examined in the
neighbourhood of Bombay.   In both cases they consist of
vast excavations hewn out in the solid body of a hill or
mountain, and are decorated with huge figures which indicate the same powers of nature, or serve as emblems to
denote the same qualities in the ruling spirits of the universe.

As a further proof of this hypothesis, we are informed
that the sepoys who joined the British army in Egypt
under Lord Hutchinson imagined that they found their own
temples in the ruins of Dendera, and were greatly exaspe-
rated at the natives for their neglect of the ancient deities,
whose images are still preserved.   So strongly, indeed,
were they themselves impressed with this identity, that
they proceeded to perform their devotions with all the ceremonies practised in their own land.   There is a resemblance, too, in the minor instruments of their superstition,
—the lotus, the lingam, and the serpent,—which can hardly
be regarded as accidental ; but it is, no doubt, in the immense extent, the gigantic plan, the vast conception which
appear in all their sacred buildings, that we most readily
discover the influence of the same lofty genius, and the en

deavour to accomplish the same mighty object. The excavated temple of Guerfeh Hassan, for instance, reminds every traveller of the cave of Elephanta. The resemblance, indeed, is singularly striking; as are, in fact, all the leading principles of Egyptian architecture to that of the Hindoos. They differ only, it has been observed, in those details of the decorative parts, which trifling points of difference in their religious creeds seem to have suggested to each; but many even of the rites and emblems are precisely the same, especially those of the temples dedicated to Iswara, the Indian Bacchus. In truth, in most respects they are so much alike that the same workman might almost be supposed to have superintended the execution of them in both countries. In India and in Egypt the hardest granite mountains have been cut down into the most striking, if not the most beautiful, fronts of temples adorned with sculpture. In both countries large masses of rock have been excavated into hollow chambers, whose sides are decorated with columns and statues of men and animals carved out of the same stone; and in each are found solid blocks of many hundred tons weight, separated from the adjoining mountain and lifted up into the air. By whom and by what means these wonderful efforts have been accomplished is a mystery sunk too deep in the abyss of time ever to be revealed. To Greece neither country is indebted for any part of its architecture, while she has evidently taken many hints from them. Except at Alexandria and Antinoë, no edifice strictly Grecian appears in Egypt. But we need only compare the monolithic temples of Nubia with those of Mahabulipoor, the excavations of Guerfeh Hassan with those of Elephanta, and the grottoes of Hadjur Silsili, as described by Pococke, with the caverns of Ellora, to be convinced that these sacred monuments of ancient days derived their origin from the same source.[*]

A resemblance of a corresponding nature has been discovered in the religious usages of the Chinese, compared with those of the Egyptians, particularly in what is called the feast of lamps,—a festival annually observed by the latter people, and graphically described by Herodotus in his

[*] See Legh's Journey in Egypt and Nubia, and Quarterly Review, vol xvi. p. 18

second book. This coincidence in a ceremony so little likely to suggest itself to the minds of men who had no intercourse with one another, led M. de Guignes to conclude that the first inhabitants of China must have been a colony from Egypt. But it is easy to account for all such facts upon a much more obvious as well as a more rational hypothesis. No one can have failed to remark, that among the most ancient nations there is a great similarity in point of tradition, habits, opinions, knowledge, and history. The Babylonians, the Egyptians, the Assyrians, the Hindoos, and the descendants of Abraham held many things in common respecting the creation of the world, the great deluge, the dispersion of the human race, and the first institution of laws and religious worship. Hence we may conclude that the general agreement in these particulars, which we contemplate among the more primitive tribes of mankind, ought to be ascribed to the instruction which they had received while as yet they were but one family, or to the traditionary tenets which had spread with the diverging lines of their generations, though derived originally from the same primeval source.

But by far the most striking point of resemblance between the inhabitants of Egypt and of India is the institution of castes,—that singular arrangement which places an insuperable barrier between different orders of men in the same country, and renders their respective honours, toils, and degradation strictly hereditary and permanent. Before the invention of letters, indeed, mankind may be said to have been perpetually in their infancy; whence arose the expedient, founded in a view of the public good, of compelling sons to cultivate the arts which had originated in their family, and to follow the professions whereby their fathers had acquired distinction. In allusion to the four classes into which the natives are divided, the Hindoos maintain that, of their god, Nara-Yana, the mouth became a priest, he arm was made a soldier, the thigh was transformed into a husbandman, and from his feet sprang the servile multitude. The narrative of Herodotus bears evidence to the same institution at an early period among the Egyptians. He indeed divides the fourth caste into several subordinate sections,—tradesmen, shepherds, interpreters, and pilots, and thereby presents the appearance of a still more minute distinction than prevails in the East; but his statement, when compared with that of Diodorus Siculus at a later epoch, removes every shadow of doubt in regard to the identity of the principle from which this political arrangement must have originally proceeded. The last-named historian reduces the orders to three,—priests, including men of rank; the military; and artisans. It is obvious, however, that as husbandmen and labourers are omitted, we must comprehend in the third grade all the classes who practise those arts which are necessary to the subsistence, the comfort, and the ornament of human life.

We may also mention, as in some degree connected with the division of labour now described, that medical science, even before the days of Herodotus, must have been very carefully studied, if we may draw such a conclusion from the fact that, at the period when he wrote, one physician was confined to one disease. There are, he adds, a great many who practise this art; some attend to disorders of the eyes, others to those of the head; some take care of the teeth, others are conversant with all diseases of the intestines; while many attend to the cure of maladies which are less conspicuous.* The historian could not have mentioned a circumstance more characteristic of a people advanced to a high degree of civilization. Of the Babylonians, among whom he also travelled, he relates that they have no professors of medicine, but that they carry their sick into some public square, with the view of getting advice from any one who may happen to have been afflicted with the same illness. The passengers in general, says he, interrogate the sufferer in regard to the nature of his malady, in order that, if any one of them has been attacked with a similar disease himself, or seen its operation on a third person, he may communicate the process by which his own recovery was effected, or by which, in any other instance, he has known the distemper to be removed. No one may pass by a diseased individual in silence, or without inquiry into the symptoms of his complaint.†

But, to return to the main subject now before us, we may take leave to express our conviction that, in proportion as the antiquities of Egypt shall be brought into a clearer

* Herodotus, Euterpe, chap. 84. † Ib. Clio, chap. 197.

light, the evidence will become more satisfactory in favour of an early intercourse between Hindoostan and the upper regions of the Nile. It is already ascertained that the arts, as practised in the Thebaid, and even in the neighbourhood of Memphis, must have descended from Ethiopia,—the style of sculpture in the latter being in several respects superior to any specimen of that kind of workmanship hitherto discovered in Egypt. The temples, too, on the banks of the river above the cataracts bear a closer resemblance to those of India than the corresponding edifices in the lower parts of the country, while they exhibit the undoubted marks of a more remote antiquity. The same conclusion is further supported by the celebrity which the Ethiopians had acquired in the earliest age that tradition or poetry has revealed to us. The annals of the Egyptian priests were full of them. The nations of Asia, in like manner, on the Tigris and Euphrates, mingled Ethiopian legends with the songs which commemorated the exploits of their own heroes. At a time, too, when the Greeks scarcely knew Italy or Sicily by name, the virtues, the civilization, and the mythology of the Ethiopians supplied to their poets a subject of lofty description. Homer, both in the Iliad and Odyssey, relates that Jupiter, at a certain season of the year, departed from his chosen seat on Olympus to visit this remote and accomplished people. For twelve days the god was absent in their pious and hospitable region. It is probable that some annual procession of the priests of Ammon up the Nile, to the primitive scene of their worship, was the groundwork of this legend adopted into the popular creed of the older Greeks. Diodorus himself expresses a similar opinion, when he states that the Ethiopians were said to be the inventors of pomps, sacrifices, solemn assemblies, and other honours paid to the gods; that is, that they were the religious parents of the Egyptians, to whom the countrymen of Homer and Hesiod looked up as to their instructers in sacred things as well as in the principles of civil polity. It has therefore been thought probable that ancient Meroe was the original seat of the religion, the political institutions, the arts, and the letters, which afterward shed so bright a lustre on the kingdom of the Pharaohs.*

* Heeren's Ideas on the Politics and Commerce of Ancient Nations.

There is nothing more remarkable in the history of Egypt than that the same people who distinguished themselves by an early progress in civilization, and who erected works which have survived the conquests of Persia, the triumphs of Roman art, and all the architectural labours of Christianity, should have degraded their fine genius by the worship of four-footed beasts, and even of disgusting reptiles. The world does not present a more humbling contrast between the natural powers of intellect and the debasing effect of superstition. Among the Jews, on the other hand,—a people much less elevated by science and mechanical knowledge,—we find a sublime system of theology, and a ritual which, if not strictly entitled to the appellation of a reasonable service, was yet comparatively pure in its ordinances, and still further refined by a lofty and spiritual import. It has been said of the Hebrews, that they were men in religion, and children in every thing else. This observation may be reversed in the case of the Egyptians; for, while in the greater number of those pursuits which give dignity to the human mind, and perpetuate the glories of civilized life, they made a progress which set all rivalry at defiance,—in their notions and adoration of the invisible Powers who preside over the destinies of man, they manifested the imbecility, the ignorance, and the credulity of childhood.

In reviewing the annals of the great nations of antiquity, it is interesting to observe that nearly all the knowledge we possess of their manners and institutions may be attributed to a circumstance so very trivial as the choice which they made of their materials for building. As the rise of Egyptian power and wisdom preceded a long time the era of letters, the history of the more ancient kings, like that of the Babylonians and Assyrians, must have been lost, had the architectural monuments of the former people not been constructed of more imperishable substances than were to be found in the alluvial plains of Mesopotamia. In connexion with these reflections, we are naturally led to remark, that the recent discoveries in hieroglyphics justify the hope that the darkness which has so long hung over the annals and chronology of Egypt will be at length so far dispelled as to enable the historian to ascertain at least the order of events and the succession of monarchs.

C

CHAPTER II.

Physical Properties and Geographical Distribution of Egypt.

General Description of Egypt—Origin of the Name—Opinions of the Ancients—Egypt the Gift of the Nile—Depth of the Soil—Attempts to ascertain the mean Rate of Deposition—Opinions of Shaw, Savary, Volney, and Bruce—Speculations of the French Philosophers—Proof that Egypt has acquired an Elevation of Surface—Fear of Dr. Shaw in regard to the eventual Sterility of the Land—Constancy of the Inundations—Frauds by the Government—Qualities of the Water—Analysis of the Mud—Accident witnessed by Belzoni—Seasons in Egypt—Heat—Infrequency of Rain—The Winds, Simoom—The Political Geography of Egypt—Mouths of the Nile—Natron Lakes—Waterless River.

THE physical qualities of Egypt are not less remarkable than its stupendous works of art and its early civilization. It presents itself to the eye of the traveller as an immense valley, extending nearly 600 miles in length, and hemmed in, on either side, by a ridge of hills and a vast expanse of desert. Viewed as an alluvial basin, it owes its existence entirely to the Nile, which flows through it from south to north, conveying annually to the inhabitants the main source of their agricultural wealth, salubrity to their climate, and beauty to their landscape. The breadth of the cultivable soil varies, of course, according to the direction of the rocky barriers by which its limits are determined,—spreading, at some parts, into a spacious plain; while at others it contracts its dimensions to less than two leagues. The mean width has been estimated at about nine miles; and hence, including the whole area from the shores of the Delta to the first cataract, the extent of land capable of bearing crops has been reckoned to contain ten millions of acres.

The learning of geographers has long been employed in the intricate field of etymology to discover the origin of the term by which Egypt is known among the moderns. It is asserted, by the Greeks, that a celebrated king of this name bequeathed it to his dominions, which had formerly passed under the appellation of Aöria, or the land of heat and blackness. In the sacred writings of the Hebrews it is called Mizraim, evidently the plural form of the oriental noun Mizr, the name which is applied to Egypt by the Arabs of the present day. The Copts retain the native word Chemia, which, perhaps, has some relation to Cham, the son of Noah; or, as Plutarch insinuates, may only denote that darkness of colour which appears in a rich soil or in the human eye. Mizraim, it ought also to be observed, was one of the children of Cham; and it is therefore not improbable that the epithet applied to his inheritance may have arisen from the respect usually paid to the founders of nations. Bruce remarks that Y Gypt, the term used by the Ethiopians when they speak of Egypt, means the country of canals,—a description very suitable to the improved condition of that singular valley under her ancient kings. At all events, it is perfectly clear, that in the heroic age of Greece the word Egyptus was employed in reference to an ancient sovereign, to the land, and also to the river.

The Nile, we may observe, was described, even among the descendants of Jacob, by the term Sichor, which also signifies black; and hence the Greeks called it Melas, and the Latins Niger, words which express the very same idea. But it is worthy of remark, as one of the many instances in which the perceptions of the ancients as to colour are not clearly comprehended in our days, that the modern name, used by the Arabs, denotes blue; the very tint, perhaps, which was indicated by Plutarch when he compared it to the organ of vision. The Greeks, indeed, who interpreted all languages on the principles recognised by their own, derived this epithet from an imaginary event, the reign of King Nileus. But this hypothesis is disproved by the familiar fact that the great Abyssinian branch is denominated by the inhabitants, in their vernacular tongue, the Bahr-el-Nil, the Blue River, or more commonly the Bahr-el-Azrek, an appellation almost strictly synonymous.

The stream itself, as if it were doomed for ever to share the obscurity which covers the ancient history of the land to which it ministers, still conceals its true sources from the eager curiosity of modern science. The question which was agitated in the age of the Ptolemies has not yet been

solved; and although 2000 years have elapsed since Eratosthenes published his conjectures as to the origin of the
principal branch, we possess not more satisfactory knowledge on that particular point than was enjoyed in his days
by the philosophers of Alexandria. The repeated failures
which had already attended the various attempts to discover
its fountains convinced the geographers of Greece and
Rome that success was impossible, and that it was the will
of the gods to conceal from all generations this great secret
of nature. Homer, in language sufficiently ambiguous,
describes it as a stream descending from heaven. Herodotus made inquiry in regard to its commencement, but soon
saw reason to relinquish the attempt as altogether fruitless.
Alexander the Great and Ptolemy-Philadelphus engaged in
the same undertaking, and despatched persons well qualified
by their knowledge for the arduous task; but who, nevertheless, like the great father of history himself, travelled
and inquired in vain. Pomponius Mela was doubtful
whether it did not rise in the country of the antipodes:
Pliny traced it in imagination to a mountain in the Lower
Mauritania, while Euthemenes was of opinion that it proceeded from the borders of the Atlantic, and penetrated
through the heart of Africa, dividing it into two continents.
Virgil appears to have favoured a conjecture, which has also
found supporters at a later period, that the Nile proceeded
from the East, and might be identified with one of the great
rivers of Asia.

Quaque pharetratæ vicinia Persidis urget,
Et viridem Ægyptum nigra fœcundat arena,
Et diversa ruens septem discurrit in ora
Usque coloratis amnis devexus ab Indis.—*Georg.* iv. 290.

And where the stream from India's swarthy sons,
Close on the verge of quivered Persia runs,
Broods o'er green Egypt with dark wave of mud,
And pours through many a mouth its branching flood.
                                        SOTHEBY.

Lucan indulges in his usual mysticism, and appears satisfied that, by a decree of the fates, the glory of no nation will
ever be increased by drawing aside the veil in which the
Naiads of this mighty stream have been pleased to conceal
themselves. The conceptions of Lucretius, the poet of
physical nature, were perhaps more correct, although

obviously founded upon a fortunate conjecture rather than derived from actual research.

Ille ex mstiferâ parti venit amnis, ab Austro
Inter nigra virûm, percoctaque secla calore,
Exoriens penitus mediâ ab regione diei.—Lib. vi. 721.

While rolls the Nile adverse
Full from the south, from realms of torrid heat,—
Haunts of the Ethiop tribes; yet far beyond
First bubbling distant, o'er the burning line.—Goon.

It is worthy of notice that the judgment formed by Herodotus in respect to the course of this celebrated river coincides, in a great degree, with the conclusions held by many modern authors. He remarks that, without including the section between Syene and the Mediterranean, the progress of the Nile is known to the extent of four months' journey, partly by land and partly by water; for it will be found on experience that no one can go in less time from Elephantiné to the country of the Automolians. There is no doubt, he adds, that the Nile rises in the west; but beyond the people just mentioned all is uncertainty, this portion of Africa being, from the excessive heat, a rude and uncultivated desert. The Nile, he elsewhere observes, certainly rises in Libya, which it divides; and if it be allowable to draw, from things which are well known, conclusions respecting those that are more obscure, it takes a similar course with the Danube. But of the fountains of the former river, washing, as it does, the savage and uninhabitable wilds of Libya, no one can speak with precision.[*]

From other circumstances mentioned in the second book of his history, there is little doubt that Herodotus believed the Niger and the Nile to be the same river, or, at least, that the water which was carried to the centre of the African continent by the one was discharged into the sea through the mouths of the other. At the present moment there is no hypothesis in regard to these streams which rests on a better foundation. It is no longer disputed that the left branch, the Bahr-el-Abiad or White River, constitutes the principal body of the Nile, and that it flows towards Egypt from the west or south-west. Mr. Browne was informed that it issues from a lofty ridge situated to the south of

[*] Euterpe, 31. 33, 34.

C 2

Darfûr, called in the language of the country Djibbel-el-
Kumri, or Mountains of the Moon. But it is important to
observe that the south winds are there the hottest and driest
of any, and bring along with them thick clouds of dust.
This shows that there is no high chain within a great distance in the direction now described; for the winds, before
they can be possessed of such qualities, must sweep over a
great extent of sandy desert.

The source of the Bahr-el-Abiad cannot, therefore, be
sought in the meridian of Darfûr, unless we consent to remove it far beyond the equator. Besides, Mr. Jackson was
informed that travellers have passed by water from Tim-
buctoo to Cairo,—a circumstance which, if true, proves
either that the Niger and the Nile are the same, or that there
must be intermediate streams, forming, between the two
rivers just named, a communication resembling that which
was found by Humboldt to connect the Orinoco with the
Amazons. Nor is it a slight circumstance, in weighing the
evidence on both sides of this question, to be reminded that
the quantity of mud brought down by the Nile cannot be
washed annually from the rocky channel of a mountain-tor-
rent. This fact was employed by Bruce as the basis of his
argument against those writers who ascribe the increase of
the Delta to the depositions of the river, being founded on
his personal observation of the Bahr-el-Azrek in its course
through the greater part of Abyssinia. It is therefore certain that the White River cuts a passage through a considerable extent of rich soil before it approaches the granite
range which bounds the western extremity of Nubia. The
tropical rains collect on the table-lands of the interior, where
they form immense sheets of water or temporary lakes.
When these have reached a level high enough to overflow
the boundaries of their basins, they suddenly send down
into the rivers an enormous volume of fluid impregnated with
the soft earth over which it has for some time stagnated.
Hence the momentary pauses and sudden renewals in the
rise of the Nile,—hence, too, the abundance of fertilizing
slime, which is never found so copious in the waters of rivers
which owe their increase solely to the direct influence of the
rains.*

* Malte Brun vol. iv. p 8

There is a fact, however, which ought not to be omitted, as being of some value in the determination of the problem now before us; namely, that the White River begins to swell three or four weeks before the Abyssinian branch receives any accession of water. This may be thought to indicate that the source of the Bahr-el-Abiad must be farther south than the springs which Bruce reached in the meadows of Geesh; for it is well known that the rainy season in every part of the torrid zone accompanies the vertical position of the sun. But from these considerations, perhaps, as also from many others which might be adduced, we ought only to conclude that the most learned geographers are still very much in the dark relative to the origin of the magnificent stream to which Africa owes its chief distinction, as well as in regard to the geological phenomena of that remarkable kingdom from which the civil historian derives his clearest views of the primitive state of the western world.

It is an observation as old as the days of Herodotus, that Egypt is the gift of the Nile. This historian imagined that all the lower division of the country was formerly a deep bay or arm of the sea, and that it had been gradually filled up by depositions from the river. He illustrates his reasoning on this subject by supposing that the present appearance of the Red Sea resembles exactly the aspect which Egypt must have exhibited in its original state; and that, if the Nile by any means were admitted to flow into the Arabian Gulf, it would, in the course of twenty thousand years, convey into it such a quantity of earth as would raise its bed to the level of the surrounding coast. I am of opinion, he subjoins, that this might take place even within ten thousand years; why then might not a bay still more spacious than this be choaked up with mud, in the time which passed before our age, by a stream so great and powerful as the Nile ?*

The men of science who accompanied the French expedition into Egypt undertook to measure the depth of alluvial matter which has been actually deposited by the river. By sinking pits at different intervals, both on the banks of the current and on the outer edge of the stratum, they ascertained satisfactorily,—first, that the surface of the soil

* Euterpe, chap. 11

declines from the margin of the stream towards the foot of the hills; secondly, that the thickness of the deposite is generally about ten feet near the river, and decreases gradually as it recedes from it; and, thirdly, that beneath the mud there is a bed of sand analogous to the substance which has at all times been brought down by the flood of the Nile. This convex form assumed by the surface of the valley is not peculiar to Egypt,—being common to the banks of all great rivers where the quantity of soil transported by the current is greater than that which is washed down by rain from the neighbouring mountains.   The plains which skirt the Mississippi and the Ganges present in many parts an example of the same phenomenon.

An attempt has likewise been made to ascertain the rate of the annual deposition of alluvial substance, and thereby to measure the elevation which has been conferred upon the valley of Egypt by the action of its river.   But on no point are travellers less agreed than in regard to the change of level and the increase of land on the seacoast.   Dr. Shaw and M. Savary take their stand on the one side, and are resolutely opposed by Bruce and Volney on the other.   Herodotus informs us, that in the reign of Mœris, if the Nile rose to the height of eight cubits, all the lands of Egypt were sufficiently watered; but that in his own time,—not quite nine hundred years afterward,—the country was not covered with less than fifteen or sixteen cubits of water. The addition of soil, therefore, was equal to seven cubits at the least, or a hundred and twenty-six inches, in the course of nine hundred years.   "But at present," says Dr. Shaw, "the river must rise to the height of twenty cubits,—and it usually rises to twenty-four,—before the whole country is overflowed.   Since the time, therefore, of Herodotus, Egypt has gained new soil to the depth of two hundred and thirty inches.   And if we look back from the reign of Mœris to the time of the deluge, and reckon that interval by the same proportion, we shall find that the whole perpendicular accession of the soil, from the deluge to A. D. 1721, must be 500 inches; that is, the land of Egypt has gained 41 feet 8 inches of soil in 4072 years.   Thus, in process of time, the whole country may be raised to such a height that the river will not be able to overflow its banks; and Egypt consequently, from being the most fertile, will, for want of the annual inundation, become one of the most barren parts of the universe."*

Were it possible to determine the mean rate of accumulation, a species of chronometer would be thereby obtained for measuring the lapse of time which has passed since any monument, or other work of art in the neighbourhood of the river, was originally founded. In applying the principle now stated, it is not necessary to assume any thing more than that the building in question was not placed by its architect under the level of the river at its ordinary inundations,—a postulatum which, in regard to palaces, temples, and statues, will be most readily granted. Proceeding on this ground, the French philosophers hazarded a conjecture respecting a number of dates, of which the following are some of the most remarkable.

1. The depth of the soil round the colossal statue of Memnon, at Thebes, gives only 0.106 of a mètre (less than four inches) as the rate of accumulation in a century, while the mean of several observations made in the valley of Lower Egypt gives 0.126 of a mètre, or rather more than four inches. But the basis of the statue of Memnon was certainly raised above the level of the inundation, by being placed on an artificial mound; and excavations made near it show that the original height of that terrace was six mètres (19.686 feet) above the level of the soil. A similar result is obtained from examining the foundations of the palace at Luxor. Taking, therefore, 0.126 of a mètre, the mean secular augmentation of the soil, as a divisor, the quotient, 4760, gives the number of years which have elapsed since the foundation of Thebes was laid. This date, which of course can only be considered as a very imperfect approximation to the truth, carries the origin of that celebrated metropolis as far back as 2960 years before Christ, and consequently 612 years before the deluge, according to the reckoning of the modern Jews. But the numbers given there differ materially from those of the Samaritan text and the Septuagint version; which, carrying the deluge back to the year 3716 before Christ, make an interval of seven centuries and a half between the flood and the building of Thebes. Though no distinct account of the age of that

* Shaw's Travels, vol. ii. p. 235.

city is to be found in the Greek historians, it is clear from Diodorus that they believed it to have been begun in a very remote period of antiquity.[*]

2. The rubbish collected at the foot of the obelisk of Luxor indicates that it was erected fourteen hundred years before the Christian era.

3. The causeway which crosses the plain of Siout furnishes a similar ground for supposing that it must have been founded twelve hundred years anterior to the same epoch.

4. The pillar of Heliopolis, six miles from Cairo, appears, from evidence strictly analogous, to have been raised about the period just specified; but as the waters drain off more slowly in the Delta than in Upper Egypt, the accumulation of alluvial soil is more rapid there than higher up the stream; the foundations, therefore, of ancient buildings in the former district will be at as great a depth below the surface as those of much greater antiquity are in the middle and upper provinces. But it is obvious that to form these calculations with such accuracy as would render them less liable to dispute, more time and observation would be requisite than could be given by the French in the short period during which they continued in undisturbed possession of Egypt. One general and important consequence, however, arising from their inquiries, can hardly be overlooked or denied; namely, that the dates thus obtained are as remote from the extravagant chronology of the ancient Egyptians, as they are consistent with the testimony of both sacred and profane history, with regard to the early civilization of that interesting country.[†]

But little or no reliance can be placed on such conclusions, because it is now manifestly impossible to ascertain, in the first instance, whether the measures referred to by the ancient historians were in all cases of the same standard;

---

[*] Diod. Sic. lib. i. c. 15, ἀμφισβητεῖται δ᾽ ἡ κτίσις της πολεως ταυτης, ὁυ μονον παρα τοις συγγραφευσιν, ἀλλα και παρ᾽ ἀυτοις τοις κατ᾽ Αίγυπτον ἱερευσι.

[†] See article "Egypt" in Encyclopædia Metropolitana. The grounds which may be alleged for giving a preference in point of chronology to the Samaritan text, or even to the Septuagint, and the singular approximation to the former, resulting from a mean taken between it, the Hindoo, and the Chinese epochs, are ably stated by Klaproth in his *Asia Polyglotta*, 25-29.

and, secondly, whether the deposition of soil in the Egyptian valley did not proceed more rapidly in early times than it does in our days, or even than it has done ever since its effects first became an object of philosophical curiosity. That the level of the land has been raised, and its extent towards the sea greatly increased since the age of Herodotus, we might safely infer, as well from the great infusion of earthy matter which is held in suspension by the Nile when in a state of flood, as from the analogous operation of all large rivers, both in the old continents and in the new. There is, in truth, no good reason for questioning the fact mentioned by Dr. Shaw, that the mud of Ethiopia has been detected by soundings, at the distance of not less than twenty leagues from the coast of the Delta.

Nor is there any substantial ground for apprehending, with the author just named, that, in process of time, the whole country may be raised to such a height that the river will not be able to overflow its banks; and consequently that Egypt, from being the most fertile, will, for want of the annual inundation, become one of the most barren parts of the universe. The fears of the learned traveller might have been removed by the following reflections. As the formation of land in the Delta proceeds at a quicker rate than in the higher parts of the river, the issue of water into the sea becomes, year after year, less rapid, and consequently less copious; the current is retarded by the accumulation of mud; the mouths are successively choked by the increasing masses of sand and soil; and hence, in the course of ages, the stream, creating a barrier against its own escape, is thrown back upon the adjoining valley, and becomes the willing servant of the agriculturist from Rosetta to the Cataracts. The same opinion is expressed by Lucretius in the following verses :—

Est quoque, uti possit magnus congestus arenæ
Fluctibus aversis oppilare ostia contra,
Cùm mare permotum ventus ruit intus atenam:
Quo sit uti pacto liber minus exitus amnis,
Et proclivus item fiat minus impetus undis.--Lib vi. v. 724.

Then ocean, haply, by the undevious breeze
Blown up its channel, heaves with every wave
Heaps of high sands, and dams its wonted course.
Whence narrower, too, its exit to the main,
And with less force the tardy stream descends.

While this cause continues to operate in checking the velocity of the inundation in the northern division of the country, the entrance of the river at Philoe is gradually facilitated by the removal of those obstructions which, in ancient times, secured to Nubia the advantages of an annual irrigation such as Egypt now enjoys, and which still partially oppose the motion of the descending flood.   The traveller discovers on both sides of the Nubian valley many traces of an extended cultivation which no longer exists. The ridge of rocks which formerly crossed the line of the river, and gave rise to the magnificent falls, the sound of which was heard at the distance of so many leagues and stunned the neighbouring inhabitants, has been insensibly corroded and worn down by the action of the rushing water, and presents in these days only a few tokens of its original extent.   A similar effect, which time will produce on the cliffs of Niagara, will be attended with a similar result on the chain of lakes which terminate in Erie,—the contents of which will at length find their way to the ocean along the bed of the St. Lawrence.   In the remote ages of the future, the immense valleys now occupied by Superior, Michigan, and those other inland seas which form so striking a feature in North America, will be covered with flocks, herds, and an agricultural population, and only watered by a fine river passing through their centre.   In this way the interior of every continent is imperceptibly drained, and new tracts of alluvial land are added to its extremities.

That Egypt was raised and augmented in the manner described above is rendered manifest by a variety of considerations.   It is particularly deserving of notice, as suggested by Dr. Shaw and confirmed by the French, that whereas the soil of other level countries is usually of the same depth, we find it in Egypt to vary in proportion to its distance from the river,—being in some places near the banks more than thirty feet, while at the extremity of the inundation it does not exceed six inches.   Another circumstance which fortifies the same conclusion is the practice long since become necessary of raising mounds to protect their cities from the violence of the waters.   It is not to be imagined that the natives, accustomed to the annual swelling of their river, would build their towns within the limits even of its greatest elevation.   On the contrary, it is believed that they were wont to place their cities on artificial eminences, to guard against the inconvenience of the summer flood, and particularly to exempt from its ravages their temples and public monuments. But it is every where admitted that some of the finest of their ancient towns are at present under the level of the inundation; while the most laborious efforts have in other parts become indispensable to prevent, by embanking, the destruction of their sacred buildings. Memphis, it is presumed, has been covered by the increasing soil, after having been abandoned by its inhabitants, who had found the use of mounds unavailing. Bubastis, when about to fall a prey to the same destroyer, was rebuilt on higher ground; but the beautiful temple, as it could not be removed, was left in its original position, and was accordingly looked down upon from every part of the new city. Heliopolis, in like manner, as we are informed by Strabo, was erected upon an eminence; but at present the land is elevated around it to such a degree that it appears situated in a plain, which, moreover, is inundated every year to the depth of six or eight feet.[*]

This source of fertility to Egypt depends exclusively, as every reader knows, upon the periodical rains which drench the table-land of Abyssinia and the mountainous country which stretches from it towards the south and west. The ancients, some of whom indeed entertained very absurd notions respecting the cause of this phenomenon, were generally in the right as to its physical origin,—expressing their belief that the annual overflow of the Nile was closely connected with the climate of Ethiopia, that receptacle of clouds and vapour. Plutarch states most distinctly that the increase of the Egyptian river is owing to the rains which fall in Abyssinia. Even the Arabs had arrived at the same conclusion long before any European found his way into the country.[†] More than seven hundred years ago, a failure in the inundation was announced to the farmers of Egypt by a clerical envoy from the chief city of Ethiopia; who, after having stated that the season in the hill country had been unusually dry, advised them to expect and prepare for the unwonted lowness of the Nile, which actually occurred.

[*] Shaw, vol. ii. p. 229.
[†] History of Egypt by Abdollatiph, quoted by Shaw, vol. ii. p. 215.

It is impossible to find any where among terrestrial objects a more striking instance of the stability of the laws of nature than the periodical rise and fall of this mighty river. We know, by the testimony of antiquity, that the inundations of the Nile have been the same with respect to their height and duration for thousands of years; which, as Humboldt remarks, is a proof well worthy of attention, that the mean state of humidity and temperature does not vary in that vast basin.* The rise of the water is so regular that the inhabitants of Lower Egypt look for its arrival with the same degree of confidence as if the blessings which it brings along with it depended upon causes within their own control.

The value attached to this gift of nature is esteemed so great as to be made the subject of political regulation, and the main source of public revenue. When it rises to sixteen cubits, the prosperity of the country and the wealth of the exchequer are secure. But, unfortunately, influenced by avaricious motives, the power of a despotic government is employed to mislead their own people in the first instance, and, through that channel, the more scientific nations of Europe, in regard to the actual rise of the inundation. It has been suspected that the notices issued by the guardians of the Mekyas, or Nilometer, have a reference to the taxes which the ruler of Egypt intends to levy, rather than to the real increase of the fertilizing fluid from which they are to be derived. It was first suspected by Niebuhr, and afterward fully ascertained by the French, that the number of cubits announced in the daily proclamation of the height of the river is not to be relied upon. The real state of the inundation is concealed for political purposes; and as a proof of this, it is mentioned by M. Girard, that, in 1801, when the public crier gave notice that the water had attained twenty-three cubits two inches, it stood in reality at only eighteen cubits. Hence the difficulty of obtaining an accurate statement on this head, and the impossibility of comparing with suitable exactness the fluctuations of the river in ancient and modern times.

Considering how much the Egyptians owe to the Nile, it is not surprising that in rude ages they should have been induced to make it an object of worship. Not only does it supersede the labour of the plough and the necessity of collecting manure, but it also supplies an abundance of that element which is the most necessary to human existence and comfort, and which to a native of Egypt is, at the same time, a medicine and a luxury. The Egyptian, in short, like the Hindoo, finds his chief solace in his beloved river. Its water is preferred to the most costly beverage ; he even creates an artificial thirst, that he may enjoy the delight of quenching it ; and, when languishing under disease, he looks forward to the approaching inundation as the season of renovated health and vigour. Nor is this predilection to be ascribed to bigotry or ignorance. On the contrary, we find that Europeans are equally loud in their eulogies on the agreeable and salubrious qualities of the Nile. Giovanni Finati, for example, who was no stranger to the limpid streams of other lands, sighed for the opportunity of returning to Cairo, that he might once more drink its delicious water, and breathe its mild atmosphere. Maillet, too, a writer of good credit, remarks, that it is among waters what champaign is among wines. The Mussulmans themselves acknowledge that if their prophet Mohammed had tasted it, he would have supplicated Heaven for a terrestrial immortality, that he might enjoy it for ever.

The Copts, with the feeling natural to Christians of the Greek communion, have fixed upon the 24th of June, the festival of St. John, as the day which affords the first decisive token of the annual flood. Travellers, however, inform us that in ordinary years, it is not till the first week in July the rise can be distinctly marked. It is true, that at a much earlier part of the season there is a temporary swell in the current, occasioned by partial rains which fall within the tropics soon after the vernal equinox ; but the real inundation does not commence till the period already mentioned, and even then very imperceptibly. By the middle of August it has reached half its elevation, but it is not at the highest till towards the last days of September. It then continues stationary about two weeks, when it begins gradually to subside. By the 10th of November it has fallen one-half, from which period it diminishes very slowly till the 15th or 16th of the following May, when it is understood to have reached its lowest ebb. During the increase the water first acquires a green colour, sometimes pretty deep ; and after thirty or forty days this is succeeded by a brownish red. These changes are probably owing to the augmentations it receives from different temporary lakes in succession, or from the rains which fall at various distances on the table-lands in the interior of Africa.

The mud of the Nile upon analysis gives nearly one-half of argillaceous earth, with about one-fourth of carbonate of lime ; the remainder consisting of water, oxide of iron, and carbonate of magnesia. On the very banks the slime is mixed with much sand, which it loses in proportion as it is carried farther from the river, so that at a certain distance it consists almost entirely of pure argil. This mud is employed in several arts among the Egyptians. It is formed into excellent bricks, as well as into a variety of vessels for domestic use. It enters also into the manufacture of tobacco-pipes. Glass-makers employ it in the construction of their furnaces, and the country people cover their houses with it. As it contains principles favourable to vegetation, the cultivators consider it as a sufficient manure for such places as have not been saturated by the overflowing of the river.

Although the Nile is almost without exception the minister of good to Egypt, there are yet cases in which the excess of its waters has occasioned no small loss both of life and property. In September, 1818, Belzoni witnessed a deplorable scene, owing to the river having risen three feet and a half above the highest mark left by the former inundation. Ascending with uncommon rapidity it carried off several villages, and some hundreds of their inhabitants. Expecting an unusual rise, in consequence of the scarcity of water the preceding season, the Arabs had had recourse to their wonted expedient of erecting fences of earth and reeds round the villages, to keep the water from their houses. But on this occasion the pressure of the flood baffled all their efforts. Their cottages, built of earth, could not stand one moment against the current, but were, as soon as the water touched them, levelled with the ground. The rapid stream carried off all that was before it ; the inhabitants of all ages, with their corn and cattle, were washed away in an instant. In Upper Egypt, where the villages are not raised above the level even of the ordinary inundations, the natives depend for their safety upon artificial barriers. At Agalta, whither he went to procure the assistance of the caimakan, or magistrate, he found the said functionary in great alarm, expecting every hour to be swept away by the Nile. " There was no boat in the village, and should the water break down their weak fences, the only chances of escape was by climbing the palm-trees, till Providence sent some one to their relief. All the boats were employed in carrying away the corn from villages that were in danger. Both in Upper and Lower Egypt the men, women, and children are left to be the last assisted, as their lives are not so valuable as corn, which brings money to the pasha. As this village was then four feet below the water, the poor Fellahs were on the watch day and night round their fences. They employed their skin-machines, or bags, to throw out the water which rose from under the ground; but if their fences should be broken down all would be lost." At another village described by the traveller, the distress of the people was very great. Some of them had taken refuge on a spot where there were only a few feet of land uncovered; and the water, he adds, was to rise twelve days more, and after that to remain twelve days at its height, according to the usual term of the inundation.*

It was probably to prevent the occurrence of such catastrophes, as well as to turn to a beneficial purpose the superfluous waters of the Nile, that the lake of Mœris, and other similar receptacles, were formed by the ancient kings of Egypt. Although the valley of Fayoum supplied a natural basin for the grand reservoir now mentioned, yet as the canal which connected it with the river, together with the numerous dams which were necessary to regulate the current during the rise and fall of the inundation, were the fruit of human labour, we shall postpone the description of it till we come to the chapter on the Works of Ancient Art.

We have already remarked that Egypt is indebted for her rich harvests to the mould or soil which is deposited by the river during the annual flood. As soon as the waters retire the cultivation of the ground commences. If it has imbibed the requisite degree of moisture, the process of agriculture is neither difficult nor tedious. The seed is scattered over the soft surface, and vegetation, which almost immediately succeeds, goes on with great rapidity. Where

the land has been only partially inundated, recourse is had
to irrigation, by means of which many species of vegetables are raised even during the dry season. Harvest follows
at the distance of about six or eight weeks, according to
the different kinds of grain,—leaving time in most cases for
a succession of crops, wherever there is a full command of
water. The cold season begins with December, and continues about two months. Spring appears in the first days
of February, when the fruit-trees blossom, and the atmosphere acquires a delightful warmth. The period of summer
may be said to commence in June, and to end at the close
of September, although the transition from the one season
to the other is so gradual that it is impossible to define the
exact limits of either. During these four months the heat
is intense, the fields to which the swelling river has not
attained are parched like a desert, and no green leaf is seen
but such as are produced by artificial irrigation. Autumn,
which is only marked by a slight diminution of temperature,
commences about the middle of October, when the leaves
fall, and the Nile retires within its channel; and till the
approach of that season which, from its relation to the rest
of the year, must be called winter, the face of the country
resembles a beautiful meadow diversified with lively colours.
Thus is realized the description of Volney, who observed
that Egypt assumed in succession the appearances of an
ocean of fresh water, of a miry morass, of a green level
plain, and of a parched desert of sand and dust.*

For various reasons, especially the want of wood and
the low elevation of the whole plain from Rosetta to Assouan,
the average degree of heat in Egypt is considerably greater
than in many other countries situated in the same latitude.
In summer, as long as the sun remains above the horizon,
the atmosphere is inflamed, the sky is cloudless and sparkling, and the heat is rendered supportable only by the profuse perspiration which it excites. At Cairo, the medium
temperature during that season has been estimated at
ninety-two degrees of Fahrenheit's thermometer. On
some occasions it has been known to rise as high as one
hundred and twelve degrees; but such an intensity of heat
is usually of short continuance, and almost never expe-

* Travels, vol. ii. p. 10.

rienced except in the more confined districts of the Saïd. At sunset the wind falls, the air becomes cooler, and the vapour suspended in the atmosphere during the day is deposited in an abundant supply of dew. As the evening advances, a thin mist darkens the horizon, and spreads over the watery grounds; but during the night it becomes scarcely perceptible, and in the morning, when the sun has attained a certain elevation, it gradually ascends in the form of flaky clouds.

The copious evaporation, which necessarily takes place in a country distinguished one-half of the year by excessive heat and moisture, is hardly ever restored to the soil in the shape of rain. The clouds, it is true, sometimes collect in dark masses, and the atmosphere exhibits all the meteorological symptoms, which in other climates indicate rain; but a shower, notwithstanding, is a very rare occurrence in Egypt. When this phenomenon does occur, it continues only a few minutes, and seems counteracted by some affinities, chymical or electrical, too powerful to be overcome by the ordinary principle of gravity. In the Delta rain is occasionally seen during the cool part of the year; but above Cairo it is almost never witnessed at any season. Thunder and lightning are still more infrequent, and are, at the same time, so completely divested of their terrific qualities that the Egyptians never associate with them the idea of destructive force, and are quite unable to comprehend how they should ever be accompanied with either fear or injury. Showers of hail descending from the hills of Syria, and sweeping along the plains of Palestine, are sometimes known to reach the confines of Egypt. But the production of ice is so extremely uncommon, that, on one occasion when it appeared in the low country, the Arabs collected it with the greatest care, and sold it, at a high price, to the European merchants of Alexandria.

The course of the wind, so variable in our climate, is almost strictly periodical on the banks of the Nile. In point both of strength and duration, the northerly breezes predominate,—blowing nearly nine months in the year. They continue with little intermission from May till September; but about the autumnal equinox they veer round to the east, where they remain nearly six weeks, with only slight deviations. About the end of February the gale assumes a southerly direction, and fluctuates exceedingly till the close of April, when it again yields for a time to a more powerful current from the eastward.

The southerly winds are the most changeable, as well as the most unhealthy; traversing the arid sands of Africa, uninterrupted by rivers, lakes, or forests, they arrive in Egypt fraught with all the noxious exhalations of the desert. At their approach, the serene sky becomes black and heavy; the sun loses its splendour, and appears of a dim violet hue; a light warm breeze is felt, which gradually increases in heat till it almost equals that of an oven. Though no vapour darkens the air, it becomes so gray and thick with the floating clouds of impalpable sand that it is sometimes necessary to use candles at noonday. Every green leaf is instantly shrivelled, and every thing formed of wood is warped and cracked. The effect of these winds on the animal creation, too, is not less pernicious, sometimes even occasioning immediate death by sudden squalls which attack the victim before he is aware. The breathing becomes quick and difficult, the pores of the skin are closed, and a feverish habit is induced, owing to suppressed perspiration. The increasing heat pervades every substance; and water itself, no longer cool, is rendered incapable of mitigating the intolerable sensation by which the whole body is oppressed. Dead silence reigns in the streets; the inhabitants, by confining themselves to their houses, vainly attempt to elude the showers of dust, which is so fine and penetrating that, according to the oriental expression, it will enter an egg through the pores of the shell.*

These are the hot winds of the desert, termed by the Arabs *simoom*, and by the Turks *samiel*, and which have so often proved fatal to whole caravans, and even to large armies. When they continue longer than three days their effects become quite insupportable, especially to persons of a full habit of body. It is worthy of notice, at the same time, that the southerly breeze which, in the spring of the year, is attended with an intolerable heat, is, during the winter, noted above all others for an intense and penetrating cold. In the latter season the rays of the sun fall more

* Antis's Observations on Egypt; Volney's Travels, vol. ii. p. 61. Dr. Leyden on Egypt, in Murray's Africa.

obliquely on the desert, and the current of air which descends on Egypt is chilled by the snowy mountains of Abyssinia.

Such are the principal phenomena which characterize the climate of Egypt,—a country in the very atmosphere of which nature seems to have adopted new and singular arrangements. In that country, distinguished by an uncommon regularity of the seasons and of all the changes which the atmosphere presents, these meteorological facts were first ascertained with philosophical accuracy. But though the observations of the ancient sages of Thebes and Memphis, engraved on immense masses of granite, have defied the ravages of time and the still more destructive hand of man, we can only view the characters with regret, and lament that a wise and learned people may utterly perish before the monuments of their power and science have entirely passed away.

Egypt is usually divided into Upper and Lower, the latitude of Cairo presenting in our day the line of demarcation. But besides this distinction there is another of great antiquity, to which frequent allusion is made by the Greek and Roman authors, namely, that of the Delta, the Heptanomis, and the Thebaid. According to this distribution, the first of the provinces just mentioned occupied the seacoast of the Mediterranean ; the third the narrow valley of Upper Egypt ; while to the second was allotted the intermediate space, which seems to have been divided into seven districts or cantons. At a later period when Egypt became subject to the Romans, the Arcadia of that people corresponded nearly to the ancient Heptanomis ; and, about the conclusion of the fourth century, the eastern division of the Delta, between Arabia and the Phatnitic branch of the Nile, as high as Heliopolis, was erected into a new province under the name of Augustamnica. In modern times the Arabs have changed the classical appellation of Thebaid into Saïd, or the high country ; the Heptanomis into Vostani ; and the Delta into Bahari, or the maritime district.

The following table exhibits a succinct view of the territorial distribution of Egypt as recognised by modern geographers and the actual government of the country :—

I.—THE SAÏD, OR UPPER EGYPT.
1. Province of Thebes.
2. ————— Djirgeh.
3. ————— Siout.

II.—THE VOSTANI, OR MIDDLE EGYPT.
1. Province of Fayoum.
2. ————— Beni Souef.
3. ————— Minieh.

III.—THE BAHARI, OR LOWER EGYPT.
1. Province of Bahireh
2. ————— Rosetta.
3. ————— Damietta.
4. ————— Gharbiyeh.
5. ————— Menouf.
6. ————— Mansoura.
7. ————— Shafkeyeh.

The frequent alteration of terms by nations using different languages has produced considerable obscurity in geographical details, as well as a most inconvenient variety in the spelling of proper names. The cities which flourished during the different periods of the Persian, Grecian, Roman, and Saracenic dynasties were not only erected on the sites of more ancient edifices, but under the Turkish and Mamlouk domination, their positions have been partially changed; and thus, splendid towns celebrated in history have been buried in their own ruins, and the traveller searches for them in vain within the circuit of their ancient walls.

Nor is this vicissitude confined to the works of human art. Even the great lineaments of nature undergo a gradual change, and thereby render the descriptions of early authors almost unintelligible to the modern traveller. The mouths of the Nile, for example, have often deserted their channels, and the river has entered the sea at different points. The seven estuaries known to the ancients were:
—1. The Canopic mouth, corresponding to the present outlet from the Lake Etko, or, according to others, that of the Lake of Aboukir or Maadée; but it is probable that, at one time, it had communications with the sea at both these

places. 2. The Bolbitine mouth at Rosetta. 3. The Sebenitic, probably the opening into the present Lake Burlos. 4. The Phatnitic or Bucolic at Damietta. 5. The Mendesian, which is lost in the Lake Menzaleh, the mouth of which is represented by that of Debeh. 6. The Tanitic or Saitic, which seems to have some traces of its termination to the east of the Lake Menzaleh, under the modern appellation of Om-Faridjé. The branch of the Nile which conveyed its waters to the sea corresponds to the canal of Moez, which now loses itself in the lake. 7. The Pelusiac, which seems to be represented by what is now the most easterly mouth of Lake Menzaleh, where the ruins of Pelusium are still visible.*

Of these communications with the sea, the Nile, it is well known, maintains at the present day only the second and the fourth,—the others having been long choked up with mud, or with the earth which falls from the crumbling banks. The cultivation of the Delta has been contracted in a similar proportion; for in Egypt, wherever the water of the river is withheld, the desert extends or resumes its dominion, covering the finest fields with barren sand and useless shrubs.

Our description of the physical aspect of this singular country would not be complete did we fail to mention the Valley of the Natron Lakes, and that of the Waterless River. In the former of these there is a series of six basins, bounded on the one side by a lofty ridge of secondary rocks, which perhaps proves the means of concentrating the saline deposite which has given celebrity to the place. The banks and the waters are covered with crystallizations, consisting of muriate of soda or sea-salt, and of natron or carbonate of soda. When a volume of water contains both these salts, the muriate of soda is the first to crystallize, and the carbonate is then deposited in a separate layer. But in some instances, the two crystallizations are observed to choose, without any assignable cause, distinct localities in different parts of the same lake.

The Waterless River, called by the Arabs Bahr-bela-Maieh, presents itself in a valley which runs parallel to the one just described, and is separated from it only by a line

* Malte Brun, vol. iv. p. 23; Mém. sur l'Egypte, vol. i. p. 165; Mém. sur les Bouches du Nil, par Dubois-Aymé.

of elevated ground. It has been traced from the neighbourhood of the Mediterranean through the desert country which
stretches to the westward of Fayoum. In the sand with
which its channel is every where covered, trunks of trees
have been found in a state of complete petrifaction, and also
the vertebral bone of a large fish. Jasper, quartz, and
petrosilex have likewise been observed scattered over the
surface; and hence some learned persons have thought
that these fragments of rock, which do not belong to the
contiguous hills, have been conveyed thither by a branch of
the Nile, which it is more than probable once passed in this
direction, and discharged itself into the sea at some distance
to the westward of Alexandria. But this question, which
belongs more properly to a subsequent part of our volume,
will be discussed at some length in connexion with the opinions of those writers who have most recently examined the
borders of Lake Mœris.*

CHAPTER III.

Civil History of Ancient Egypt.

Obscurity of Egyptian Annals—Variety of Hypotheses—Reign of Menes
determined; his Actions—Account of Osymandias; his Palace and
Tomb—Chronological Tables—Invasion of the Shepherds—Quotation
from Manetho—Mistake as to the Israelites—Indian Tradition in
regard to the Conquest of Egypt by Pastoral Chiefs—The Origin of
the Pyramids—Hatred of Shepherds entertained by the Egyptians in
time of Joseph—The Reign of Mœris—Accession of Sesostris; his
Exploits; Proofs of his warlike Expedition; the Magnificence of his
Buildings; his Epitaph—Invasion by Sabaco the Ethiopian or Abyssinian—By Sennacherib—By Nebuchadnezzar—By Cyrus—And complete Subjugation by Cambyses—The Persian Government—Conquest
of Egypt by Alexander the Great—Ancient Dynasties—The Ptolemies—
The Romans—The Saracens.

IT is our intention in this chapter to give an outline of
Egyptian history from the earliest times down to the accession of the Saracenic princes,—an epoch at which the

* Belzoni, vol. ii. p. 168; Denon, vol i. p. 224.

power and splendour of the more ancient governments were oppressed by a weight of barbarism which has not yet been removed.

In regard to this interesting subject, we may confidently assert that there is no portion of the remoter annals of the human race more obscure from the want of authentic records, or more perplexed by groundless conjecture and bold speculation. He who begins his inquiries with the establishment of the Egyptian monarchy, and proposes to sail down the stream of time accompanied and guided by the old historians, soon discovers the numerous obstacles which must impede his course. The ancient authors from whom he seeks information require of him to carry back his imagination to an era many thousand years prior to the existence of all written deeds ; and they then gravely introduce him to the gods and demigods who had once condescended to dwell on the banks of the Nile, and to govern the fancied inhabitants of that fertile region.

If, impatient of the fables related to him respecting supernatural personages, the inquirer should ask who was the first human sovereign who reigned over Egypt, he is encouraged by being told that his name was Menes, and that his history is not altogether unknown. But he soon finds out that the exploits of this prince greatly resemble the achievements of the god Osiris, and that the limits between mythology and the simple annals of a mortal race are not yet fully established. Fatigued with vain conjectures, and still unable to separate facts from fiction, he may resolve to change his plan, and flatter himself with the hope of being able to thread his way through the dark labyrinth of Egyptian chronology. Adopting the philosophical rule, he determines to proceed from the known to the unknown ; and, selecting some comparatively recent and well-attested fact, of which the date is considered as certain, he obtains possession of one end of the chain, which he trusts he may succeed in tracing, link after link, until he shall arrive at the other extremity.

But this method, however ingeniously conceived, has not hitherto been attended with a corresponding success. The chronologer pursues his way, trusting now to one guide, and at another time to a second, who appears to have opened the path under a clearer light ; but, unfortunately,

E

he soon becomes convinced that the authorities who oppose
im, in whatever direction he may choose to proceed, are
more numerous than those who favour him with their aid,
and on whose reputation he had thought it safe to rely.
As he advances, he is further dismayed by the unwelcome
discovery that all his guides become more and more ignorant, and also that their confidence increases in proportion
to the obscurity in which they are enveloped.   Their statements abound with fictions sufficient to stagger the strongest belief.   He is now satisfied that absolute truth cannot
be obtained on such uncertain ground, and therefore consents to imitate all those who have gone before him,—to
build conjectures instead of establishing facts ; to admit
what is probable where he cannot find demonstration ; and,
finally, to allow what is possible where he cannot reach
unquestionable evidence.   His difficulties augment as he
removes farther from the point whence he had originally
started.   Like the traveller who sets out upon a journey
when the day is closing, the light grows more feeble at
every step he takes, and the shades of night fall blacker and
thicker around him, until he is at length shrouded in total
darkness.*
   But to a certain extent, at least, the history of ancient
Egypt can be placed on credible grounds, and even be rendered capable of throwing light upon the condition of contemporary kingdoms.   We must at once relinquish the regal
gods and the thirty-six thousand years of their government,
as only the indication perhaps of some physical principle,
or, more probably, the expression of a vast astronomical
cycle.   The sun, moon, and other leaders of the celestial
host may, according to the ancient mythology, be supposed
to have ruled over Egypt before it became fit for the habita-
tion of mortals ; or the authors of this hypothesis may be
thought to have had nothing more serious in view than the
gratification of their fancy in the wilds of that terra incog-
nita, which, in every quarter of the globe, stretches far beyond the boundaries of authentic history.
   But as the reign of Menes marks the limits of legitimate
inquiry in this interesting field, and as all correct notions of
Egyptian chronology must rest upon the determination of

* See "Origines," by Sir William Drummond, vol. ii. p 250.

the period at which that monarch exercised the supreme power, we shall lay before our readers an abridged view of such opinions on this subject as seem the most worthy of their attention. Here, we need not add, we must confine ourselves to mere results; it being quite inconsistent both with our limits and our object to enter into the learned arguments by which different authors have laboured to fortify their conclusions. But to those readers who are desirous of entering more deeply into the question, we earnestly recommend the works of Hales and Dr. Prichard, the latest and unquestionably the ablest writers on this obscure though very important branch of historical inquiry.

Menes, then, began his reign,

```
* According to Dr. Hales ...........2412 years B. C.
† ————————— Old Chronicle........2231 —————
‡ ————————— Eratosthenes.........2290 —————
§ ————————— Eusebius ............2258 —————  } or 2202;
‖ ————————— Julius Africanus .....2218 —————
¶ ————————— Dr. Prichard.........2214 —————
```

As the actions of this monarch were conveyed to posterity through the uncertain channel of tradition, little reliance can be placed upon the accuracy of the details. Herodotus informs us that he protected from the inundations of the Nile the ground upon which Memphis was afterward erected. Before his age the river flowed close under the ridge of hills which borders the Libyan desert, whence, it is more than probable, a large branch of it, at least, made its way through the valley of Fayoum into the Mediterranean. To prevent this deviation, he erected a mound about twelve miles south from the future capital of Egypt; turned the course of the stream towards the Delta; and led it to the sea at an equal distance from the elevated ground by which on either side the country is bounded. Menes is moreover said to have been a great general, to have made warlike expeditions into foreign countries, and to have fallen a prey at last to the voracity of a hippopotamus.

Among the principal authorities on which the reign of Menes has been determined is the following statement of

* New Analysis of Ancient Chronology, vol. iv. p. 418.
† Ibid. vol. iv. p. 407.   ‡ Prichard's Egyptian Antiquities.
§ New Analysis, vol. iv. p. 417.   ‖ Ibid.
¶ Egyptian Antiquities, p. 91.

Josephus, who had better means of becoming acquainted with the works of Manetho than were enjoyed by Syncellus, Africanus, or Eusebius. He assures us that Menes lived many years before Abraham, and that he ruled more than 1300 years before Solomon.* Now the father of the faithful was born 2153, and the son of David ascended the throne of Israel 1030 years before the Christian era. These facts, combined with the account which is given in the old chronicle of the dynasty of kings which proceeded from Misraim or Misor, seem to justify the conclusions of modern chronology.

The Greek historian further mentions that the priests recited to him, from books, three hundred and thirty sovereigns, successors of Menes, among whom were eighteen Ethiopian princes and one queen called Nitocris. But as none of these monarchs were distinguished by any acts of magnificence or renown, he abstains from encumbering his pages with the unmeaning catalogues of their appellations and titles. He makes one exception in favour of Mœris, famed for the excavation of the lake which still bears his name, and of which an account will be given in a subsequent chapter.

To assist the recollection of the reader on this rather intricate subject, we shall abridge, from the New Analysis of Chronology, a list of the kings who fill up the space between the accession of the first human monarch of Egypt and the death of Mœris :—

FIRST DYNASTY, EGYPTIANS, 253 YEARS.

	Y.	B. C.
Menes and his successors, ending with Timaus	253	2412

SECOND DYNASTY, SHEPHERD KINGS, 260 YEARS.

	Y.	B. C.
1. Salatis, Silites, or Nirmaryada	19	2159
2. Baion, Byon, or Babya	44	2140
3. Apachnes, Pachman, or Ruchma	37	2096
First Pyramid begun about		2005
Abraham visits Egypt about.................		2077
4. Apophes...................................	61	2059
5. Janias or Sethos	50	1998
6. Assis or Aseth	49	1948
Expulsion of the Shepherds...............	260	1899

THIRD DYNASTY, NATIVE KINGS, 251 YEARS.

	Y.	B. C.
Alisphragmuthosis, &c.	37—	1899
Joseph appointed Governor or Regent	9—	1872
Jacob's Family settle in Goshen	215—	1863
Death of Joseph		1792
Queen Nitocris ....,...............		1743
Exode of the Israelites	251—	1648

FOURTH DYNASTY, 340 YEARS.

1. Amosis, Tethmosis, or Thummosis	25—1648
2. Chebron	13—1623
3. Amenophis I.	20—1610
4. Amesses	21—1589
5. Mephres	12—1567
6. Misphragmuthosis	25—1554
7. Thmosis or Tethmosis	9—1528
8. Amenophis II.	30—1518
9. Orus or Horus	36—1488
10. Acencbris	12—1452
11. Rathosis	9—1440
12. Acencheres I.	12—1421
13. Acenchères II.	20—1418
14. Armais or Harmais	4—1398
15. Ramesses	1—1394
16. Harmesses	66—1393
17. Amenophis III. or Mœris	19—1327
Death of Mœris	340—1308*

The most interesting event that occurred during this long
interval was the invasion of Egypt by the Shepherds, which,
according to the chronology we have here adopted, took
place two thousand one hundred and fifty-nine years before
the birth of Christ. Manetho, the historian already mentioned, inserted in his work a very intelligible notice of the
misfortune which had befallen his country at that early period; the accuracy of which cannot be called in question,
except in the point where he is supposed to identify the
savage invaders from the East with the peaceful family of
Jacob, who were invited to settle in the land of Goshen.
The fragment has been preserved by Josephus in his tract
against Apion, and contains the following statement :—

"We had formerly a king named Timaus. In his reign,
God, upon what account I know not, was offended with us

* Vol. iv. p. 418. We have omitted the odd months.

and unexpectedly men from the East, of obscure origin,
boldly invaded the kingdom and subdued it without a contest. Having mastered the former rulers, they barbarously
burnt the cities, demolished the temples of the gods, and
treated all the inhabitants most cruelly; massacring the
men, and reducing the women, and children to slavery.
They next appointed one of their leaders king, whose name
was Salatis. He resided in Memphis, and imposed a tribute on the Upper and Lower Egypt, and put garrisons in
the most important places. But chiefly he secured the
eastern parts of the country, foreseeing that the Assyrians,
who were then most powerful, would be tempted to invade
the kingdom likewise. Finding, therefore, in the Saite-
nome, a city placed most conveniently on the north side of
the Bubastic channel, which in an ancient theological book
is called Avaris, he repaired and fortified it very strongly,
and garrisoned it with two hundred and forty thousand soldiers. Hither he used to come in summer to furnish them
with corn and pay, and he carefully disciplined them for a
terror to foreigners. He died after he had reigned nineteen
years.*

"The next, called Baion, reigned 44 years; and after
him Apachnes, 36 years and three months; then Apophes,
61 years; and Janias, 50 years and one month; and after
him Assis, 49 years and two months. These six were their
first kings, who were continually at war with the Egyptians,
and wished of all things to eradicate them.

"At length the native Egyptian princes rebelled against
these tyrants, and, after a tedious warfare, drove them out
of the rest of Egypt, and shut them up in Avaris, where
they had collected all their cattle and plunder, and besieged
them with an army of 480,000 men. But, despairing of
success, the Egyptians concluded a treaty with them, and
they were suffered to depart unmolested from Egypt, with
all their households, amounting to 240,000 souls, and their
cattle. Accordingly they crossed the desert; but being
afraid to return home on account of the Assyrian power,
which then held Asia in subjection, they settled in the country of Judæa, and there built Jerusalem."

Josephus imagined that this narrative describes the his-

* Avaris, or Abaris, "the Pass," was afterward called Pelusium.

tory of his own ancestors, the children of Israel. But it is much more probable that the people who were thus expelled from Egypt were the fathers of the Philistines, who occupied the eastern shores of the Mediterranean, and occasionally extended their power as far as the banks of the Euphrates. Every.one knows that, in the language of Western Asia, the term *pali* denotes shepherds, and *stan* or *sthan* means land; and accordingly the compound word Pali-stan, literally signifies Shepherd-land, or the country of shepherds. It is therefore extremely probable that the warlike nation who so frequently disputed with the descendants of Abraham the possession of the Syrian border were the progeny of the royal herdsmen who so long subjected to their thrall the rich territory of Lower and Middle Egypt.

The remembrance of the Shepherd expedition is not yet extinct even among the tribes of Central India. In one of the sacred books of the Hindoos, quoted by Captain Wilford, a record is preserved of two remarkable migrations from the East in remote times; first of the Yadavas, or "sacred race," and afterward of the Pali or Shepherds. These last, we are told, were a powerful tribe, who, in ancient days, governed the whole country, from the Indus to the mouth of the Ganges, and are called Pali-bothri by Pliny, and Pali-putras in the annals of Hindoostan. They were besides an active, enterprising, and roving people, whò, by conquest and colonization, gradually spread themselves over a great part of Asia, Africa, and Europe. Crossing from the shores of the Persian Gulf, they took possession of Arabia, as well as of the lands on the western shore of the Red Sea; in the latter their country was, by the Greeks and Romans, called Barbaria. This term was derived from *berber*, a shepherd, according to Bruce, who describes them as a distinct race from the natives, with long hair and dark complexions, living in tents, and shifting their cattle from place to place for the convenience of pasturage. They seem, in fact, to be the eastern Ethiopians, as distinguished from the western both by Homer and Herodotus.[*]

It is well known that the historian just quoted describes the inhabitants of the Syrian Palestine as having, according

* Asiatic Researches, vol. iii. p. 46; Bruce's Travels, vol. ii. p. 21; Iliad, i. v. 423; Odyss. i. v. 22; Herod. lib. vii.

to their own account, migrated from the Erythræan Sea to the shores of the Mediterranean, where they afterward applied themselves to navigation and commerce. How extensively they spread themselves both in Europe and Asia appears from the cities and places which still retain their name. Thus, a Palestine, or Palesthan, was found on the banks of the Tigris, most probably their original settlement; the town of Paliputra stood on the Hellespont; the river Strymon in Thrace was surnamed Palestinus; the Palestini and the town Philistia were situated on the river Po in Italy; and the god of shepherds, among the Latins, was denominated Pales.*

The following extract from an article in the Asiatic Researches, contributed by the learned soldier already named, will tend to strengthen the opinion now universally entertained by the ablest writers, that the shepherds who invaded Egypt had migrated from a distant country in the East:—

"An ancient king, called Chatura-Yána, passed a hundred years in a cavern of Chrishna-giri, the Black Mountain, on the banks of the Cali, performing the most rigorous acts of devotion. At length Vishnu appeared to him, and promised him that he should have a son, whom he was to name *Tamovatsa*. This prince when he succeeded his father was warlike and ambitious, but wise and devout. He prayed to Vishnu to enlarge his empire, and the god granted his request. Hearing that Misra-sthan (the land of Egypt) was governed by a powerful but unjust prince called Nirmaryada, he, with a chosen army, invaded that country without any declaration of war, and began to administer justice among the people, to give them a specimen of a good king; and when Nirmaryada sent to expostulate, he treated his remonstrance with disdain. This brought on a bloody battle of three days, in which the Egyptian king was killed. The conqueror, who fought like another Parasa Rama, then took possession of the kingdom of Misra, and governed with perfect equity. Babya Vatsa, his son, devoted himself to religion, and resigned his crown to his son Rucma Vatsa, who tenderly loved his people, and so highly improved his country that, from his just revenues, he amassed an incredible treasure. His wealth was so great that he raised

* Herod. lib. i. c. 5; Hales's New Analysis, vol. iv. p. 427.

three mountains, called Rucm-adri, Rujat-adri, and Retu-adri, or the mountain of gold, of silver, and of gems."*

In this legend, says Dr. Hales, we trace the distorted features of the Egyptian account. By an interchange of characters, Tamo is the Timaus of Manetho, a quiet and peaceable prince, who was invaded without provocation by this Nirmaryada of Cushite race, called Salatis by Manetho, and Silites by Syncellus. His son Babya is evidently the Baion of Manetho. The third king was surnamed Ruchma from his immense wealth, which he collected by oppressing the Egyptians, though he tenderly loved his own people the Shepherds. Wishing either to extirpate the natives or to break down their spirits by hard and incessant labour, he employed them in constructing those stupendous monuments of ancient ostentation and tyranny. The Pyramids, which are obviously the *mountains* indicated in the Hindoo records, were, it is presumed, originally cased with yellow, white, or spotted marbles, brought from the quarries of Arabia.

From this Hindoo record we seem fully warranted in ascribing the building of the first and greatest pyramid to Apachnes, the third of the Shepherd kings, and of the rest to his successors. This conclusion is still further confirmed by the tradition of the native Egyptians, communicated to Herodotus, that " they were built by one Philitis, a shepherd, who kept his cattle in those parts, and whose memory was held in such abhorrence that the inhabitants would not even repeat his name nor that of his brother who succeeded him." It is interesting to observe that the vindictive feeling of an oppressed people has preserved the original title of the Shepherds in the foreign term Philitis; the etymology of which, as derived from the Sanscrit Pali, and branching out into all the epithets applied to a celebrated people in Syria, we have already endeavoured to explain.†

The hostile spirit entertained by the Egyptians against their barbarian conquerors continued unabated in the age of the patriarch Joseph, when shepherds were still held as an " abomination,"—a fact which of itself goes far to prove

* Asiatic Researches, vol. iii. p. 225.
† See above, page 55.—New Analysis of Ancient Chronology, vol. iv. p. 469; Herodotus, book ii. c. 128.

that the celebrated inroad of the Pastoral kings must have taken place before this favourite son of Jacob was carried as a slave into the house of Potiphar. But it is not surprising that the exode of the Israelites should have been confounded by historians with the expulsion of the more ancient invaders. The Hebrews were employed in tending cattle as well as the oriental Pali; and, in other respects, they were not less disliked by the people, to whom their increasing numbers had rendered them formidable. The military array, too, assumed by the followers of Moses, and the pursuit directed by the Egyptian monarch in person, throw an air of resemblance over the two events. But it is manifest, notwithstanding, that the family of Jacob cannot be identified with that warlike host which subdued Lower Egypt, overturned the throne of Memphis, and placed the sceptre in the hands of a powerful dynasty of kings, who exercised supreme power during the long period of two hundred and sixty years. The departure of the Israelites did not take place until the lapse of two centuries and a half had again consolidated the government of the Pharaohs, and improved the resources of the nation. But the true exode of the chosen people, with all the demonstrations of miraculous agency by which it was accomplished, is too well known to require from us even the most abbreviated narrative; we therefore proceed to complete the outline of Egyptian history in a department not quite so familiar to the common reader.

Passing over Mœris, whose peaceful labours will be described hereafter, we arrive at the era of his renowned son, the accomplished and victorious Sesostris. In the history of this hero fiction has exhausted all her powers to darken and exaggerate; and the little light which remained to guide us to the appreciation of facts has been nearly all obscured by the clouds of chronological error which, from time to time, have been spread over his reign. In placing his accession at the beginning of the thirteenth century before Christ, we follow Hales, being satisfied that his conclusions are worthy of greater confidence than those of every other writer who preceded him in the study of time; and as our object in this chapter is to fix dates rather than to describe actions, we shall mention the grounds upon which we believe that Sesostris ascended the throne of Egypt at the epoch just stated. Such an exposition will appear more necessary when it is considered that Eusebius imagined this conqueror to be the immediate successor of the Pharaoh who was drowned in the Red Sea at the exode of the Israelites, and that he began his famous expedition while the descendants of Jacob were still wandering in the desert of Arabia. In this untenable opinion the Bishop of Cæsarea has been followed by Usher and Playfair. Sir John Marsham, on the other hand, identified Sesostris with the Shishak of Scripture who invaded Judæa,—a notion which received the concurrence of Sir Isaac Newton, and has been adopted by many writers of inferior reputation. That the reign of the son of Mœris belongs to an intermediate period may be proved from the following considerations :—

Herodotus relates that Sesostris was succeeded by Pheron and this last by Proteus, in whose time Troy was taken; and, according to Manetho, Sesothis was succeeded by Rampses, and Rampses by Ramesses, in whose reign also Troy was taken. Therefore Sesothis and Sesostris were obviously the same person; and it is equally clear that his accession could not have been much earlier than 1283, or a century before the destruction of Troy, reckoning three reigns equivalent to three mean generations. This agrees sufficiently with the date which we have selected.

Again, in his fourth book, Herodotus states that Targitaus founded the Scythian kingdom about a thousand years at most before the invasion of Darius Hystaspes, or, in other words, about 1508 before the Christian era. But we learn from the historian Justin that Timaus, the sixth king in succession from Targitaus, encountered Sesostris, and checked or defeated him at the river Phasis. Reckoning these six reigns equivalent to mean generations, or 200 years, the accession of Sesostris could not be earlier than 1308 B. C.

In the third place, Herodotus mentions that Sesostris founded the kingdom of Colchis near Pontus, and left a colony there, consisting of such of his soldiers as were weary of service; and we are informed by Apollonius Rhodius that the posterity of the Egyptian governor subsisted at Æa, the capital of Colchis, for many generations. This governor was the father of Æetes, who was the father of Medea, the mistress of Jason in the Argonautic expedition, which, it is well known took place about 1225 B. C.; that is, seventy-four years after Sesostris returned from his Asiatic campaigns.[*]

The confirmation thus afforded to the Egyptian chronology by historical facts, incidentally mentioned by Grecian writers, is extremely satisfactory, and illustrates the soundness of the principle upon which our system is constructed. It is deserving of notice, at the same time, that the hero whose exploits fill so large a space in the traditional story of ancient Egypt has been placed, by the researches of Champollion, at the beginning of the thirteenth century before the reign of Augustus Cæsar, and thereby most distinctly identified with the great Sesostris, the conqueror of the world.

Diodorus is our principal authority for the warlike achievements of this celebrated monarch. His first expedition after he came to the throne was against the Abyssinians, whom he reduced to the condition of tributaries. He then turned his arms against the nations who dwelt on either shore of the Red Sea, advanced along the Persian Gulf, and finally, if we may trust to the accuracy of our historian, marched at the head of his troops into India, and even crossed the Ganges. Directing his face towards Upper Asia, he next subdued the Assyrians and Medes; whence, passing to the confines of Europe, he ravaged the land of the Scythians, until he sustained the reverse above alluded to at the hands of Timaus, their valiant prince, on the banks of the Phasis. Want of provisions, and the impenetrable nature of the country which defended the approaches to ancient Thrace, compelled him to relinquish his European campaign. He accordingly returned to Egypt in 1299 B. C., being the ninth year of his military enterprise.

Making due allowance for the exaggeration which always takes the place of authentic records, we are nevertheless disposed to maintain that the history of Sesostris cannot be wholly reduced to fiction, nor ascribed entirely to the mythological wanderings of Bacchus or Osiris. We are assured, on the personal evidence of Herodotus and Strabo, that the pillars erected by the Egyptian leader still remained in their

---

[*] Herod. book ii. c. 103; book iv. c. 5, 6, 7; Justin, lib. i. c. 1; Apoll. Rhod. lib. iv. p 272; Hales, vol. iv. p. 429.

days, and even that they were actually inspected by them in Syria, Palestine, Arabia, and Ethiopia. The inscription which these proud monuments every where bore was to the following effect :—

"Sesostris, King of Kings, and Lord of Lords, subdued this country by his arms."

Another circumstance corroborative of the general accuracy of the old annalists has been already mentioned,—the establishment of an Egyptian colony in the province of Colchis. The descendants of this military association, presenting the dark complexion and woolly hair of Africa, were long distinguishable from the natives of the district among whom they dwelt. Nay, it is possible, we believe, at the present day, to find among the Circassians certain families whose blood might be traced to the soldiers of Sesostris, and whose features still verify the traditional affinity which connects them with the ancient inhabitants of the Nile.

It is usual, in all countries, that the fame of a popular monarch shall be increased by having ascribed to him, not only all the heroic deeds which have been transmitted by the chroniclers of the olden time, but that he shall be regarded by the multitude as the founder of all the magnificent palaces and gorgeous temples of which the remains still continue to testify that their nation was once wealthy and powerful. On this account it is not improbable that Sesostris, under the several names or titles of Osymandias, Ramesses, Sethosis, and Sethon, has had attributed to him the merit of erecting several splendid edifices which are due to sovereigns of a less imposing celebrity. At all events, it is not doubted by any one that both Memphis and Thebes owed some of their finest structures to the conqueror of Asia; and it is even recorded by his panegyrists, that the riches and the immense number of prisoners which crowned his successes in the East enabled him to decorate all the towns of Egypt without exacting from his native subjects any portion of their labour or revenue. Memphis, the new capital, was enlarged and ornamented with the most profuse expenditure. The statues, the temples, and the obelisks which adorned it are described by historians in their most pompous language; but the infelicity of its situation, which

F

exposed it to the inundations of the Nile, has so completely
obliterated all traces of its existence as to have created a
question among antiquaries as to the precise spot on which
it stood.   Thebes, on the contrary, which enjóyed a more
secure position, and was perhaps built of more lasting materials, displays at the present day the magnificence of her
princes, combined with the learning and taste which distinguished her inhabitants.

The Palace, or Sepulchral Temple (for the ruins of the
two have been confounded), appears to have been an edifice of
exquisite workmanship as well as of vast extent.   In front
there was a court of immense size; adjoining which there
arose a portico four hundred feet long, the roof of which was
supported by figures fifteen cubits in height.   This portico
led into another court similar to the first, but more superb,
and adorned with statues of great magnitude, which are said
to have represented the king and certain members of his
family.   Amid a numerous succession of halls and galleries
the chisel had sculptured with wonderful art the triumphs
of the sovereign, the sacrifices which he had offered, the
administration of justice in his courts of law, and such
other functions as were appropriated to the head of a great
nation.   But the tomb, properly so, called, is especially
remarkable for the astronomical emblems which it exhibits.
It is encompassed with a golden circle three hundred and
sixty-five cubits in circumference, to represent the number
of days comprehended in the year. · The rising and setting
of the stars are likewise depicted with considerable accuracy, and show that great attention was already paid to the
motions and periods of the heavenly bodies.   Thus it is
rendered manifest, that whatever doubt may exist as to the
identity of Sesostris and Osymandias, or in regard to the
period at which one or other ascended the throne, the light
of civilization and the improvement of the arts had made
great progress in Upper Egypt more than thirteen centuries
before the Christian era.   The statue of the monarch himself represented in a sitting posture, was considered by the
ancients as the largest in the country.   The foot alone was
seven cubits in length; and the following epitaph appropriated this gigantic work of art to the renowned commander
whose name it was meant to perpetuate :—

"I am Osymandias, King of Kings; if any one desire to know what a prince I am, and where I lie, let him excel my exploits."

The successors of this great prince, for several generations, did not perform any remarkable action, nor allow their ambitious views to extend beyond the limits of their native kingdom. Perhaps it might be said that the power of Egypt was not more than sufficient to defend her own borders against the erratic hordes who constantly threatened her on the east, and the more regular armaments of Abyssinia, which occasionally made an inroad from the south. About 770 B. C. Sabaco the Ethiopian descended the Nile, and drove Anysis from the throne. Sixty years later, Sennacherib, King of Assyria, meditated the conquest of the same country, and had actually entered its territories, when his immense host was destroyed by a Divine visitation.

Disgusted with the weakness or misfortune of their sovereigns, the Egyptians made the experiment of an oligarchy of twelve governors, who directed the administration about fifteen years. But, in 619 B. C., Pharaoh Neche was elevated to an undivided throne. His reign is remarkable for the success he obtained against Jerusalem, which he took, and against the good prince Josiah, whom he slew. He made several attempts to connect, for the purposes of commerce, the Nile with the Red Sea; and afterward accomplished what must have been then esteemed the still more arduous enterprise of circumnavigating Africa, from the Strait of Babelmandeb to the Mediterranean.

About this period the Assyrian monarchy, which had acquired an ascendant over all the neighbouring nations from the Euphrates to the shores of the Great Sea, became formidable also to Egypt. Nebuchadnezzar on more than one occasion made the weight of his power to be felt on the banks of the Nile; but the conquest of the whole of that country was reserved for the great Cyrus, who marshalled under his standard nearly all the states of Western Asia. It appears, however, that the liberal policy of this famed warrior restored to the Egyptians, as well as to the Jews, a certain degree of national independence,—a boon which the former were thought to have abused so much that one of the first measures adopted by his successor had for its object their entire and permanent subjugation.

The effects produced upon Egypt by the victories of Cambyses are too important to be passed over with so slight a notice as that now given. It should seem that the way was paved for him by the treachery of two great officers, who sought revenge for a personal insult by throwing open the kingdom to a foreign enemy. When, however, the Persian monarch appeared before Pelusium, he found that preparations had been made for a vigorous resistance ; but, availing himself of the miserable superstition of the garrison, he placed their sacred animals in front of his army, and advanced to the attack. The city surrendered without opposition. A general engagement, which ensued immediately afterward, terminated in the total discomfiture of Psammenitus and the reduction of Memphis. The conqueror disgraced his triumph by the most wanton cruelties, and particularly by putting to death the son of the king, together with two thousand individuals of high rank. He also gave vent to his rage against the priests and religion of the country, on suspicion that they were employed to undermine his authority. Regardless of public opinion, he gave orders to slay the bull Apis, the object of so much veneration among all classes ; and, because the magistrates and guardians of the temple interposed to prevent this horrible sacrilege, he slew the one and scourged the other. A similar feeling dictated the mad attempt to seize the consecrated fane of Jupiter Ammon, situated in the Greater Oasis. The loss of half his army, the disaffection of the remainder, and the universal hatred of his new subjects, compelled him to return to Persia, where he soon afterward became the victim of accident or of conspiracy.

The government of Persia, interrupted only by a series of unsuccessful revolts, was maintained during more than two hundred years ; at the end of which Alexander the Great, who soon afterward wrested from the hands of Darius the sceptre of the empire itself, took possession of the kingdom of the Pharaohs, now one of its most remote provinces.

Before we proceed to the history of the Grecian rulers, we shall present a tabular view of the several dynasties from the death of Mœris to the accession of the first Ptolemy.

FIFTH DYNASTY, 342 YEARS.

		Y.	B. C.
1.	Sethos, Sesostris, or Osymandias....................	32	1366
2.	Rampses or Pheron...................................	61	1275
3.	Cetes, Proteus, or Ramesses...........................	50	1214
4.	Amenophis IV...	40	1164
5.	Rampsinites	42	1124
6.	Cheops or Chemmis	50	1062
7.	Cephrenes, Cephres, or Sesah	56	1032
8	Mycerinus or Cherinus	10	976
	His death..	342	966

SIXTH DYNASTY, 293 YEARS.

		Y.	B. C.
	A chasm..................................	151	966
1.	Bocchoris or Asychis	44	815
2.	Anysis	2	771
3.	Sabacon or So }	50	769
	Anysis again {	6	719
4.	Sebecon or Sethos..............................	40	713
	Sennacherib invades Egypt............................		711
	End of the period...................................	293	673

SEVENTH DYNASTY, 148 YEARS.

		Y.	B. C.
1.	Twelve contemporary kings..........................	15	673
2.	Psammeticus I...................................	39	658
3.	Nekus or Pharaoh Necho.........................	16	619
4.	Psammis.......................................	6	603
5.	Apries or Pharaoh Hophra	28	597
6.	Amasis	44	569
	Cyrus conquers Egypt		535
7.	Psammenitus. First revolt of Egypt, (6 mo.)		525
		148	

EIGHTH DYNASTY, PERSIAN KINGS, 112 YEARS.

		Y.	B. C.
1.	Cambyses reduced Egypt }	38	525
	First Persian Administration {		
2.	Darius Hystaspes. Second revolt of Egypt...............	3	487
3.	Xerxes reduces Egypt }	24	484
	Second Persian Administration {		
4.	Artaxerxes Longimanus. Third revolt	4	460
	Reduces Egypt }	43	456
	Third Persian Administration {		
	Herodotus visits Egypt................................		448
5.	Darius Nothus. Fourth revolt.......................	112	413

NINTH DYNASTY, EGYPTIAN KINGS, 81 YEARS.

Y. B. C.

1. Amyrtæus .... 6—413
2. Pausiris .... 6—407
3. Psammeticus II .... 6—401
4. Nephereus .... 6—395
5. Acoris .... 14—389
6. Nectanebus .... 12—375
7. Tachus or Tacos .... 2—363
8. Nectanebus .... 11—361.
   Ochus reduces Egypt } .... 18—350
   Fourth Persian Administration }

Alexander conquers Egypt .... 81—332

Upon the division of the Persian empire, Egypt fell to Ptolemy Lagus, one of Alexander's generals, who, when he ascended the throne, assumed the cognomen of Soter. Our limits will not permit us to describe at length the character of this prince, nor to set forth the numerous obligations which literature and philosophy continue to bear to his memory. His establishment of the celebrated Alexandrian Library, and his marked encouragement of men of letters, are too well known to require illustration; and perhaps the royal munificence which he displayed in providing so splendid an asylum for learning was more than equalled by the discrimination which he manifested in the choice of individuals to preside over its interests and to promote its progress. While inviting to his court and placing in his schools those characters who were, the most distinguished of the age for their scientific acquirements, Ptolemy nevertheless showed himself the greatest philosopher that adorned Alexandria. To the knowledge of books he joined the more valuable knowledge of men and of business; and was thereby qualified to direct the pursuits of science to practicable objects, as well as to withdraw the speculations of the learned from the insane metaphysics in which they were wont to indulge, in order to engage them in the more profitable studies of criticism, history, geometry, and medicine. The countenance shown to Demetrius Phalerius, and the employment to which he turned his accomplished mind, reflect greater honour upon the memory of Soter than all the magnificence of the Serapeion, or even the patriotic object contemplated in the structure of the Pharos.

His son Philadelphus succeeded to an inheritance of great

honour, but of much anxiety; for, being raised to the throne in place of his eldest brother Ceraunus, he was long exposed to the fear of domestic treason and of foreign war. But a reign of thirty-eight years enabled him to consolidate his power, and even to purchase the gratitude of his subjects, by executing many public works of great utility. He conveyed the waters of the Nile into the deserts of Libya, completed the lighthouse at the harbour of Alexandria, and laboured to improve the navigable canals which connected his capital with the Red Sea and the Mediterranean. The only stain upon his administration arose from the pitiful revenge inflicted on the librarian Demetrius, for having advised the former king to allow the succession to proceed in the natural course, and to settle the crown on his first-born son.

The third Ptolemy found it necessary to begin his reign with a Syrian war, which, in his own time, produced no memorable results, though, it would appear, it opened up to his successor a path to renown as a conquerer in the East. The latter is said not only to have chastised the insolence of Seleucus, and extended his conquests beyond the Euphrates, but even to have carried his arms to the confines of Bactria. Among the spoils which Euergetes—the title bestowed upon him by his people—acquired in the course of his victories, was a prodigious number of statues, images of gold and silver, and other instruments of worship, which Cambyses had carried away from the palaces and temples of Egypt.

It was in the year 221 before our era that Ptolemy Philopater mounted the throne of his father in the due course of succession. In his reign the Syrians recovered the provinces which the more fortunate arms of his predecessor had added to the Egyptian territory; the Jews were inhumanly persecuted; and the general affairs of the kingdom fell into confusion and disorder. A slave to his passions, and addicted to cruelty, he sunk under a ruined constitution at the early age of thirty-seven.

The minority which followed was of considerable importance, inasmuch as it proved the occasion of introducing formally into Egypt the powerful influence of the Roman government. As Ptolemy Epiphanes was only five years old at the death of his father, the kings of Syria and Macedon determined to dismember and divide his dominions; on which account the guardians of the prince applied to the Western Republic to interpose her authority in the cause of justice, and to prevent the undue aggrandizement of two ambitious monarchs.

This request was readily granted; and, that the interests of the Egyptian court might not suffer from delay, Marcus Æmilius Lepidus set sail for Alexandria to assume the direction of affairs. Meanwhile ambassadors were despatched to Antiochus and Philip, charged with the determination of the senate, and instructed to make known the line of policy which the Roman government had resolved to pursue. But the peace and happiness which were thus secured to the people ceased almost as soon as this feeble ruler took the sceptre into his own hand. He became corrupt, and they became disaffected. Various conspiracies were formed and defeated; but at length the attempt of an assassin succeeded, and Epiphanes was cut off in the twenty-ninth year of his age.

The government was seized by the queen, a Syrian princess, named Cleopatra, in behalf of her son, who was only six years old. Her partiality for her native court, and the influence of her brother Antiochus, threatened the peace of Egypt and even its independence, when the Romans again interposed to defeat the ambitious schemes of Syria. But the young Ptolemy, distinguished by the title of Philometer, was so completely in the power of his uncle that the inhabitants of Alexandria raised to the throne a younger prince, upon whom they conferred the surname of Euergetes, though, at a later period, he was better known by the epithet Physcon, a term expressive of unwieldy corpulence. The brothers at length divided the kingdom, and exercised a separate and independent sovereignty; Cyrene and Libya being ceded to the younger, while the other retained that original portion of Egypt which was considered as more strictly hereditary.

Philometer, at his death, left an infant son, who has been denominated Ptolemy the Seventh, but who never attained to the possession of power. To secure the tranquillity of the nation, a union between the widow of the late king and Euergetes the Second was recommended by the Romans, and immediately adopted; the right of succession, on the demise of his uncle, being reserved to the young prince. But the jealousy of the cruel monarch soon put an end to his life, with the view, it might be presumed, of clearing the way for the accession of one of his own sons. He next repudiated his queen, whom he subsequently drove into Syria, and thereby involved his country in the hazard of a war with Demetrius, the rival and enemy of Egypt. Science and learning, intimidated by the horrors which oppressed the kingdom, were observed to take flight from their ancient seat, and to seek an asylum in other lands. The seminaries of Alexandria were deserted by the most distinguished professors, who, together with the principal inhabitants of the maritime district, found themselves menaced with imprisonment or death. Nor was it until after the lapse of twenty-nine years that Physcon, detested for his crimes and feared for his sanguinary disposition, finished his earthly career, leaving his crown to be disputed by three sons, Appion, Lathyrus, and Alexander. This reign will appear interesting in the eye of the philosophical historian, from the fact, which the Egyptians could no longer conceal from themselves, that the influence of Rome was daily gaining ground in their councils, and already securing the foundations of that dominion which she afterward formally usurped.

Through the influence of Cleopatra, who had returned from her Syrian exile, Alexander was preferred to the throne. But as the claims of Lathyrus were acknowledged by a majority of the people, he was encouraged to assert his right by force of arms; and having succeeded in driving his younger brother into a foreign country, he inflicted a severe punishment upon the insurgents of Upper Egypt, who had, during the political dissensions of the new capital, endeavoured to establish their independence. The inhabitants of the Thebaid had long felt themselves overlooked. The rising glory of Memphis had first obscured the splendour of the ancient metropolis; while, more recently, the importance of Alexandria, both as a place of learning and of commerce, had attracted to a still greater extent the wealth and population of the kingdom. It is not surprising, therefore, that the citizens of Thebes should have entertained the desire of recovering some share of the distinction of which they had been gradually deprived, and, at the same time, of securing to the Egyptians a seat of government at a greater distance from the arms and intrigues of their warlike neighbours. In suppressing this spirit of disaffection, Lathyrus is accused of an excessive severity, in which he emulated the destructive policy of Cambyses, and reduced the remains of the venerable city to a heap of ruins.

His death, in the year eighty-one before Christ, relieved the apprehensions of the people, and opened a path for the accession of Cleopatra, his only child, whose gentle sex and manners gave the promise of a happy reign. This cheering anticipation might have been realized, had there not existed another claimant for the same honour in the person of Alexander, the son of her father's brother. Cleopatra was, without doubt, the legitimate sovereign, and was acknowledged as such by nearly all her subjects; but the councils which now directed the affairs of Egypt emanated from the shores of the Tiber. The Romans, who at first acted only as umpires, had already begun to enlarge their views, and to claim a right to interpose with their advice, and even with their arms. Sylla at this period discharged the office of dictator, and, in virtue of his high prerogative as master of the commonwealth, prescribed an arrangement to the competitors for the Egyptian crown. Cleopatra became the wife of her cousin Ptolemy, Alexander the Second, and thereby, it was hoped, had finally united the rival interests of the two branches of the royal family. But this measure produced not the auspicious results which were expected to arise from it. The ambitious youth, impatient of an equal, murdered his young wife, and seized the undivided sovereignty, which he appears to have occupied several years. At length he was compelled to flee from the indignation of his subjects to the coast of Tyre; where, just before his death, he made a will, by which he bequeathed Egypt to the Roman senate and people.

The next who assumed and disgraced the title of Ptolemy, was a son of Lathyrus, who, from the excellence of his performances on the flute, was surnamed Auletes. This weak prince proved a tool in the hands of the Romans, and evidently lent himself to accomplish their favourite design of reducing Egypt to the condition of a province dependent on the republic. The leading men at court, who had no difficulty in penetrating his intentions, expelled him from the throne, and placed the sceptre in the hand of his daughter Berenice. To defend themselves still further against the intrigues of Rome, they proposed to marry their young sovereign to the King of Syria,—hoping that the combined forces of the two kingdoms would prove more than a match for the legions usually stationed beyond the Hellespont. But the premature death of Antiochus defeated this wise project. Auletes was restored through the interest of the celebrated Pompey, and conducted into his capital by Mark Antony, a commander hardly less renowned. After a series of oppressions and cruelties, among which may be mentioned the murder of Berenice, he terminated a shameful reign by an early death,—intrusting his surviving children to the care and tuition of the Roman government.

Among the infants thus left to the protection of the senate, were the famous Cleopatra and her brother Ptolemy Dionysius. As soon as these princes came of age, they were raised to the throne, and associated in the government. But their friendship and union were of short continuance ; and each having the support of a numerous party, their dissensions almost necessarily terminated in a civil war. Cleopatra was compelled to seek refuge in Syria ; soon after which event, Julius Cæsar, who by his victory at Pharsalia had already made himself master of the commonwealth, appeared in Egypt to complete his conquest, and to quell the intestine commotions by which the whole of that kingdom was distracted. She lost no time in repairing to Alexandria, where she was secretly introduced into the presence of the Roman general. This able soldier and politician immediately restored to her the share of power which she had formerly possessed,—issuing a decree, in the name of the senate, that Ptolemy Dionysius and his sister Cleopatra should be acknowledged as joint sovereigns of Egypt. The partisans of the young king, being dissatisfied with this arrangement, had recourse to a military stratagem, by which Cæsar and his attendants were nearly destroyed. A war ensued soon afterward, which ended in the death of Ptolemy and the complete establishment of the Romans, not less as conquerors than as guardians of the children of Auletes.

But it was not consistent with Egyptian decorum that

Cleopatra should reign without a colleague, and, therefore, to satisfy the prejudices of the people, her youngest brother, not more than eleven years of age, was placed beside her on the throne. Such a nomination could not be regarded in any other light than as a show of limiting the power of the queen; and even this apparent check on her authority was soon removed by the murder of the child, who fell a victim to the furious passions which at that period dishonoured the descendants of the great Ptolemy.

But the term of their dynasty was now fast approaching. The assassination of the conqueror of Pharsalia, and the subsequent defeat of Mark Antony, raised the fortunes of Octavianus above the reach of the most powerful of his rivals, and at length invested him with the imperial purple, as the acknowledged head of the Roman world. Cleopatra made her escape from his revenge in a voluntary death; for suspecting that he intended to wound her feelings, by assigning to her a place in the train of captives who were to adorn his triumph at Rome, she found means to put an end to her life by the bite of a poisonous reptile. With her ended the line of Grecian sovereigns, which had continued two hundred and ninety-six years.

As a province of the Roman empire, the history of Egypt can hardly be separated from that of the mighty people by whose deputies it was now to be governed. It was, indeed, occasionally disturbed by insurrections, and sometimes even by foreign war; but it was, notwithstanding, retained with a firm grasp both against domestic and external foes, until the decline of power compelled the successors of Augustus to withdraw their legions from the extremities of the empire, to defend the provinces on the Tiber and the Danube. Adrian, in the beginning of the second century, spent two years in Egypt, during which he laboured to revive among the natives the love of letters and the beauties of archi tecture. Severus, too, at a somewhat later period, made a similar visit, when, like his predecessor, he exerted himself to relieve the burdens and improve the condition of the great body of the people. In particular, he countenanced every attempt that was made to repair the ancient monuments, as also to replenish the museums and libraries at Alexandria with books, instruments, and works of art; and, above all, to withdraw the minds of the more contemplative from the dangerous pursuits of magic and the contemptible deceptions of astrology. The reigns of Claudius and of Aurelian were slightly agitated by the pretensions of Zenobia, Queen of Palmyra, who, as a descendant of the Ptolemies, announced herself the sovereign of Egypt. Her army advanced to the frontiers, and even gained some advantages over the Romans; but her troops being at length steadily opposed by the legions of Syria, she sustained a total defeat, and was carried captive to Rome.

When, at a later period, the emperor Probus visited Egypt, he executed many considerable works for the splendour and benefit of the country. The navigation of the Nile, so important to Rome itself, was improved; and temples, bridges, porticoes, and palaces were constructed by the hands of his soldiers, who acted by turns as architects, as engineers, and as husbandmen. On the division of the empire by Diocletian, Egypt was reduced to a very distracted state. Achilleus at Alexandria, and the Blemmyes, a savage race of Ethiopians, defied the Roman arms. The emperor, resolved to punish the insurgents, opened the campaign with the siege of Alexandria. He cut off the aqueducts which supplied every quarter of that immense city with water, and pushed his attacks with so much caution and vigour, that at the end of eight months the besieged submitted to the clemency of the conqueror. The fate of Busiris and Coptos was even more melancholy than that of Alexandria. Those proud cities,—the former distinguished by its antiquity, the latter enriched by the passage of the Indian trade,—were utterly destroyed by the arms of the enraged Diocletian.*

The introduction of Christianity was marked by repeated outrages among the people, and even by such commotions as threatened to shake the stability of the government. The adherents of the old superstition resisted, on some occasions, the destruction of their temples and the contemptuous exposure of their idols; while, in more than one instance, the Christian ministers, with a larger share of zeal than of discretion, insulted their opinions, and even set at defiance the authority of the civil magistrate when interposed to preserve the public peace. But, after the

* Gibbon, vol. i. chap. 6.

G

conversion of Constantine, the power of the church was
effectually exerted to co-operate with the provincial rulers
in supporting the rights of the empire, and in repelling the
inroads of the barbarians from the east and south.   Nor
was it till a new religion arose in Arabia, and gave birth to
a dynasty of warlike sovereigns, that Egypt, wrested from
its European conquerors, was forced to receive more arbitrary masters, and submit to a severer yoke.   This era,
however, constitutes the point in our historical retrospect
at which we announced our intention to interrupt the narrative, until we shall have laid before the reader an account
of the arts, the literature, and commerce of the ancient
Egyptians.

CHAPTER IV.

Mechanical Labours of the Ancient Egyptians.

The Magnitude of Egyptian Edifices—Their supposed Object connected
with the Doctrine of the Metempsychosis—Proposal made to Alexander the Great—Lake Mœris; its Extent—The Narrative of Herodotus; supported by Diodorus and Pomponius Mela—Opinion that the
Nile originally flowed through the Valley of the Dry River—Facts
stated by Denon; and by Belzoni—Lake Mœris not a Work of Art—
The River of Joseph, and Canals connecting it with the Nile—Pyramids; Account by Herodotus; Researches of Davison; of Caviglia;
of Belzoni; Dimensions of Pyramids—Sphinx; Exertions of Caviglia
—Monolithic Temple—Tombs—Reflections.

THE history of Egypt presents nothing more wonderful
than the magnitude and durability of the public works
which were accomplished by her ancient inhabitants. Prodi-
gal of labour and expense, her architects appear to have
planned their structures for the admiration of the most
distant posterity, and with the view of rendering the fame
of their mechanical powers coeval with the existence of
the globe itself. It has been suspected, indeed, that the
omnipotent spirit of religion mingled with the aspirations
of a more earthly ambition in suggesting the intricacies of
the Labyrinth, and in realizing the vast conception of the

Pyramids. The preservation of the body in an entire and uncorrupted state during three thousand years, is understood to have been connected with the mythological tenet that the spirit by which it was originally occupied would return to animate its members, and to render them once more the instruments of a moral probation amid the ordinary pursuits of the human race. The mortal remains even of the greatest prince could hardly have been regarded as deserving of the minute care and the sumptuous apparatus which were employed to save them from dissolution, had not the national faith pointed to a renewal of existence in the lapse of ages, when the bodily organs would again become necessary to the exercise of those faculties from which the dignity and enjoyment of man are derived. There can be no doubt, therefore, that Egypt was indebted to the religious speculations of her ancient sages for those sublime works of architecture which still distinguish her above all the other nations of the primitive world.

It must at the same time be acknowledged that, in all countries comparatively rude, vastness of size takes precedence of all other qualities in architectural arrangement. As a proof of this, it will not be denied that even the Pyramids sink into insignificance when compared with an undertaking proposed by Stesicrates to Alexander the Great. Plutarch relates that this projector offered to convert Mount Athos into a statue of the victorious monarch. The left arm was to be the base of a city containing ten thousand inhabitants; while the right was to hold an urn, from which a river was to empty itself into the sea. But our object in this chapter is not to describe the fanciful dreams of a panegyrist; but to give an account of works which were actually effected, and of which the remains continue at the present day to verify at once the existence and the grandeur.

We shall begin with Lake Mœris, which, although, upon the whole, it owes more to nature than to art, is nevertheless well worthy of notice, both for its great extent and for its patriotic object. Herodotus, our best authority for its original appearance, informs us that the circumference of this vast sheet of water was three thousand six hundred stadia, or four hundred and fifty miles,—that it stretched from north to south,—and that its greatest depth was about

three hundred feet.   He adds that it was entirely the pro-
duct of human industry ; as a proof of which, he states that
in its centre were seen two pyramids, each of which was
two hundred cubits above and as many beneath the water,
and that upon the summit of both was a colossal statue,
placed in a sitting attitude.   The precise height of these
pyramids, he concludes, is therefore four hundred cubits, or
six hundred Egyptian feet.

The waters of the lake, he continues, are not supplied
by springs : on the contrary, the ground which it occupies
is of itself remarkably dry ; but it communicates by an
artificial channel with the Nile,—receiving during six
months the excess of the inundation, and during the other
half of the year emptying itself back into the river.   Every
day during the latter period the fishery yields to the royal
treasury a talent of silver,—whereas, as soon as the ebb
has ceased, the produce falls to a mere trifle.   " The inhabitants affirm of this lake, that it has a subterraneous passage
westward into the Libyan Desert, in the line of the mountain which rises above Memphis.   I was anxious to know
what became of the earth which was dug out of the lake,
and made inquiry at those who dwelt on its shores."   The
answer given to this very natural question seems to have
imposed on the credulity of the historian.   They assured
him that the soil was carried to the river, and washed down
by the current into the sea,—an explanation with which he
was perfectly satisfied.

In reference to this narrative, which exhibits the usual
characteristics of truth and simplicity, we may remark that
it is substantially confirmed by the statements of Diodorus
Siculus and of Pomponius Mela.   According to the former
of these writers, the circumference of the lake was exactly
that which has been already quoted from the more ancient
historian ; while the latter magnifies it to the extent of five
hundred miles.   They all agree in representing that its
object must have been to save the country from the effects
of an excessive inundation, and at the same time to reserve
a supply of moisture for the arid lands in the vicinity, or for
the wants of a dry season in the Delta.   It may, however,
be thought probable that it was rather to prevent an evil
than to secure a benefaction ; for we find that the water

has not only a disagreeable taste, but is almost as salt as
the sea,—a quality which it is supposed to contract from
the nitre with which the surrounding land is every where
impregnated.

Last century, according to Dr. Pococke, Lake Mœris was
about fifty miles long and ten broad. The older French
writers estimated its circumference at a hundred and fifty
leagues,—a result not materially different from that of the
English traveller. Mr. Browne, who was more lately in
Egypt, thought that the length did not exceed thirty or forty
miles, and that the greatest breadth was not more than six.
It is hence manifest that the limits of this inland sea have
been much contracted; and, moreover, that the process of
diminution is still going on at a rate which is distinctly per
ceptible. In ancient times, there can be no doubt, the water
covered a large portion of the valley of Fayoum, and probably, when the inundation exceeded certain limits, found an
outlet from the eastern extremity along the valley of the
Bahr-bela-Maieh. It is equally manifest that the level of
the Nile itself must, in those days, have been higher than
it is at present, and that the branch which is now called
Joseph's River must have conveyed no small share of its
flood along the foot of the Libyan hills. At the remote
epoch when the Delta was a bay of the Mediterranean, the
main current of the descending flood would naturally seek
an issue in the direction of those very hollows which continue to display the most convincing evidence that they were
long washed as the channel of a mighty stream.

That the Nile originally flowed through the valley of the
Dry River is admitted by the most intelligent among modern
travellers. M. Denon, for example, regards as proofs of this
fact the physical conformation of the adjoining country,—
the existence of the bed of a river extending to the sea, but
now dry,—its depositions and incrustations,—the depth of
the lake,—its extent,—its bearing towards the north on a
chain of hills which run east and west, and turn off towards
the north-west, sloping down to follow the course of the
valley of the dry channel, and likewise the Natron Lakes.
And, more than all the other proofs, the form of the chain
of mountains at the north of the Pyramid which shuts the
entrance of the valley, and appears to be cut perpendicularly, like almost all the mountains at the foot of which the

Nile flows at the present day,—all these offer to the view a channel left dry, and its several remains.*

The opinion that the river of Egypt penetrated into the Libyan Desert, even to the westward of Fayoum, is rendered probable by some observations recorded in the second volume of Belzoni's Researches. In his journey to the Oasis of Ammon, he reached one evening the Bahr-bela-Maieh. "This place is singular and deserves the attention of the geographer, as it is a *dry river*, and has all the appearance of water having been in it,—the bank and bottom being quite full of stones and sand. There are several islands in the centre; but the most remarkable circumstance is, that, at a certain height upon the bank, there is a mark evidently as if the water had reached so high: the colour of the materials above that mark is also much lighter than those below. And what would almost determine that there has been water there, is that the island has the same mark, and on the same level with that on the banks of the said dry river. I am at a loss to conjecture how the course of this river is so little known, as I only found it marked near the Natron Lakes, taking a direction of north-west and south-east, which does not agree with its course here, which is from north to south as far as I could see from the summit of a high rock on the west side of it. The Arabs assured me that it ran a great way in both directions, and that it is the same which passes near the Natron Lakes. If this be the case, it must pass right before the extremity of the Lake Mœris, at the distance of two or three days' journey in a western direction. This is the place where several petrified stumps of trees are found, and many pebbles with moving or quick water inside."†

In its present contracted dimensions, the Lake of Mœris is called by the Arabs the Birket-el-Karoun, and is recognised at once as a basin formed by nature, and not by art. The details collected by Herodotus, and the other writers of Greece and Rome, must therefore have applied to the works which were necessary not only to connect the Nile with the lake, but also to regulate the ebb and flow of the inundation. The canal, called Joseph's River, is about a hundred and twenty miles in length; which, when it enters

* Denon, vol. i. p. 163.   † Belzoni, vol. ii. p. 163.

the valley of Fayoum, is further divided into a number of subordinate branches, and supplied with a variety of locks and dams. There were two other canals communicating between the lake and the stream, with sluices at their mouths, which were alternately shut and opened as the Nile rose or fell. These, we may presume, were the achievements of Mœris; which, when they are regarded as the work of an individual, having for their object the advantage and comfort of a numerous people, may justly be esteemed a far more glorious undertaking than either the Pyramids or the Labyrinth.

In no circumstance, indeed, do the arts and civilization of ancient Egypt appear more manifest than in the care which was taken to improve the productive qualities of the soil by means of irrigation. A slight inspection of the plain of Fayoum, even in its present neglected state, affords the most convincing evidence that, in the days of the Pharaohs, no degree of labour was accounted too great, provided it could secure to the agriculturist a share in the blessing annually communicated by the Nile.

Near Beni Souef, in Middle Egypt, the river passes close under the foot of the Arabian hills, and leaves on the western side a large extent of fertile land. At this place the excellence of the system followed by the ancients is most distinctly perceived. The soil deposited during the inundation, as we have elsewhere observed, accumulates fastest near the river, and forms a ridge about a mile and a half broad, which is above the level of the water at all seasons. Between this elevation and the hills there is produced a similar rising of the surface; so that from the Nile to the rocky barrier which bounds the Libyan Desert, there are two ridges and two depressions. Hence two kinds of canals became requisite,—large ones in the bottom of these hollows, and a smaller class branching off on either side, to water the intermediate grounds. To render these last available, dikes of considerable magnitude were, at certain distances, constructed across the current of the main canals, which served both as dams to retain the water for a sufficient time, and as roads from village to village. Between Siout and Fayoum, accordingly, where the distance from the Nile and the mountains is the greatest, several principal canals, parallel to the river, were dug in ancient times; among which, the most remarkable were the Bahr Yousef, and another called the Hatn,—the line of which last, however, cannot be so distinctly traced at the present day. In the same district there were eleven large mounds or dikes; besides a considerable number of smaller size,—all provided with sluices to regulate the issue of water according to the state of the crops and the height of the inundation.

This precaution, on some occasions, must have been absolutely necessary. Belzoni tells us that the year in which he visited Fayoum an extraordinary overflow of the Nile sent such a quantity of water into the Lake Mœris that it rose twelve feet higher than it had ever been known by the oldest fisherman on its banks. Denon, in like manner, remarks, that if it were not for the dikes which stop the inundation, the great swells would soon convert the whole province into an inland sea,—an event which had nearly taken place about forty years ago, during an unusually high flood, when the river rose over the banks of Ilahon, and created an apprehension that it would lay the plain under water, or resume the channel which it had evidently occupied in remote ages. To remedy this inconvenience, a graduated mound has been raised near the village just named, where there is also a sluice erected, which, as soon as the inundation has got to the proper height to water the province without drowning it, divides the mass of fluid; taking the quantity necessary for irrigation, and turning aside the remainder by forcing it back into the river through other canals of a deeper cut, directed to a lower section of the stream.

We have already suggested that the great work of King Mœris is to be sought for not in the lake which bears his name, but in the immense excavations which connected it with the Nile, and in the mounds, the dams, and the sluices which rendered it subservient to the important purposes of irrigation. Enough still remains to enable the reader to form some judgment of the extent and magnificence of the original undertaking. The French philosophers describe Fayoum, the ancient name of Arsinoë, as being of an oval figure, and forming a low table-land, gradually sloping towards the north and the south. Along the highest part of the ridge runs the Bahr Yousef as far as

Medinet-el-Fayoum, the capital of the province, where it branches off into a great number of smaller streams. Its bed is here cut through the solid rock, and shows that the Egyptians in old times were well acquainted with the principles of levelling. About five miles within the valley there is a bridge of ten arches running parallel with Joseph's River, which, serving as a dam when the inundation is low, lets the water pass when it is high, and is probably the sluice mentioned by Strabo and other ancient authors.

In a direction nearly due north from the bridge just described, there is a canal, now usually dry, but which, at the height of the flood, carries the water as far as the village of Tamieh, situated on the east side of the lake,—a distance of about twenty-two miles. This cut must have been formed through a bed of continuous rock, as appeared on sinking a shaft into the mud, which in some places was found twenty-three feet deep. Tamieh, which formerly stood on the edge of Mœris, is now six miles from it,—an additional proof that the extent of the lake is very much contracted. In fact, so much neglected are the various channels which, after disburdening the Nile of its superfluous waters, used to carry them into this western valley, that the limits of the cultivable land are becoming every year more narrow; the Birket-el-Karoun is gradually retiring from its shores; and the approach of the desert towards the river is more and more facilitated.

The observations of Belzoni during his journey to the Oasis give much probability to the opinion that the reign of civilization had, at an early age, extended far into the Libyan waste. Ruins of towns, and other tokens of an improved population, meet the eye from time to time; masses of sand cover the monuments of an age comparatively enlightened, and deform plains which, there is every reason to believe, were at one time the scene of agricultural industry, of the arts, and of law. A similar inference might be drawn from an examination of the country which stretches to the southward of Tripoli; where are still to be found the relics of magnificent buildings, mixed with the shingle of the desert, and affording to the barbarians who now traverse that wilderness a constant triumph over the achievements of polished life. We ought not, therefore, to give way to an undue haste in concluding that the descriptions of Lake Mœris left to us by the ancient authors are much exaggerated. The pyramids mentioned by Herodotus, if we may form a judgment from the remains of those which still stand at the entrance of the valley, were built of brick, and may therefore long ago have yielded to the solvent power of the atmosphere, supplying perhaps part of those ruins which are at present found scattered along the beach. It is not to be imagined that they were placed in the deep basin formed by nature, and which is still occupied by the Birket-el-Karoun, but rather in that division of the lake which was prepared by art for the reception of the annual flood, at the period when Mœris changed the course of the Nile from its more ancient channel.*

The Labyrinth is also mentioned by Herodotus as one of the greatest wonders of Egypt, and the most surprising effort of human ingenuity and perseverance. " It exceeds, I can truly assert, all that has been said of it ; and whoever takes the trouble to examine them will find all the works of Greece much inferior to this, both in regard to workmanship and expense. The temples of Ephesus and Samos may justly claim admiration, and the Pyramids may individually be compared to many of the magnificent structures erected by the Greeks ; but even these are inferior to the Labyrinth. It is composed of twelve courts, all of which are covered ; their entrances are opposite to each other, six to the north and six to the south ; one wall encloses the whole. The apartments are of two kinds ; there are fifteen hundred above the surface of the ground, and as many beneath,—in all three thousand. Of the former, I can speak from my own knowledge and observation ; of the latter, only from the information which I received. The persons who had the charge of the subterraneous apartments would not suffer me to see them, alleging that in these were preserved the sacred crocodiles, and the bodies

* Belzoni, vol. ii. p. 150-158; Jomard Déscrip. de l'Egypte, vol. ii. p. 8-43; Strabo, xvi. c. 1 ; Nouvelles Annales des Voyages, xi. p. 133 ; Pococke's Travels in the East ; Wilford in Asiatic Researches, vol. iii. p. 245.

The words of Pliny are remarkable in regard to the extent of Lake Mœris, as compared with its limits in his own day :—" Inter Arsinoitem autem et Memphetem *lacus fuit*, circuitu ccl. M.p., aut, ut Mutianus tradit ccccl. M p. et altitudinis L. pass., manu factas a rege qui fecerat, Mœridis appellatus." P. 69.

of the kings who constructed the Labyrinth. Of these, therefore, I presume not to speak; but the upper apartments I myself examined, and I pronounce them to be among the greatest triumphs of human industry and art. The almost infinite number of winding passages through the different courts excited my warmest admiration. From spacious halls I passed through smaller chambers, and from them again to large magnificent courts almost without end. The ceilings and walls are all of marble, the latter richly adorned with the finest sculpture; and around each court are pillars of the same material, the whitest and most polished that I ever saw. At the point where the Labyrinth terminates stands a pyramid one hundred and sixty cubits high, having large figures of animals engraved on the outside, and an entrance to the interior by a subterraneous path."*

The same historian relates that this stupendous edifice was constructed beyond the Lake Mœris, near the City of Crocodiles, now better known as Arsinoë, or the Medinet-el-Fayoum. He ascribes the design of the building to a determination of the twelve kings, who at that period governed Egypt, to leave behind them a monument worthy of their fame; and hence, perhaps, the number of the courts and gates by which the Labyrinth was distinguished.

Diodorus says that it was built as a sepulchre for Mendes, while Strabo intimates that it only stood near the tomb of the monarch who erected it. Pomponius Mela, again, speaks of it as having been constructed by Psammeticus; but as Mendes or Imandes is mentioned by several writers, it is probable that he was the king of the particular province in which the Labyrinth was placed, and who, as possessing the greatest influence and authority, might have his funeral monument set apart from the rest. It is, however, more worthy of notice that, although no other traveller gives so minute an account as has been supplied by Herodotus, the testimony of ancient times tends decidedly to support the main facts contained in his narrative. Strabo, for instance, describes the passages in the Labyrinth as being so numerous and artfully contrived that it was impossible to enter any one of the palaces, or to leave it, without a guide. Pliny,

* Lib. v. c. 9; Herodotus, book ii. chap. 148.

too, makes a reference to the Egyptian Labyrinth, which
proves, at least, his conviction that it was worthy of the
fame universally received concerning it, as also that it was
the pattern of all the similar works which had been attempted in different parts of Europe.

But it must not be concealed that the curiosity of the
moderns, who have employed themselves in searching for
the remains of this superb structure, has been very generally disappointed; and, of consequence, that there is a
great difference of opinion among them as to its local position.   Larcher and Gibert, after a long investigation of the
subject, have determined the situation of the Labyrinth to
have been at Senures ; while Pococke, Banier, and Savary
follow the ancient historians in placing it beyond Arsinoë,
in the direction of the Libyan Desert, and on the shore of
Lake Mœris. Amid the ruins of Karoun, accordingly,
the attention of certain French travellers was particularly
fixed by the appearance of several narrow, low, and very
long cells, which, it was thought, could have had no other use
than that of 'containing the sacred crocodiles ; and these
have, therefore, been imagined to correspond with the remains of the great building in question. But this supposition is not confirmed by the more diligent researches of
Belzoni. Speaking of the place, he says, "I observed
several pieces of white marble and granite, which has given
me reason to think that there must have been some building of considerable importance in this place, for they must
have had more trouble to convey it hither than to any part
of Egypt, in consequence of the distance. But whatever
remains of beauty might be seen in this town, it does not
appear that this was the site of the famous Labyrinth, nor
any thing like it ; for, according to Herodotus and Pliny,
there is not the smallest appearance which can warrant the
supposition that any such edifice was here. The Labyrinth was a structure of three thousand chambers, one-half
above and one-half below. The construction of such an
immense building, and the enormous quantity of materials
which must have been accumulated, would have yet left
specimens enough to have shown where it had been erected,
but not the smallest trace of any such thing is any where
to be seen. The town was about a mile in circumference,

with the temple in its centre, so that I could not see how the Labyrinth could be placed in this situation."*

He is more inclined to adopt an opinion, founded on the narrative of the Roman naturalist, that this sumptuous monument of ancient taste must have stood in the neighbourhood of Terza, at the west end of the Lake Mœris. He there observed several blocks of white stone and red granite, which evidently must have been taken from edifices of great magnitude. Reflecting on the description of Pliny, who places the Labyrinth in that very situation, he made the most diligent search among the remains of antiquity, to ascertain whether the marble fragments bore any evidence of the exquisite workmanship ascribed to the famed structure of Psammeticus. He admits that he saw not the smallest appearance of an edifice either on the ground or under it, but, at the same time, he beheld through all that part of the country a "great number of stones and columns of beautiful colours, of white marble and of granite." These materials of a splendid architecture he observed scattered about for the space of several miles, some on the road, and some in the houses of the Arabs, and others put to various uses in the erection of huts. It was not, therefore, without very plausible reasons that he arrived at the conclusion already stated; and we are satisfied that most of his readers will concur with him in the opinion that, by tracing those interesting ruins to their source, the site of the Labyrinth might yet be discovered. It is true, that having been but little elevated above the ground, the building may be already buried to a great depth under the mass of soil and sand which is constantly accumulating in all parts of the valley.†

Nothing is more certain than that the level of the lake, as well as of the adjoining land, must have been raised considerably since the first era of historical records. Belzoni himself observed, in one part of Mœris, pillars and ruins of ancient buildings now nearly under water; and it is well known that the present rulers of Egypt have more than once found it necessary to erect new dikes upon the ancient mounds, to obviate the effects of an excessive inundation. Denon, too, remarks that at the mouth of this

* Belzoni, vol. ii. p. 156. † Ibid. vol. ii. p. 161–166.

H

valley the remains of villages overwhelmed by the sand
may be every where discovered ; adding, that nothing is so
melancholy to the feelings as to march over these ruins, to
tread under foot the roofs of houses and the tops of mina-
rets, and to think that these were once cultivated fields,
flourishing gardens, and the habitations of man. Every
thing living has disappeared, silence is within and around
every wall, and the deserted villages are like the dead,
whose skeletons strike with terror.*

When these circumstances are considered, it will be
allowed, both that there is good evidence for the existence
of an ancient building of great magnificence on the shores
of Lake Moeris, and also that the changes to which the
neighbouring soil is constantly subjected render the discovery of the Labyrinth, more especially the subterraneous
chambers, an undertaking of the utmost uncertainty. From
what still remains under our eyes, we are justified in be-
lieving almost every thing of Egyptian grandeur, when the
object of the architect was to do honour to the gods, or to
preserve the memory of a beneficent king.

Of the wonderful people, indeed, who inhabit the banks
of the Nile, there is nothing more remarkable than that
their greatest efforts were made at a time when, in regard
to religious faith, they were in the grossest ignorance and
darkness, and that, when light sprang up around them, their
power, their taste, or their zeal seemed to decay,—yielding
to the domination of barbarian tribes, who were indebted to
them for all their knowledge, as well as for their superstition. Persia added nothing to the arts or architectural improvement of Egypt ; the Greeks presumed not to rival
their masters in the construction of temples, pyramids, and
labyrinths ; and the propagation of the true religion, under
the Roman emperors, put an end to the lofty imaginations
which the subjects of the Pharaohs were wont to realize in
their national structures. Christianity, which blesses every
land where it is cordially received, contributed most of all
to the extinction of that spirit which had impelled the
Egyptians to undertake and carry into effect designs so
vast and imperishable as those which still call forth the astonishment of the traveller. The days of their mythology

* Denon, vol. ii. p. 218.

were those of their proudest glories, and, we may add, of
their greatest happiness and freedom. The blind belief in
the divine origin of their monarchs, as also the inspiring
dogma that the soul was to return to its ancient tenement
in the flesh, encouraged them to erect monuments which
might resist the pressure of ten thousand years, and carry
the fame of their authors to the very threshold of eternity.
But when the exercise of their primitive superstition was
no longer allowed, and another faith was introduced in its
place, the temples were gradually abandoned, and the spirit
of the Egyptians, unsubdued by the severest political oppression, yielded at length to a more prevailing power,
which directed their hopes and fears to the contemplation
of loftier and more spiritual objects.*

But whatever doubt may exist in respect to the situation
and remains of the Labyrinth, there can be none relative
to the next great object of Egyptian art which we are
about to introduce to the reader. The Pyramids, during
several thousand years, have attracted the curiosity of the
traveller, and given rise to much learned disquisition;
while so great is their magnitude, and so durable the material of which they are constructed, that they present to the
moderns the same subject of study which was contemplated
by Herodotus, Eratosthenes, Diodorus, and Strabo. Pursuing the plan we have hitherto followed, we shall first extract from the oldest Greek historian the tradition which prevailed in his days, and then draw from other sources the
most probable account of the origin, the date, the intention,
and the actual appearance of those famous buildings.

Herodotus, it is well known, ascribes the largest of the
Pyramids to Cheops, a tyrannical and profligate sovereign.
"He barred the avenues to every temple, and forbade the
Egyptians to offer sacrifice to the gods; after which, he
compelled the people at large to perform the work of slaves.
Some he condemned to hew stones out of the Arabian
mountains, and drag them to the banks of the Nile; others
were stationed to receive the same in vessels, and transport
them to the edge of the Libyan Desert. In this service a
hundred thousand men were employed, who were relieved
every three months. Ten years were spent in the hard

* Webster, vol. ii. p. 221.

labour of forming the road on which these stones were to
be drawn—a work, in my estimation, of no less difficulty
and fatigue than the erection of the Pyramid itself. This
causeway is five stadia in length, forty cubits wide, and its
greatest height thirty-two cubits; the whole being composed of polished marble, adorned with the figures of animals. Ten years, as I have observed, were consumed in
forming this pavement, in preparing the hill on which the
Pyramids are raised, and in excavating chambers under the
ground. The burial-place which he intended for himself
he contrived to insulate within the building, by introducing
the waters of the Nile. The Pyramid itself was a work of
twenty years; it is of a square form, every side being eight
plethra in length, and as many in height. The stones are
very skilfully cemented, and none of them of less dimen
sions than thirty feet.[*]

"The ascent of the Pyramid was regularly graduated by
what some call steps, and others altars. Having finished
the first tier, they elevated the stones to the second by the
aid of machines constructed of short pieces of wood; from
the second, by a similar engine, they were raised to the
third; and so on to the summit. Thus there were as many
machines as there were courses in the structure of the Pyramid, though there might have been only one, which, being
easily manageable, could be raised from one layer to the
next in succession; both modes were mentioned to me, and
I know not which of them deserves most credit. The summit of the Pyramid was first finished and coated, and the
process was continued downward till the whole was completed. Upon the exterior were recorded, in Egyptian
characters, the various sums expended in the progress of
the work, for the radishes, onions, and garlic consumed by
the artificers. This, as I well remember, my interpreter

---

[*] We have departed from the common translation of this passage,
which, it must be acknowledged, is shrouded in some degree of obscurity. In Beloe's version, and even in Larcher's, to which he appears to
have been much indebted, the reader is led to conclude that the object
of the architect, in forming leads or canals from the Nile, was to surround the Pyramids themselves with water; whereas it appears that
the real intention was to place in an island, or, in other words, to enclose
with the sacred stream the repository of the royal corpse in the interior
of the building—τας ἐποίεετο ϑηκας ἑαυτῳ ἐν νησῳ, διωρυκα τοῦ Νειλου
ἐσαγαγων.—Euter. 124.

informed me amounted to no less a sum than one thousand six hundred talents. If this be true, how much more must it have cost for iron tools, food, and clothes for the workmen!—particularly when we consider the length of time they were employed in the building itself, besides what was spent on the quarrying and carriage of the stones, and the construction of the subterraneous apartments.

"According to the account given to me by the Egyptians, this Cheops reigned fifty years. He was succeeded on the throne by his brother Cephrenes, who pursued a policy similar in all respects. He also built a pyramid, but it was not so large as his brother's, for I measured them both. It has no subterraneous chambers, nor any channel for the admission of the Nile, which, in the other pyramid, is made to surround an island where the body of Cheops is said to be deposited. Thus, for the space of one hundred and six years, the Egyptians were exposed to every apecies of oppression and calamity; not having had, during this long period, permission to worship in their temples. Their aversion for the memory of these two monarchs is so great, that they have the utmost reluctance to mention even their names. They call their pyramids by the name of Philitis, who, at the epoch in question, fed his cattle in that part of Egypt."

It is from the last circumstance mentioned by Herodotus that the very reasonable conclusion has been formed by Bryant, Dr. Hales, and others, in regard to the people by whom the Pyramids are supposed to have been erected. We have already explained the connexion which subsists between the term Pales, Phalis, or Philitis, and the Shepherd kings who, having invaded Egypt from the east, possessed that country as masters during more than a hundred years, and who, upon being expelled by the indignant natives, settled on the adjoining coast of Syria under the denomination of Philistines. It is manifest, at first sight, that the dynasty of princes to whom these stupendous works are ascribed were foreigners, and also that they professed a religion hostile to the animal worship of the Egyptians; for it is recorded by the historian, with an emphatic distinctness, that, during the whole period of their domination, the temples were shut, sacrifices were prohibited, and the people subjected to every species of oppression and calamity. Hence it follows that the date of the Pyramids

H 2

must synchronise with the epoch of the Shepherd kings,—those monarchs who were held as an abomination by the Egyptians, and who, we may confidently assert, occupied the throne of the Pharaohs during some part of the interval which elapsed between the birth of Abraham and the captivity of Joseph.

The reasoning now advanced will receive additional confirmation, when we consider that buildings of the pyramidal order were not uncommon among the nations of the East, having probably some connexion with the principles of that more refined and lofty adoration which directed the feelings of its votaries to the magnificence of the heavenly host, and to the influence supposed to be exercised by their aspect and movements on the destiny of man. At the present day there are pyramids in India,—and more especially in Benares, where there is one formed of earth and covered with bricks. An edifice of the same kind has been observed at Meduri in Egypt, constructed in different stories or platforms, diminishing in size as they rise in height, until they terminate in a point,—the exact pattern, it is said, which was supplied by the followers of Budha in the plan of their ancient pyramids, as these have been described by European travellers, on the banks of the Indus and the Ganges. Such, too, is understood to have been the form of the Tower of Babel, the object of which may have been to celebrate the mysteries of Sabaism, the first and purest superstition of the untaught mind. Mr. Wilford informs us, that on his describing the great Egyptian Pyramid to several very learned Brahmins, they declared it at once to have been a temple ; and one of them asked if it had not a communication with the river Nile. When he answered that such a passage was mentioned as having existed, and that a well was at this day to be seen, they unanimously agreed that it was a place appropriated to the worship of Padma Devi, and that the supposed tomb was a trough which, on certain festivals, her priests used to fill with the sacred water and lotus-flowers.*

The most probable opinion respecting the object of these vast edifices is that which combines the double use of the sepulchre and the temple,—nothing being more common in

* Asiatic Researches, vol. iii. p. 430.

all nations than to bury distinguished men in places consecrated by the rites of divine worship. If Cheops, Suphis, or whoever else was the founder of the great Pyramid, intended it only for his tomb, what occasion was there, says Dr. Shaw, for such a narrow sloping entrance into it, or for the well, as it is called, at the bottom, or for the lower chamber with a large niche or hole in the eastern wall of it, or for the long narrow cavities in the sides of the large upper room, which likewise is incrusted all over with the finest granite marble,—or for the two antechambers and the lofty gallery, with benches on each side, that introduce us into it? As the whole of the Egyptian theology was clothed in mysterious emblems and figures, it seems reasonable to suppose that all these turnings, apartments, and secrets in architecture were intended for some nobler purpose,—for the catacombs or burying-places are plain vaulted chambers hewn out of the natural rock—and that the deity rather, which was typified in the outward form of this pile, was to be worshipped within. *

The present aspect of the Pyramids renders it doubtful whether they were ever fully completed, or whether the apparent dilapidation of the external parts ought not to be altogether ascribed to the injuries of the atmosphere and the hands of barbarian conquerors. It is presumed, that a pile of this description was not regarded as entirely finished until it was coated over with polished stone, so as to fill up the vacancies occasioned by the diminution of the successive layers of the building, and to render the surface quite smooth and uniform from the foundation to the summit. Herodotus states, in the clearest terms, that, after the structure was raised to its full height, the artisans began to finish it from the top downwards. In the second Pyramid, accordingly which bears the name of Cephrenes, a considerable portion of the original casing still remains; confirming the accuracy of the ancient historian as to the general plan of all such edifices, and affording, at the same time, the means of understanding that part of his narrative in which he asserts that a great quantity of the stone was brought from the Arabian side of the Nile, and even from the neighbourhood of the Cataracts. It has been ascertained by several modern

* Travels, vol. ii. p. 201.

travellers that the main body of the huge masses now under consideration is composed of rocks still found in the immediate vicinity; we must therefore infer that the granite and porphyry used for casing the exterior, as well as for the decorations of the chambers within, are to be identified with the materials described by the Halicarnassian, and which Strabo and Pliny more usually designate as precious stones and marble.*

The number of pyramids scattered over Egypt is very great; but by far the most remarkable are those at Djizeh, Sakhara, and Dashour. The first of these places, which is situated on the west side of the Nile, about ten miles from its bank, and nearly in the latitude of Grand Cairo, is distinguished by possessing the three principal edifices described by Herodotus, and which are still regarded as the finest monuments of this class that are to be seen in any part of the world. It is noticed by every author who from personal observation has described these wonderful works of art, that the sense of sight is much deceived in the first attempt to appreciate their distance and their magnitude. Though removed several leagues from the spectator, they appear to be quite at hand; and it is not until he has travelled some miles in a direct line with their bearing that he becomes sensible both of their vast bulk and also of the pure atmosphere through which he had viewed them. They are situated on a platform of rock about a hundred and fifty feet above the level of the surrounding desert,—a circumstance which at once contributes to their being well seen, and also to the discrepancy that still prevails among the most intelligent travellers as to their actual height.

The effect now alluded to is well described by Dr. Richardson. "We had viewed them from several points of observation on the opposite side of the river, and all along the whole course of the canal kept constantly looking at them; but our recollections were so occupied with exaggerated descriptions of their enormous dimensions that every look was followed by disappointment; the eye always encountered something less than the mind expected it to see;

* It is worthy of notice that every stone which admitted of a fine polish and shone in the light was called marble, from μαρμαιρειν, to glisten or shine.

and, now that we were, comparatively speaking, at their base, and looking up from the low sandy bank to the Pyramids on the rocky elevation above, our idea of their magnitude was not increased. 'Even those of the party who exercised the greatest self-control, and scarcely cast a look on those ancient piles during the whole time of our approach, felt disappointed with the diminished grandeur of their appearance.'[*]

It was not, in short, until their eyes became accustomed to the outline of the stupendous pile of masonry that they could form an estimate of its real dimensions; after which they were hardly able to convince themselves that such enormous structures were really the work of human hands. In most parts of Europe, the refraction occasioned by a moist climate raises distant objects above the true angle of vision, and confers upon them an apparent magnitude, which a nearer inspection never fails to correct. But in Egypt, on the contrary, the air of which is extremely dry and transparent, the atmospherical effect is reversed, and, accordingly, the first glance of the Pyramids from the banks of the Nile is usually felt to form a striking contrast to all the preconceived notions of the traveller.

The largest Pyramid stands on an elevation free all round, on which account the accumulation of sand in contact with it is less than might have been apprehended. It has, however, suffered much from human violence, immense heaps of broken stones having fallen down on each side, which form a high mound towards the middle of the base. The corners are pretty clear, where the foundation is readily discovered, particularly at the north-west angle; but it is impossible to see straight along the line of the base on account of these heaps of rubbish. Hence, as has been already suggested, the difficulty of making an exact measurement, and the frequent disagreement of the results; it being impracticable, without removing the sand and fallen stones, to run a straight line all the way in contact with the building. Dr. Richardson paced one side at a little distance from the wall, and found it two hundred and forty-two steps; whence he conjectures that the extent of seven hundred feet, usually assigned to it, is not far from the truth.

* Travels along the Mediterranean and Parts Adjacent, vol. i. p. 112.

The entrance into the Pyramid is on the north side, and is nearly in the centre, about an equal distance from each angle; being, at the same time, elevated about thirty feet above the base, probably that it might be more difficult for a conqueror to discover it, and less liable to be blocked up with sand. The ascent to it is over a heap of stones and rubbish, that have either fallen from the Pyramid, or been forced out and thrown down in the various efforts made at successive periods to find a passage into the interior. This heap at present rises considerably above the entrance, which is a small orifice not more than three feet and a half square: it is lined above and below, and on either side, with broad flat rocks of red granite, smooth and highly polished. The flags in the bottom of the passage are formed with alternate depressions and elevations, in order to afford a firm footing to the person descending; but this, it is presumed, is a modern operation, because the depressions are not smooth and polished like the rest of the stones.

After advancing nearly a hundred feet into the entrance, which slopes downward at an angle of about twenty-six degrees, the explorer finds an opening on the right-hand, which conducts him up an inclined plane to the queen's chamber, as travellers have agreed to call it,—an apartment seventeen feet long, fourteen feet wide, and twelve feet high to the point on which the roof is suspended. Ascending a similar passage, but somewhat steeper than the first, he perceives another chamber of larger dimensions, being thirty-seven feet two inches long, seventeen feet two inches wide, and about twenty feet in height. This is denominated the king's chamber,—but upon no better authority than we can discover than the caprice of tourists already converted into a local tradition. Its magnificence, however, entitles it in some degree to the distinction which it has obtained. It is lined all round with large slabs of highly-polished granite, reaching from the floor to the ceiling; this last being formed of nine immense flags which stretch from wall to wall. Towards the west end of the room stands the sarcophagus, which likewise consists of red granite highly polished, but without either sculpture or hieroglyphics. Its length is seven feet six inches, while the depth and width are each three feet three inches. There is no lid, nor was there any thing found in it except a few fragments of the stone with which the chamber is decorated.

As this room does not reach beyond the centre of the Pyramid, Dr. Richardson suggests the very probable opinion that there are other passages leading to other chambers in communication with it; the entrance to which would, it is very likely, be found by removing some of the granite alaba which serve as wainscoting to the walls. To present to the eye a uniform surface in the interior of an apartment was one of the devices usually employed by an architect in old times when he wished to conceal from an ordinary observer the approach to a secret retreat,—reserving to himself and his employer the knowledge of the particular stone which covered the important orifice, as well as the means of obtaining a ready access.

A third chamber, still higher in the body of the Pyramid than either of the two just mentioned, was discovered by Mr. Davison, who about sixty years ago was British consul at Cairo. Having on one of his visits observed a hole in the top of the gallery, he resolved to ascertain the object of it, and whether it led to any apartment which had not yet been described. For this purpose he made seven short ladders in such a manner as to fasten one to another by means of four wooden pins,—the whole set, when joined, being about twenty-six feet in length. When all the parts were put together, the ladder entered enough into the hole to prevent it from sliding on the side of the gallery. He then mounted, and found a passage two feet four inches square, which turned immediately to the right. He entered a little way, with his face on the ground, but was obliged to retire on account of the passage being in a great measure choked with dust and bats' dung, which in some places was near a foot deep. He first thought of clearing a path by throwing the dirt down into the gallery; but, foreseeing that this would be a work of some time, he determined to make another effort to enter, which was attended with more success than the first. He was able to creep in, though with much difficulty, not only on account of the lowness of the passage, but likewise the quantity of dust which he raised. When he had advanced a little way, he discovered what he supposed to be the end of the approach. His surprise was great when he reached it, to find to the right a straight passage into a long, broad, but low place, which he knew, as well by the length as the direction of the entry he had come in at, to be immediately above the large room. The stones of granite which are at the top of the latter form the bottom of this; but are uneven, being of unequal thickness. The room is four feet longer than the one below; in the latter you see only seven stones, and a half of one on each side of them; but in that above the nine are entire, the two halves resting on the wall at each end. The breadth is equal with that of the room below. The covering of this, as of the other, is of beautiful granite, but it is composed of eight stones instead of nine, the number in the room below. At this stage of the investigation Mr. Davison was joined by some of his attendants, who, being a great deal troubled with the dust and want of air, soon retired. At length, after having measured and examined every part of the chamber, he also descended by the ladder, satisfied that no more could be accomplished without the accession of greater strength and means.*

The same room was entered and explored a few years ago by Mr. Caviglia, to whose enterprising spirit the antiquaries of Egypt are under great obligations, but without adding any thing to our knowledge of its structure or intention. He remarks, that the sides of the chamber were coated with red granite of the finest polish; and he ascertained that the unevenness of the floor was occasioned by its being formed of the individual blocks of syenite which constitute the roof of the chamber below; hence they must be wedged in on the principle of the arch. The bats' dung, which in the time of Mr. Davison was a foot in depth, had now increased to a foot and a half.

But it is extremely doubtful, even after these laborious endeavours, whether we have yet made farther progress in dissecting the structure of the Pyramid than was attained by the Greeks and Romans two thousand years ago; for it is worthy of notice that every recess which has been explored in modern times bears marks of having been examined by former adventurers. We find, besides, that the narrow entrance into the great Pyramid was known to

* Memoirs relating to European and Asiatic Turkey, edited from MS. Journals by Robert Walpole, M. A. p. 354.

Strabo, which he tells us had a stone placed at the mouth of it to be removed at pleasure. The same author likewise, as well as Herodotus, was acquainted with the subterraneous chambers, and Pliny has left a description of the well. It is true that they declined to enter into many particulars which could hardly fail to have met their observation, —an omission which we are justified, at least in the case of Herodotus, in attributing to certain superstitious notions of their sanctity and mysterious uses.

The account given by Mr. Davison of his descent into the well, now alluded to, is so interesting that we cannot withhold from the reader an outline of his proceedings. Conceiving it to be very deep, he provided himself with a large quantity of rope, one end of which he tied round his waist; and letting down a lantern attached to a small cord, he resolutely prepared to follow. With no small difficulty he prevailed on two of his servants and three Arabs to hold the line,—the latter assuring him that there were ghosts below, and that he never could hope to return. Taking with him a few sheets of paper, a compass, a measure, and another lighted candle, he commenced the descent, and soon reached the bottom of the first well or shaft. Here he found, on the south side, at the distance of about eight feet from the place where he landed, a second opening, which descended perpendicularly to the depth of five feet only; and at four feet ten inches from the bottom of this he discovered a third shaft, the mouth of which was nearly blocked up with a large stone, leaving an opening barely sufficient to allow a man to pass. Here he dropped down his lantern, not only with the view of ascertaining to what depth he was about to proceed, but also to determine whether the air were pernicious or otherwise. The shaft, however, was so tortuous that the candle soon became invisible; but the consul was not to be discouraged, as nothing less than a journey to the bottom would satisfy his eager curiosity. His main difficulty arose from the superstitious dread of the Arabs, who could hardly be prevailed upon to go down and hold the rope. After many prayers, and threats, and promises of money, and of all the treasure which might be found in the well, the avarice of one man so far overcame his terror that he ventured to descend;

I

though, on reaching the bottom, "he stared about him pale and trembling, and appeared more like a spectre than a human being."

Mr. Davison now pushed forward with the rope round his body, being convinced, from the distant view of the lantern which he had let down, that this well was somewhat deeper than the first. Having proceeded a little farther than half-way to the spot where the candle had rested, he came to a grotto about fifteen feet long, four or five wide, and nearly the height of a man. From this place the third shaft or well was sloping; and, by throwing down a stone, he ascertained it to be of much greater depth than the others. But, still resolved to persevere, he pushed the lantern a little before him, and set out afresh on his journey, calling to the Arab to loosen the rope gently, and availing himself of little holes made in the rock, obviously with the purpose of aiding a descent. At length, the shaft beginning to return a little more to the perpendicular, he arrived speedily at the bottom, where he found all farther passage precluded by a large accumulation of sand and rubbish.

Having reached this point, our adventurer began to reflect on two circumstances which had not before occurred to him, either of which would have agitated weaker nerves. The first was, that the multitude of bats which he had disturbed might put out his candle; and the second, that the immense stone on the mouth of the pit might slip down and close the passage for ever. On looking about the bottom he found a rope-ladder, which, though it had lain there sixteen years, was as fresh and strong as if perfectly new. It had been used, as is conjectured, by Mr. Wood,— the author of a work on the ruins of Balbec and Palmyra, —to assist his progress downwards; but he, it is concluded, must have stopped short at the grotto. When Mr. Davison, on his return, had reached the bottom of the first shaft, the candles fell and went out; upon which "the poor Arab thought himself lost." He laid hold of the rope, as his master was about to ascend, declaring that he would rather have his brains blown out than be left alone there with the Devil. "I therefore permitted him," says the consul, "to go before; and, though it was much more difficult to ascend than to descend, I know not how it was, but he scrambled up a hundred times more quickly than he had come down."[*]

The depth of the first shaft was twenty-two feet; of the second twenty-nine; and of the third, ninety-nine; which, with the five feet between the first and second, makes the whole descent one hundred and fifty-five.[†]

It is somewhat remarkable that the dimensions assigned to the well by Pliny were eighty-six cubits,—an approximation to the truth which must remove all doubt from the mind of every candid reader that the honour of detecting the intricacies of the great Pyramid was not reserved to the moderns. The Romans appear to have taken a considerable interest in the architectural antiquities of Egypt, the names of their favourite princes being inscribed on the monuments; and hence it might have been inferred that this, one of the greatest works of the ancient world, would not fail to attract their attention.

The latest and the most complete survey, however, made of the hidden caverns of the Pyramid of Cheops, is that accomplished by Mr. Caviglia, the spirited foreigner already mentioned. In his first attempt to sound the depths of the celebrated well, he descended as far as Mr. Davison had done, and with nearly similar results. But he was by no means satisfied with the issue of his labour. Observing that the ground under his feet gave a hollow sound, he suspected that there must be some concealed outlet. He accordingly determined to resume operations; and with this view he hired several Arabs, whom he employed in drawing up the rubbish from the bottom with baskets and cords. In a short time, however, owing to the extreme reluctance of these people to work, he was compelled to suspend his undertaking until an order from the Kaiya-bey was procured, which had the effect of subduing their indolence, and, to a certain degree, of removing their prejudices. It is not,

* In the letter to M. Varsy, of which the above is an abridgment, Mr. Davison remarks, "Vous avez beau dire que j'aurais dû regarder comme honorable d'être enseveli dans un dè ces fameux monumens qui n'ont été destinés que pour les grands rois. Je vous avoue franchement, Monsieur, que je n'avais pas la moindre ambition à cet égard. Bien au contraire, j'étais cent fois plus content de sortir et revoir le jour."

† See Walpole's Memoirs, p. 350, for the narrative of Mr. Davison; and Quarterly Review, vol. xix. p. 392, which contains an original communication from Mr. Salt.

indeed, surprising that the natives should have manifested reluctance to labour in circumstances so appalling; being confined in a place where, owing to the impurity of the atmosphere, no light would burn longer than half an hour, and where the heat was so intense as to threaten suffocation. At length, in fact, it became so intolerable that one Arab was carried up nearly dead, and several others, on their ascending to the surface, fainted away; so that, at last, in defiance of the command laid upon them, they almost entirely abandoned the task, declaring that they were willing to work, but not to die for him.

Thus opposed and disappointed, Mr. Caviglia next turned his attention to the clearing of the principal entry or passage into the Pyramid, which, from time immemorial, had been so blocked up as to oblige those who ventured within its orifice to creep on their hands and knees. His chief object in this undertaking was to improve the ventilation of the interior,—a purpose which he not only carried into effect, but, moreover, in the course of his labours, he made the unexpected discovery that the main passage leading from the entry did not terminate in the manner asserted by Maillet, and believed by all his successors. On the contrary, having removed several large masses of calcareous stone and granite, apparently placed there to obstruct all farther progress, he found that it still continued in the same inclined plane downwards, was of the same dimensions, and had its sides worked with the same care as in the portion above, though filled up nearly to the top with earth and fragments of rock. After clearing it out to the length of a hundred and fifty feet, the air became again so impure, and the heat so suffocating, that he had once more the same difficulties to encounter with regard to the Arabs. Even his own health was at this time visibly impaired, and he was attacked with a spitting of blood; but nothing could induce him to desist from his interesting researches.

After the lapse of the third month from the time at which he began his toils, he had excavated as far as two hundred feet in the new passage without any thing particular occurring, when, shortly afterward, a door on the right-hand was discovered, from which, in the course of a few hours, a strong smell of sulphur was perceived to issue. Mr. Caviglia, having now recollected that when at the bottom of the well, in his first enterprise, he had burned some sulphur for the purpose of purifying the air, conceived it probable that this doorway might communicate with it,—an idea which, in a little time, he had the pleasure of seeing realized, by discovering that it opened at once upon the bottom of the well, where he found the baskets, cords, and other implements, which had been left there on his recent attempt at a farther excavation. This discovery was so far valuable as it afforded a complete circulation of air along the whole passage, and up the shaft of the well, and thereby obviated all danger for the future, arising from the noxious condition of the atmosphere.[*]

But the passage did not terminate at the doorway which opened upon the bottom of the well. Continuing to the distance of twenty-three feet beyond it, in the same angle of inclination, it became narrower, and took a horizontal direction for about twenty-eight feet farther, where it opened into a spacious apartment immediately under the central point of the Pyramid. This new chamber is sixty-six feet long by twenty-seven broad, with a flat roof; and, when first entered, was found nearly filled with large stones and rubbish, which Mr. Caviglia succeeded in removing. The

---

[*] It is amusing to contrast the indefatigable exertions of this individual, whose sole motives were derived from an enlightened curiosity and a desire to benefit the literary world, with the cautious procedure of Colonel Coutelle, one of Buonaparte's military savans:—" J'arrival à l'extrémité, mais non pas à point où s'étaient arrêtés les ouvriers: le fond était rempli de terre et de cailloux ronlés; j'en remplis une de mes poches; ensuite je pris toutes les mesures dont j'avais besoin. Mais déjà ma lumière était pâle; ma respiration plus genée; le thermomètre de Reaumur était audessus de 25 degrés," &c. After filling one of his pockets with the rubbish which impeded his progress into the secret apartments of the Pyramid, the gallant colonel withdrew, uttering imprecations against the detestable atmosphere, which at once affected his breathing and raised the thermometer.—Descrip. de l'Egypt. Antiquitiés, vol. ii. p. 39.

The same writer informs us that the French, hoping to find many antiquities fresh and undesecrated in the interior of a pyramid not yet touched, adopted the resolution of demolishing one of the third or fourth class from top to bottom. It is stated that every layer of stone was from a yard to a yard and a half in depth, and that all the blocks, being of a dimension proportioned to their thickness, weighed about twelve thou sand pounds (6000 kilogrammes) a piece. But, after having advanced about half way in the process of demolition, they were obliged to relinquish the enterprise; leaving, says the colonel, the fruit which would have indemnified their toils to be reaped by those who were to come after them

platform of the floor, which is dug out of the rock, is irregular, nearly one-half of the length from the east end being level, and about fifteen feet from the ceiling; while in the middle it descends five feet lower, in which there is a hollow space, bearing all the appearance of the commencement of a well or shaft. From this point it rises to the western end; so that at the extremity there is scarcely room between the floor and the roof for a man to stand upright, the whole chamber having the appearance of an unfinished excavation. Mr. Salt, however, is disposed to think, after a careful comparison of it with other subterranean apartments which have been disfigured by the combined effects of time and the rude hands of curious visiters, that it may once have been highly wrought, and used, perhaps, for the performance of solemn and sacred mysteries.. Some Roman characters, rudely formed, had been marked with the flame of a candle on the rock, part of which, having mouldered away, rendered the words illegible. The same gentleman had flattered himself that this chamber would turn out to be the one described by Herodotus, as containing the tomb of Cheops, which was insulated by a stream drawn from the Nile; but the want of an inlet for the sacred fluid, and the elevation of the floor thirty feet above the level of the river at its highest inundation, put an end to this delusive opinion. From an expression of Strabo, however, purporting that the passage from the entrance leads directly down to the chamber which contains the sarcophagus, he thinks, and perhaps justly, that this apartment was the only one known to the Greek geographer.

On the south side of this spacious excavation there is a passage just wide and high enough for a man to creep along on his hands and knees, continuing horizontally in the rock for fifty-five feet; but there it abruptly terminates. Another opening at the east end of the chamber commences with a kind of arch, and runs about forty feet into the solid rock of the Pyramid. A third passage is mentioned, but so obscurely that we cannot ascertain either its direction or dimensions. It is not, however, to be imagined that these passages had no object, or that they originally terminated at the point where the curiosity of modern travellers meets a check from the accumulation of rubbish, or, perhaps, from the intervention of a regular portcullis, such as Belzoni encountered in the second Pyramid. Dr. Richardson, indeed, insinuates that the avenues in question have not been actually explored by, several writers who have thought proper to describe them,—a charge which, we are satisfied, does not apply to Caviglia, whose exertions were only limited by the utmost bounds of human energy and perseverance.

Before we proceed to some more general observations on the history and comparative magnitude of the Pyramids, we shall present to the reader a short account of the discoveries made by Belzoni in the interior of that which bears the name of Cephrenes.

As Herodotus, whose fidelity has been generally approved by the investigations of more recent times, gave assurance that there were no chambers in this edifice, a long time had passed without any attempt being made to penetrate its outer walls. In fact, such an undertaking was regarded as equally romantic and impracticable. The French philosophers who accompanied the invading army led by Buonaparte made several endeavours to find an entrance, but, perceiving no trace in the building which could encourage the belief that it had ever been perforated, they left it in despair. The resolution of Belzoni, however, a private unassisted individual, achieved a conquest over the mystery of ancient art, which the power and ingenuity of a great nation had relinquished as beyond the reach of human means. His success in detecting the sepulchral labyrinths of Thebes inflamed him at once with the desire and the confidence of discovering a passage into the secret chambers of Cephrenes, the reputed founder of the second Pyramid.

His first attempt was not attended with an adequate degree of success, while the labour and expense which it entailed upon him were so great as would have cooled the ardour of a less zealous antiquary. He began by forcing a passage, which he was soon obliged to abandon, as equally hopeless to himself and dangerous to the persons employed. But this disappointment only increased his desire to accomplish an object on which he had staked his happiness as well as his reputation. Observing minutely the exterior of the Great Pyramid, he satisfied himself that the passage was not placed exactly in the middle of the building, but that it ran in a straight line to the eastern side of what is called the king's chamber; which being in the centre of the Pyramid, he conjectured that the entrance must be as far from the middle of the face as is the distance from the centre of the chamber to the east end of it. Having made this. clear and simple observation, he concluded, that, if there were any chamber in the second Pyramid, the orifice could not be at the spot where he had begun his excavation, but, calculating by the position of the passage in the first, nearly thirty feet farther east.

Encouraged by these new views, he returned to his task, and was immediately delighted to observe, that at the very place where he intended to recommence operations, there was a hollow on the surface of the building. Any traveller, says he, who shall hereafter visit the Pyramids may plainly perceive this concavity above the true entrance. Summoning his Arabs, he forthwith resumed his toils; and so correct was his measurement that he did not deviate more than two feet from the mouth of the passage which was to admit him into the recesses of this vast edifice. The native workmen were indeed as skeptical as ever, entertaining not the slightest expectation that any approach would ever be discovered, and occasionally muttering their opinion of him in the expressive term *magnoon*, which, in their language, denotes madman or fool.

After clearing away a great deal of rubbish, and cutting through massy stones, he had the satisfaction to see the edge of a block of granite,—the material used for casing the passages in the Pyramid of Cheops,—inclining downward at the same angle as in the latter building, and pointing towards the centre. On the following day three large slabs were discovered, one on each side, and the third on the top,—indicating very distinctly that the object of his search was now about to be realized. In a few hours, accordingly, the right entrance into the Pyramid was opened,—proving to be a passage four feet high, and three feet six inches wide, formed of granite, and descending a hundred and four feet towards the centre, at an angle of twenty-six degrees. Nearly all this passage was filled with large stones which had fallen from the upper part, and, as the floor slopes downwards, they had slid on till some larger than the rest stopped the way.

The next portion of his task, was to remove this rubbish, which had extended even to the entrance of the chamber At length he reached a portcullis, which, being a fixed block of stone, at first sight appeared to obstruct all further progress into the interior. "It stared me in the face," said Mr. Belzoni, "and said *ne plus ultra*,—putting an end, as I thought, to all my projects;" for it made a close joint with the groove at each side, and on the top it seemed as firm as the rock itself which formed the passage. On a close inspection, however, he perceived that, at the bottom, it was raised about eight inches from the lower part of the groove which was cut beneath to receive it; and he found by this circumstance that the large slab before him was nothing more than a barrier of granite, one foot three inches thick. Having observed a small aperture at the top, he thrust a straw into it upwards of three feet,—a discovery which convinced him that there was a vacuum prepared to receive the portcullis. The raising of it, indeed, was a work of no small difficulty. As soon, however, as it was elevated high enough for a man to pass, an Arab entered with a candle, and announced that the place within was very fine. A little more room enabled our adventurer to squeeze his person through, when he exclaims,—"After thirty days I had the pleasure of finding myself in the way to the central chamber of one of the two great Pyramids of Egypt, which have long been the admiration of beholders."*

As his main object was to reach the centre of the building, he advanced in that direction, along a passage cut out of the solid rock, six feet in height, and six feet six inches broad. At length he reached a door at the centre of a large chamber. "I walked slowly two or three paces, and then stood still to contemplate the place where I was. Whatever it might be, I certainly considered myself in the centre of that Pyramid which, from time immemorial, had been the subject of the obscure conjectures of many hundred travellers, both ancient and modern. My torch, formed of a few wax candles, gave but a faint light: I could, however, clearly distinguish the principal objects. I naturally turned my eyes to the west end of the chamber, looking for the

* Researches and Operations in Egypt and Nubia, vol. i. p. 417.

sarcophagus, which I strongly expected to see in the same situation as that in the first Pyramid; but I was disappointed when I saw nothing there. The chamber has a pointed or sloping ceiling, and many of the stones had been removed from their places evidently by some one in search of treasure. On my advancing towards the west end, I was agreeably surprised to find that there was a sarcophagus buried on a level with the floor."

Upon examining more minutely the chamber into which he had entered, he found it to be forty-six feet in length, sixteen feet three inches wide, and twenty-three feet six inches high. It is hewn out of the solid rock from the floor to the roof, which last is composed of large slabs of calcareous stone, meeting in the centre at an angle corresponding to that of the Pyramid itself. The sarcophagus is eight feet long, three feet six inches wide, and two feet three inches deep in the inside. It is surrounded by large blocks of granite, apparently to prevent its removal, which could not be effected without great labour. The lid had been drawn to one side; so that the receptacle, be it fount or grave, was half open. It is manufactured of the very finest granite; but, like the other in the Pyramid of Cheops, it presents not a single hieroglyphic. Inspecting the inside solely with the view of finding some inscription which would throw light on the history and intention of this mighty edifice, he did not at first observe that there were bones mixed with the sand and gravel which it contained. These fragments of an animal body, being afterward sent to London, were ascertained to belong to the bovine species, and have been very generally supposed to be the remains of a sacred bull,—an object of veneration among the ancient Egyptians. On the sides of the chamber, which were carefully examined, Mr. Belzoni observed many scrawls executed with charcoal; all of which, however, were in a character quite unknown to him, and already become so faint that they were in some places nearly illegible, and rubbed off on the slightest touch.

On the wall at the west end of the chamber he perceived an inscription, which has been translated as follows:—

"The Master Mohammed Ahmed, lapicide, has opened them; and the Master Othman attended this (opening), and the King Ali Mohammed, from the beginning to the closing up."*

Mr. Belzoni admits that the letters were far from being distinct. The transcriber was a Copt, whom he induced to go from Cairo for the purpose, not having sufficient confidence in his own pen. He adds, however, that not being satisfied with his protestations of accuracy, though the inscription was copied under his own eyes, he invited other persons, who were esteemed the best Arabic scholars in the country, to lend their aid, and particularly to compare the transcript with the original on the wall. They found it all perfectly correct and intelligible, except the concluding word, which was acknowledged to be obscure; but, says he, if it be considered how much that word resembles the right one, we shall find a good sense, and the whole inscription made out. The circumstance, too, supposed to be here recorded,—that the Pyramid was closed up after having been opened by the agents of King Ali Mohammed,—corresponds exactly to the facts of the case, and affords a strong corroboration of the conjectural emendation proposed by the translator.

It is remarkable that in this Pyramid, as well as in the larger one, there is a pit or shaft which descends to a lower part of the building. At the bottom of this opening there were so many stones as nearly to choke up its entrance; but, after removing these, Mr. Belzoni found the passage running towards the north, as formerly, at an angle of twenty-six degrees. It continued in this direction, and with the same slope downwards, forty-eight feet and a half, where it joined a horizontal passage fifty-five feet in length, still running north. Half-way up this avenue on the right is a recess eleven feet long and six deep. On the left, opposite to it, is another entry twenty-two feet in length, with a descent of twenty-six degrees towards the west. Before he proceeded any farther northwards, he went down this passage, where he found a chamber thirty-two feet long, nine feet nine inches wide, and eight feet six inches in height. This apartment contains many small blocks of stone, some

* This is the version of Mr. Salame, who says, "The Arabic to which I gave the meaning of these last words 'to the closing up' is not spelled correctly in the paper I saw,—a fault which I attribute to the transcriber from the stone."

not more than two feet in length. It has a pointed roof like that before mentioned, though it is cut out of the solid rock. On the walls and ceiling are some unknown inscriptions similar to those in the upper chamber.

Reascending to the horizontal passage, he discovered at the end of it a portcullis, which must have originally possessed the same construction as the one, already described; but the plate of granite which had served as a door was taken down, and is still to be seen under the rubbish which encumbers the approach. Beyond this point he entered into a lane which runs forty-eight feet in a direction parallel to the one above, and, in fact, appears to issue from the Pyramid near its base. If this supposition be well founded, it will follow that the monument of Cephrenes has two entrances,—an inference, we presume, which might be extended to that of Cheops, where there are several passages without any outlet hitherto discovered. The immense mass of broken stones and sand which surrounds the foundation of the larger edifice has all along prevented such a minute examination of its lower parts as might have enabled the scientific antiquary to connect the internal structure with the general plan and uses of the building. Hence it is extremely probable that apertures will be found in all the four sides conducting to the centre, at different angles of inclination, and establishing a communication among the various chambers which the Pyramids contain.

After these details, it is impossible to refrain from an expression of admiration so justly due to the perseverance and ability of Mr. Belzoni. It was truly observed by Mr. Salt, that the opening of this Pyramid had long been considered an object of so hopeless a nature that it is difficult to conceive how any person could be found sanguine enough to make the attempt; and, even after the laborious discovery of the forced entrance, it required great resolution and confidence in his own views to induce him to continue the operation, when it became evident that the enterprise of his predecessors, possessed of greater means, had completely failed. Of the discovery itself Belzoni has given a very clear description, and his drawings present a perfect idea of the entrances, passages, and chambers. Of the labour of the undertaking no one can form an idea. Notwithstanding the masses of stone which he had to remove, and the hardness of the materials which impeded his progress, the whole was effected entirely at his own risk and expense.[*]

It is manifest, from the inscription discovered by Belzoni, as well as from the state of the chambers in the two larger Pyramids, that they had both been opened at the distance of many years. Dr. Shaw, on the authority of an Arabian author, mentions that the one attributed to Cheops was entered about ten centuries ago by Almamon, the renowned caliph of Babylon. It is added that the explorers found in it, towards the top, a chamber with a hollow stone, in which there was a statue like a man, and within it the body of a man, upon which was a breastplate of gold set with jewels. Upon this breastplate there was a sword of inestimable price; and at its head a carbuncle of the bigness of an egg, shining like the light of the day; and upon the human figure were characters written with a pen, which no man understood.[†]

[*] What must be the feelings of every candid person who reads the following statement, which we give in the words of the discoverer himself:—
"One thing more I must observe respecting the Count de Forbin. On his return from Thebes I met him at Cairo, in the house of the Austrian consul. I had begun the task of opening the Pyramids, and had already discovered the false passage. The count requested, in a sort of sarcastic manner, when I had succeeded in opening the Pyramid, which no doubt he supposed I never would, that I would send him the plan of it, as he was about setting off for Alexandria the next day, and thence to France. I thought the best retaliation I could make was to send him the desired plan, and I did so as soon as I opened the Pyramid, which was in a few days after his departure. Would any one believe that the noble count, on his arrival in France, gave out that he had succeeded in penetrating the second Pyramid of Djizeh, and brought the plan of it to Paris? Whether this be the fact or not will appear from the following paragraph taken from a French paper now in my possession:—'On the 24th of April, Monsieur le Compte de Forbin, director-general of the Royal Museum of France, landed at the lazaretto of Marseilles. He came last from Alexandria, and his passage was very stormy. He has visited Greece, Syria, and Upper Egypt. By a happy chance, some days before his departure from Cairo, he succeeded in penetrating into the second Pyramid of Djizeh. Monsieur Forbin brings the plan of this important discovery, as well as much information on the labours of M. Drovetti at Karnac, and on those which Mr. Salt, the English consul, pursues with the greatest success in the valley of Boban-el-Malook, and in the plain of Medinet Abou. The Museum of Paris is going to be enriched with some of the spoils of Thebes, which Monsieur Forbin has collected in his travels.'
"Was this written," exclaims Belzoni, "by some person in France, in ridicule of the Count de Forbin, or is it an attempt to impose on the public by a tissue of falsehoods?"—Vol. i. p. 393.
[†] Shaw's Travels, vol. ii. p. 207, and Pyramidographia by Mr. Greaves.

It is in like manner recorded by Abdollatiph, that when Mélec-Alaziz-Othman-ben-Yousouf succeeded his father, he allowed himself to be persuaded by some foolish courtiers to throw down the Pyramids, and that he sent thither sappers, miners, and quarriers, under the direction of proper officers, with orders to overturn the red one, that, namely, ascribed to Mycerinus, and which is known to have been coated with highly-coloured granite. To execute the instructions with which they were charged, they encamped on the adjoining ground, and collected a great number of labourers, whom they maintained at an enormous expense. There they remained eight whole months, exerting themselves to the utmost in order to fulfil their commission; but their most strenuous endeavours with picks and levers above, and with ropes and cables below, could not remove more than one or two stones a-day. When a block was thrown down, there was the additional labour of breaking it into fragments and carrying it aside; and one of the engineers is reported to have said, that, although he were to get ten thousand pieces of gold, he could not readjust one of these stones in its proper place. At length they abandoned the attempt, without demolishing the magnificent structure, or even, as the historian thinks, without materially reducing its dimensions. The date of this barbarous project is usually placed about the end of the twelfth century.

Several other caliphs are named by Makrisi and Abdollatiph as having meditated the demolition of these great works. Saladin, for example, charged his emir, Karakoush Asadi, to build the citadel and walls of Cairo,—instructing him, at the same time, to consider Memphis and the Pyramids as the most suitable quarry for obtaining materials. Hence, it is conjectured, the coating of the large edifice of Cheops, two-thirds of that of Cephrenes, and the greater part of some of the smaller ones, have been carried away, and can now only be sought for in the immense causeway, and the innumerable arches which he constructed between these monuments and the Nile, or in the citadel, the mosques, and the battlements of the capital. The remains of this causeway are still to be seen; the finer portion of it, however, that was upon the lower ground, has been swept away by the overflowing of the Nile. Some authors have supposed it to be the relics of the great road described by Herodotus, used for transporting the stones consumed in the construction of the Pyramids. But we are informed that a very slight inspection of the material, as well as of the style in which the building has been completed, will satisfy every one qualified to judge that this opinion is not founded in truth. Abdollatiph, in fact, a contemporary writer, states, in the plainest terms, that it was constructed by Asadi, one of the emirs of Salah-Eddin-Yousouf, the son of Job, commonly called Saladin the Great.[*]

The opening of the Great Pyramid has, by many oriental writers, been ascribed to the Caliph Abdalla Mamour, the son of Haroun Al Raschid; and they state that he employed for the accomplishment of his object, fire, vinegar, and other chymical solvents. Others attribute this achievement to the Caliph Mohdi, whose name was Mohammed. The latter is not improbably the sovereign whose reputation is embalmed in the inscription, copied by the direction of Belzoni, under the title of King Ali Mohammed; and as it is recorded that he attended the opening of *them*,—in the plural number,—it is certainly not unreasonable to conclude that it was he who first penetrated into the interior of both, and who is, consequently, chargeable with much of the unnecessary dilapidation which accompanied his fruitless labours.

Considering the immense toil as well as uncertainty which attend the exploration of the Pyramids, we cannot be surprised at any difference of opinion that may happen to prevail in regard to the various apertures, passages, and chambers which occupy the interior. But it is much less easy to reconcile the mind to the discrepancy which perplexes almost every book of travels, in reference to the magnitude of the buildings themselves. For instance, the following table exhibits only a small portion of the error which applies to the measurement, or estimated bulk, of these famous structures; and yet the difference is so great as to justify the suspicion that the standard used by the several writers could not be the same, or that the summit

[*] Travels along the Mediterranean and Parts Adjacent. By Robert Richardson, M.D.—Vol. i, p. 130.

of the principal structure has been considerably lowered since the days of Herodotus.

	Height of the Great Pyramid.	Length of the Side.
ANCIENTS.	*Feet.*	*Feet.*
Herodotus	800	800
Strabo	625	600
Diodorus	600	700
Pliny	—	708
MODERNS.		
Le Brun	616	704
Prosper Alpinus	625	750
Thevenot	520	612
Niebuhr	440	710
Greaves	444	648
Davison	461	746
French Savans	440 (470 Eng.)	704

NUMBER OF LAYERS OR STEPS.

Greaves	207
Maillet	208
Albert Lewenstein	260
Pococke	212
Belon	250
Thevenot	206
Davison	206

Davison not only numbered the layers, but gives the height of every one of them separately, from the bottom to the top. Grobert, a member of the French Academy, appears to have proceeded in a similar manner, counting the steps individually, and measuring their thickness. But it is obvious, that if they did not make an allowance in every instance for any deviation of the surface of the step from the plane of the horizon, the result would not coincide with the actual height of the Pyramid. As an approximation, however, we may assume that the structure in question is four hundred and eighty feet high, on a base of seven hundred and fifty feet in length; or, in other words, covering an area of about eleven acres, and rising to an elevation of 127 feet above the cross of St. Paul's cathedral.

Mr. Belzoni, whose solitary exertions accomplished more than the united band of philosophers attached to the French army, ascertained the dimensions of the second Pyramid to be as follows:—

	Feet.
The Base	693
Perpendicular height	456
Coating from the top to the place where it ends	140

Before we leave these memorable relics of ancient grandeur, we must revert to a circumstance which is too remarkable to be passed over. In all the pyramids that have been opened, which at Djizeh and Sakhara amount at least to six, the entrance has always been found near the centre on the northern face, and the passage as uniformly proceeding downwards from it, at an angle which never varies. Greaves makes the inclination in that of Cheops to be 26°, while Caviglia has determined it at 27°; which last we have observed to be common to all the sloping passages in the edifice just specified. He found the same angle on opening one of the small pyramids towards the south, at the end of the passage of which were two chambers, leading one out of the other, and both empty. The same conclusion was formed by Belzoni in regard to the Pyramid of Cephrenes. The angle in all the sloping channels was 26°. With much apparent reason, therefore, has it been conjectured that this coincidence could not be accidental. It must have been the work of design, executed for some special purpose; and nothing more readily presents itself to the mind, as an object worthy of so much care, than the uses of astronomy, to which the priests of ancient Egypt are known to have been greatly addicted.

Pauw suggested that the pyramids, as well as the obelisks, were temples raised to the god of day, because one of their sides is in all cases turned to the east. If, then, nothing more were apparent than the exact position of these buildings in reference to the four cardinal points of the compass, it would of itself be sufficient to stamp the character of the Egyptians at a very remote age as at least practical astronomers. But when to this are added the delineation of the twelve signs of the zodiac, the traces of which are still visible at Esneh and Dendera, the naming of the principal stars, and the grouping of the constellations, there can remain no doubt that the science of the priesthood was chiefly employed in marking the times and paths of the celestial host. When, too, we find that all the learning of

K 2

Thales, by which he was enabled to calculate eclipses, and determine the solstitial and equinoctial points, was acquired from the Egyptian clergy six hundred years before the Christian era ; that at a later period Eratosthenes was found qualified to measure a degree of the meridian, and from the result to deduce the circumference of the earth to an extraordinary degree of accuracy ; and that the day of the summer solstice was then, and probably at a much earlier epoch, so nicely observed by means of a well dug at Syene, from the surface of which the sun's disk was reflected entire,— we cannot hesitate to receive any hypothesis which assumes an astronomical purpose, in accounting for the architectural prodigies of ancient Egypt.

It is indeed quite consistent to suppose that the priests, in the construction of these stupendous monuments, would avail themselves of the means thus offered of connecting their sacred duties with their favourite study, and of combining the sentiments of piety with the sublime conceptions of astronomy. Among other benefits which this union has conferred upon posterity is that of having fixed with precision the faces of the Pyramids, from which, as Pauw has observed, "we know that the poles of the earth have not changed." But there is reason to think that the Pyramids were made subservient to a more immediate and important use in the science of astronomy, namely, to correct the measurement of time. This object, it may be conceived, was in contemplation when the main passages leading from the northern sides were formed. These approaches, as we have repeatedly remarked, are invariably inclined downwards, in an angle of about 27°, with the plane of the horizon, which gives a line of direction not far removed from that point in the heavens where the polar star now crosses the meridian below the Pole. The observation of this, or some other star, across the meridian, would give them an accurate measure of sidereal time,—a point of the first importance in an age when, it is probable, no other instruments than rude solar gnomons, or expedients still more imperfect, were in use. Indeed it would not be easy to devise a method more effectual for observing the transit of a star with the naked eye, than that of watching its passage across the mouth of such a lengthened tube ; and it is manifest that some one of these luminaries, when in the meridian below the Pole, must have been seen in the line of a passage inclined at an angle of twenty-six or twenty-seven degrees.

These remarks were suggested by an incidental notice in the short memorandum of the measurements made by Mr. Caviglia :—"One no longer sees the pole-star at the spot where the main passage ceases to continue in the same inclination, and where one begins to mount." From this expression it is naturally concluded that he must have seen the pole-star when at the bottom of the main passage; and, if so, we have not yet got the true measure of the angle which these passages form with the horizon. This would be very desirable, as it could not fail to lead to most important results ; especially if it should be found that the difference of the angles in the approaches of the Pyramids of Djizeh, Sakhara, and Dashour correspond to the difference of the latitude of these several places. We might then be almost certain that they were intended for the purpose of observing the passage, over the meridian, of some particular star, whose altitude, when below the Pole, was equal to the angle of the passage. If this suggestion should be well founded, it would not be difficult, by calculation, to determine which of the stars within the Arctic circle might be seen to pass across the mouths of the shafts about the supposed time of building the Pyramids, and thereby to fix, with more precision than has been hitherto attained, the period at which these stupendous structures were erected.[*]

Dr. Richardson is disposed to call in question the soundness of this hypothesis,—observing that the supposition of the passage being intended as "an astronomical instrument for measuring sideral time is scarcely tenable. Pyramids are prodigiously expensive and unmanageable machines ; and the passage, being so carefully sealed at the entrance, precluded all possibility of using them as such."[†] But, in reply to this rather hasty stricture, it may be sufficient to remark that no one has ever maintained they were meant solely for astronomical uses. The constant occurrence of

* Quarterly Review, vol. xix. p. 405 ; Greave's Pyramidographia Belzoni's Researches, vol. i. p. 416.
† Travels along the Mediterranean, vol. i. p. 122.

a fact, however, so little likely to be accidental could hardly
fail to suggest that it must have been intended to serve
some purpose ; and we therefore agree with the ingenious
writer who first advanced the hypothesis, in ascribing the
uniform inclination of the passages in the two large Pyramids to some object quite unconnected with the mere
facility of descent.

Having occupied so much space with this description of
the monuments of Djizeh, we must rest satisfied with a
mere reference to those of Abousir, Sakhara, and Dashour.
Every one knows that, in point of magnitude, these are
much inferior to the former, though still entitled to rank
very high as the remains of a great people, whose glory
unfortunately is now almost entirely reflected from the
ruins of their ancient works. It is deserving of notice, at
the same time, that these smaller pyramids are generally
coated with a material different from the body of the edifice ;
and, moreover, that, so far as they have been inspected, in
their structure and internal distribution they bear a striking resemblance to the more stupendous erections at Djizeh.

Our account of the mechanical productions of ancient
Egypt would be incomplete did we not mention the great
Sphinx, which has always been regarded as an accompani-
ment, and sometimes even as a rival to the Pyramids. The
latest information in regard to this stupendous figure was
obtained from the persevering labours of Mr. Caviglia,
whose name has been already mentioned with so much
honour. After the most fatiguing and anxious endeavours,
during several months, he succeeded in laying open the whole
statue to its base, and exposing a clear area extending to a
hundred feet from its front. It is not easy, says Mr. Salt,
who witnessed the process of excavation, for any person
unused to operations of this kind, to form the smallest idea
of the difficulties which he had to surmount, more especially when working at the bottom of the trench ; for, in
spite of every precaution, the slightest breath of wind, or
concussion, set all the surrounding particles of sand in motion, so that the sloping sides began to crumble away, and
mass after mass to come tumbling down, till the whole surface bore no unapt resemblance to a cascade of water.
Even when the sides appeared most firm, if the labourers
suspended their work but for an hour, they found on their

return that they had the greatest part of it to do over again.
This was particularly the case on the southern side of the
paw, where the whole of the people,—from sixty to a hundred,—were employed for seven days without making any
sensible advance, the sand rolling down in one continued
torrent.

But the discovery amply rewarded the toil and expense
which were incurred in revealing the structure of this wonderful work of art. The huge paws stretched out fifty feet
in advance from the body, which is in a cumbent posture ;
fragments of an enormous beard were found resting beneath
the chin ; and there were seen all the appendages of a
temple, granite tablet, and altar, arranged on a regular
platform immediately in front. On this pavement, and at
an equal distance between the paws of the figure, was the
large slab of granite just mentioned, being not less than
fourteen feet high, seven broad, and two thick. The face
of this stone, which fronted the east, was highly embellished with sculptures in bas-relief, the subject representing
two sphinxes seated on pedestals, and priests holding out
offerings, while there was a long inscription in hieroglyphics most beautifully executed ; the whole design being
covered at top, and protected, as it were, with the sacred
globe, the serpent, and the wings. Two other tablets of
calcareous stone, similarly ornamented, were supposed,
together with that of granite, to have constituted part of
a miniature temple, by being placed one on each side of the
latter, and at right angles to it. One of them, in fact, was
still remaining in its place ; of the other, which was thrown
down and broken, the fragments are now in the British Museum. A small lion, couching in front of this edifice, had
its eyes directed towards the Sphinx. There were, besides,
several fragments of other lions rudely carved, and the fore-
part of a sphinx of tolerable workmanship ; all of which,
as well as the tablets, walls, and platforms on which the
little temple stood, were ornamented with red paint,—a
colour which would seem to have been, in Egypt as well
as in India, appropriated to sacred purposes. In front of
the temple was a granitic altar, with one of the four projections or horns still retaining its place at the angle.
From the effects of fire evident on the stone, this altar, it is
manifest, had been used for burnt-offerings. On the side

of the last paw of the great Sphinx were cut several indistinct legends in Greek characters, addressed to different deities. On the second digit of the same was sculptured, in pretty deep letters, an inscription in verse; of which the subjoined translation was given by the late Dr. Young, whose extensive knowledge of antiquities enabled him at once to restore the defects of the original, and to convey its meaning in Latin as well as in English:*

On the digits of the southern paw were only discovered a few of the usual dedicatory phrases in honour of Harpocrates, Mars, and Hermes. One inscription gives, as Mr. Salt reads it, to the Emperor Claudius the extraordinary appellation of the "good spirit" (ἀγαθὸς δαίμων),—an instance of flattery which can only be outdone by that of another inscription discovered in Upper Egypt, where Caracalla is styled "most pious" (piissimus), on the very same stone from which the name of his murdered brother Geta had probably been erased by his own hand. On another small edifice, in front of the Sphinx, was a legend with the name of Septimius Severus, in which that of Geta was

---

* Σον δεμας ἐκπαγλον τευξαν θεοι αἰεν ἐοντες
Φειδαμενοι χωρης πυριδα μαχομενης· κ. τ. λ.

Tuum corpus stupendum struxerunt dii sempiterni,
   Parentes terrae triticum pinsenti;
In medium erigentes arvensis tabulae
   Insulae petrosae arenam detrudentes:
Vicinam pyramidibus talem se posuerunt viam,
Non Œdipodis homicidam, sicut ad Thebas,
   Sed Deae Latonae famulam purissimam
Sedule observantem desideratum bonum regem,
Terrae Egyptiae venerandum ductorem,
Caelestem magnum imperatorem (diis affinem)
Similem Vulcano, magnanimum (fortissimum)
Validum in bello, et amabilem inter cives
Terram laetari (omnigenis epulis jubentem),

Thy form stupendous here the gods have placed,
   Sparing each spot of harvest-bearing land;
And with this mighty work of art have graced
   A rocky isle encumbered once with sand:
Not that fierce Sphinx that Thebes erewhile laid waste,
   But great Latona's servant, mild and bland:
Watching that prince beloved who fills the throne
Of Egypt's plains, and calls the Nile his own,
That heavenly monarch who his foes defies:
Like Vulcan powerful, and like Pallas wise.

obliterated as in the former, and as it also is on the triumphal arch erected by the same emperor at Rome. The former inscription, however, is not to Claudius, but to his successor Nero, as may be distinctly traced in the first line as it now appears.[*]

We have entered more particularly into these details on account of an error into which Dr. Clark has fallen respecting the share of merit due to the French in uncovering the body of the Sphinx. He states, without the slightest hesitation, that the academicians who followed the camp of Buonaparte laid open the whole pedestal of this statue, as well as the cumbent or leonine part of the figure, which were before entirely concealed by the sand; adding that, instead of answering the expectations raised concerning the work upon which it was supposed to rest, the pedestal proves to be a wretched substructure of brick-work and small fragments of stone, put together like the most insignificant piece of modern masonry, and wholly out of character, both with respect to the prodigious labour bestowed upon the statue itself and the gigantic appearance of the surrounding objects. Now, every one who has glanced into the splendid publication, to the contents of which the several philosophers contributed in their respective departments, knows well that the French never uncovered more than the back of the Sphinx,—that they never pretended to have seen the pedestal,—and that there is, in fact, no brick-work in any way connected with that celebrated statue. M. Denon saw nothing but the head and neck; and M. Gobert, who was constantly stationed at the Pyramids, says, in his Memoir, that he succeeded in laying bare the back to such an extent as was sufficient to determine the measurement; affirming that the figure was cut out of a salient angle of the mountain, and is accordingly one solid piece of rock. It is true that the paws, which are thrown out fifty feet in front, are constructed of masonry; but it is neither insignificant, nor in the least degree resembling modern workmanship. This, however, could not be known either to the French or to Dr. Clark. Perhaps, after all,

* For the above account of Caviglia's discoveries, as he himself has not published any thing, the reader is indebted to the several communications forwarded by Mr. Salt from Egypt to the late editor of the Quarterly Review.

the hint has been taken from Pococke, who remarks, in regard to the body of the Sphinx, that what some have taken for joinings of the stones, are nothing more than veins in the rock. Hence the suspicion that the hands of the builder were employed in constructing the supposed pedestal or platform on which the statue rests.

We may remark in passing, that the scientific corps commissioned by Buonaparte to illustrate the history and antiquities of Egypt effected almost nothing in either department. Compelled to follow the movements of the army, which was at no time in undisturbed possession of the country, they could not engage in those tedious operations, which, as has been proved by the experience of Belzoni and Caviglia, were absolutely necessary to success in any attempt to analyze the structure of the vast edifices which invite the curiosity of the traveller. It is not denied that, in the great work published under the patronage of the French government, there is much valuable information connected more or less directly with the ancient state of Egypt; but it is no less true, that nearly all the dissertations which occupy its splendid volumes might have been written by men who had never quitted Paris, nor seen any other document besides those which are supplied by the Greek and Roman authors. This remark applies, in the strictest sense, to the long article by M. Jomard on the Pyramids. It is a mere abridgment of the descriptive narrations left by Herodotus, Diodorus, Strabo, Pliny, Ammianus, and by some later writers of the Arabian school. In regard to the Sphinx, again, we subjoin in a note the sum of all the intelligence which is conveyed to the readers of Europe by the renowned philosophers of Napoleon the Great.[*]

We know not whether it will be consolatory to the reader

---

[*] Son élévation, d'environ 13 mètres au-dessus du sol actuel, reste comme *témoin* et comme mesure de l'enlèvement des pierres qui a été fait à la superficie pour dresser cette partie de la montagne. La croupe, à peine sensible, semble seulement tracée sur le sol dans une longueur de près de 22 mètres; et le côté que nous avons voulu découvrir, en faisant enlever le sable que les vents ont accumulé jusqu'au niveau de la montagne, ne nous a offert, sur une profondeur de 9 à 10 mètres environ, aucune forme régulière : quant à l'excavation qui avait été remarquée sur la tête, elle n'est profonde que de 2 mètres 924 millimètres, d'une forme unique et irrégulière.—*Description de l'Egypte*, vo. ii. p. &c. *Antiquités*.

to be informed, that this remarkable statue is again as much under the dominion of the desert as it was half a century ago; and, consequently, that it now meets the eye of the Egyptian traveller shrouded in sand to the same depth as before. Dr. Richardson relates that the wind and the Arabs had replaced the covering on this venerable piece of antiquity, and hence that the lower parts were quite invisible. "The breast, shoulders, and neck, which are those of a human being, remain uncovered, as also the back, which is that of a lion; the neck is very much eroded, and, to a person near, the head seems as if it were too heavy for its support. The headdress has the appearance of an old-fashioned wig, projecting out about the ears, like the hair of the Berberi Arabs; the ears project considerably, the nose is broken, the whole face has been painted red, which is the colour assigned to the ancient inhabitants of Egypt, and to all the deities of the country except Osiris. The features are Nubian, or what, from ancient representations, may be called ancient Egyptian, which is quite different from the negro feature. The expression is particularly placid and benign; so much so, that the worshipper of the Sphinx might hold up his god as superior to all the other gods of wood and stone which the blinded nations worshipped."*

He adds that there is no opening found in the body of the Sphinx whereby to ascertain whether it is hollow or not; but we learn from Dr. Pococke that there is an entrance both in the back and in the top of the head, the latter of which, he thinks, might serve for the arts of the priests in uttering oracles, while the former might be meant for descending to the apartments beneath.†

As to the dimensions of the figure, Pococke found the head and neck,—all that were above ground,—to be twenty-seven feet high; the breast was thirty-three feet wide; and the entire length about a hundred and thirty. Pliny estimated it at a hundred and thirteen feet long, and sixty-three in height. According to Dr. Richardson, the stretch of the back is about a hundred and twenty feet, and the elevation of the head above the sand from thirty to thirty-five,—a result which accords pretty nearly with the measurement of Coutelle. It is obvious, at the same time, that

* Travels, vol. i. p. 154.   † Vol. i. p. 44.

the discrepancy in these reports as to the elevation of the figure must be attributed to the varying depth of the sand, which appears to have accumulated greatly since the days of the Roman naturalist. The Sphinx was entire in the time of Abdollatiph, who describes its graceful appearance and the admirable proportion in the different features of the countenance, which excited his astonishment above every thing he had seen in Egypt. Makrizi states that it was mutilated by the Sheik Mohammed, who, in the spirit of a true Mussulman, thought himself bound to destroy all images, and every thing indeed which bore the slightest resemblance to a living creature. He was called: the Faster,—an expression which denoted his rigid adherence to the rules of his church; while his attack on the Sphinx, and on the stone-lions at the gates of Cairo, established his reputation as a furious bigot.

The learned have indulged in the utmost latitude of conjecture respecting the design of such figures. As they are all found placed near temples and consecrated buildings, it has been justly inferred that their emblematical form must have had some relation to the theological opinions or religious rites of the ancient Egyptians. According to some authors, the countenance of a beautiful woman, combined with the body of a lion or other animal, intimated the alluring aspect with which vice at first assails the unwary, and the besotted monsters which she makes them when caught in her fangs. Others, again, have regarded them as astronomical symbols, marking the passage of the sun from the sign Leo into that of Virgo, and thereby shadowing forth the happy period when the overflowing of the Nile diffuses the blessings of health and plenty throughout the whole land. To us the import of this vast hieroglyphic appears somewhat more profound and mystical. The philosophers of the East, who accustomed themselves to view the created universe as the effect of a certain mysterious generation, naturally regarded the First Cause as combining both sexes, as exercising, in a manner entirely incomprehensible to the human intellect, the male and the female energies, and thereby becoming the parent of every thing that exists. It will, accordingly, be found that to the Sphinx are ascribed attributes which do not belong to a man or to a woman singly, and which cannot be united in the same figure out representing that imaginary hermaphrodite which the refined speculation of the orientals has enshrined in the darkest recesses of their mystic theology.* On a subject, however, so far removed from the ordinary path of investigation, in modern times, and so little likely either to instruct or amuse, it may be sufficient to have suggested materials for reflection to such as are inclined to enter at greater length upon such abstruse inquiries.

Connected with the stupendous undertakings of the Egyptian architects, there is an occurrence mentioned by Herodotus, to which we shall merely direct the attention of the reader. Alluding to a temple erected at Sais in honour of Minerva, the historian observes that what, in his opinion, was most of all to be admired, was a sanctuary brought by Amasis from Elephantiné, consisting of one entire stone. The carriage of it employed two thousand men, all sailors, for the whole period of three years. The length of this edifice, if it may be so called, was twenty-one cubits, the width fourteen, and the height eight. It was placed at the entrance of the temple; and the reason assigned for its being carried no farther is, that the architect, reflecting upon his long fatigue, sighed deeply, and thereby alarmed the superstition of the king, who considered it as a bad omen. Some, however, affirm, that one of the men employed in working a lever was crushed to death,—an event which discouraged Amasis, and induced him to desist from his enterprise.†

We know that the practice of erecting monolithic temples, or sanctuaries hollowed out in a single stone, was very general in Egypt; some striking specimens being still preserved in the higher parts of the country. But we question whether the power of modern mechanics could remove from

---

* Les Sphinx des Egyptiens ont les deux sexes, c'est à dire qu'ils sont femelles par devant, ayant une tête de femme,—et mâles derrière.... C'est une remarque que personne n'avait encore faite. Il resulte de l'inspection de quelques monumens, que les artistes Grecs donnaient aussi des natures composées à ces êtres mixtes, et qu'ils faisaient même des sphinx barbus, comme le prouve un bas-relief en terre cuite conservé à la Farnesina. Lorsque Herodote nomme les sphinx des androsphinges, il a voulu designer par cette expression la duplicité de leur sexe. Les sphinx qui sont aux quatre faces de la pointe de l'obelisque du soleil, sont remarquables par leurs mains d'hommes armées d'ongles crochus, comme les griffes des bêtes féroces.—Winkelman.

† Herodotus, lib. ii. c. 175.

the quarry, and convey to the distance of four hundred miles, a mass of rock thirty-two feet long, twenty-one broad, and twelve in height. It is only in a nation where the Pyramids continue to bear witness to the astonishing effects produced by labour and perseverance that such things must not be pronounced incredible. The obelisks, too, some of which adorn more than one capital city in Europe, prove that the resources of the Egyptian engineer are not to be measured by the progress of similar arts, at the same period, in any part of Italy or Greece.

But our limits forbid us to indulge in details. We hasten, therefore, to leave the vast cemetery which surrounded the ancient Memphis, and of which the Pyramids may be considered as the principal decorations, by noticing the researches of Mr. Salt and his coadjutor Caviglia, in the ruined edifices or tombs which crowd the neighbourhood of Djizeh. Viewed from the monument of Cheops, they appear in countless multitudes, scattered without order among the larger buildings, as the graves in a churchyard round the church, and extend towards the north and south along the left bank of the Nile, as far as the eye can reach. These remains of antiquity were noticed by Pococke and other travellers, but were not till lately examined with the attention which they appear to deserve. They are described as being generally of an oblong form, having their walls slightly inclined from the perpendicular inwards,— the peculiar characteristic of ancient Egyptian architecture—flat roofed; with a sort of parapet round the outside formed of stones, rounded at the top, and rising about a foot and a half above the level of the terrace. The walls are constructed of large masses of rock of irregular shape, seldom rectangular, though neatly fitted to each other, somewhat in the manner of the Cyclopean structures, as they are called, which are found in various parts of Greece.

The first of these mausoleums examined by Mr. Caviglia was found to have the inside walls covered with stucco, and embellished with rude paintings, one of which, though much defaced, evidently represented the sacred boat, while another displayed a procession of figures, each carrying a lotus in his hand. At the southern extremity were several mouldering mummies laid one over the other in a recumbent posture. Many of the bones remained entire, and among

the rest was a scull with part of its cloth covering inscribed
with hieroglyphics. The second edifice he explored had
no paintings, but contained several fragments of statues.
In one of the chambers were found two pieces of marble
composing an entire figure, almost as large as life, in the
act of walking, with the left leg stretched forward, and the
two arms hanging down and resting on the thighs. From
the position of this statue, and from that of a pedestal and
the foot of another figure, in a different chamber, both facing
the openings into the respective apartments, Mr. Salt is of
opinion that they were so placed for the express purpose
of being seen by the friends of the deceased from an adjoining corridor; the statues themselves bearing, as he
thinks, evident marks of being intended for portraits of the
persons whom they were meant to represent. The several
parts were marked with a strict attention to nature, and
coloured after life, having artificial eyes of glass or transparent stones, to give them the air of living men. A head
was discovered, but it did not exactly fit the statue in question, though it probably belonged to the foot and pedestal;
but its chief value consisted in its similarity in style and
features to that of the Sphinx, having the same facial line,
the same sweetness of expression and marking in the mouth,
and the same roundness and peculiarity which characterize
the rest of the countenance,—circumstances which tend to
prove its great antiquity. In removing the fragments, eight
hours were employed in enlarging the opening of the chamber to enable the workmen to force them through; whence
it is evident that the statue must have been placed in its cell
before the edifice was completely finished. The same observation, indeed, applies to the Pyramids; the sarcophagus,
and other remains of art contained in which, must have been
introduced before the passages were lined with granite,
the space being now too contracted to admit of their conveyance in a perfect state. We are informed by Mr. Salt
that many of the fragments found in these tombs, composed
of alabaster as well as of the hardest rock, give a much
higher idea of Egyptian sculpture than has usually been
entertained; the utmost attention being shown by the artist
to the anatomical properties of the human figure, to the
swell of the muscles and the knitting of the joints.

In a third of these stone edifices was a boat of a large

size, sculptured with a square sail, different from any now employed on the Nile. In the first chamber of this building were paintings, in bas-relief, of men, deer, and birds,—the men engaged in planning and preparing certain pieces of furniture, hewing blocks of wood, and pressing out skins either of wine or oil. The top of the second chamber is hollowed out in the form of an arch. In this apartment, it is added, the figures and hieroglyphics are exceedingly beautiful. On the right is represented a quarrel between some boatmen, executed with great spirit; and, a little farther on, a number of men engaged in the different pursuits of agriculture,—ploughing, hoeing up the ground, bringing in their corn on asses, and storing it in the magazines. On the west are several vases painted in the most vivid colours; and on the south a band of musicians playing on the harp, flute, and a species of clarionet, together with a group of dancing women, tinged of a yellow colour, as is the case in most of the temples of Upper Egypt. In the same structure are two other chambers, one unembellished, the other having carved on its walls a variety of figures and hieroglyphics. In a fifth of these mortal dwellings were similar inscriptions on a thick coat of white plaster, executed, as it would appear, with a wooden stamp or mould.

Many others of these ancient sepulchres were cleared out, and found to consist of a number of different apartments, variously disposed, but similarly decorated with carvings and paintings, according, perhaps, to the wealth or caprice of those who erected them; one, in particular, from the delicacy of its colours, its general, pleasing aspect, and superior style of execution, was deemed deserving of the closest attention. It is further observed, that, in all of them, there were discovered fragments of bitumen, great quantities of mummy-cloth and of human bones, which seemed to remove all doubt of their having served the purpose of entombing the dead. A very important circumstance yet remains to be noticed. In some one apartment of all these monumental edifices was a deep shaft or well, from the bottom of which a narrow passage conducted to a subterraneous chamber. One of these shafts, cleared out by Mr. Caviglia, was sixty feet deep, and in the room a little to the south of the lower extremity of the pit was standing, without a lid, a plain but highly-finished sarcophagus, of the same dimensions nearly

as that in the Pyramid of Cheops, though still more exqui-
sitely polished. This discovery supplies a strong argument
in support of the opinion that all the Pyramids were used as
sepulchres, whatever may have been their primary and more
important object.

As to the comparative antiquity of the mausoleums just
described, Mr. Salt entertained an opinion different from
that of most writers; considering the ground in which they
stand as the burial-place of the kings of Egypt prior to the
construction of the Pyramids, and as having been connected
with Heliopolis before the seat of government was transferred to Memphis. The more general belief, however, is,
that these edifices are not only much more recent than the
vast structures which they surround, but that in a majority
of cases they are composed of the coating of the Pyramids,
removed from their surface either by violence or by the
effects of time. As a confirmation of this view, it may be
stated that the walls of these tombs are formed of the same
kind of stones which were used for coating the more majestic monuments; and covered with hieroglyphics, as were
also the casings of the Pyramids at a remote epoch. On
these last Abdollatiph says that he himself saw as many
inscriptions as would fill ten thousand volumes; and other
authors have recorded the same fact in language equally
strong. A circumstance mentioned by Mr. Salt appears to
us to be completely decisive of the question. He saw a
stone, bearing an inscription of hieroglyphics and figures,
built into one of the walls upside down,—a fact which
proves beyond a doubt that it had constituted a part of
some other structure before it was placed in its present
position. It is probable, too, that the little mounds which
diversify the surface of the neighbouring country were originally buildings of the same description, but of a still higher
antiquity; and that they have gradually mouldered down
into the shape they now exhibit, under the pressure of age
and the wasting influence of the elements.

In examining the interesting district which includes
Djizeh, Abousir, Sakhara, and Dashour, and which may
even be regarded as extending to the borders of Lake Mœris,
the contemplative spirit finds itself in a great city of the
dead,—reading the annals of a mighty people, the impressions of whose power and genius are most closely associated

with emblems of mortality,—whose thoughts must have been constantly occupied with the value of posthumous fame, and who appear to have spent their lives in preparing a receptacle for the body after all its earthly attachments should have passed away. At the present hour, the wide plain of Memphis is in the possession of those who urged its labours or presided over its affairs three thousand years ago. The peasant or the traveller, accordingly, who seeks a dwelling in that desolate region, must enter the precincts of a tomb, and share an apartment with bones which have been insensible during many centuries, and be surrounded with figures and inscriptions which point to events not recorded in any other history. No nation of the ancient world has so successfully perpetuated its existence through the medium of death. The actual inhabitants of Egypt sink into insignificance when compared with the mouldering dust of their ancestors; and the proudest edifices which they have raised since the days of the Pharaohs produce not on the mind of the spectator any other feeling than that the sons have gradually degenerated from the power or ambition of their fathers.

We reserve for another chapter an account of the ruins, more strictly architectural, which continue to adorn the sites of the ancient cities, especially in the upper division of the kingdom.

CHAPTER V.

The Literature and Science of the Ancient Egyptians.

Remains of Egyptian Literature scanty but valuable—Meaning of Hieroglyphics—Picture-writing—Progress towards an Alphabet; Illustrated by the Hebrew and other Oriental Tongues—Different Modes of Writing practised by the Egyptians, Epistolographic, Hieratic, and Hieroglyphic properly so called—Discovery of Rosetta Stone—Researches of Dr. Young and Champollion—The Practice of Chinese in rendering Words Phonetic—The Advantages of the Hieroglyphical Method—Discoveries of Mr. Salt—Anecdote of King Thamus—Works of Thoth or Hermes—Quotation of Clemens Alexandrinus—Greeks learned History from Egypt—The Numerical System of the Ancient Egyptians—The Arabians derived their Arithmetical Signs from Egyptians.

THE materials for this section of our work are neither abundant nor various; but they are, nevertheless, extremely satisfactory, and point out, in a manner free from all ambiguity, the first steps taken by man in his attempts to communicate his thoughts through the medium of written language. The literature of ancient Egypt, we must admit, does not, like that of Greece, call forth our admiration by splendid poems and regular histories; nor, like that of the Hebrews, by preserving the events of the primeval world in a record sanctioned by the Spirit of Eternal Wisdom. But, notwithstanding, in the brief notices which have come down to our age of the methods adopted by the early Egyptians for giving permanency to their conceptions, we have a treasure which, to the philosopher, is more valuable than the sublime verses of Homer, and, in a merely grammatical point of view, not inferior to the inspired narrative of Moses itself. We allude to the system of hieroglyphics; the knowledge of which is very important, both as exhibiting authentic specimens of picture-writing—the original expedient of the rude annalist—and also as indicating the path which led to that nobler invention—the use of an alphabet.

The term hieroglyphic literally denotes sacred sculpture, and was employed by the Greeks in reference to those figures and inscriptions which they found engraven on the

temples, sepulchres, and other public buildings of Egypt.
The practice, however, out of which it arose, appears to be
common to the whole human race in the first stage of civilization; being dictated to them by necessity, and suggested
by the most obvious associations. Man learns to paint
before he attempts to write; he draws the outline of a figure
long before he is able to describe an event; he confines his
representations to the eye during ages in which he can find
no more direct means of addressing the understanding, or
of amusing the fancy. In the infancy of society, all communication not strictly verbal is carried on through the
medium of picture-writing; and this imperfect method
continues in all countries until a happy accident, or the
visit of a more refined people, makes known the secret of
alphabetical notation.

When, for example, the Spaniards first landed on the
shores of America, the event was announced to the inhabitants of the interior by rough drawings of men, arms, and
ships; some specimens of which have been preserved by
Purchas, to whose laborious diligence we are indebted for
the best account of European discovery and conquest in the
western hemisphere. But, generally speaking, the aid of
an alphabet so completely supersedes the more primitive
usage, that, in most countries, all traces of the latter are
speedily forgotten; and it is only by a remote and rather
indistinct species of reasoning that the philosophical grammarian endeavours to connect the refined literature of a
polished age with the rude efforts of the savage to imbody
his thoughts in external signs. The monuments of Egypt,
from their extreme durability, supply a history which nowhere else exists of the successive steps which conduct
mankind from the first point to the last in the important
art now under our consideration. Our limits will not permit us to enter into an investigation which would itself
occupy an entire volume; we shall therefore confine ourselves to a general statement of first principles, and to
such an illustration of them as may prove intelligible to the
young reader, who may not have other opportunities of
studying this important subject.

The first and simplest expedient, then, is that already
mentioned, of attempting to convey and perpetuate the
knowledge of an event by forming a rude picture of it,

The inconvenience inseparable from such a method would soon suggest the practice of reducing the delineation, and of substituting a sword for an armed man, a flag for an invading host, and a curved line for a ship. In the earlier stages of contraction, the abbreviated forms would still retain a faint resemblance to the original figure; but in process of time, as the number of ideas and relations increased, the signs would deviate farther from the likeness of an object, and assume more and more the character of a conventional mark, expressive of thought as well as of mere existence. At this era, however, which may be regarded as the second in order, every sign would continue to be a separate word, denoting some individual thing, together with all the circumstances and associated reflections which could be conveyed by so imperfect a vehicle.

It is worthy of notice that the language of China retains the aspect now described at the present day. Attached to old habits, or repelled from imitation by the contempt which usually attaches to ignorance, the people of that vast empire refuse to adopt the grammatical improvements of Europe, which would lead them to analyze their written speech into its alphabetical elements. Their composition, accordingly, still consists of a set of words or marks expressive of certain ideas; becoming, of course, more complicated as the thoughts to be conveyed are more numerous or subtile, and requiring, at length, a great degree of very painful and unprofitable study to comprehend their full import.

The third and most valuable movement in the progress of grammatical invention is that which provides a sign for expressing a sound instead of denoting a thing, and dissects human speech into letters instead of stopping at words. The apparatus for accomplishing this object appears to have been at the first sufficiently awkward and inconvenient. In order to write the name of a man, for example, the ingenuity of the Egyptian philologist could suggest nothing more suitable than to arrange, in a given space, a certain number of objects, the initial letters of which, when pronounced, would furnish the sounds required. For instance, if a person following that scheme of notation wished to record that Pompey had landed in Egypt, he would describe the action by the wonted signs employed in picture-writing; but to express the appellation of the general, he would find

It necessary to draw as many objects as would supply in the first letters of their names, *P*, *o*, *m*, *p*, *e*, *y*. In writing the word London, on this principle, we might take the figures of a *lion*, of an *oak*, of a *net*, of a *door*, of an *oval*, and of a *nail*; the initial sounds or first letters of which words would give the name of the British capital.

After a certain period there arose, from this modified hieroglyphic, a regular alphabet constructed so as to represent and express the various sounds uttered by the human voice. This invention, being subsequently communicated to the Greeks, contributed in a great measure to their improvement, and laid the foundation of their literary fame. The gift of Cadmus, who conveyed sixteen letters across the Mediterranean, is celebrated in the traditional history of the nation upon whom it was conferred; and hence the arrival of that renowned adventurer from the coast of Egypt continues to be mentioned as the epoch when civilization and a knowledge of the fine arts were first received by the barbarians of eastern Europe. The trading communities which had already stationed themselves on the shores of Syria were probably, as we have elsewhere suggested, the medium of intercourse between Egypt and Greece—a supposition which enables us to account for the similarity observed by every scholar in the more ancient form of their alphabetical characters. But, whatever ground there may be for this conjecture, there is no doubt that the process detected in the Egyptian monuments reveals the important secret which the philosophical grammarian has so long laboured to discover.

As a proof, and at the same time an illustration of the argument now advanced, we may recall to the mind of the oriental student that the alphabet of the Hebrew, as well as of the other cognate tongues, is in fact a list of names, and that the original form of the letters bore a resemblance to the objects which they were used to express. Aleph, Beth, Gimel, which in the common language of the country denoted an ox, a horse, a camel, were at first pictures or rude likenesses of a dwelling and of the two animals just specified; proceeding on the very familiar system, not yet exploded in books for children, where an ass, a bull, and a cat are associated with the first three letters of the Roman alphabet. The process of abbreviation, which is rapidly

applied by an improving people to all the technical properties of language, soon substituted an arbitrary sign for the
complete portrait, and restricted the use of the alphabetical
symbol to the representation of an elementary sound.

But in Egypt the use of the hieroglyph was not entirely
superseded by the invention of an alphabet. For many
purposes connected with religion, and even with the more
solemn occupations of civil life, the emblematical style of
composition continued to enjoy a preference; on a principle
similar to that which disposes the Jew to perform his worship in Hebrew, and the Roman Catholic in Latin. There
appears also to have been a mixed language used by the
priests, partaking at once of hieroglyphics and of alphabetical characters; which, in allusion to the class of men
by whom it was employed, was denominated hieratic.
Hence, in process of time, the Egyptians found themselves
in possession of three different modes of communication—
the hieroglyphic, properly so called, the hieratic, and the
demotic or common. This distinction is clearly recognised
in the following well-known passage extracted from the
works of Clemens Alexandrinus.

Those who are educated among the Egyptians, says he,
learn first of all the method of writing called the epistolographic; secondly, the hieratic, which the sacred scribes
employ; and, lastly, the most mysterious description, the
hieroglyphic, of which there are two kinds,—the one denoting objects, in a direct manner, by means of the initial
sounds of words; the other is symbolical. Of the symbolical signs one class represents objects by exhibiting a
likeness or picture; another, by a metaphorical or less complete resemblance; and a third, by means of certain alle-
gorical enigmas. Thus,—to give an example of the three
methods in the symbolical division,—when they wish to
represent an object by the first, they fix upon a distinct resemblance; such as a circle, when they want to indicate
the sun, and a crescent when their purpose is to denote the
moon. The second, or metaphorical, allows a considerable
freedom in selecting the emblem, and may be such as only
suggests the object by analogous qualities. For instance,
when they record the praises of kings in their theological
fables, they exhibit them in connexion with figurative allu-
sions which shadow forth their good actions and benign

M

dispositions. In this case the representation is not direct but metaphorical. Of the third method of symbolical writing, the following will serve as an example : they assimilate the oblique course of the planets to the body of a serpent, but that of the sun to the figure of a scarabæus.*

In the above extract there is mention made of that species of hieroglyphics which expresses objects by the *initial letters*,—a remark that is now perfectly intelligible, but which, till the year 1814, presented a most perplexing enigma to the ablest scholars in Europe. It does not properly belong to the business of this chapter to give a history of the various steps which finally led to a discovery of the path that promises to conduct the scholar to the richest treasures of Egyptian learning ; but as the subject is of considerable interest, and affords at the same time a striking instance of the success which hardly ever fails to reward an enlightened perseverance, we shall enter into a few details.

When the French were in Egypt they discovered, in the foundation of a fort near Rosetta, a block or slab of basalt, which presented an inscription in three distinct languages, namely, the sacred letters, the letters of the country, and the Greek. The first class obviously comprehends the hieroglyphic and hieratic, the mode of writing used by the priests ; while the second not less manifestly identifies itself with what Clemens calls the epistolographic, and which is now usually particularized as demotic or enchorial. Unfortunately a considerable part of the first inscription was wanting ; the beginning of the second, and the end of the third, were also mutilated ; so that there were no precise points of coincidence from which the expounder could set out in his attempt to decipher the unknown characters. But the second inscription, notwithstanding its deficiencies near the beginning, was still sufficiently perfect to allow a comparison to be made of its different parts with each other, and with the Greek, by the same method which would have been followed if it had been entire. Thus, on examining, in their relative situation, the parts corresponding to two

* We have given a paraphrase rather than a literal version ; the original not admitting of a strict rendering without sacrificing the sense of the author, which alone we have endeavoured to retain.

passages of the Greek inscription in which *Alexander* and *Alexandria* occurred, there were soon recognised two well-marked groups of characters resembling each other, which were therefore considered as representing these names. A variety of similar coincidences were detected, and especially that between a certain assemblage of figures and the word Ptolemy, which occurred no fewer than fourteen times; and hence, as the Greek was known to be a translation of the Egyptian symbols, the task of the decipherer was limited to a discovery of the alphabetical power of the several marks, or objects, which denoted that particular name. It was by pursuing this path that success was ultimately attained. It was satisfactorily made out that hieroglyphics not only expressed ideas, or represented things, but also that they were frequently used as letters; and that, when employed for the last of these purposes, the names of the several objects in the language of the country supplied the alphabetical sounds which composed any particular word.

The first steps which led to this important discovery were made by Dr. Young, who ascertained that certain figures in the group, corresponding to the word Ptolemy, were used alphabetically, and represented sounds. Hence the distinction of *phonetic* hieroglyphics, as opposed to those which are understood to denote objects only. A key was thereby found for unlocking the storehouses of Egyptian learning, which had remained inaccessible to many generations; and, whether the treasure shall prove equal in value to the expectations which have been entertained of it, there is now the greatest probability that the famed wisdom of one of the most ancient nations of the world shall be rendered familiar to the modern reader. Already, indeed, history and chronology have received essential aid from the investigations of recent travellers, guided by the light which has just been revealed. The names of some of the most distinguished Egyptian princes, even of the Pharaonic dynasties, have been deciphered from monuments erected during their respective reigns. The canon of Manetho, which it had become so common to treat with contempt, has been verified in many points; and in this way the titles of several monarchs which had been abandoned as fabulous, including Misphragmuthosis, Amenophis, Ramesses, and Sesostris, are once more restored to the page of authentic history, and to their place in the succession of Egyptian sovereigns.

Nothing, perhaps, connected with this interesting subject is more surprising than that the priests of Heliopolis and Memphis should have continued the use of imitative and symbolic hieroglyphics so long after they had become acquainted with the more convenient apparatus of alphabetical writing. But this fact, which might otherwise appear incredible, finds a counterpart in the practice of the Chinese, who, as we have already mentioned, retain even at the present day a modified species of hieroglyphics,—a literary notation that denotes things or ideas instead of expressing sounds,—and which they likewise can render phonetic at pleasure. When, for example, they have occasion to indicate any foreign combination of vocal sounds, such as the name of a European object or person, they attach a certain mark to their words, and thereby convert them into letters; the initial consonant of the several terms supplying the successive alphabetical articulations necessary to form the noun in question. At this stage all the difficulty of the invention is conquered. The moment that men have learned to denote, by a visible sign, a sound instead of a sensation or an event, they have acquired possession of an alphabet; and then nothing more is requisite except to abbreviate the figures so as to make them convenient for the rapid uses of ordinary life,—to dismiss the picture, in short, and substitute an arbitrary mark, according to the practice of European nations. But the ancient Egyptians, like the modern Chinese, thought proper to rest satisfied with one-half of the advantages which their ingenuity had earned; continuing, for ages after the knowledge of phonetic characters, to intersperse them with the imitative and symbolical figures which in every other country those others have completely superseded.

Leaving it to the historian of this remarkable discovery to detail the incidents which accompanied the investigations of Dr. Young, Silvestre de Sacy, Akerblad, Salt, and Champollion, we confine ourselves to the statement of the important fact, that, from a copious induction of instances, extending in some cases to several hundreds for a single character, the last of these authors has completely ascertained that every *phonetic* hieroglyph is the image of some physical object whose name, in the spoken language of Egypt, begins with the sound or letter which the sculptured figure was destined to represent. Thus the image of an eagle, which in the Coptic is *Ahôm*, became the sign of the vowel A; that of a small vase, called *Berbe* in Egyptian, stood for the consonant B; that of a hand, *Tot*, represented the letter T; that of a hatchet, *Kelebin*, was the sign of the consonant K; that of a lion or lioness, *Labo*, the sign of the consonant L; that of a nycticorax, *Mouladj*, the sign of M; that of a flute, *Sebiandjo*, the sign of the consonant S; that of a mouth, *Rô*, the sign of the consonant R; and the abridged image of a garden, *Shené*, the sign of the compound articulation Sh.

It is obvious from the statement now made, that, as there are a great many objects the names of which begin with the same letter, an author using phonetic hieroglyphics must have had a wide field in which to select his characters. Some of the letters were in fact represented by fifteen and even by twenty-five different figures. M. Champollion is of opinion that, in writing the articulated sounds of a word, the Egyptians chose, among the great number of characters which they were at liberty to employ, those figures which by their qualities represented such ideas as had a relation to the object which they meant to express. For example, in designating the name of Noub, one of their deities, they selected, to express the letter B, the figure of a ram in preference to any other sign, because the ram was by itself a symbol of this deity; so much so, indeed, that we often find him represented under the figure of a man, with the head of that animal. For the same reason, to express the letter N, they chose from among the several characters employed for the purpose the sign of a vase, because it was usual to represent this god with one of these vessels lying at his feet. Again, the lion, which in Coptic was called Labo, stood for the letter L; and though this sound was represented by several other signs, the Egyptians, in writing the name of Ptolemy, and afterward of the Roman emperors, uniformly employed the figure of that noble animal, to denote, no doubt, the corresponding qualities in their powerful and magnanimous sovereigns.

An author was thus enabled to combine with a name the

character of the individual to whom it applied,—possessing through these means a fund of the most delicate flattery or panegyric. Perhaps it may have been solely for such reasons that hieroglyphics continued to be used for inscriptions and legends, in preference to the bare notation of alphabetical signs, long after the superior convenience belonging to the latter, for merely literary purposes, must have been universally appreciated.

We may observe, too, that in writing hieroglyphics the figures may be placed in four different ways, and are often found so arranged on the same monument. They are either in perpendicular lines, and may be read from right to left or from left to right; or they are in a horizontal direction, following the same variety as to the mode of reading. Two rules, however, have been given to determine which way any inscription or papyrus is to be deciphered. The first is, that in hieroglyphical manuscripts the characters are for the most part placed in perpendicular lines; while in sculptures and paintings, especially when they refer to persons, the signs are situated horizontally. The second rule, equally general and equally useful, is, that every inscription, manuscript, or legend of any kind whatever, is to be read from the side towards which are turned the heads of the animals or the angular edges of the characters. Thus a line of hieroglyphics is like a regular procession, in which all the images of the several objects follow the march of the initial sign; and it is probably to point out this direction that all the figures of men and lower animals, whether birds, reptiles, insects, or quadrupeds, have been designed in profile.

After what has been narrated, it is scarcely necessary to observe, that the learning of an Egyptian, like the similar acquirements of a modern Chinese, would be measured by the number of hieroglyphic or ideographic signs which he was able to interpret. This remark, it is true, applies almost exclusively to the figurative and symbolic classes which, instead of sounds, denoted things or qualities. But as there were scarcely any pieces of composition executed entirely in phonetic characters, and without a considerable intermixture of the two others, the means of acquiring knowledge among the subjects of the Pharaohs must have been extremely limited. Perhaps, at a more advanced period of hieroglyphical discovery, we shall find that many of the signs which are at present esteemed symbolical were also used alphabetically,—an expectation which has unquestionably been rendered more probable by the recent investigations of Champollion among the ancient monuments of Egypt.

This indefatigable author has arrived at the following conclusions, founded on personal research, and supported by the results published by other travellers:—

1. That the phonetic hieroglyphic alphabet can be applied with success to the legends of every epoch indiscriminately, and is the true key of the whole hieroglyphical system.

2. That the ancient Egyptians constantly employed this alphabet to represent the sound of the words in their language.

3. That all hieroglyphical inscriptions are composed of signs, which, for the greatest part, are purely alphabetical.

4. That these alphabetical signs are of three different kinds,—the demotic, hieratic, and hieroglyphical, strictly so called.

And, *lastly*, that the principles of this graphic system are precisely those which were in use among the ancient Egyptians. The hieroglyphical alphabet which he has already discovered includes nearly nine hundred characters, some of which are exclusively phonetic, but the greater number appear also to combine the properties of the figurative and the symbolical orders.

We cannot leave this interesting subject without mentioning a discovery made by Mr. Salt, which proves that phonetic characters were in use as early as the reign of Psammeticus,—an inference, indeed, which has been since extended to a much remoter period of Egyptian history. It had occurred that, as these characters were applied to the names of foreign monarchs,—the Ptolemies and Roman emperors,—so, in all probability, if known at the time, they would likewise have been made use of in expressing the names of the Ethiopian sovereigns who had previously held the country in subjection. The result proved the soundness of this conjecture. From some sketches made at Abydos, he was fortunate enough to decipher the name of ΣΑΒΑΚΟ or ΣΑΒΑΚΟΘΘ, with the same termination which was afterward found in ΑΜΕΝΩΘ; and in an inscription

taken from the back of a small portico at Medinet Abou, he
discovered the name of TIRAKA, who, he imagines, can be
no other than "Tirhakah, King of Ethiopia, who came out
to make war against Sennacherib, king of Assyria."[*]

If this supposed identity be admitted, it will prove that
the phonetic characters were in use more than seven hundred years before Christ, and it would also establish the
reign of a sovereign named in the Bible, of whose existence
some learned men have been inclined to doubt. Nor did
Mr. Salt's discoveries stop here. Upon the high granitic
rocks of Elephantiné, and also on a large column in front
of the great Temple of Karnac, he made out, with the
utmost ease, from beneath the obtrusive name of a Ptolemy
the appellation of ΠΞΑΜΙΤΙΚ written phonetically. This
name is also sculptured on one of the smaller temples at
Eleithias and on the Campensian obelisk, as well as on that
in Monte Citorio. But we have already remarked that the
use of phonetic symbols can be satisfactorily traced back
as far as the reign of Misphragmuthosis,—fifteen centuries
at least before the Christian era.[†]

Some readers, it is presumed, will value this discovery
more because it seems to withdraw the veil which had long
concealed the origin of alphabetical writing, than for any
light which it may prove the means of throwing upon the
literature of the ancient Egyptians. There can be no doubt
that the Greeks were accustomed to attribute to the priests
of the Nile the merit of having first introduced the knowledge of letters as the representatives of vocal sounds.
Plato, for example, relates, that, during the reign of King
Thamus, his secretary Thoth came to lay before him the
discoveries he had made, among which was the invention

* 2 Kings, chap. xix. v. 9.
† We refer, once for all, to the following treatises as the sources of
our information on hieroglyphics:—The article " Egypt," in Supplement
to Ency. Brit. An Account of some Recent Discoveries in Hieroglyphical
Literature and Egyptian Antiquities, &c. by Thomas Young, M.D., F.R.S.
Lettre à M. Dacier, rélative à l'Alphabet des Hiéroglyphes Phonétiques,
&c. par M. Champollion le Jeune. Précis du Système Hiéroglyphique
des Anciens Egyptiens, &c. par le même Auteur. Lettres à M. le Duc
de Blacas d'Aulps, &c., rélatives au Musée Royal Egyptien de Turin.
Essay on Dr. Young's and M. Champollion's Phonetic System of Hieroglyphics, &c.; by Henry Salt, Esq. Article " Hieroglyphics," in Edin.
Review, vol. xiv. p. 96. Lectures on the Elements of Hieroglyphics and
Egyptian Antiquities; by the Marquis Spineto.

of the alphabet; and he consulted the king whether it might be expedient to make it public. His majesty, who saw the full value of the discovery, was particularly opposed to the plan of recommending it to general use, and, like a true politician, concealed the real cause, while he assigned one more remote and secondary, why he wished that it should be kept secret. He therefore told his ingenious minister, that if the new mode of writing should be divulged, the people would no longer pay any attention to hieroglyphics; and as these would consequently be soon forgotten, the invention would, in its effects, prove one of the greatest obstacles to the progress of knowledge.

Whatever may be the precise meaning of the passage now quoted, it seems reasonable to infer from it, that in the days of Plato the Greeks ascribed to the philosophers of Egypt the honour of having devised a system of phonetic signs, which finally superseded the cumbrous expedient of writing by pictures. It may likewise be concluded, although on grounds somewhat different, that hieroglyphics were not invented after the use of letters had become known, with the view of concealing mysteries from the multitude, but that they were in fact the original mode of communication employed by all nations in the rude beginnings of society. To suppose that they were introduced for the sake of enhancing the paltry knowledge possessed by the priests, or for confining the lights of science to the privileged orders of the state, is an hypothesis contradicted by the most authentic historical records; while to assert that the Egyptians had letters before they had hieroglyphics is not less absurd, says Spineto, than to affirm that they danced before they could walk. On this question the only difficulty we have to encounter is, to explain why they continued so long, in their public monuments and more solemn transactions at least, to use the ancient method after they had become acquainted with a scheme of notation so much better suited to all the purposes of literature. Perhaps certain notions of sanctity, similar to those entertained by the Jews in regard to the name of the Supreme Being, may have prevented the priests of Pharaoh from revealing the attributes of their gods in the vulgar idiom of the country.

In reference to the knowledge actually acquired of the literature of ancient Egypt by means of the late discove-

ries in hieroglyphics, we are not entitled to speak in boastful
or very confident language. The wasting hand of time,
which has rendered its effects visible even on the Pyramids,
has entirely destroyed the more perishable materials to
which the sages of Thebes and the magicians of Memphis
may have committed the science of their several generations. We know, too, that the bigotry of ignorance and of
superstition accomplished, in many cases, what the flood of
years had permitted to escape ; for which reason we must
not estimate the extent of acquirement among the wise
men of Egypt by the scanty remains of their labours which
have been casually rescued from accident and violence.
From Diodorus Siculus we receive the information that in
the tomb of Osymandias were deposited twenty thousand
volumes,—a number which is reduced by Manetho to three
thousand five hundred and twenty-five,—all of which, on
account of their antiquity or the importance of their subjects, were ascribed to Theth or Hermes, who, it is well
known, united in his character the intelligence of a divinity
with the patriotism of a faithful minister.

Of these works, which unquestionably belong to a very
remote antiquity, we have a short account supplied by a
Christian bishop, Clemens of Alexandria, who appears to
have devoted much attention to the learning of the ancient
Egyptians. "In that country," he tells us, " every individual cultivates a different branch of philosophy,—an arrangement which applies chiefly to their holy ceremonies.
In such processions the singer occupies the first place, carrying in his hand an instrument of music. He is said to be
obliged to learn two of the books of Hermes ; one of which
contains hymns addressed to the gods, and the other the
rules by which a prince ought to govern. Next comes the
Horoscopus, holding a clock and the branch of a palm-tree,
which are the symbols of astrology. He must be completely
master of the four books of Hermes which treat of that
science. One of these explains the order of the fixed stars ;
the second, the motion and phases of the sun and moon ;
the other two determine the times of their periodical rising.
Then follows the Hierogrammatist or sacred scribe, with
two feathers on his head, and a book and ruler in his
hand, to which are added the instruments of writing, some
ink and a reed. He must know what are called hiero-

glyphics, and those branches of science which belong to
cosmography, geography, and astronomy, especially the
laws of the sun, moon, and five planets ; he must be acquainted with the territorial distribution of Egypt, the course
of the Nile, the furniture of the temples and of all consecrated places. After these is an officer denominated Sto-
listes, who bears a square-rule as the emblem of justice, and
the cup for libations. His charge includes every thing
which belongs to the education of youth, as well as to sacrifices, first-fruits, selecting of cattle, hymns, prayers, religious pomps, festivals, and commemorations ; the rules for
which are contained in ten books. This functionary is
succeeded by one called the prophet, who displays in his
bosom a jar or vessel, meant for carrying water,—a symbol
thought to represent the deity, but which, more probably,
had a reference to the sacred character of the Nile. He is
attended by persons bearing bread cut into slices. The duty
of the prophet made it necessary for him to be perfectly
acquainted with the ten books called sacerdotal, and which
treat of the laws of the gods, and of the whole discipline of
the priesthood. He also presides over the distribution of
the sacred revenue ; that is, the income arising from the
performance of pious rites, and dedicated to the support of
religious institutions. Hence, there are forty-two books of
Hermes, the knowledge of which is absolutely necessary ;
of these, thirty-six, containing the whole philosophy of the
Egyptians, are carefully studied by the persons whom we
have mentioned ; and the remaining six are learned by the
Pastophori, or inferior priests, as they belong to anatomy,
to nosology, to instruments of surgery, to pharmacy, to the
diseases of the eye, and to the maladies of women."*

This distribution of the sciences does not enable us to
determine either the principles on which they were founded
or the extent to which they were pursued. We possess a
better criterion in the perfection to which the people of
Egypt, at a very early period, had carried some of those
arts which have a close dependence upon scientific deductions. The prodigies of Thebes could not have been accomplished by a nation ignorant of mathematics and chymistry ;
nor could the pyramids, the obelisks, and the monolithic

* Clemen. Alexandria. Strom. lib. vi. p. 632.

temples, which still meet the eye of the traveller in almost
every spot between Elephantine and the mouths of the Nile,
have been raised without the aid of such mechanical powers
as have their origin in the calculations of philosophy.

It seems possible that, in the lapse of ages, a country
shall lose the science upon which the arts must have been
founded, while the arts themselves shall remain as an hereditary bequest from father to son. The Chinese are in such
a condition at present ; and so perhaps were the Egyptians
immediately before the Macedonian conquest. But as the
practical excellence of several of the arts in China satisfies
us that the light of scientific knowledge must at one time
have shone in that vast empire, so might we be convinced,
on the same grounds, that the artisans of Egypt were
instructed by men who had made great progress in the
various branches of natural philosophy. We are in fact
informed by Manetho, that one of the Pharaohs, the grand-
father of Psammeticus, and the sage Petosiris his contemporary, wrote valuable treatises on astronomy, astrology,
and medicine. The last of these works is mentioned even
by Galenus and Aëtius, while that on astronomy is alluded
to both by Eusebius and Pliny ; though it is not improbable
that they were altered by the sophists of Alexandria who
began to flourish under the reigns of the Ptolemies. It is
asserted that the royal author and his philosophical colleague undertook to explain the creation of the world, as
well as the influences exerted upon the human frame by the
heavenly bodies ; but when we reflect upon the channel
through which this account has reached us, we must not
draw hasty conclusions in regard to the physics of the
ancient Egyptian school.

Tatian relates that the Greeks learned how to write history from perusing the Egyptian annals. This assertion
appears to be well founded ; it being manifest, that from the
most remote antiquity the latter people had adopted the
custom of transmitting to posterity the memory of past
events. Originally they seem to have written their chroni-
cles in verse, and inscribed them on stones in hieroglyphical
characters ; but at a certain time after the invention of the
alphabet, they adopted prose and began to form regular
books, though they still retained the custom of celebrating,
in lyric measure, the praises of their gods and heroes. It

seems, indeed, according to the account of the industrious and learned Zoega, who has collected all the authorities of ancient writers on this subject, that historical treatises were very numerous in Egypt, and that the care of copying them constituted one of the principal duties which devolved upon the sacred scribes. Herodotus himself informs us, that he acquired all his knowledge of their country from the priests, who read to him from a book the names of three hundred and thirty kings who had reigned between Menes and Sesostris. Theophrastus, too, who may be regarded as writing from personal knowledge, concurs in the views just stated. Manetho, again, assures his readers that he compiled his work from authentic records. Diodorus, a writer of the highest credit, refers not only to histories in the Egyptian language, but to commentaries and illustrations,—a fact confirmed by Josephus and Strabo, the latter of whom even praises the simplicity of their style. It was from these sources that the Greek authors, Eratosthenes, Agatharchides, Artemidorus, Syncellus, Apollonides, Asclepiades, compiled their histories of Egypt. Besides, we ought not to forget that the Grecian writers who visited the land of the Pharaohs found it already in a state of decay both as to knowledge and power. The priests had lost much of the learning for which their ancestors were celebrated, and no longer enjoyed the privileges which dignified their order prior to the invasion of Cambyses. A library at Thebes, so early as the reign of Osymandias, proves that before the Trojan war a taste for reading had spread over a large portion of Egyptian society. There was a similar establishment at Memphis, in the temple of the god Phtha, from which Naucrates, a wretched scribbler, accuses Homer of having stolen the Iliad and Odyssey, and of having afterward published them as his own. Such a charge evidently refutes itself, but it nevertheless tends to confirm the conclusion drawn from it by ancient writers, in regard to the early civilization and literary habits of the Egyptians. The patronage bestowed by the first of the Ptolemies was, therefore, in strict accordance with the pursuits of the people whom the fortune of war had appointed them to govern. The splendid collection of books at Alexandria was formed by those politic sovereigns as one of the means whereby they might procure popularity,—a motive which reflects no less honour on the character of their subjects than on their own penetration and beneficence.

Nor is it undeserving of notice, that in the most brilliant period of Alexandrian literature, a large share of attention was bestowed upon the antiquities of Egypt. Nearly three centuries before our era, the works of authors then esteemed ancient were sought for with eagerness, and made the subject of laborious commentary. Heyne, in a very ingenious treatise on the sources whence Diodorus probably derived the materials of his history, has mentioned a long list of writers who preceded the Sicilian, as compilers on the affairs of that interesting kingdom.[*] In this way we see the erudition of the older nation reflected from the works of their successors in a comparatively recent age; on which account we think it not too bold to maintain that most of the scientific and literary acquirements which distinguished the Greeks, while the rest of Europe was in a state of barbarism, were derived from their intercourse with the scholars of Thebes and Memphis. In fact, at one time, no Greek was accounted truly learned until he had sojourned a certain period on the banks of the Nile; conversed with the philosophers on the mysteries of their science; studied the laws, the government, and the institutions of the most remarkable people that ever existed; examined and explored their everlasting monuments; and become in some measure initiated in the wisdom of the Egyptians.

Connected with the subject of this chapter, and not a little important in itself, is an inquiry, which has lately engaged a good deal of attention, into the Egyptian method of arithmetical notation. The principal writers who have favoured the world with their opinions on this interesting monument of antiquity are, M. Jomard, whose name has been already mentioned as the author of an essay on the Pyramids, Dr. Young, M. Champollion, and Dr. Kosegarten, who, about two years ago, published a treatise on the literature of ancient Egypt.[†]

This system, we are told, is neither literal, like the Grecian and Roman, nor altogether figurate, like the Arabic, but

[*] De Fontibus Historiarum Diodori.
[†] De Prisca Ægyptiorum Litteratura Commentatio Prima; quam scripsit Joannes Godoffredus Kosegarten, S. S. Theol. Doct., ejusdemque et Lit. Orient. in Academia Gryphisvaldensi Prof. Vimariæ, 1828.

something intermediate between them. It is constructed
upon principles altogether peculiar, and 'expressed by means
of certain characters or signs, which, although perfectly
distinct from those which are employed in the graphic system, are nevertheless framed upon a strict analogy to them,
and adapted with much nicety to the particular form of
composition in which they happen to be used. As there
were three forms of writing among the ancient Egyptians,
—the hieroglyphic, the hieratic, and the enchorial or demotic,—so, in like manner, there were three forms of notation used by them; one adapted to each of these particular
kinds of composition, and now known by the name of the
variety to which it belongs. But as the hieroglyphic or
monumental writing is the basis of the two other classes,
so, in the system of numerical expression, the hieratic is a
modified form of the hieroglyphic, and the demotic of the
hieratic. In the last two, however, there is this peculiarity,
—that separate modes of notation are employed to designate
the days of the month, and that, in both these modes,
several of the numerals which we now denominate Arabic
are distinctly recognised. This very remarkable fact has
been so strikingly exemplified by such writers as have examined the Egyptian notation in detail, as to leave no doubt
whence our modern symbols originated. It does not indeed
appear very clearly which of the three forms was used, in
preference to the others, in scientific computations. But,
judging from analogy, it is probable that the demotic notation, like the demotic writing, was employed in the common
transactions of life; while, with respect to scientific calculations, all that can be gathered from such monuments as
the zodiacs of Dendera and Esneh amounts to nothing
more than the fact that the numerical expressions are uniformly accommodated to the particular kind of writing in
which they occur.

By the labours of several distinguished antiquaries who
have applied themselves to the study of Egyptian literature,
the hieroglyphic signs of numbers from one to a thousand
have been ascertained beyond the possibility of doubt or
error: and as these constitute the simplest of the three
forms of notation in use among the ancient Egyptians, we
shall endeavour to represent them in such a manner as to
render the principle of their arrangement as intelligible as
our means will admit.

The nine digits are not formed upon the Arabic scheme of having a separate mark for each, but simply by repeating the sign of unity as often as there are units in any digit from one to nine. Thus the former is represented by a short thick stroke ❘; *two* by a couple of such strokes ❘❘; *three* by ❘❘❘; and so on to ten : the higher digits, however, *seven, eight,* and *nine,* being represented frequently by strokes arranged in double columns, obviously for the purpose of saving space. The mark or sign for *ten* is ∩; and all the intermediate numbers between ten and twenty are made up by units affixed to the symbol for ten ; thus ∩❘ is eleven, ∩❘❘ is twelve, ∩❘❘❘ is thirteen, and so on. *Twenty* is expressed by two tens ∩∩ ; and the intermediate numbers between twenty and thirty, in the same way precisely as those between ten and twenty. *Thirty* is represented by three tens, ∩∩∩ ; *forty* by four tens, ∩∩∩∩ ; and so on to a hundred ; the tens in sixty, seventy, eighty, and ninety, being, like the higher digits, generally arranged in double columns. From a *hundred,* the mark or sign for which is 9, to a *thousand,* the numbers ascend exactly upon the principle already explained in regard to the preceding part of the scale. Thus 200 is represented 99 ; 300 999 · and so on to a thousand, the symbol of which is ⟨⟩ .

'Such is the hieroglyphical form of notation ascertained by a vast number of readings and comparisons ; and from what has been already stated, as well as from the nature of the signs themselves, and the principle upon which they are combined, it seems pretty evident that they could never have been employed except in monumental inscriptions, for which alone they are adapted. To say nothing of other objections, the method is by far too operose for ordinary purposes, and never could. have been applied, with any degree of success, either to civil affairs or to scientific computations. To denote, for example, the present year, 1831, it would require, according to this scheme, no fewer than thirteen figures, ⟨⟩999999999∩ ∩ ∩❘. At the same time, the high antiquity of this method of numeration is manifest from the simplicity of the principle upon which the scale is constructed, no less than from the age of the monuments on which the inscriptions have been discovered.

The hieratic form, which is the most complete of all, possesses some very remarkable peculiarities; but as it passes naturally into the demotic or enchorial, and has a much closer affinity to that than to the hieroglyphic, we shall confine our account of it to a mere exposition of the principle on which the scheme is made to rest. The digits, omitting the variations, which are of little importance, are represented thus :—

1	**】**	6	三
2	Ч	7	心
3	Щ	8	ヨ
4	Щ	9	Հ
5	Հ		

Ten is represented by the Greek lambda direct or reversed 入 or ⟨. The sign of a hundred is 〕, of two hundred ⟩, of three hundred 〃, of four hundred ⁗; while 500, 600, 700, 800, 900, are represented respectively by combining the signs of 200 and 300; of 300 and 300; of 300 and 400; of 400 and 400; and 300 thrice repeated. The mark for 1000 is the sanpi of the Greeks. 5; the symbol of 10,000 is 2, while 100,000 is represented by the sign of a hundred combined with that of 1000.

So much for the common numbers of the hieratic scale. But there is also a peculiar and distinct set of numerical signs for the days of the month; which are not a little interesting, as exhibiting the source whence the Arabians derived three or four of the figures which that people afterward introduced into the western world; thus conferring upon Europe one of the greatest benefits it ever received, at the hand either of conqueror or of sage, the art of printing alone excepted. These numbers resolve themselves into three decades, the first of which is as follows;

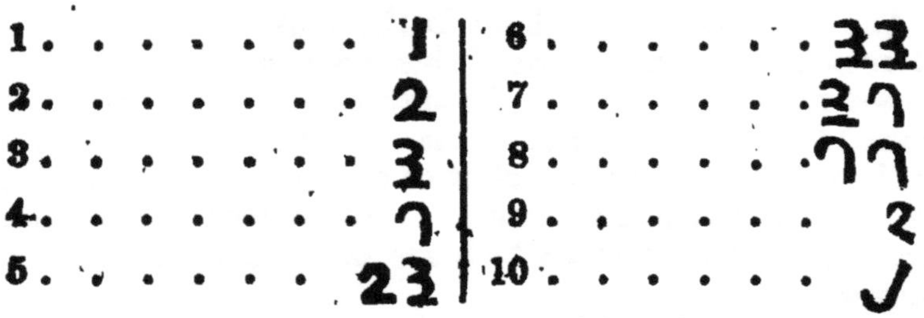

1	𝟏	6	33
2	2	7	�３ㄱ
3	ㄥ	8	ㄱㄱ
4	ㄱ	9	2
5	23	10	ノ

The numbers composing the second decade, or from ten to twenty, are represented by combining the symbol of 10 with the digits in succession, thus ⟋, 11; ⟋, 12; ⟋, 13;

and so on to twenty, the mark or sign of which is ⟋. Lastly, from twenty to thirty, the numbers are represented in the same way precisely as from ten to twenty, ⟋, 21;

⟋, 22; ⟋, 23. So much, then, for the hieratic notation in both its parts, which is evidently in many respects a great improvement upon the hieroglyphic, the source whence it was primarily derived.

The demotic form of notation is not so perfectly understood as the method just described; there being a blank from 13 to 20, and from 60 to 100, the intervening numbers not having been yet determined by actual discovery. The signs or marks bear a great resemblance to those of the hieroglyphic class, of which they are obviously a copy:—

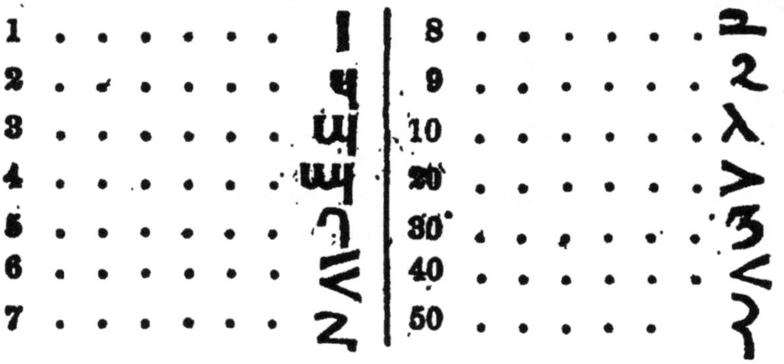

1	𝐈	8	二
2	ㄩ	9	2
3	Ⅲ	10	ㅅ
4	Ⅲ	20	⟨λ
5	Ⅵ	30	⟨3
6	⟨Ⅳ	40	⟨⟨
7	ᱬ	50	⟩

The history of the various steps by which Champollion and others arrived at the knowledge of the numerical system of the Egyptians is extremely interesting, and affords an instance, almost as striking as that of phonetic hieroglyphics, of the triumph of genius, combined with perseverance, over difficulties which appeared entirely insuperable. Accident, it is true, contributed in both cases to diffuse a light over the subject, which could not have been struck out by dint of unaided sagacity. The Rosetta stone enabled our antiquaries to accomplish what the learning of Clemens and the ingenuity of Warburton had failed to make known; and, in the latter inquiry, the appearance of a neglected papyrus, containing the translation of an ancient deed, supplied the means of determining the value of a long list of numerical signs.

There can be little doubt that it was to Egypt the Saracens were indebted for the scheme of arithmetical notation which they subsequently communicated to the scholars of Europe. Thus it is rendered more than probable that to the same people we owe two of the most important inventions which could be employed in the service of learning,—an alphabet, and a regular scale of numbers suited to the profoundest investigations of science. Justly, indeed, has it been remarked, as a most striking fact in the history of the human mind, that the only two discoveries which no one has ever claimed as his own are precisely those which succeeding ages have found it impossible to extend or improve, and which, at the period of their first introduction, were as complete and as universal in their application as they are at the present moment. It is hardly less surprising that the Greeks, who were indebted to the Egyptians for the elements of almost all those sciences which they afterward so much advanced, should have failed to discern the manifold conveniences attached to their numerical system. Some centuries, however, had passed away before they were induced to adopt it from a people comparatively barbarous, but who, like themselves, had profited by their vicinity to that fountain of knowledge which so long beautified and enriched the country of the Pharaohs.[*]

* To the authorities mentioned in the text we feel satisfaction in adding an article, in a recent number of the Westminster Review, on the "Egyptian Method of Notation," to which we acknowledge ourselves under great obligations. See also "Remarques sur les Signes Numériques des Anciens Egyptiens.' Par E. Jomard. Description de l'Egypte, vol. ii. p. 57. Antiquités."

A review of the literature of this ancient nation might seem to require that we should give an account of the theological opinions entertained by the priests, as well as of the doctrines received by the multitude, relative to the nature of the human soul, and a future state of reward and punishment. But it must be apparent that the object of our undertaking precludes all such discussion, as being at once too abstruse and too extensive in its ramifications. It may therefore be sufficient to observe that the popular religion of Egypt, like that of all pagan tribes, was directed towards those qualities in the physical system of the universe upon which the permanence of the animal kingdom is known to depend. The generative and prolific powers, under their various forms, and as affecting every description of organized matter, were worshipped as the Universal Parent, whose names were multiplied according to the changing aspect of nature, and whose attributes, when personified, gave birth to a thousand subordinate divinities. The tenet of the metempsychosis appears to have regulated the faith of the people so far as it applied to the effect of their conduct on their future condition. The soul was understood to expiate the sins committed in the human body, or to enjoy the rewards due to pureness of living, in a succession of transmigrations during three thousand years; at the end of which it was expected to resume its former tenement, and to discharge once more the functions of an earthly existence.

Again, as to the poetry, the eloquence, and the polite literature of that remarkable people, we are still too ignorant of the Coptic to form an accurate judgment. But there is reason to hope that the example presented by M. Quatremère to the scholars of Europe will not be neglected—that the spoken language of the Egyptians will at length receive a degree of attention equal to its importance—and, consequently, that the productions of the poets and orators of Thebes, the passionate effusions of the lover and the patriot, may yet be added to the stores of English learning.

In respect to the arts of the ancient Egyptians, we shall have a better opportunity of introducing a few observations in the following chapter, where we intend to bring before the reader a view of some of the more striking remains of their taste and skill, as collected from the descriptions of recent travellers.

CHAPTER VI.

Remains of Ancient Art in various Parts of Egypt.

General Magnificence of Remains—Alexandria—Pillar—Cleopatra's Needle—Catacombs—Memphis—Beni Hassan—Hermopolis Magna—Antinopolis—Siout—Sepulchral Grottoes—Temple of Antæopolis—Abydos—Dendera or Tentyra—Magnificent Temple and Portico—Elegant Sculptures—Zodiac and Planisphere—Opinions as to their Antiquity—Thebes—The Gateway or Propylon at Luxor—Magnificent Sculptures—Karnac—The Temple; its Approaches and splendid Gateways; its vast Extent—Temples at Dair and Medinet Abou—The Memnonium—Statue of Memnon—Tombs—Herment—Esneh—Eleithias—Striking Representations of Domestic Life—Edfou—Hadjar Silsili—Koum Ombos—Es Souan—Quarries of Syené—Island of Elephantiné—Concluding Remarks.

WE have purposely made a distinction between those immense works which display the gigantic plans and mechanical resources of the ancient Egyptians, and the specimens of the finer arts of architecture, statuary, and painting which still delight the eye of the scientific traveller amid the ruins of Thebes, Dendera, and Ebsamboul. No view of Egypt would be complete without such an outline as we now propose to exhibit; for it is not possible in any other way to connect the history of that remarkable country with its proud monuments of ancient taste and grandeur, or to render credible the sublime descriptions which have been transmitted to us by philosophers as well as by poets. The remains which still indicate the site of its oldest capital present the most unequivocal proof of its early civilization, and of the high degree of power which the inhabitants had attained by means of their knowledge. Its origin is lost in the obscurity of time, being coeval perhaps with the people who first took possession of the country; but, to give an idea of its great antiquity, it may be sufficient to remark that the building of Memphis, the date of which even stretches beyond the limits of authentic history, was the first attempt made to rival its magnificence and prosperity. Alluding to one portion of that splendid city, Champollion expresses himself in the following terms:—"All that I had seen, all that I had admired on the left bank, appeared miserable in comparison with the gigantic conceptions by which I was surrounded. I shall take care not to attempt to describe any thing; for, either my description would not express the thousandth part of what ought to be said, or, if I drew even a faint sketch, I should be taken for an enthusiast or perhaps for a madman. It will suffice to add, that no people, either ancient or modern, ever conceived the art of architecture on so sublime and so grand a scale as the ancient Egyptians. Their conceptions were those of men a hundred feet high; and the imagination, which in Europe rises far above our porticoes, sinks abashed at the foot of the 140 columns of the hypostyle hall at Karnac."

The traveller from Europe usually lands at Alexandria, a city which in any other part of the world except Egypt would be denominated ancient. The pillar which graces that capital of the Grecian kings was long associated with the name of Pompey the Great; but an inscription upon it has, in modern times, been distinctly made out, which proves that its last dedication was to the Emperor Diocletian by a prefect who happened to bear the same name as the rival of Julius Cæsar. We have just insinuated that it was no uncommon occurrence, during the successive dynasties which governed the Egyptians, to carve the titles of princes on palaces, temples, and obelisks which had existed a thousand years before their accession to power; whence it must appear that nothing can be more fallacious, as a test of antiquity, than the names which are found in inscriptions, even in those of the hieroglyphic class. Mr. Salt, we have already mentioned, traced the appellation of one of the Ptolemies engraved over that of Psammeticus—the sovereign, it is probable, in whose reign the original building was erected.

The Alexandrian pillar stands upon a pedestal twelve feet high, which has obviously been formed of stones previously used for some other purpose. The shaft is round, about ninety feet in length, and surmounted by a Corinthian capital which adds ten feet more to the elevation. The column, we believe, is one block of porphyry, although it has more usually been described as consisting of syenite or Egyptian granite. It is nine feet in diameter, with a perceptible entasis, but without hieroglyphics; remarkably well cut, and very little injured by the effects of time. No one, however, can fail to perceive that the shaft does not correspond with the capital, base, and pedestal, which are extremely poor both in execution and taste.

It is to be deeply regretted that the architectural beauties of this celebrated monument are not a little defaced by the undue freedoms which have been used by certain European visiters. One of the latest writers on the subject informs us, that what with black paint and red ochre, pitch and sand, the pedestal and the lower part of the shaft may now rival the party-coloured mantle of Jacob's favourite son. It was in vain to look for any of Diocletian's inscriptions, since the scribbling of those who had ascended to the top had obliterated all other traces. It appears, that in March, 1827, the officers of the Glasgow, ship of war, by means of flying a kite, had passed a string over the top of the column —to this they fastened a cord, and eventually a rope-ladder. Their example has been followed by the crew of almost every king's ship since stationed in that port. Breakfasts have been given, and letters written on the top, and even a lady has had courage to ascend. But the national flag having on one occasion been left by a party, the governor took so much offence as to prohibit all such frolics for the time to come.*

There is a want of unanimity among travellers as to the precise import of the inscription on this famous pillar. M. Quatremère has ascertained that there was in the time of Diocletian a prefect whose name was Pompeius, and thereby afforded a strong corroboration to the opinion of those who think that the monument was raised in honour of that emperor by one of his deputies. But Dr. Clarke read the Greek characters so as to substitute Adrian instead of Diocletian ; and found out, at the same time, that the name of the commander who dedicated the pillar was Posthumus rather than Pempeius. The greater number, however, follow the version which retains the latter appellation, and which by that means accounts so easily for the vulgar error in regard to the object of the erection.

We are informed by Denon, that the earth about the

* Travels in the C——mea.—A similar feat was accomplished in 1777 by an English captain. See Irwin's Voyage.

foundations of the pillar having been dug away, two fragments of an obelisk of white marble were discovered to
have been added to the original substructure. These, Dr.
Clarke thinks, must have been intended merely to maintain
the base in its adjusted-position until the pedestal could be
raised upon it, and that they were not meant to contribute
to the support of the column. It is chiefly deserving of
notice, however, that the block on which the pedestal rests
is inscribed on the four sides with hieroglyphics, the figures
or characters of which, being inverted, show that it has
been turned upside down; thus affording a complete proof
that the stone must have belonged to some more ancient
work, which was probably in ruins before the pillar was
erected in its present site.

In a remote, unfrequented part of the city stands the obe
lisk well known by the name of Cleopatra's Needle, and
which is described as a fine piece of granite covered with
hieroglyphics. There were originally two of these, apparently brought from Heliopolis or Thebes to adorn the entrance to the palace of the Ptolemies. About twelve years
ago, when Dr. Richardson visited Alexandria, the one stood
erect, the other lay prostrate on the ground; but, in regard
to the latter, he remarks that it was mounted on props, and
seemed as if "prepared for a journey." It has been since
removed, with the view of being conveyed to England,
though it has not yet, so far as we have been able to learn,
reached its destination. The dimensions are sixty-four
feet in length, and eight feet square at the base.

Alexandria presents many other remains of sumptuous
buildings, of which there is no tradition among the inhabitants on which any reliance can be placed. On each side
of what appears to have been one of the principal streets
are still to be seen rows of stately marble columns, all overturned and neglected. They are conjectured to be the
relics of a magnificent colonnade which extended between
the gates of the Sun and Moon, and was regarded as one
of the most striking ornaments of the city; but in the
hands of the Turks, as some author has observed, every
thing goes to decay, and nothing is repaired. Wherever an
excavation is made, an arch, a pillar, or a rich cornice indicates that a splendid structure had once occupied the
ground, but can supply no information as to the object, the

date, the name, or the founder. For miles the suburbs are
covered with the ruins of the ancient town. Heaps of
brick and mortar, mixed with broken shafts and mutilated
capitals, cover immense vaults, which, serving as reservoirs
of water, are replenished on every overflow of the Nile.
Perhaps much of this devastation, as well as of the ignorance which prevails respecting it, may be attributed to the
effects of that fatal earthquake which swallowed up 50,000
of the inhabitants, and threw down the loftiest of their
edifices. But on such subjects all inquiry is vain, for the
traveller finds that the degraded beings who now occupy
the wrecks of this superb metropolis are equally indifferent
and ill-informed as to every event which preceded their own
times.

The Catacombs of Alexandria present nothing very remarkable, being in a condition nearly as ruinous as the city
whose dead they were intended to receive. The real entrance to these subterraneous abodes is unknown ; the present passage opening from the seashore like the approach
into a grotto. The most of the chambers are so entirely
choked up with sand that it is extremely difficult to crawl
into them even on the hands and knees. Their form, as
well as the doors, pilasters, and sarcophagi, show them to
be the work of Grecian artists ; but, although in size they
are fully equal to the Egyptian catacombs, yet in the article
of decoration they are not once to be compared to them.
All along the shore of the western harbour are numerous
sepulchres of inconsiderable note, some of them under the
rock ; many are merely cut into it, and open to the air ;
and not a few are under the level of the sea. Several baths
are likewise exhibited in this quarter, which as usual are
assigned to Cleopatra ; but such of them as are now to be
seen are equally small and incommodious, and of a description far too inferior to countenance the supposition that
they had ever been used by her whose beauty and accomplishments triumphed over the heroes of Rome.*

In ascending the Nile we shall take no notice of Cairo,
because the works which it exhibits do not serve to illustrate the principles of the arts, or to display the remains of
the grandeur for which the ancient Egyptians are cele-

* Richardson's Travels, vol. i. p. 21

brated. We should willingly detain the reader at Memphis, did any relics of its magnificence occupy the ground on which it once stood, to gratify the rational curiosity its name cannot fail to excite. But we shall only quote from an old writer a description of that capital as it appeared in the twelfth century. "Among the monuments of the power and genius of the ancients," says Edrisi, "are the remains still extant in old Misr or Memphis. That city, a little above Fostat, in the province of Djizeh, was inhabited by the Pharaohs, and is the ancient capital of the kingdom of Egypt. Such it continued to be till ruined by Bokht-nasr (Nebuchadnezzar); but many years afterward, when Alexander had built Iskanderiyeh (Alexandria), this latter place was made the metropolis of Egypt, and retained that pre-eminence till the Moslems conquered the country under Amru ebn el Aasi, who transferred the seat of government to Fostat. At last El Moezz came from the west and built El Cahirah (Cairo), which has ever since been the royal place of residence. But let us return to the description of Memf, also called old Misr. Notwithstanding the vast extent of this city, the remote period at which it was built, the change of the dynasties to which it has been subjected, the attempts made by various nations to destroy even the vestiges, and to obliterate every trace of it by removing the stones and materials of which it was formed,—ruining its houses, and defacing its sculptures; notwithstanding all this, combined with what more than four thousand years must have done towards its destruction, there are yet found in it works so wonderful that they confound even a re-flecting mind, and are such as the most eloquent would not be able to describe. The more you consider them the more does your astonishment increase; and the more you look at them the more pleasure you experience. Every idea which they suggest immediately gives birth to some other still more novel and unexpected; and as soon as you ima-gine that you have traced out their full scope, you discover that there is something still greater behind."

Among the works here alluded to, he specifies a mono-lithic temple, similar to the one mentioned by Herodotus, adorned with curious sculptures. He next expatiates upon the idols found among the ruins, not less remarkable for the beauty of their forms, the exactness of their proportions, and perfect resemblance to nature, than for their truly astonishing dimensions. We measured one of them, he says, which, without including the pedestal, was forty-five feet in height, fifteen feet from side to side, and from back to front in the same proportion. It was of one block of red granite, covered with a coating of red varnish, the antiquity of which seemed only to increase its lustre.[*]

The ruins of Memphis, in his time, extended to the distance of half a day's journey in every direction. But so rapidly has the work of destruction proceeded since the twelfth century, that few points have been more debated by modern travellers than the site of this celebrated metropolis. Dr. Pococke and Mr. Bruce, with every show of reason, fixed upon Metrahenny, an opinion which was opposed by Dr. Shaw, who argued in favour of Djizeh. But the investigations of the French appear to have decided the question. At Metrhainé, one league from Sakhara, we found, says General Dugua, so many blocks of granite covered with hieroglyphics and sculptures around and within an esplanade three leagues in circumference, enclosed by heaps of rubbish, that we were convinced that these must be the ruins of Memphis. The sight of some fragments of one of those colossuses, which Herodotus says were erected by Sesostris at the entrance of the temple of Vulcan, would, indeed, have been sufficient to dispel our doubts had any remained. The wrist of this colossus, which Citizen Coutelle caused to be removed, shows that it must have been forty-five feet high.[†]

The ruins of Beni Hassan, although comparatively a modern place, bear decided marks of antiquity; the materials of the principal buildings having been conveyed from some more ancient town,—a practice which appears to have become frequent under the Ptolemies as well as in the earlier times of the Roman ascendency. The grottos, however, which were once the abodes of holy hermits, are the most striking remains of this village, and are remarkable for paintings, of which Mr. Hamilton has given an elaborate account. The ceilings of these chambers are

[*] Abdollatiph's Abridgment of Edrisi, translated by M. Silvestre de Sacy. Encyclopædia Metropolitana, article Egypt.
[†] Courrier de l'Egypte. A plan of the ruins is given by M. Jacotin in the Description de l'Egypte.

generally arched, while others are supported by columns cut out of the rock, having a truly Egyptian character, and the appearance of four branches of palm-trees tied together. The largest is sixty feet in length, and forty in height; to the south of it are seventeen smaller apartments, and probably the same number to the north. Ten columns originally supported this large chamber, four of which are fallen down. There were two other rooms of nearly similar dimensions, from which, as in the former case, there were doorways leading into inferior apartments, suggesting the idea of halls surrounded by cells for the private accommodation of the inmates.

Ashmonein, the ancient Hermopolis Magna, is now reduced to the state of a village, though the remains of its former magnificence may yet be traced over an area four miles in circumference. The portico of a temple is described by Mr. Leigh, who saw it in the year 1813, as quite perfect. It consists of twelve massive columns, which are not built of cylindrical blocks of stone, but each block is formed of several pieces so neatly joined together that, where they are not injured by time, it is difficult to discover the junction of the several fragments. The columns are arranged in two rows, distant from each other twelve feet; and the roof is formed of large flags of stone, covered with stucco and beautifully ornamented. The columns and the whole interior of the portico have been painted; among the colours red, blue, and yellow seem to predominate. The hieroglyphics on the plinths are different on each front, but they are the same on every plinth on the same front. The capitals, which in some degree represent the tulip in bud, are let into the columns. Several other shafts of granite are scattered about near the temple, bearing a distinct evidence to its original extent and grandeur.

We pass by Antinopolis or Sheikh Ababdé, because its features unequivocally denote its modern origin, and fix its larger buildings to the time of the Romans. It is said to have been erected by the emperor Hadrian in memory of Antinous, who perished in the Nile; and it has been remarked that its colonnades, triumphal arches, baths, and amphitheatres are as little in unison with the surrounding objects, and as foreign to the soil in which they stand, as was the new capital raised by the same people at Tr ves, on the banks of the Moselle.

Siout, which is now esteemed the metropolis of Upper Egypt, is better stored with the relics of former days, consisting, however, of tombs and sepulchral grottos rather than of the more lively monuments of antiquity, the palaces and temples of the victorious Pharaohs. Norden describes at some length those primeval repositories of the dead, which are excavated in the mountains about half a league from the modern town. Passing a gateway, the visiter enters a large saloon supported by hexagonal pillars hewn out of the rock itself. The roofs are adorned with paintings, which can be distinguished sufficiently well even at present ; and the gold that was employed in the decoration glitters on all sides. There are perceived here and there some openings which lead to other apartments ; but the accumulation of sand and rubbish prevents all ingress. He suggests that there are three tiers of tombs, approachable by separate avenues from the outside,—an opinion which is confirmed by Sir F. Henniker, who observed in the second story an excavation of 168 feet by 78, the entrance of which was ornamented with some costly sculptures. Denon, indeed, assures us that all the inner porches of these grottoes are covered with hieroglyphics : " Months," says he, " would be required to read them, even if one knew the language, and it would take years to copy them. One thing I saw by the little daylight that enters the first porch,—that all the elegancies of ornament which the Greeks have employed in their architecture, all the wavy lines and scrolls, and other Greek forms, ar here executed with taste, and exquisite delicacy. If one of these excavations were a single operation, as the uniform regularity of the plan of each would seem to indicate, it must have been an immense labour to construct a tomb. But we may suppose that such a one, when finished, would serve for ever for the sepulture of a whole family, or even race, and that some religious worship was regularly paid to the dead ; else, where would have been the use of such laboured ornaments in the form of inscriptions never to be read, and a ruinous, secret, and buried splendour. At different periods, or at annual festivals, or when some new inhabitant was added to the tombs, funereal rites were doubtless performed, in which the pomp of ceremony might vie with the magnifi sense of the place. This is the more probable, as the richness of decoration in the interior forms a most striking contrast with the outer walls, which are only the rough natural rock. I found one of these caves with a single saloon, in which were an innumerable quantity of graves cut in the rock in regular order; they had been ransacked with the view of procuring mummies, and I found several fragments of their contents, such as linen, hands, feet, and loose bones. Besides these principal grottoes, there is such a countless number of smaller excavations that the whole rock is cavernous, and resounds under the foot."*

The temple at Antæopolis, the modern Gau-el-Kebir, is well deserving of attention, and more especially as it is fast mouldering into a heap of ruins. The portico, in the year 1813, consisted of three rows, each of six columns, eight feet in diameter, and, with their entablature, sixty-two feet high. This structure, which, from its situation in a thick grove of palm-trees, is perhaps the most picturesque in Egypt, stands close to the banks of the Nile, whose waters have already undermined some part of it, and threaten to wash the whole away. The columns, architraves, and indeed every stone of the building, are covered with hieroglyphics in bas-relief. At the farthest extremity of the temple is an immense block of granite of a pyramidal form, twelve feet high, and nine feet square at the base, in which a niche has been cut, seven feet in height, four feet wide, and three deep. It is hollowed out, as if for [the reception of a statue, though Mr. Leigh imagined that the cavity was meant as a chest or depository for the sacred birds.

In the year 1817, many overturned stones and pillars were lying on the brink of the river, or had fallen into its channel. Of the portico just described only one column remained standing, presenting a shaft from forty to fifty feet in height, wrought into panels, and surmounted with a capital like the calix of a flower. The space between each of the compartments was occupied by rows of hieroglyphics; and the compartments themselves were filled with figures of Osiris, Isis, and Anubis, receiving offerings under different forms. A column, which seemed to have recently fallen down at its side, consisted of the same number of stones, and was sculptured in a similar manner.

* Denon, vol. i. p. 150.

Two years afterward, the fine vestibule of antæopolis was entirely levelled with the ground. The Nile, in this part of its course, had long been advancing towards the eastern side of the valley, and washing away the foundations of such buildings as stood upon its right bank : when, in the year just mentioned, in consequence of an unusually high inundation, it completed the work of destruction, reducing this splendid monument of ancient piety to a mass of ruins.[*]

As our object in this survey of ancient buildings and ruined cities is not confined to a mere topographical description, we omit several small towns situated on either bank of the Nile, because they no longer present any re mains of art to connect them with the period to which our retrospect extends. In ascending the Thebaid, however, we are arrested by the interesting relics of Abydos, the modern Arabat, supposed by Strabo to have been the residence of Memnon ; although in the days of this geographer it was already reduced to a paltry village. A few blocks and columns of granite continue to assure the traveller that the desolate region which he has entered was once the scene of splendour and an active population. A large building, too, of the highest antiquity, convinces him that Abydos must have held a distinguished place among the cities of Upper Egypt. Mr. Hamilton tells us that this edifice appeared entire, but was so much choked up with sand that it was extremely difficult either to enter the apartments or to examine the architecture. The area which it occupied was nearly a rectangle of 350 feet by 150. The pillars were conjectured to be about thirty feet in height ; which did not, however, exhibit any remarkable sculptures or paintings. One peculiarity of this building could not be observed without interest.—"From the west point we could enter into seven chambers of similar dimensions, measuring thirty-six feet in length, sixteen feet and a half in width, and five feet six inches in height ; the only instance of the kind I have ever witnessed of undoubted Egyptian architecture. The arches, however, are not constructed on the principle of the arch, and cannot therefore be adduced as any evidence of such principles having been known to, and put in practice

* Leigh, p. 96; Richardson, vol. 1 p. 178; Encyclop. Metropol. Egypt.

by the Egyptians. The architraves, or rather rafters of the rooms, as well as the upper layer of stones on each side-wall, are cut out so as to resemble an arched roof; and perhaps they are thus executed in imitation of those which the same people used to form for the catacombs and sepulchres which they excavated in the rocks."*

Four hundred paces farther north are the traces of another building, which appears to have been a temple, though little now remains but the fragments of three granite gateways. In size it has been much inferior to the edifice just described, being only 250 feet in length, and 120 feet wide. Such ruins seem to justify the conclusion, which has been drawn by recent travellers, that Arabat represents the ancient Abydos, and also that the great structure is the Memnonium celebrated by Strabo.

As the sand continues to gain ground all along the precincts of the western desert, the difficulty of entering this palace of Memnon is every year increased. In 1821, when Sir F. Henniker visited Egypt, the external lineaments of the building were so entirely obliterated that it was not easy to imagine a building could be concealed in the spot where he was directed to seek for it. On the roof, which alone occupies nearly as much space as the neighbouring village, he paced fifty-four long steps on stones that have never yet been removed, though he observed signs of destruction at either end. There are some small chambers in the pile, in which the colour of the painting is so well preserved that doubts immediately arise as to the length of the time it has been done. The best works even of the Venetian school betray their age; but the colours, here supposed to have been in existence two thousand years before the time of Titian, are at this moment as fresh as if they had been laid on an hour ago. The stones of which this fabric is built measure in some cases about twenty-two feet in length; the span of the arch is cut in a single stone;

* Hamilton's Egyptiaca, p. 259. This author remarks, "Savary's pompous account of Abydos is a fictitious narrative of a place he never saw, and bears more resemblance to the remains at Dendera than to any other in Egypt. It is composed of the description of this place by M. Chevalier, Governor of Chandernagore, improved by a few embellishments of his own invention.

a portico is still visible ; each individual part is of exquisite workmanship, but badly put together. This writer agrees with Mr. Hamilton in the opinion that the ancient Egyptians did not understand the principle of the arch. One chamber, in particular, appears to demonstrate at once their intention and their inability,—the span of the arch being cut in two stones, each of which bears an equal segment of the circle. These placed together would naturally have fallen, but they are upheld by a pillar placed at the point of contact,—an expedient which leaves no doubt that in this point of architectural invention the subjects of the Pharaohs had. not attained their usual success. If, says Sir Frederick, those who raised the Pyramids and built Thebes, and elevated the obelisks of Luxor, had been acquainted with the principle of the arch, they would have thrown bridges across the Nile, and have erected to Isis and Osiris domes more magnificent than those of St. Peter's and St. Paul's.*

It was in one of the inmost chambers of the larger edifice at Abydos that Mr. W. Bankes, in 1818, discovered a large hieroglyphical tablet containing a long series of royal names, as was evident from the ring, border, or, as the French call it, the cartouche, which surrounds such inscriptions. On examination, it proved to be a genealogical table of the immediate predecessors of Ramesses the Great, the Sethos or Sethosis of Manetho, the Sesoosis of Diodorus, and the Sesostris of Herodotus. A careful comparison of it with other documents has enabled M. Champollion to ascertain, with a considerable degree of probability, the period in which the sixteenth and following dynasties mentioned by Manetho must have occupied the throne. The epochs thus determined, though still liable to some objections, are supported by so many concurrent and independent testimonies as to warrant the expectation, now entertained by many chronologists, that they will ultimately be established beyond the reach of controversy.†

Dendera, which is commonly identified with the ancient Tentyra, presents some very striking examples of that

* A Visit to Egypt, p. 112.
† Encyclopædia Metropolitana, *article* Egypt.

sumptuous architecture which the people of Egypt lavished upon their places of worship. The gateway in particular which leads to the temple of Isis has excited universal admiration. Each front, as well as the interior, is covered with sculptured hieroglyphics, which are executed with a richness, a precision, elegance of form, and variety of ornament, surpassing in many respects the similar edifices which are found at Thebes and Philoe. The height is forty-two feet, the width thirty-three, and the depth seventeen. "Advancing along the brick ruins," says Dr. Richardson, "we came to an elegant gateway or propylon, which is also of sandstone, neatly hewn, and completely covered with sculpture and hieroglyphics remarkably well cut. Immediately over the centre of the doorway is the beautiful Egyptian ornament usually called the globe, with serpent and wings, emblematical of the glorious sun poised in the airy firmament of heaven, supported and directed in his course by the eternal wisdom of the Deity. The sublime phraseology of Scripture, 'the Sun of Righteousness shall rise with healing on his wings,' could not be more emphatically or more accurately represented to the human eye than by this elegant device." The temple itself still retains all its original magnificence. The centuries which have elapsed since the era of its foundation have scarcely affected it in any important part, and have impressed upon it no greater appearance of age than serves to render it more venerable and imposing. To Mr. Hamilton, who had seen innumerable monuments of the same kind throughout the Thebaid, it seemed as if he were now witnessing the highest degree of architectural excellence that had ever been attained on the borders of the Nile. Here were concentrated the united labours of ages, and the last effort of human art and industry, in that uniform line of construction which had been adopted in the earliest times.

The portico consists of twenty-four columns, in three rows; each above twenty-two feet in circumference, thirty-two feet high, and covered with hieroglyphics. On the front, Isis is in general the principal figure to whom offerings are made. On the architrave are represented two processions of men and women bringing to their goddess, and to Osiris, who is sitting behind her, globes encompassed with cows' horns, mitred snakes, lotus flowers, vases, little boats, graduated staffs, and other instruments of their emblematical worship. The interior of the pronaos is adorned with sculptures, most of them preserving part of the paint with which they have been covered. Those on the ceiling are peculiarly rich and varied, all illustrative of the union between the astronomical and religious creeds of the ancient Egyptians; yet, though each separate figure is well preserved and perfectly intelligible, we must be more intimately acquainted with the real principles of the sciences, as they were then taught, before we can undertake to explain the signs in which they were imbodied.

The sekos, or interior of the temple, consists of several apartments, all the walls and ceilings of which are in the same way covered with religious and astronomical representations. The roofs, as is usual in Egypt, are flat, formed of oblong masses of stone resting on the side-walls; and when the distance between these is too great, one or two rows of columns are carried down the middle of the apartment, on which the huge flags are supported. The capitals of these columns are very richly ornamented with the budding lotus, the stalks of which, being extended a certain way down the shaft, give it the appearance of being fluted, or rather scalloped. The rooms have been lighted by small perpendicular holes cut in the ceiling; and, where it was possible to introduce them, by oblique ones in the sides. But some idea might be formed of the perpetual gloom in which the apartments on the ground-floor of the sekos must have been buried, from the fact, that where no side-light could be introduced, all they received was communicated from the apartment above; so that, notwithstanding the cloudless sky and the brilliant colours on the walls, the place must have been always well calculated for the mysterious practices of the religion to which it was consecrated. On one corner of the roof there was a chapel or temple twenty feet square, consisting of twelve columns, exactly similar in figure and proportions to those of the pronaos. The use to which it may have been applied must probably remain one of the secrets connected with the mystical and sometimes cruel service in which the priests of Isis were employed, though it is by no means unlikely that it was meant as a repository for books and instruments collected

P

for the more innocent and exalted pursuits of practical astronomy.

Towards the eastern end of the roof are two separate sets of apartments, one on the north and the other on the south side of it. The latter consists of three rooms, the first of which is only remarkable for the representation of a human sacrifice. A man, with the head and ears of an ass, is kneeling on the ground, tied with his hands behind him to a tree, with two knives driven into his forehead, two in the shoulders, one in his body, and another in the thigh. Five priests, with the heads of dogs and hawks, are in a row behind him, each having a knife in his hand. The deity, before whom the mactation is about to be performed, is clothed in a long white garment, and holds in his right hand the crook or crosier, with the flagellum.

The ceiling of the next room is divided into two compartments by a figure of Isis in very high relief. In one of them is the circular zodiac; in the other a variety of boats with four or five human figures in each; one of whom is in the act of spearing a large egg, while others are stamping with their feet upon the victims of their fury, among which are several human beings. Near this scene a large lion, supported by four dog-headed figures, each carrying a knife, may be regarded as an additional type of the sanguinary purposes for which the apartment was used. The walls of the third room are covered with the several representations of a person,—first at the point of death lying on a couch; then stretched out lifeless upon a bier; and finally, after being embalmed. As these sculptures are much more defaced than the others, it is very difficult to decipher their details. But the ensigns of royalty and the presence of the deity are, in general, clearly discernible; on which account it is not improbable that the scenes may bear an allusion to the death of some sovereign of the country who was honoured as the patron of religion or of science.

The western wall of the great temple is particularly interesting for the extreme elegance of the sculpture,—as far as Egyptian sculpture is susceptible of that character, —for the richness of the dresses in which the priests and deities are arrayed, and even of the chairs in which the latter are seated. Here are frequent representations of men who seem prepared for slaughter or just going to be put to death. On these occasions one or more appear, with their hands or legs tied to the trunk of a tree, in the most painful and distorted attitudes.

The grand projecting cornice, one of the most imposing features of Egyptian architecture, is continued the whole length of this and the other walls; a moulding separates it from the architrave; and, being carried down the angles of the building, gives to the whole a solid finished appearance, combined with symmetry of parts and chasteness of ornament.

In a small chapel behind the temple, the cow and the hawk seem to have been particularly worshipped, as priests are frequently seen kneeling before them presenting sacrifices and offerings. In the centre of the ceiling is the same front face of Isis in high relief, illuminated, as it were, by a body of rays issuing from the mouth of the same long figure, which, in the other temples, appears to encircle the heavenly bodies. About two hundred yards eastward from this chapel is a propylon of small dimensions, resembling in form that which conducts to the great temple, and, like it, built in a line with the wall which surrounds the sacred enclosure. Among the sculptures on it, which appear of the same style but less finished than those on the large temple, little more is worthy of notice than the frequent exhibition of human slaughter by men or by lions. Still farther towards the east there is another propylon, equally well preserved with the rest, about forty feet in height, and twenty feet square at the base. Among the sacred figures on this building is an Isis pointing with a reed to a graduated staff held by another figure of the same deity, from which are suspended scales containing water animals; the whole group, perhaps, being an emblem of her influence over the Nile in regulating its periodical inundations.

The enclosure within which all the sacred edifices of Dendera, with the exception of the last propylon, are contained, is a square of about a thousand feet. It is surrounded by a wall which, where best preserved, is thirty-five feet in height, and fifteen feet thick. The crude bricks of which it is built were found to be fifteen inches and a half long, seven and three-quarters broad, and four inches and three-quarters thick. There have been at certain intervals projections of the wall or towers; but it is difficult to say whether for purposes of defence or strength.*

Dr. Richardson observes, in reference to the sculptures on the temple of Dendera, that "the female figures are so extremely well executed that they do all but speak, and have a mildness of feature and expression that never was surpassed." Every thing around appears to be in motion, and to discharge the functions of a living creature; being, at the same time, so different from what is ever seen in Europe that the mind is astonished, and feels as if absolutely introduced to personages of the remotest ages, to converse with them, and to witness the ceremonies by which they delighted to honour their gods. The temple at Dendera, says this author, is by far the finest in Egypt; the devices have more soul in them; and the execution is of the choicest description. After walking round it, and considering its peculiar beauty and ornament, one is astonished to find that there is no exact transcript or model of it in England.

France has done much to make the world acquainted with Egyptian antiquities, and had the agents she employed performed their work with fidelity, would have been entitled to our warmest gratitude; but the rubbish was never cleared away from the walls or from the interior of this temple; and being unable to give the whole of any one building, they represent it in patches, and those so incorrectly, that no person, on examining them, can be sure whether he is studying the compositions of the ancient Egyptians or of the modern French; so that no part of their work can serve as an unsuspected guide to the student of antiquities on the banks of the Nile.

As Dr. Richardson is one of the latest travellers who have published upon Egypt, we are induced to give his description of the inside of the magnificent fane now under our consideration. "The first apartment has three columns on each hand, all covered with sculpture and hieroglyphics, and surmounted at the top, like those already mentioned, with the head of Isis Quadrifrons. The walls behind the columns are equally enriched, so that there is not a spot the eye can rest on but addresses to the mind a tale of interest and wonder; though no man can read or unfold its precise

* Hamilton's Egyptiaca, p. 196-204.

meaning, yet each forms to himself some conjecture of the story, and is pleased with the constant exercise of his mind. Passing on we entered another apartment which has no columns, but the walls are decorated in the same manner: then we moved into a third, which was equally so, and from thence passages go off to small handsome side-chambers, equally ornamented with figures, and stars, and hieroglyphics, and a sort of chain-work along the ceiling, of a blue colour. The passage to the right leads to an easy handsome stair, by which to ascend to the top of the building; we continued our way, however, straight forward, and entered another chamber, in the centre of which stands the sanctuary, or holiest apartment, all of them rich in sculpture and hieroglyphics. Never did I see a greater field for thought or reflection, and never did I regret more the want of time than in visiting the superb temple of Dendera."*

The enthusiasm of a Frenchman seeks expressions still more elevated to give utterance to his feelings. " I wish," exclaims Denon, " that I could here transfuse into the soul of my reader the sensations which I experienced. I was too much lost in astonishment to be capable of cool judgment; all that I had hitherto seen served here but to fix my admiration. This monument seemed to me to have the primitive character of a temple in the highest perfection. I felt that I was in the sanctuary of the arts and sciences. How many periods presented themselves to my imagination at the sight of such an edifice! How many ages of creative ingenuity were requisite to bring a nation to such a degree of perfection and sublimity in the arts; and how many more of oblivion to cause these mighty productions to be forgotten, and to bring back the human race to the state of nature in which I found them on this very spot! Never was there a place which concentred in a narrower compass the well-marked memorial of a progressive lapse of ages. What unceasing power, what riches, what abundance, what superfluity of means must a government possess which could erect such an edifice, and find within itself artists capable of conceiving and executing the design of decorating and enriching it with every thing that speaks to the eye and the understanding! Never did the labour of man show me

* Travels, vol. i. p. 205

the human race in such a splendid point of view; in the ruins of Tentyra the Egyptians appeared to me giants. I wished to take every thing on paper, but I could hardly venture to begin the work: I felt that, not being able to raise my powers to the height which was before my admiring eyes, I could only show the imperfection of the imitative art. I was confused by the multiplicity of objects, astonished by their novelty, and tormented by the fear of never again visiting them. On casting my eyes on the ceilings, I had perceived zodiacs, planetary systems, and celestial hemispheres, represented in a tasteful arrangement: I saw that the Supreme Being, the First Cause, was every where depicted by the emblems of his attributes; and I had but a few hours to examine, to reflect on, and to copy what it had been the labour of ages to conceive, to put together, and to decorate. With my pencil in my hand, I passed from object to object, distracted from one by the inviting appearance of the next, constantly attracted to new subjects, and again torn from them. I wanted eyes, hands, and intelligence vast enough to see, copy, and reduce to some order the multitude of striking images which presented themselves before me. I was ashamed at representing such sublime objects by such imperfect designs, but I wished to preserve some memorial of the sensations which I here experienced, and I feared that Tentyra would escape from me for ever; so that my regret equalled my present enjoyment. I had just discovered, in a small apartment, a celestial planisphere, when the last rays of daylight made me perceive that I was alone here, along with my kind and obliging friend General Beliard, who, after having satisfied his own curiosity, would not leave me unprotected in so deserted a spot. We galloped on and regained our division. —In the evening, Latournerie, an officer of brilliant courage and of a refined and delicate taste, said to me, ' Since I have been in Egypt deceived in all my expectations, I have been constantly heavy and melancholy, but Tentyra has cured me: what I have seen this day has repaid me for all my fatigues; whatever happens to me in the event of this expedition, I shall all my life congratulate myself at having embarked in it, to have obtained the remembrance of this day, which I shall preserve all the rest of my existence.' "*

* Travels in Upper and Lower Egypt, vol. i. p. 295

This extract will afford the means of judging how far the members of the French Institute had an opportunity of examining the buildings of which they have undertaken to give at once a description and a copy. Denon himself admits, that as their troops were engaged in pursuit of an enemy constantly mounted, the movements of the division were invariably both unforeseen and complicated; and consequently that he was sometimes obliged to pass rapidly over the most interesting monuments, and at other times to stop where there was nothing to observe.[*]

We must not, however, omit to mention that at a subsequent period Denon returned to this interesting scene of antiquities, when he copied the zodiac and the celestial planisphere which have excited so much discussion among the philosophers of Europe. He copied also the rest of the ceiling, which is divided into two equal parts by a large figure that seems to be an Isis; her feet resting upon earth, her arms extended towards heaven, while she appears to occupy all the space between. In another part of the ceiling is a large figure, probably representing heaven or the year, with its hands and feet on the same level, and unfolding, with the curvature of the body, fourteen globes, placed on as many boats, distributed over seven beads or zones, separated from each other by numberless hieroglyphics, but too much covered with stalactites and smoke to allow of its being taken.

All the world knows that the French mathematicians discovered in these astronomical drawings, compared with the corresponding emblems at Esneh, certain proofs of an antiquity usually thought inconsistent with the chronology of the sacred writings. Signor Visconti published some calculations on the subject, which drew from M. de Lalande a series of remarks, inserted in the "Connaissances des Tems" for the year 1807. These authors agree in the conclusion that the zodiac of Dendera must have been formed in the first century of the Christian era, or, at latest, before the year 132 of our epoch. Mr. Hamilton discovered two facts which tended greatly to confirm the opinion now stated; the one fixing the reign of Tiberius as the period to which may be assigned the construction of the building;

* Preface, p. iii.

the other affording the most satisfactory proof that the summer solstice was in Cancer when the zodiac was carved; whence it follows that the date in question could not be far removed from the birth of Christ.

The coincidence here between the deductions of the astronomer and the observations of the traveller is very striking, and strengthens our confidence in the accuracy of both. But the speculations which follow on the celestial planisphere, as they assume a wider range, have not produced the same unanimity. From certain figures which are introduced, De Lalande is of opinion that it must have been composed at the time when the summer solstice was in the *middle* of the sign Cancer, or, in other words, about three thousand years ago; and he refers his readers to the arguments he has adduced in another work, to prove that it was about the period just mentioned when the system of the heavens was constructed, in which Eudoxus, eight hundred years afterward, and Aratus his follower, described the sphere. While, however, he attributes this antiquity to the Dendera zodiac, he has no hesitation in allowing the probability that the temple itself within which it is engraved may be of a much later date.

From another process of calculation into which our limits forbid us to enter, Mr. Hamilton infers that we cannot assign to this astronomical picture an antiquity less remote than four thousand five hundred years, the period the sun must have taken to pass through the two adjacent signs of Leo and Cancer, according to the annual precession of the equinoxes. He adds, indeed, in a note, that if we place the sun in the middle of Leo at the time of the solstice when this zodiac was constructed, we shall then assign to it only the antiquity of three thousand two hundred years; that is, fourteen hundred years before the Christian era. This would leave a space amply sufficient for the acquisition of astronomical knowledge between the deluge and the date specified.*

The reasonings and conclusions of which we have now presented an outline have drawn upon their authors a load of calumny by no means justifiable on any of the grounds which a generous and candid criticism is wont to assume.

* Hamilton's Egyptiaca, p. 215.

The positions, indeed, which they laboured to establish, are liable to attack from various quarters; and especially because these are founded on a very incorrect copy of the astronomical sculptures which they undertook to explain. Denon appears to have spent but one day amid the ruins of Dendera, on a task which would have required the uninterrupted employment of several weeks; and accordingly it is now nowhere denied that his drawings do not exhibit an exact representation either of the zodiac or of the planisphere. Dr. Richardson, who had an opportunity of comparing the French work with the original, admits the elegance of the execution, but declares that "it is perfectly foppish, and not the least Egyptian in its style or manner It is, besides, extremely incorrect both in the drawing of the figures and in the hieroglyphics, as well as in the number of stars which accompany them; which last are both fewer in number and differently arranged from what we found them to be in the ceiling. In point of sentiment it is equally inaccurate; the several authors having imparted to the human figure an insipid and babyish expression, which one would not have expected from the companions of Napoleon; and which is as foreign to the Egyptian character as the aspect of a child or an insipid coxcomb is to that of the Theseus, the Memnon, or the Apollo."[*]

We cannot, however, agree with this facetious traveller that the ceiling at Dendera has no connexion whatever with astronomy, but is merely a congregation of gods and goddesses, mythological beings, and religious processions. Perhaps there may be a scheme of general physics involved in the multifarious emblems displayed in the temple,—a theory of production and reproduction, of which the principles continue unknown,—but it is still more probable that the veneration shown by all ancient nations to the host of heaven, and an effort to trace their paths or positions in the immense regions of space, called forth the genius of the artist and the wealth of the pious in the ornaments of Tentyra.

Our object in this chapter, we have already remarked, is not to illustrate the opinions of the Egyptians, but to pre-

sent a record of their taste and ability in the fine arts. For
this purpose no portion of their labours, since Thebes was
trodden under foot and the Labyrinth disappeared, could be
more happily selected than the ruins of Dendera. Its
columns, statues, sculptures, and hieroglyphics, are the
admiration of the most refined people at present on the face
of the earth. Travellers who can agree in nothing else
unite in extolling the wonders of the temple and portico.
The ardent Frenchman and the more phlegmatic native
of Britain are equally enthusiastic in their expressions
of delight and astonishment. Even Belzoni, who was
accustomed to the grandest sights, acknowledges that the
majestic appearance of the temple and the variety of its
ornaments had such an effect on him, that he seated himself on the ground, and for a considerable time was lost in
admiration.[*]

It is generally admitted that the monuments of Tentyra
do not possess the same degree of antiquity which belongs
to the buildings of Thebes. As a proof of this, it is mentioned that the basis of the large temple in the former
place stands upon a terrace which is still fifteen feet above
the level of the neighbouring country; while similar ter-
races at Thebes are only on a level with the surface of the

---

[*] Narrative, vol. i. p. 52. When at Dendera Mrs. Elwood relates
that "here we in vain searched for the famous circular zodiac, which,
by the descriptions of the temple we had read, we were aware must be
in this neighbourhood; but, after a great number of pantomimic signs
had passed between us, the Arab guide made us understand it had been
taken away; and this we subsequently found was positively the case, a
Frenchman having carried it off to Cairo! What a Goth! to dismantle
this majestic building for the purpose, in a manner more rude than even
the Turks themselves! We, however, saw the spot where—alas! that
I should say—it *had* been. C——observed that the figures in the temple closely resembled those he had seen in India; and in fact it was
here that the sepoys, when brought into Egypt, prostrated themselves
in adoration, thinking they saw their own deities before them, which
proves there is a strong affinity between the worship of the ancient
Egyptians and that of the modern Hindoos."—*Narrative of a Journey
Overland from England to India*, vol. i. p. 213.

It is generally known that the zodiac, the removal of which occasioned
so much indignation to this lady, has been some time in Paris. The
rivalry which animates the tourists and philosophers of France and
England threatens to inflict upon the interesting remains of Egyptian
art a greater injury than they have sustained from the ravages of two
thousand years, and from the assaults of all the barbarian conquerors
who have possessed the country from Nebuchadnezzar to Mohammed Ali.

Nile, above which they were, beyond a doubt, once greatly elevated. Visconti, therefore, and after him Belzoni, inferred that the temple at Dendera was not older than the time of the Ptolemies, or perhaps that of the Romans; but Jollois, on the contrary, expresses his firm conviction, that from the style and execution of the sculptures, they cannot have been made subsequently to the invasion under Cambyses, and were probably at least as old as the tomb of Psammis, who lived in the time of Josiah, king of Judah.

It is obvious, when we reflect that Tentyra was built at a considerable distance from the river, the argument drawn from the elevation of the soil occasioned by the annual flood, does not apply to the question at issue; while the inscriptions found on many of the ancient monuments of Egypt cannot be understood in any other sense than as a rededication of the fabric to a popular monarch,—a practice sanctioned by the usage of all ages. But, on other accounts, we concur in the views of Belzoni in regard to the date of the principal edifices now under consideration.

Leaving Dendera, however, we proceed to Thebes, the remains of which, though not possessed of greater elegance and beauty, are usually regarded with a larger share of interest. The vast extent of the ruins is itself a subject of profound attention. The ancient city extended from the ridge of mountains which skirt the Arabian Desert to the similar elevation which bounds the valley of the Nile on the west, being in circumference not less than twenty-seven miles. But its actual situation may perhaps be more successfully represented to the fancy by the descriptions of those who have recently examined it, and whose first impressions, though recorded in language which may seem inflated, supply, it is probable, a faithful picture of the manifest desolation for which alone it is now celebrated. The following paragraph, extracted from the work of Denon, the friend and companion of Buonaparte, is sufficiently striking:—

"At nine o'clock, in making a sharp turn round a projecting point, we discovered all at once the site of the ancient Thebes in its whole extent. This celebrated city, the size of which Homer has characterized with the single expression of the *hundred-gated*,—a boasting and poetical phrase which has been repeated with so much confidence for so many centuries;—this illustrious city, described in a few pages dictated to Herodotus by Egyptian priests, that have since been copied by every historian,—celebrated by the number of its kings, whose wisdom had raised them to the rank of gods,—by laws which have been revered without being promulgated,—by science, involved in pompous and enigmatical inscriptions,—the first monuments of ancient learning which are still spared by the hand of time;—this abandoned sanctuary, surrounded with barbarism, and again restored to the desert from which it had been drawn forth, —enveloped. in the veil of mystery and the obscurity of ages, whereby even its own colossal monuments are magnified to the imagination,—still impressed the mind with such gigantic phantoms that the whole army, suddenly and with one accord, stood in amazement at the sight of its scattered ruins, and clapped their hands with delight, as if the end and object of their glorious toils, and the complete conquest of Egypt were accomplished and secured by taking possession of the splendid remains of this ancient metropolis."*

Another traveller, less enthusiastic than Denon, describes the effect of a first sight in the following terms:—" While I was leisurely travelling along, thinking only of our arrival at Luxor, one of the party who had preceded us called to me from a rising ground to turn to the left: and having gone a few yards off the road, I beheld unexpectedly the temple of Karnac. It was long after I reached my tent ere I recovered from the bewilderment into which the view of these stupendous ruins had thrown me. No one who has not seen them can understand the awe and admiration they excite even in unscientific beholders. When I compare the descriptions of Denon and Hamilton I find them essentially correct, yet without giving me any adequate idea of the glorious reality. They fail in describing what has never been, and which, I think, never can be, described. No words can impart a perception of the profusion of pillars, standing, prostrate, inclining against each other, broken and whole. Stones of a gigantic size propped up by pillars, and pillars again resting upon stones which appear ready

* Travels in Upper and Lower Egypt, vol. i. p. 3.

to crush the gazer under their sudden fall; yet, on a second view, he is convinced that nothing but an earthquake could move them; all these pillars, covered with sculpture, perhaps three thousand years old, though fresh as if finished but yesterday,—not of grotesque and hideous objects, such as we are accustomed to associate with ideas of Egyptian mythology, but many of the figures of gods, warriors, and horses, much larger than life, yet exhibiting surpassing beauty and grace."[*]

The modern Egyptians, either with the view of obtaining materials at little expense of labour, or in order that their hovels might be secure from the periodical inundations of the river, are commonly found to have built their villages on the ruins of an ancient temple or palace, even on the very summit of the roof and most elevated part of the walls. Hence the grandeur of Thebes must now be traced in four small towns or hamlets,—Luxor, Karnac, Medinet Abou, and Gornoo. Following the best authorities, which, in this case, are usually the most recent, we proceed to lay before the reader a brief description of the principal buildings which time and barbarism have spared within the precincts of this celebrated capital.

In approaching the temple of Luxor from the north, the first object is a magnificent gateway, which is two hundred feet in length, and the top of it fifty-seven feet above the present level of the soil. In front of the entrance are two of the most perfect obelisks in the world, each consisting of a single block of red granite. They are between seven and eight feet square at the base, and more than eighty feet high; many of the hieroglyphical figures with which they are covered being an inch and three-quarters deep, cut with the greatest nicety and precision. Between these obelisks and the propylon are two colossal statues, also of red granite; they are nearly of equal size, but, from the difference of the dress, it is inferred that the one was a male, the other a female figure. Though buried in the ground to the chest, they still measure about twenty-two feet from thence to the top of their mitres.

* Narrative of a Journey from Calcutta to Europe. By Mrs. Charles Lushington, p. 61.

Q

On the eastern wing of the north front. of the propylon
there is sculptured a very animated description of a remarkable event in the campaigns of some Egyptian conqueror.
The disposition of the figures and the execution of the whole
picture are equally admirable, and far surpass all ideas that
have ever been formed of the state of the arts in Egypt at
the era to which they must be attributed. The moment
chosen for the representation of the battle is that when the
troops of the enemy are driven back upon their fortress, and
the Egyptians, in the full career of victory, are about becoming masters of the citadel.

The commander, behind whom is borne aloft the royal
standard, is of a colossal size, and advances in a car drawn
by two horses. His helmet is adorned with a globe, and
has a serpent at each side. He is in the act of shooting an
arrow from a bow, which is full stretched; around him are
quivers, and at his feet a lion in the act of rushing forward.
There is a great deal of life and spirit in the form and attitude of the horses, which are at full gallop,—feathers
waving over their heads, and the reins fastened round the
body of the conqueror. Under the wheels of the car, and
under the hoofs and bellies of the horses, are crowds of
dead and wounded men. On the side of the enemy horses
are seen in full speed with empty cars; others heedless of
the rein; and all at last rushing headlong down a precipice
into a broad and deep river which washes the walls of the
town. The expression here is exceedingly good. Nowhere has the artist shown more skill than in two particular
groups; in one of which the horses, arrived at the verge
of the precipice, instantly fall down, while the driver, cling-
ing with one hand to the car, the reins and whip falling
from the other, and his whole body trembling with despair,
is about to be hurled over the backs of his steeds. In the
other, the horses still find a footing on the side of the hill,
and are hurrying forward the charioteers to inevitable destruction.

Immediately in front of the conqueror are several cars in
full speed for the walls of the town; but even in these the
warriors are not beyond the reach of the arrows darted from
his unerring bow; and when wounded they look back on
their pursuer as they fall. Farther on, more fortunate fugitives are passing the river; in which are mingled horses,

chariots, arms, and men, expressed in the most faithful manner, and represented in all attitudes. Some have already reached the opposite bank, where their friends, who are drawn up in order of battle but have not courage to engage in fight, drag them to the shore. Others, having escaped by another road, are entering the gates of the town amid the shrieks and lamentations of those within. Towers, ramparts, and battlements are crowded with inhabitants, who are chiefly bearded old men and women. A party of the former are seen sallying forth, headed by a youth whose different dress and high turban mark him out as some distinguished chieftain; while on either side of the town are observed large bodies of infantry, and a great force of chariots issuing from the gates, and advancing apparently by different routes to attack the besiegers.

The ardour with which the hero of the piece is advancing has already carried him far beyond the main body of his own army, and he is there alone, among the slain and wounded who have sunk under his powerful arm. Behind this scene the two lines of the enemy join their forces, and attack in a body the army of the invaders who move on to meet them. Besides the peculiarity of the incidents recorded in this interesting piece of sculpture, there may be traced an evident distinction between the short dresses of the Egyptians and the long robes of their oriental enemies, whether Indians, Persians, or Bactrians;—the different forms of the car or chariot,—the Egyptian containing two warriors, the foreign vehicle being loaded with three; and, above all, the difference of the arms,—the soldiers of Sesostris having a bow and arrows, while their antagonists vibrate spears or brandish short javelins.

At one extremity of the western wing of the propylon the beginning of this engagement appears to be represented; the same monarch being seen at the head of his troops advancing against the double line of the enemy, and first breaking their ranks. At the other extremity of the same wing the conqueror is seated on his throne after the victory, holding a sceptre in his left hand, and enjoying the barbarous pleasure of beholding eleven of the principal captives tied together in a row with a rope about their necks. The foremost stretches out his hands imploring pity; another is on his knees just going to be put to death by the hands of

two executioners; while above them is the vanquished
monarch with his hands bound behind him to a car, about
to be dragged in triumph before the conqueror.

In the rear of the throne different captives are suffering
death in various ways; some like the Briareus, the execu-
tioner holding them by the hair of the head; others dragged
by chariots, or slain by the arrow or the scimitar. Next
appears in view the conqueror's camp, round which are
placed his treasures, and where his servants are preparing
a feast to celebrate the victory.

"It is impossible," says Mr. Hamilton, "to view and to
reflect upon a picture so copious and so detailed as this I
have just described, without fancying that I saw here the original of many of Homer's battles, the portrait of some of the
historical narratives of Herodotus, and one of the principal
groundworks of the description of Diodorus: and, to complete the gratification, we felt that, had the artist been better
acquainted with the rules of perspective, the performance
might have done credit to the genius of a Michael Angelo
or a Julio Romano. To add to the effect, in front of this
wall had been erected a row of colossal figures of granite;
fragments of some of them, still there, sufficiently attest
their size, their character, and the exquisite polish of the
stone."

All this magnificence and cost, the reader is aware, are
lavished on a gateway. On passing it the traveller enters a
ruined portico of very large dimensions; and from this a
double row of seven columns, with lotus capitals, two-and-
twenty feet in circumference, conducts him into a court one
hundred and sixty feet long, and one hundred and forty
wide, terminated at each side by a row of columns; beyond
which is another portico of thirty-two columns, and then
the adytum, or interior part of the building. It is conjectured, with much plausibility, that this is the edifice to which
the description of Diodorus applies as the palace or tomb
of the great Osymandias; allowance being made for his
embellishments, in which he has introduced some of the
more striking features that distinguish the largest buildings
of Thebes.

Karnac, which is about a mile and a half lower down, is
regarded as the principal site of Diospolis, the portion of
the ancient capital which remained most entire in the days

of Strabo. The temple at the latter place has been pronounced, in respect to its magnitude and the beauty of its several parts, as unique in the whole world. Mr. Hamilton admits that, in regard to its general plan, the distribution of the entrances, and the interior of the building, the descriptions of Pococke and Denon are tolerably accurate. But he adds, that without personally inspecting this extraordinary structure, it is impossible to have any adequate notion of its immense size, or of the prodigious masses of which it consists. This edifice has twelve principal entrances, each of which is composed of several propyla and colossal gateways, besides other buildings attached to them, in themselves larger than most other temples. The sides of some of these are equal to the bases of the greater number of the pyramids in Middle Egypt, and are built in the rustic style, each layer of stone projecting a little beyond that which is above it. One of the propyla is entirely of granite, adorned with the most finished hieroglyphics. On each side of many of them have been colossal statues of basalt and granite, from twenty to thirty feet in height,—some in the attitude of sitting, others standing erect. The avenues of sphinxes that lead in several directions to the propyla, one of which was continued the whole way across the plain to the temple at Luxor, nearly two miles distant, correspond to the magnificence of the principal structure. And the body of the temple, which is preceded by a large court, at whose sides are colonnades of thirty columns in length, and through the middle of which are two rows not less than fifty feet high, consists, first, of a prodigious hall or portico, the roof sustained by one-hundred and thirty-four pillars, some of which are twenty-six feet in circumference, and others thirty-four. Next appear four beautiful obelisks, marking the entrance to the adytum, near which the monarch is represented as embraced by the arms of Isis. This sanctuary consists of three apartments, entirely of granite. The principal room is in the centre; it is twenty feet long, sixteen wide, and thirteen feet high. Three blocks of granite form the roof, which is painted with clusters of stars, on a blue ground. The walls are likewise covered with painted sculptures, of a character admirably suited to the mysterious purposes to which th chamber was sometimes devoted.[*]   Beyond this are other porticoes and galleries, which have been continued to a third propylon, at the distance of two thousand feet from that at the western extremity of the temple.

This is certainly the building which Diodorus Siculus attempts to describe as the most wonderful and most ancient of the four temples at Thebes, remarkable for their magnitude and beauty.   In enumerating its colossal proportions, he says that it was thirteen stadia—a mile and a half—in circumference ; forty-five cubits high; and the walls twenty-four feet thick ; adding, that the ornaments, riches, and workmanship which combined to embellish it corresponded to its vast extent.   The above dimensions, however great, are, we may add, in many instances found to fall short of the truth.

It were needless, says the author from whose work we have abridged this account, to enumerate with a more minute detail the different apartments, the columns, the colossal statues, the gateways, or the obelisks of this immense edifice.   Denon concludes the partial description which he has attempted, by declaring that "one is fatigued with writing, one is fatigued with reading, one is stunned with the thought of such a conception.   It is hardly possible to believe, after having seen it, in the reality of the existence of so many buildings collected on a single point, in their dimensions, in the resolute perseverance which their construction required, and in the incalculable expenses of so much magnificence. . On examining these ruins, the imagination is wearied with the idea of describing them.   Of the hundred columns of the porticoes alone of this temple, the smallest are seven feet and a half in diameter, and the largest twelve.   The space occupied by this circumvallation contains lakes and mountains.   In short, to be enabled to form a competent idea of so much magnificence, it is necessary that the reader should fancy what is before him to be a dream, as he who views the objects themselves occasionally yields to the doubt whether he be perfectly awake."[†]

[*] Herodotus, Clio, c. 182.

[†] On est fatigué d'écrire, on est fatigué de lire, on est épouvanté de la pensée d'une telle conception ; on ne peut croire, même après l'avoir vu, à la réalité de l'existence de tant de constructions réunies sur un même

The dimensions of the great edifice at Karnac are about 1200 feet in length and 420 in width. But the principal fane, grand and imposing as it is, sinks into nothing when compared with the extent and number of the buildings which surround it,—the prodigious gateways of polished granite, covered with sculpture and adorned with colossal statues,—the subordinate temples which any where else would be esteemed magnificent piles,—and the avenues, which approach it from almost every point of the compass, miles in length, and guarded by rows of sphinxes, of vast size, cut out of single blocks of syenite. The field of ruins at Karnac is about a mile in diameter. Probably the whole of this space was once, in the prouder days of Thebes, consecrated entirely to the use of the temple. There are traces of walls considerably beyond this, which, we may presume, enclosed the city in its greatest extent; but, after the seat of government was withdrawn, the capital removed to Memphis, and the trade removed to another mart, the inhabitants narrowed the circle of their defences, and built their houses within the limits of the sacred confines.*

But Luxor and Karnac represent only one-half of ancient Thebes. On the western side of the river there are several structures, which, although they may be less extensive, are equal, if not superior, in their style of architecture. We cannot, however, enter upon a description of the temples at Dair and Medinet Abou. Suffice it to observe, that the propylon of the latter is about 175 feet long, and very richly adorned with the usual embellishments of sculpture and inscriptions. The temple itself is in length somewhat more than five hundred feet, while the cella is nearly a hundred and fifty broad without the walls. The Memnonium, the ruins of which give a melancholy celebrity to northern Dair, is still more remarkable, and is perhaps one of the most ancient in Thebes. This beautiful relic of antiquity looks to the east, and is fronted by a stupendous propylon, of which 294 feet in length are still remaining. The main edifice has been about 200 feet wide, and 600

point, à leur dimensions, à la constance obstinée qu'a exigée leur fabrication, aux dépenses incalculables de tant de somptuosité —Tome II p. 226.

* Richardson's Travels, vol. ii. p. 96.

feet long; containing six courts and chambers, passing from side to side, with about one hundred and sixty columns thirty feet high. All the side-walls have been broken down, and the materials of which they were composed carried away; nothing remaining but a portion of the colonnade and the inner chambers, to testify to the traveller what a noble structure once occupied this interesting spot.

There is a circumstance mentioned by a recent visiter, which is too important to be overlooked in detailing the unrivalled grandeur of ancient Thebes. The temple at Medinet Abou was so placed as to be exactly opposite to that of Luxor, on the other side of the Nile; while the magnificent structure at Karnac was fronted by the Memnonium or temple of Dair: and hence all these grand objects formed so many stages or prominent points in the religious processions of the priests. Though the tabernacle of Jupiter dwelt at Karnac, the proper Diospolis, yet it was carried over the river every year, and remained a few days in Libya; and we find, from a general estimate, that there was a space of between nine and ten miles, over which they might exhibit the pomp and parade of their superstition, both going and returning. Almost every part of the road through this immense theatre was lined with sphinxes, statues, propyla, and other objects calculated to inflame the ardour of devotion; and in all the imposing ceremonies of pagan idolatry, it is impossible to conceive any thing more impressive than the view which must have burst upon the sight of the enraptured votaries when, at the close of the solemnity of bringing back their god, they entered the grand temple of Karnac, to replace him in his shrine, with harps and cymbals, and songs of rejoicing. *

In the Memnonium there is still to be seen the statue of Osymandias, Memnon, or Sesostris. It is pronounced to be by far the finest relic of art which the place contains, and to have been once its brightest ornament, though at present it is thrown down from its pedestal, laid prostrate on the ground, and shattered into a thousand pieces. It is about 26 feet broad between the shoulders, 54 feet round the chest, and 13 feet from the shoulder to the elbow.

* Richardson vol. ii. p. 95.

There are on the back and both arms hieroglyphical tablets extremely well executed, which identify this enormous statue with the hero whose achievements are sculptured on the walls of the temple.

This figure has sometimes been confounded with that which bears the name of Memnon, and which has been so long celebrated for its vocal qualities. This last, however, is one of the two statues vulgarly called Shamy and Damy, which stand at a little distance from Medinet Abou, towards the Nile. These, we are told, are nearly equal in magnitude, being about 52 feet in height. The thrones on which they respectively rest are thirty feet long, eighteen broad, and between seven and eight feet high. They are placed about forty feet asunder; are in a line with each other; and look towards the east, directly opposite to the temple of Luxor. If there be any difference of size, the southern one is the smaller. It appears to be of one entire stone. The face, arms, and front of the body have suffered so much from studied violence that not a feature of the countenance remains. The headdress is beautifully wrought, as also the shoulders, which, with the back, continue quite uninjured. The massy hair projects from behind the ears like that of the Sphinx. The sides of the throne are highly ornamented with the elegant device of two bearded figures tying the stem of the flexible lotus round the ligula. The colossus is in a sitting posture, with the hands resting upon the knees. On the outside of each of the limbs there is a small statue, with spiked crowns on their heads, and the arms down by the side. They stand up in front of the pedestal, and reach nearly to the knee. The legs of the great statue are divided, and between the feet there is another diminutive figure whose head does not rise higher than the two just described.

The other statue, which stands on the north side, appears to be that of the vocal Memnon. It presents the same attitude as its companion, with a similar figure between the feet and on each side of the legs. It has, however, been broken over at the waist,—an effect which was reported to Strabo to have been produced by an earthquake. In his time the head with the disrupted half of the body, lay on the ground; the other half remaining in the original position, which it still occupies. The part that had been

broken off is now carried away, and the figure is again
completed by courses of common sandstone, forming the
back, neck, and head. It is entirely fashioned like the
upper part of the other, having several hieroglyphics and
other emblems sculptured between the shoulders; but, as
the stone is not susceptible of such elegant workmanship,
no attempt has been made to imitate the drapery which
adorns its more fortunate neighbour. Upon that portion
of the more celebrated statue which still remains, or rather
upon the side of the throne, the ornament of the two
bearded figures tying the lotus round the stalk of the ligula,
with the accompanying hieroglyphics, are as fresh and distinct as on the other. The drapery, too, as far as can
now be determined, must have been originally the same
in both.

"But," says Dr. Richardson, "what characterizes this
as the statue of vocal celebrity are the numerous inscriptions, both in Greek and Latin, in verse and prose, with
which it is covered; all of them attesting that the writers
had heard the heavenly voice of Memnon at the first dawn
of day,—feeble indeed at first, but afterward becoming
strong and powerful like a trumpet. We searched with
eagerness for the name of the illustrious geographer quoted
above; but, if ever it was there, it is now among the many
illegibles that no human eye can decipher. Julia Romilla,
Cecilia Treboulla, Pulitha Balbima, and many others, attest
that they heard the voice of the Memnon, when along with
the Emperor Hadrian and his royal consort Sabina, whom
they seem to have accompanied in their tour throughout the
country. One person writes,—I hear (audio) the Memnon;
and another person,—I heard the Memnon sitting in Thebes
opposite to Diospolis."*

We know not whether the fact now mentioned will
receive any explanation from the circumstance that the
material of which the statues are composed is a quartzy
sandstone, highly crystallized, and containing a considerable
portion of iron. When struck it gives a metallic ring,—the
kind of sound which used to be attributed to the Memnon.
It is singular, at all events, that the belief of its former
vocality still lingers in the tradition of the country; for the

* Travels, vol. ii. p. 41

Arabs continue to call it Salamat, or the statue that bids good morning.*

It is evident that these statues stand on either side of an avenue leading to a place of worship, and that they were followed by a series of other colossal figures, the remains of some of which are still visible. The temple, whose approach they were appointed to guard, was uncovered by Mr. Salt, who at the same time brought to light a number of sphinxes, with the lion's head on the body of a human female, and in short traced the foundation and columns of a magnificent building. Belzoni, in like manner, disinterred a handsome statue of black granite, which is now within the precincts of the British museum,—affording additional evidence that the Memnon had belonged to an establishment not inferior, perhaps, even to the sublime structures of Luxor and Karnac. On this ground we are disposed to adopt the opinion of the writer whom we have just quoted, who thinks that the ruined temple now mentioned ought to be regarded as the proper Memnonium, and not the edifice which contains the statue of Osymandias.

The neighbourhood of Thebes presents another subject worthy of attention, and quite characteristic of an Egyptian capital,—the Necropolis, or City of the Dead. Proceeding on the idea that the human being only sojourns for a time in the land of the living, but that the tomb is his permanent dwelling-place, the inhabitants of this magnificent metropolis lavished much of their wealth and taste on the decoration of their sepulchres. The mountains on the western side of Thebes have been nearly hollowed out in order to supply tombs for the inhabitants; while an adjoining valley, remarkable for its solitary and gloomy aspect, appears to have been selected by persons of rank as the receptacle of their mortal remains. The darkest recesses of these pits and chambers have been repeatedly explored by travellers in search of such antiquities as might illustrate the ancient manners of the people, as well as by those mercenary dealers in mummies who make a trade of human bones, coffins, and funeral lining.

To give an idea of the magnificence lavished by the Egyptians on their burial-places, it will be enough to de-

* Richardson, v. 42.

scribe the immense vaults discovered by Belzoni, who, in excavating for curiosities, possessed a tact or instinct similar to that which leads the mineral engineer, to the richest veins of the precious metals. He fixed upon a spot at the bottom of a precipice, over which, when there happens to be rain in the desert, a torrent rushes with great fury; and after no small degree of labour he reached the entrance of a large and very splendid tomb. This hall, which is extremely beautiful, is twenty-seven feet long and twenty-five broad; the roof being supported by pillars fully four feet square. At the end of it is a large door which opens into another chamber twenty-eight feet by twenty-five, having the walls covered with figures, which, though only drawn in outline, are so perfect that one would think they had been done only the day before. Returning into the entrance-hall, he observed a large staircase descending into a passage. It is thirteen feet long, seven and a half in width, and has eighteen steps, leading at the bottom to a beautiful corridor of large dimensions. He remarked that the paintings became more perfect the farther he advanced into the interior, retaining their gloss or a kind of varnish laid over the colours, which had a beautiful effect, being usually executed on a white ground. At the end of this splendid passage he descended by ten steps into another equally superb; from which he entered into an apartment twenty-four feet by thirteen, and so elegantly adorned with sculptures and paintings that he called it the Room of Beauty. When standing in the centre of this chamber, the traveller is surrounded by an assembly of Egyptian gods and goddesses—the leading personages of the Pantheon,—whose presence was thought to honour, or perhaps to protect, the remains of the mighty dead.

Proceeding farther, he entered a large hall twenty-eight feet long, and twenty-seven broad; in which are two rows of square pillars, three on each side of the entrance, forming a line with the corridors. At either side of this hall, which he termed the Hall of Pillars, is a small chamber, the one on the right is ten feet by nine, that on the left ten feet five inches by eight feet nine inches. The former of these, having in it the figure of a cow painted, he called the Room of Isis; the latter, from the various emblematical drawings which it exhibits, was denominated the Room of

Mysteries. At the end of the hall is the entry to a large
saloon with an arched roof or ceiling, and extending to
thirty-two feet in length by a breadth of twenty-seven. On
the right of the saloon is a small chamber without any thing
in it, roughly cut as if unfinished, and destitute of painting;
on the left is an apartment with two square pillars, twenty-
five feet eight inches by twenty-two feet ten inches. These
columns are three feet four inches square, and beautifully
painted like the rest. At the same end of the room, and
facing the Hall of Pillars, he found another chamber, forty-
three feet long by seventeen six inches broad, and adorned
with a variety of columns. It is covered with white plaster
where the rock did not cut smoothly, but there is no painting
in it; and as Mr. Belzoni discovered in it the carcass of a
bull embalmed with asphaltum, he distinguished it by the
appellation of the Room of Apis. There were also seen,
scattered in various places, an immense number of small
wooden figures of mummies six or eight inches long, and
covered with mineral oil to preserve them. There were some
other figures of fine earth, baked, coloured blue, and strongly
varnished; while on each side of the two little rooms were
wooden statues standing erect, with a circular hollow inside,
as if to contain a roll of papyrus.

"But," says Mr. Belzoni, "the description of what we
found in the centre of the saloon, and which I have reserved
till this place, merits the most particular attention, not
having its equal in the world, and being such as we had no
idea could exist. It is a sarcophagus of the finest oriental
alabaster, nine feet five inches long, and three feet seven
inches wide. The thickness is only two inches, and it is
transparent when a light is placed in the inside of it. It is
minutely sculptured within and without with several hundred figures, which do not exceed two inches in height, and
represent, as I suppose, the whole of the funeral procession
and ceremonies relating to the deceased. I cannot give an
adequate idea of this beautiful and invaluable piece of antiquity, and can only say that nothing has been brought into
Europe from Egypt that can be compared with it. The cover
was not there; it had been taken out and broken into several
pieces, which we found in digging before the first entrance."[*]

* Belzoni's Narrative of Operations, &c. vol. i. p. 365. Dr. Clarke
pronounced the stone of which the sarcophagus is composed to be of a

R

The sarcophagus was placed over a staircase in the centre
of the saloon, communicating with a subterraneous passage
three hundred feet in length, which seemed to proceed
through the very heart of the mountain.   Hence, there is
reason to believe that there must originally have been two
entrances to the tomb, one of which was closed at the time
when the sarcophagus was lodged in it; for not only was
this communication obstructed by means of a wall, but
several large stones were inserted in the pavement of the
saloon, to prevent any one from perceiving either the stair
or the passage to which it leads.   In short, great pains had
been taken to conceal the chamber in which the royal corpse
was deposited.   The staircase of the entrance-hall had
been built up at the bottom, and the intervening space filled
with rubbish; while the floor was covered with large blocks
of stone, so as to deceive such individuals as might happen
to force a passage through the wall, and make them suppose
that the tomb ended at the second apartment.   The persons
who had been previously in the sepulchre, and destroyed
the cover of the sarcophagus, must have possessed a complete acquaintance with the plan and structure of that subterranean palace; for, at their departure they used such
precautions against a second discovery, that no degree of
sagacity less than the share which had fallen to Belzoni could
have defeated their object.

The walls of nearly all the apartments are decorated with
superb paintings and sculptures which we cannot undertake
to describe at length.   But, for a reason which will immediately appear, we must not pass over one wherein is represented a military procession, consisting of a great number
of figures all looking towards a man who is much superior
to them in size.   At the close of this pageant are three different sorts of people, from as many nations, evidently Jews,
Ethiopians, and Persians.   Behind them are some Egyptians without their ornaments, as if they were captives
rescued and returning to their own country, followed by
a hawk-headed figure, supposed to be their protecting
deity.

By the application of his principle for explaining phonetic

rarer and much more valuable species than alabaster. A model of this
splendid tomb was afterward exhibited in London containing the real
sarcophagus.

hieroglyphics, Dr. Young discovered among the drawings copied from this tomb the names of Necho and Psammis, kings of Egypt, who reigned towards the end of the seventh century before the Christian era. Now, it is universally known that Pharaoh-Necho' conquered Jerusalem and Babylon, and that his son Psammis or Psammuthis, as he is sometimes called, made war against the Ethiopians. Hence, we are provided with the means of understanding the object as well as the constituent parts of the procession described by Belzoni. The natives of three different countries are distinctly recognised. The Jews are readily distinguished by their physiognomy and complexion; the Ethiopians by their colour and ornaments; and the Persians by their characteristic dress, as they are so often seen engaged in battle with the Egyptians.*

There cannot, therefore, be any doubt as to the age of this splendid monument of Egyptian art; for the two Pharaohs whom it commemorates, and by the latter of whom it was probably erected, swayed the sceptre nearly two thousand five hundred years ago. What were the Greeks and Romans at that period? They were barbarians in the strictest sense of the word, or only beginning to emerge from the rudest condition in which mankind are found to cultivate the relations of social life. Many of the sepulchral chambers of Thebes are much older than that of Psammis, reaching back to the epoch when that capital was

"The world's great empress on the Egyptian plain,
That spread her conquest o'er a thousand states,
And poured her heroes through a hundred gates;
Two hundred horsemen and two hundred cars
From each wide portal issued to the wars."—Pope.

Every traveller, from Bruce down to the latest tourist who has trodden in his steps, luxuriates in the description of Gornoo, with its excavated mountains, and dwells with minute anxiety on the ornaments which at once decorate the superb mausoleums of the Beban el Melouk, and record the early progress of Egyptian science. It is lamentable, however, to find, that in the great work published under the auspices of the French government, the representations, in point of

* Dr. Richardson, vol. i. p. 281, differs from Belzoni as to the figures in the procession, but without any attempt to oppose the explanation of Dr. Young, or to call in question the antiquity of the tomb.

colouring at least, are extremely inaccurate. In the Harp Tomb, for example, the drawings of which were very accurately copied by the historian of Abyssinia and his secretary Balugani, there is a priest performing, who is dressed in a long white robe spotted or striped with red. The French artists have arrayed him in a flowing mantle of the deepest black with white stripes. The gentleman, too, who is seated on a chair at a little distance listening to the music, and habited in a short loose garment falling about half-way down the thighs, the rest of the limbs and arms being bare, the Savans have attired in a pair of blue pantaloons after the Parisian fashion, and in a waistcoat of the same colour. The headdress, moreover, which in the original reaches up to the ceiling, they have curtailed into a small bonnet, bearing a striking resemblance to the cap of liberty. In this way they have given to the group a sort of general resemblance, while in the detail the representation is as unlike as possible. They have made that blue which should be red, black which should be white, yellow which should be green, and short which should be long.*

The names of Jollois and Devilliers are affixed to the large prints of the tomb just mentioned, as vouchers for their accuracy; but there is too much reason to suspect that the labour of colouring the engravings, like the task of writing the dissertations on the antiquities of Egypt, was left to the ingenuity of artists at Paris, who had no other guide than an indistinct description. As a farther proof of this, we may mention that the painting in the ruins of the Memnonium, which represents the storming of a fort, was copied by Major Hayes, as well as by the French academicians, and that the men, who have a sort of petticoat drapery in the one, are naked in the other; our neighbours preferring what appeared to them the more picturesque representation, without paying any regard to the truth of monuments.†

When examining the tomb discovered by Belzoni, a subse-

* Richardson, vol. ii. p. 4.
† Dr. Richardson, vol. ii. p. 5, remarks, that after so many misrepresentations in the work of the Wise-men,—the French Savans,—it will not be difficult to decide whose names should precede the verb, in the very courtly inscription, "Bruce est un menteur;" and whether we might not with some degree of propriety address them; considered as a single body, in the words of the Roman bard "Nomine mutato, de te fabula narratur."

quent traveller, after observing that the colours are remarkably vivid, and that the painting has not suffered either from time or human violence, adds, " It is impossible adequately to describe the sensations of delight and astonishment which by turns took possession of our minds as we moved along the corridor, and examined the different groups and hieroglyphics that occur in every successive chamber. We had been told that what we saw was a tomb; but it required a constant effort of the mind to convince us that it was such. Only one sarcophagus in one chamber, and twelve chambers, exclusive of the long corridor, all highly ornamented, for nothing! It may have been a subterraneous temple, exhibiting the religious creed of the worshippers, or the rites of initiation. It may have been a subterraneous palace, like those of the king of the Troglodytes. But never was there such a superfluous waste, if we are to suppose that all this was done merely for the reception of one sarcophagus." Perhaps, like the chambers of imagery seen by the Jewish prophet, they were the scene of idolatrous rites performed in the dark,—an opinion which has received the countenance of Mr. Jowett, who says that the tombs of the Beban el Melouk cannot be better described than in the words of Ezekiel, " Then said he unto me, Son of man, dig now in the wall: and when I had digged in the wall, behold a door. And he said unto me, Go in, and behold the wicked abominations that they do there. So I went in and saw; and behold, every form of creeping things, and abominable beasts, and all the idols of the house of Israel, portrayed upon the wall round about." In this, as in other cases, the Hebrews were but servile imitators; the originals were in Egypt, and are still to be seen in almost all the ancient sepulchres or subterranean temples.*

We cannot leave these ancient tombs without expressing our regret that the rage for discovery in the mansions of the dead should have led to consequences so little creditable to European delicacy. The mummies have been drawn from their tombs with a rapacious and unsparing hand. The chief part of this havoc, no doubt, has been committed by the Arabs, who tear the bodies open to get at the rosin, or asphaltum, used in the embalming, which they sell at Cairo

* Richardson, vol. ii. p. 78; Jowett's Christian Researches.

to great advantage; but travellers and their agents have also had their share in this sacrilege, as it may be justly called. "It is," says Mr. Carne, "a sad and disgusting sight; the sands and the edges of the graves in some parts being strewed with bones, and even pieces of flesh thrown wantonly about. The poor Egyptians, who had slept in peace some thousands of years, have been mercilessly dealt with here, and the remains of warriors, citizens, and sages, now lie mingled together beneath the burning sun; for no retreat or sanctuary has been suffered to remain inviolate."[*]

Sir F. Henniker made a similar complaint. He tells us that the plain is strewed with broken bones, and that the coffins are used for firewood. The trouble that the Egyptians took to preserve their bodies causes their destruction, and "the race of Nilus barters for their kings." I was standing by, he adds, when the resurrection-men found a sepulchre; "they offered me the haul, unopened, for four guineas." It proved to be Grecian-Egyptian, the first of its kind hitherto discovered; including three chambers, with fourteen coffins, in each of which was placed a bunch of sycamore branches, which fell to atoms at the touch. The whole of ancient Thebes is the private property of the French and English consuls;- a line of demarcation is drawn through every temple, and these buildings, which have hitherto withstood the attacks of barbarians, will not long resist the speculation of civilized cupidity, directed by philosophers and antiquaries.[†]

Ascending the Nile, the traveller finds the valley, which had contracted above Thebes to very narrow limits, once more begin to widen, and the adjoining hills to retire. In a recess, about a mile from the river, stands the village of Herment, on the ruins of a city to which the Greeks gave the name of Hermonthis. A temple of moderate dimensions, but peculiar in its plan, and distinguished only by the beauty of its columns and sculptures, is still remaining. There is no trace of a propylon; but the walls of the pronaos are standing, though in many places much dilapidated. The cella is pretty entire, and covered with sculptures and

* Letters from the East, vol. i. p. 157.
† Notes during a Visit to Egypt, &c. p. 137.

hieroglyphics; for a description of which we must refer the reader to the authentic pages of Travels along the Mediterranean. We are assured that these works are well executed, and indicate a more ancient date than most of the temples in Egypt; and yet stones, bearing hieroglyphics, are found here placed in an inverted position, and thereby supplying ground for a reasonable conjecture that they had been brought from the ruins of edifices still older than the one in which they are now incorporated.

Esneh, the ancient Latopolis, is the next place which invites the attention of the scientific tourist. It is worthy of notice chiefly on account of a temple, the portico of which has been pronounced by Denon to be the purest fragment of Egyptian architecture, and one of the most perfect monuments of antiquity. It consists of eight columns with broad capitals, differing from each other in the ornament that they bear; in one it is the vine, in another the ivy, in a third the palm-leaf. The parts behind the portico are trivial and negligent as to their decorations. The sanctuary is totally destroyed; but, from what remains of the outer wall, there seems to have been an exterior gallery quite around the temple. The pronaos has still twenty-four columns, six rows with four in each. Various devices, resembling those at Dendera, appear on the ceiling between the columns; and in the space which separates the last row from the wall on each side, are represented the twelve signs of the zodiac, or perhaps certain astrological emblems denoting the influence of the heavenly bodies. The vicinity of Esneh, on both sides of the river, exhibits the remains of many buildings of which the history and the object have been long concealed in that darkness which still hangs over the former condition of Upper Egypt. Vestiges of primeval paganism can be traced, mingled with the more recent institutions of Christianity, but both now so much defaced by the ravages of civil war that the most diligent research fails to be rewarded with any adequate degree of success.

The grottoes of Eleithias, a town somewhat farther south and on the eastern side of the Nile, are extremely interesting, inasmuch as they represent, in the paintings with which the walls are decorated, many of the pursuits and habits that illustrate the private life of the ancient Egyptians. In this respect they are more important than even the splendid sepulchres of Thebes; the ornaments in the latter being confined to the higher ceremonies of religion, or to the shadowing forth of those physical mysteries to which their pious rites are supposed to have had an immediate reference.

The great French work, and the less pretending volume of Mr. Hamilton, supply a very particular description of the works of art at Eleithias. In the largest of the grottoes visited by our countryman, there are three statues the size of life, representing a wealthy rustic with his two wives. One side of the wall is occupied with the picture of a feast, at which the master and mistress are seated together on a chair, richly dressed,—a favourite monkey at their feet is regaling itself on a basket of grapes. A servant, part of whose livery is the skin of a leopard, appears to introduce the guests, who are sitting in rows of men and women, each with a lotus in the hand. To some of these the attendants are presenting bowls and dishes, according to the usage which still prevails in many parts of the East. Behind the visiters are tables covered with sundry kinds of food; while the banquet is enlivened by the presence of musicians and dancers. One woman is playing on a harp; another on a double flute; three others are dancing in the style of those females known at Cairo under the name of Almeh; and a small figure, apart, is performing similar motions with a sword in each hand. The master is then represented walking, attended by his servants, who, among other things, are carrying a chair, a water-jar, and a mat, to visit his labourers at work: and accordingly the artist has here depicted the mode of hoeing, ploughing, sowing, and rolling; of reaping the corn and gathering it in; of winnowing the grain, and the carriage of it to the granary; and, finally, the embarkation of bread or biscuit on board the Djerms. The farm-yard is next seen crowded with oxen, cows, sheep, goats, asses, mules, and other animals. Again, we see the vintage and the process of making wine; after which, the mode of catching and salting fish and water-fowl. Finally, fruits are presented to the master and his friends, and the whole concludes with offerings of gratitude to the gods.

In another part of the scene is the flax-harvest. The whole process of pulling the crop up by the roots, of carry-

ing it away in small bundles and combing it, is very ingeniously represented. It may be observed that the complexion of the men is invariably red, that of the women
yellow; but neither of them can be said to have any thing
in their physiognomy at all resembling the negro countenance. The labourers are dressed in a sort of scull-cap,
and in short close drawers, having very little hair on their
heads; while the looks of the others who appear to superintend them spread out at the sides, after the fashion of the
Nubians and Berberi above the Cataracts.

Next follow representations of ship-building and sailing,
with all the machinery which belonged to their simple navigation. Nor are the amusements of the fowler forgotten,
which seem to have consisted in the use of a net and a
variety of other snares. The bow and arrow appear to have
been also employed. The scene, after embracing a great
number of occupations or pastimes, to which we cannot
make a more particular allusion, closes with a funeral procession, into which all the pageantry and magnificence of
Egyptian ceremonial are introduced, accompanied with the
several emblems which were employed of old to denote the
duties of this life and the hopes of the next.[*]

Leaving the instructive grottoes of Eleithias, we proceed
to Edfou, the Apollinopolis Magna of the Greeks, which
presents several architectural remains worthy of notice.
There are two temples in a state of great preservation; one
of them consisting of high pyramidal propyla, a pronaos,
portico, and sekos, the form most generally used in Egypt;
the other is periptoral, and is at the same time distinguished
by having, on its several columns, the appalling figure of
Typhon, the emblem of the Evil Principle.

The pyramidal propylon which forms the principal
entrance to the greater temple is one of the most imposing
monuments extant of Egyptian architecture. Each of the
sides is a hundred feet in length, thirty wide, and a hundred
high. Many of the figures sculptured on it are thirty feet
in height, and are executed in so masterly and spirited a
style as to add considerably to the grand effect of the
building. In each division there is a staircase of 150 or
160 steps, which conduct the visiter into spacious apart-

* Egyptiaca, p. 92.

ments at different elevations. The horizontal sections of each wing diminish gradually from 100 feet by 30, to 83 by 30, as will appear to the eye from the accompanying plate; although the solidity and height of the propylon give it more the aspect of a fortress or place of defence than of the approach to a religious edifice. As an explanation of this peculiarity, we are told that the addition of these gateways to a temple was permitted as a favour to such of the ancient kings of Egypt as, for their pious and beneficent actions, became entitled to perpetuate their names in the mansions of their gods. The Ptolemies, who claimed the right of sovereignty from conquest, indulged in the same magnificence, and built porticoes, propyla, and even temples. Cleopatrè, in her misfortunes, is said to have removed with the most valuable part of her property to an edifice of a very extraordinary size and structure, which she had formerly erected near the fane of Isis. Most probably, as Mr. Hamilton thinks, it was a propylon of the kind just described. Nothing could be better adapted for her purpose ; inasmuch as the variety of apartments offered every convenience that could be desired, and when the small door at the bottom of the staircase was closed, it was perfectly inaccessible.

In no part of Egypt are more colossal sculptures seen on the walls of a public building than on the larger temple at Edfou. These, we are told, are extremely well executed, and in some cases the colours are still completely unchanged. Priests are seen paying divine honours to the Scarabæus, or beetle, placed upon an altar,—an insect which is said to have been typical of the sun, either because it changes its appearance and place of abode every six months, or because it is wonderfully productive.* We regret to find that both the temples, though well preserved, are almost concealed among heaps of dirt and rubbish ; indeed the terrace of the larger one is occupied by several mud cottages belonging to the villagers, and the interior chambers of the sekos are indiscriminately used as sinks, granaries, or stables.

Hadjur Silsili would not detain the traveller in his progress up the Nile, were it not for the immense quarries from which, it is very probable, were hewn at different times those remarkable columns, statues, and obelisks which lend

* Egyptiaca, p. 88; Denon, vol. ii. p. 184.

to Thebes, Dendera, and Hermonthis their chief attraction even at the present day. Sphinxes, monolithic temples, and other monuments of Egyptian architecture, in an unfinished state, are still found near the rocks out of which they were cut. There is a large mass of stone, eighteen feet in every direction, supported only by a pillar of white earth three feet in diameter,—serving as an example of that peculiar vanity which has been attributed to the Egyptians, and which made them attract the admiration of posterity by works of the boldest design, and requiring the application of the most extraordinary mechanical powers.

Koum Ombos, supposed to represent the ancient capital of the Ombite Nome, attracts notice by the remains of a magnificent temple. The façade consists of a portico of fifteen columns, five in front and three deep, thirteen of which are still standing. The ornaments above the entrances are equally rich and highly finished. Towards the north-west angle of the enclosure is a small temple of Isis, the capitals of which are square, and have on each of the four sides the countenance of the goddess beautifully carved. The sculptures on the walls are very numerous, and even now, at the end of two thousand years, preserve the brilliancy of their first colouring.*

Es Souan, a town of which the origin is comparatively modern, stands near the site formerly occupied by the ancient Syené. The decline of commercial intercourse between Egypt and Ethiopia has gradually reduced this place to the condition of a poor village, subsisting on the scanty portion of cultivable land that spreads out between the river and the rocks of the desert. On the acclivity of an adjoining hill is an ancient temple of small dimensions, and differing somewhat in form from similar monuments in Egypt; but, being buried in rubbish up to the capitals of the columns and the architrave, it has not been minutely examined by recent travellers. Pococke imagined it to be the once celebrated observatory of Syené, although no pains were taken to ascertain its precise structure or object. The position of the famous well remains equally unknown. In fact, there is no approach to agreement among observers as to

* It was dedicated in the reign of King Ptolemy and Queen Cleopatra, his sister.—See Hamilton's Egyptiaca, p. 75.

the northern limit of the torrid zone, the place where the disk of the sun was reflected from the surface of the water on the day of the summer solstice. The calculations of Bruce led him to believe that Es Souan is situated in latitude 23° 28'; whereas Nouet, a French astronomer, asserts that its true parallel is in latitude 24° 8' 6". But it ought to be kept in mind that Syené stood a little farther towards the south than the town which now represents it; while it is not improbable that the point which marked the return of the solar orb, in his annual course, may have been fixed at the remotest extremity of the ancient city.

The quarries of Syené have been long celebrated, and sufficient vestiges of them still remain to render it credible that they furnished the materials for the colossal monuments of Egypt. They are seen at the foot of the mountains on the east, and some of them are close to the river. The marks of the chisels and drills are distinctly visible, as well as of the powerful wedges with which, when the sides were cleared, the blocks were started from their bed. In one quarry there was found a half-finished obelisk between 70 and 80 feet long, and 10 feet broad. In others were columns in a rough state, possessing similar dimensions; while along the breast of the hill were observed the marks of immense blocks, thirty and forty feet in length, which had been separated from the rock.

The island of Elephantiné is much richer in architectural remains than the town we have just described. Romans and Saracens, it is true, have done all in their power to deface or to conceal them; but, as Denon remarks, the Egyptian monuments continue devoted to posterity, and have resisted equally the ravages of man and of time. In the midst of a vast field of bricks, and other pieces of baked earth, a very ancient temple is still left standing, surrounded with a pilastered gallery and two columns in the portico. Nothing is wanting but two pilasters on the left angle of this ruin. Other edifices had been attached to it at a later period, but only some fragments were remaining, which could give no idea of their form when perfect,— proving only that these accessary parts were much larger than the original sanctuary.—Could this be the temple of Cneph, the good genius, that one of all the Egyptian gods who approaches the nearest to our ideas of the Supreme

S

Being? Or is it the temple of this deity which is placed six hundred paces farther to the north, having the same form and size, though more in ruins,—all the ornaments of which are accompanied by the serpent, the emblem of wisdom and eternity, and peculiarly that of the god now named! Judging from what he had seen of Egyptian temples, M. Denon is disposed to think that this supposed fane of Cneph belongs to the class which were used in the earliest times, and is absolutely the same species of building as the temple at Gornoo, which appeared to him the most ancient in Thebes. The chief difference in the sculpture of this at Elephantiné is, that the figures have more life, the drapery is more flowing, and falls into a better form of composition.*

The fascination attending this review of the monuments of ancient art has perhaps carried us somewhat farther than is quite consistent with our plan, which compels us to abstain from minute details, however interesting and agreeable. There is no other nation in the world, if we except those on the eastern borders of Asia,—whose real history has not yet been made known to the European reader,— which could present such a retrospect at the same early period, or gratify the traveller with the display of so much magnificence and beauty. Nor must our opinion of Egyptian science, art, and general civilization be limited to the rigid inferences which alone an examination of their actual remains might appear to justify. On the contrary, we are entitled to assume the most liberal rule of reasoning in regard to the acquirements of a people who surpassed, to such an extent, all their contemporaries westward of the Arabian Desert ; and to conclude that in other matters, the memorials of which could not be conveyed to posterity by the architect or the sculptor, the priests and sovereigns of the Nile had made a corresponding progress.

For example, we are told, that in the time of Moses the land of Egypt was celebrated for fine linen,—a notice which, to a hasty reader, conveys only that simple fact, but which, to the philosopher who has reflected on the slow and gradual steps by which nations advance to maturity, suggests a state of improvement inseparable from an established government and the exercise of good laws. Our meaning

* Denon, vol. ii. p. 32.

will receive a suitable illustration from the following passage
in the works of Dr. Adam Smith: "The woollen coat
which covers the day-labourer, coarse and rough as it may
appear, is the produce of the joint labour of a great number
of workmen. The shepherd, the sorter of the wool, the
wool-comber or carder, the dier, the spinner, the weaver,
the fuller, the dresser, with many others, must all join their
different arts in order to complete even this homely production. What a variety of labour, too, is necessary in order
to produce the tools of the meanest of those workmen:
To say nothing of such complicated machines as the ship
of the sailor, the mill of the fuller, or even the loom of the
weaver, let us consider only what a variety of labour is
requisite in order to form that very simple machine, the
shears with which the shepherd clips the wool. The miner,
the builder of the furnace for smelting the ore, the feller
of the timber, the burner of the charcoal to be made use of
in the smelting-house, the brickmaker, the bricklayer, the
workmen who attend the furnace, the millwright, the forger,
the smith, must all of them join their different arts in order
to produce them. Were we to examine in the same manner
all the different parts of his dress and household furniture,
the coarse linen shirt which he wears next his skin, the
shoes which cover his feet, the bed which he lies on, together with the tools of all the different workmen employed in
producing these different conveniences, we should be sensible that, without the assistance and co-operation of many
thousands, the very meanest person in a civilized country
could not be provided, even according to what we very
falsely imagine the easy and simple manner in which he is
usually accommodated."*

Let the reader transfer this reasoning to the "fine linen"
of Egypt, and he will immediately see the conclusions to
which we have alluded. Many arts must have arrived at
great perfection before the commodity mentioned by the
Hebrew legislator could have become an object of merchandise or of foreign commerce. How much skill, too, in
the art of tempering metals was necessary to prepare tools
for the workmen who carved the hardest granite, and covered
with sculptures the walls and ceilings of the most ancient

* Wealth of Nations, vol. l. p 17.

temples! Even the improvements of modern Europe supply not means for equalling the ingenious labours of the Egyptian artists. What a series of efforts must have preceded the excellence which is preserved for our admiration in the temples of Karnac and Luxor, in the tombs of Gornoo, and even in the grottoes of Eleithias! How many generations must have contributed their share to this perfection! The contemplative mind seeks refuge in a remoter antiquity than is allowed by the annals of the neighbouring tribes of Syria and of Greece; some of whom, instead of imitating the arts which would at once have secured to them the comforts and dignity of social life, derived nothing from their intercourse with Egypt except the absurd ceremonies of a gross superstition, which degraded the understanding while it polluted the heart.

It was our intention to have entered at some length into a history of the commercial relations which appear to have subsisted at an early period between Egypt and the nations of the East, and which were maintained, during several centuries, by a regular intercourse as well by land as by the Erythræan Sea and the Arabian Gulf. But we must content ourselves with a simple reference to the learned volumes of Dr. Vincent on the Commerce and Navigation of the Ancients, and to Dr. Robertson's Historical Disquisition concerning Ancient India; where is to be found the most authentic information that we possess on this important subject, recommended, too, by very luminous and satisfactory reasoning.

CHAPTER VII.

The Civil History of Modern Egypt.

Saracenic Dynasties—Foundation of Cairo—Crusaders—Saladin the
Great—Siege of Ptolemais—Death of Saladin—Crusaders defeated—
Rise of Mamlouks—The Borghites—Monguls and Tatars—Ibrahim
Bey—Ali Bey; his Syrian Campaign; his Death and Character—
Mohammed Bey—Ibrahim and Mourad—Invasion by the French—
Defeat at Acre—Victory of Lord Nelson—Battle of Alexandria, and
Death of Abercrombie—Evacuation of Egypt by the French—Kurouf
Pasha—Mohammed Ali; Success against the Beys; appointed Pasha
—British Expedition in 1807—Massacre of Mamlouks—History of
Wahabees; defeated by Ibrahim Pasha—European Tactics introduced
—Character of Mohammed Ali.

THE enterprising spirit breathed into the Saracens by
their military prophet soon made itself felt in the rapid conquests which they effected in all the surrounding countries.
Egypt, as a province of the Roman empire which was
already about to fall in pieces by its own weight, could not
resist their arms, led by the valiant and politic Amru.
Aided by treachery this fortunate general got possession of
Alexandria; to the inhabitants of which he presented the
humiliating alternative of paying a heavy tribute year after
year, or of embracing the Mohammedan faith and submitting to its painful ritual.   At the same time the valuable
library which adorned that city fell a prey to the religious
bigotry of the conquerors, who thought that any addition
to the knowledge bequeathed to them by the author of the
Koran was either superfluous or positively sinful.

The frequent contentions which ensued during the eighth
century for the honours of the caliphate afforded to Egypt
an opportunity of occasionally asserting its independence;
but no sooner was the question of supreme power determined by arms or by treaty than it was again compelled to
submit to the will of the victor. Among the various dynasties which assumed the reins of government were the
descendants of Ali the son-in-law of the prophet, of Abbas
his uncle, and of Fatima his daughter,—who continued to

urge their respective claims during several generations, and to expel one another in their turn from the thrones of Damascus and of Bagdad.

The reader could take no interest in the obscure wars and sanguinary revolutions which were directed by the powerful families of Aglab, Ommiah, and Ikshed, who not only seized the provincial authority along the shores of the Mediterranean, but even alarmed the holy successors of Mohammed in Syria and on the banks of the Tigris. At length, towards the end of the tenth century, the chief of the Fatimite branch removed the seat of his power from Cyrene, where it had been long established, to Cahira the City of Victory, the Grand Cairo of modern times. Other princes had assumed independence in Egypt, and refused to acknowledge the temporal supremacy of the Caliph of Bagdad, though the title of the latter, in his capacity of Imaum or chief priest of the Mohammedans, was regularly recited in the daily prayers of the faithful. But the African usurper at length interdicted this mark of spiritual allegiance, and demanded as his own right all the honours which belonged to the lineal descendant of the prophet.

The eleventh century brought upon Egypt a succession of calamities. A dreadful famine, with the usual accompaniments of plague and pestilence, swept off great multitudes, especially in the maritime districts and along the Syrian border. This destructive visitation was succeeded by one hardly less to be deplored,—an inroad of the Turks, who had already descended from the extensive plains of Central Asia and found employment at the court of the caliph as mercenary soldiers. They had resolved to avenge the cause of their master on his rebellious subjects; and with this view they committed the most horrid cruelties wherever they could carry their arms, setting an example of a savage warfare long unknown to the country which they had overrun, and thereby rousing against themselves the bitterest resentment and detestation of the whole body of the people. The hosts of the crusaders arrived to complete the misery which the northern barbarians had commenced. Having reduced Pelusium these warriors advanced against Cairo, which they threatened with a similar fate; but learning that a Syrian army was on its march to cut off their retreat, they accepted a sum of money and raised the siege.

Towards the close of the twelfth century the descendants of Fatima ceased to reign over Egypt. Aladid, the last of the race, appears to have intrusted the government to the wisdom of his viziers, who, it is manifest, laboured both at home and abroad to establish their own power rather than that of their master; and as he had no near relations, his death was the signal for his ambitious minister to seat himself on the empty throne. This founder of a new dynasty was the renowned Saladin, whose name is so closely associated with the most brilliant exploits of the Mohammedan arms. He began by seizing the wealth and securing the strong places of the kingdom,—throwing at the same time into confinement all whom he suspected of being the partisans of the late monarch. Not inheriting the blood of the prophet, he did not assume the title of caliph, which implies the sacerdotal as well as the kingly office; but contented himself with the denomination of sultan, leaving the priestly duties to be discharged by some individual sprung from the sacred lineage.

Though Saladin was acknowledged as sovereign of Egypt by many of the neigbouring states, and even received the sanction of the caliph of Bagdad, his government was not yet firmly established. There were two powerful factions opposed to his authority; the adherents of Aladid's family, who wished to retain the sceptre in the Fatimite succession, and the king of Syria, who dreaded the ascendency of so warlike a neighbour. The first favoured the pretensions of an adventurer who claimed the throne, and even enabled him to appear in the field at the head of 100,000 men. But a complete victory soon relieved the new sultan from all apprehension in this quarter. The Christians, under the command of William, king of Sicily, next engaged his attention, having laid siege to Alexandria both by land and sea. Saladin flew to the relief of a place the preservation of which was so important at once to his reputation and to the success of his future plans. He had mustered a force sufficient to justify the hazard of a battle; but before he could accomplish his object, the crusaders, smitten with a sudden panic, commenced a hurried retreat, leaving behind them their stores, their baggage, and even their military engines. The court of Damascus, still cherishing a feeling of deep-rooted jealousy, endeavoured to strengthen their interests by an extended alliance among the surrounding principalities; watching eagerly for an opportunity to check the views and disappoint the ambition of the Egyptian sultan. At length they resolved to commit their cause to the fortune of war. A general engagement ensued, which terminated so decidedly in favour of Saladin that he returned from it the undisputed master of the whole of Syria.

His next cares were directed to the enlargement and fortification of Cairo, which he had determined to render a capital worthy of his extensive dominions, and fit to be compared with the more ancient cities adorned by Menes, Sesostris, and Ptolemy. He encouraged the schools and literature of the country, and in many other respects showed qualities suited to a time of peace; but he was soon torn away from his schemes of domestic improvement to the din of arms and the ravages of war. Having obtained the ascendency in Syria, he resolved to extend his power also into Palestine; and with this view he led his troops against the numerous host of the crusaders who had again joined their banners for the recovery of the Holy Land. His first efforts in the field were not attended with success. The Christians, animated with an equal courage and long accustomed to the use of their weapons, repelled the attacks of the sultan with so much fury that he saw his fine army perish before his eyes, either in the battle or while attempting to retreat across the desert into Egypt.

But his spirit could not be subdued by temporary reverses. Aided by commanders who shared his energy and ambition, he resumed offensive operations both by sea and land; recovered all the ground he had lost in the former campaign; and finally gained a decisive victory over the allied forces led by Lusignan, king of Jerusalem, and by Arnold, lord of Karac, both of whom were taken prisoners. The former was treated with respect, but the latter was put to death by Saladin's own hand, because he had inflicted many injuries on the followers of Mohammed. Ptolemais, Neapolis, Cæsarea, and other cities fell into the power of the Egyptian ruler, who, finding nothing to oppose his progress, marched to the capital, which he immediately invested. The garrison was numerous, and made a desperate defence; but after the conqueror had effected a breach in the walls, and was on the point of entering the town, the governor proposed a capitulation.

Saladin, enraged at the delay occasioned by a protracted siege, refused to accept the terms, vowing that he would sack and utterly demolish the Holy City, though almost equally venerated by Mohammedans and by Christians. His cruel threatenings roused the spirit of the defenders, who announced their resolution to put 5000 Mussulman prisoners to death, and in order that no European might be exposed to their revenge, they would also deprive of life their own wives and children. They added, that with the view of disappointing their enemy in the expectation of booty, they would destroy every thing valuable within the walls; level the rock which the disciples of the prophet held sacred; and then sally out in a body on the besiegers, either to purchase victory or to sell their lives at the dearest price. The knowledge of this resolution moved Saladin to more reasonable terms; and he consented that the garrison, as well as the inhabitants of Jerusalem, should have their lives spared on the condition of paying a liberal ransom in money.

The wars which Saladin carried on against the heroes of the Crusade do not properly fall within the limits of this volume, more especially as the scene of conflict was chosen in Syria rather than in Egypt. Suffice it to mention, that when he had succeeded in establishing his authority from Thebes to Damascus, his territories were once more invaded by a Christian armament, conducted by the Emperor of Germany, the King of France, and the celebrated Richard Cœur de Lion, the sovereign of England. The combined forces encamped before Ptolemais,—a stronghold which is better known by its modern name of Acre,—in which the sultan had collected a numerous army, and made preparations for a vigorous defence. Want of harmony among the European powers enabled him to resist their attacks a long time without incurring any serious loss; and it was not until the approach of famine had thinned his ranks and depressed the spirits of the survivors, that he consented to offer conditions. Upon the promise of refunding a part of the treasure which at different times he had extorted from the allies, he was allowed to march out with the honours of war; delivering to the victors the possession of a town, the siege of which had involved the sacrifice of three hundred thousand men, including the flower of European chivalry and the best warriors of the East.

After numerous vicissitudes of fortune, in which his active valour, aided by the jealousies that distracted the counsels of his antagonists, had generally secured to him the advantage in the field, he died in the fifty-fifth year of his age. His son, who succeeded him on the throne of Egypt, appears to have possessed his ambition without his talents. But Alcamel, to whom the sceptre fell about the beginning of the thirteenth century, threw a lustre on his reign by his success in repelling the crusaders; who for the fifth time invaded the kingdom of the sultans. Damietta had surrendered to the Christians, who, elated by the prosperous commencement of the campaign, advanced up the Nile, and meditated the entire conquest of the country. But the issue of a general action, which soon afterward took place, was so disastrous to the foreigners that they were compelled to sue for mercy, and to accept the conditions of a treaty more honourable to the clemency of the victors than to the ability of the European commanders.

Alcamel died at Damascus in 1238, and Aladel, one of his sons, was raised to the throne; but Nojmoddin, the eldest brother, laid claim to the kingdom. A bloody contest would probably have ensued had not the younger prince, in the mean time, disappeared or died,—an event which led to the peaceable accession of the senior claimant. Nojmoddin, like his predecessor, soon acquired great influence with the leaders of the Crusade; for Richard, Earl of Cornwall, perceiving that the Sultan of Egypt possessed more power than the Syrian lords of Karac and Damascus, entered into an alliance with him, and thereby ensured protection to the Christian pilgrims when on their way to the holy sepulchre.

In this unsettled state of affairs Nojmoddin passed into Syria, determined, with the help of some rude tribes who occupied the neighbouring desert, to subdue the faithless armies of Damascus. A battle, in which he found himself opposed by certain European auxiliaries, crowned his

enterprise with success, and opened up a path to still more
important advantages; but, in the mean time, a new host
of crusaders arrived at the port of Damietta, having Louis
the Ninth of France for their leader. In the absence
of the sultan, and while the nation was altogether unprepared for such an inroad, the French king made considerable
progress; several towns fell, and the inhabitants fled for
refuge into the upper part of the country. Nojmoddin,
who was busily engaged in the siege of Emessa, hastened
towards home to save his people from the horrors of an
utter conquest; but, harassed by fatigue and anxiety, he
sank by the way, leaving the government to his son, an
inexperienced youth. The enemy still pushed into the
interior, apprehending no serious opposition, when to their
surprise they found themselves in presence of a formidable
army, raised by the exertions of the sultan's widow, the
famous Shagir Aldor. Louis was defeated and taken
prisoner; while his followers, after having endured the
greatest privations, were glad to throw themselves upon
the compassion of the natives, whose fields they had laid
waste, and whose houses they had plundered.

This period is remarkable for the earliest accession to
power of that celebrated class of men called Mamlouks.
Saladin, who as a usurper put little confidence in the
native troops of Egypt, placed around his person a guard
of foreigners, composed of slaves purchased or made captives in the provinces which border on the southern shores
of the Caspian Sea. Successive sultans had increased the
power of these armed attendants by new privileges; and
hence, as has always happened in every similar case, they
acquired at length the entire disposal of the sovereign
authority. Ibeg, one of their number, became regent during
the minority of the prince; and upon the death of that boy
he married the queen-mother, and finally stepped into the
throne. Carried off by assassination he left the supreme
power to his son, who only enjoyed it during a very short
period; but notwithstanding the convulsions which inces-
santly shook the state, and the alarming progress of the
Monguls in the eastern part of the Mohammedan empire, the
Mamlouk dynasty directed the affairs of Egypt not less than
one hundred and twenty years.

But the inheritance of the Pharaohs was now doomed to

pass from the hands of one class of slaves to be seized by another not less vile and degraded. Among the captives annually brought into Egypt were numerous young men from that district of Western Asia which in our days is denominated Circassia. Being enrolled as soldiers, they were stationed in the several fortresses and strongholds which had been erected throughout the kingdom with the view of checking the insubordination of the people; and, accordingly, from the name of such castles in the Coptic tongue, they were denominated Borghites, or garrison troops, to distinguish them from those who served in the field. By a captain of this militia, whose name was Barcok, the Mamlouk dynasty, properly so called, was brought to an end, and a new race of Borghite princes elevated to the vacant throne. His valour and wisdom entitled him to the place which he usurped, and he proved a benefactor to the unhappy country which he could hardly fail to despise.

The latter part of the fourteenth century witnessed the first menaces of those warlike hordes which, under the various designations of Monguls and Tatars, carried their arms into the southern provinces of Asia, and at length conquered settlements in the richest parts of Africa and Europe. Tamerlane, who had already overrun the fine countries watered by the Tigris and Euphrates, was desirous to add Syria also to his dominions; and, with this great object in view, was directing his march towards the west, when, finding that the Sultan of Egypt had collected a strong force at Damascus to dispute his progress, he turned on his steps and sought a less formidable enemy near the sources of the river Indus. At the same time the furious Bajazet, at the head of his Ottoman levies, was spreading terror upon both sides of the Hellespont, and had approached to the very gates of Constantinople. He had, indeed, expressed his determination to reduce that city, and to found his government upon the ruins of the Roman empire; in pursuance of which plan he eagerly solicited the friendship of Barcok and the blessing of the caliph, who, in his capacity of Imaum or chief priest of the Mohammedan church, kept his usual residence at Cairo. The fate of Egypt appeared for a time inseparably connected with the policy of one or other of these warriors, who were resolved to possess it either as an allied or as a conquered province. But, fortu-

nately for the peace and independence of that country, the
armies of the rival barbarians exhausted themselves in
mutual hostilities, till, after various success on either
side, Bàjazet was taken prisoner, and Tamerlane relinquished the pursuit of military fame. Relieved from a con-
federacy which must have borne it down, Egypt preserved,
a century and a half longer, under a succession of very
feeble princes, the semblance of supreme power; when at
length, in 1517, the victorious arms of the Turks dethroned
the last of the Borghite dynasty, and reduced his kingdom
to the condition of a province.

In the most-perfect form of the Turkish government in
Egypt it consisted of a divan, or council of regency, composed of those who commanded the military bodies,—the
president, in all cases, being the pasha or viceroy. From
the Mamlouk beys, who presided over the provinces, were
chosen the Sheik el Belled, or governor of Grand Cairo;
the Janizary Aga, or commander of the Janisaries; the
Defturdar, or accountant-general; the Emir el Hadgi, or
conductor of the caravan; the Emir el Saïd, or governor of
Upper Egypt; and the Sheik el Bekheri, or governor of the
sherifs.

In the course of the sixteenth century, when Soliman the
First was involved in war with the great European powers,
the authority of the Porte in Egypt was considerably diminished, while several important changes were introduced into
the local government. The beys, who superintended the
twenty-four departments into which the kingdom was
divided, collected the revenues of their respective districts,
and thereby acquired a degree of influence which rendered
them equally insolent and formidable. The heads of the
seven military corps and the pasha becoming excessively
avaricious, courted the favour of the beys, who could enforce
the payment of tribute with severity, or remit it in part,
according to their pleasure. By indulging the members
of the regency, these officers in their turn increased in
power till they obtained the complete disposal of public
affairs. The subordinate governors had originally a few
Mamlouks or slaves at their command, for enabling them
to make their authority respected in the provinces where
they presided; but in proportion as their power was enlarged
they augmented their attendants, and by that means added

T

materially to their military strength as independent rulers.
When, too, a vacancy occurred in the government of a
province, the most influential bey had his favourite Mamlouk
appointed to the office.   Such an election still farther
augmented his authority; and by pursuing a similar course,
the most active and powerful of these chiefs acquired a continually increasing influence in the government, and their
Mamlouks at length became the only efficient soldiers in
the state.

By means similar to those now described, Ibrahim, one
of the veteran colonels of the Janizaries, succeeded, about
the middle of last century, in rendering himself in effect the
sovereign of Egypt.   He had so multiplied and advanced
his enfranchised Mamlouks, that of the twenty-four beys no
fewer than eight belonged to his household; and the influence connected with these appointments was the greater,
inasmuch as the pasha always left vacancies in the subordinate governments, in order that he might appropriate the
revenue to his own private purposes.   On the other hand,
the largesses which he bestowed on the officers and soldiers
of his corps had firmly attached them to his interest, when
Rodoan, the most powerful of the Azab colonels, devoted
himself to his cause, and thereby completed his political
ascendency.   The pasha, incapable of opposing this faction,
was no more than a phantom in the public eye, and even
the orders of the sultan himself were lightly regarded when
weighed against those of Ibrahim.   At his death, which
happened in 1757, his slaves, divided among themselves
but united against all others, continued to give the law.
Rodoan, who had succeeded to the influence of his colleague, was expelled and slain by the younger beys; and
during the period of ten years the affairs of Egypt were
managed by a cabal, whose principal motives, veiled by the
most empty pretensions of patriotism, were ambition and
revenge.   At length the celebrated Ali, one of their number,
gained a decided superiority over his rivals; and, under the
successive titles of Emir Hadgi and Sheik el Belled, and by
means which indicate the degraded condition of all classes
of the people, rendered himself absolute master of the whole
country.

The birth of Ali Bey, like that of the Mamlouks in general,
is extremely uncertain.   It is commonly believed in Egypt

that he was the son of a Circassian peasant, bought or captured as a slave when about twelve years of age, and afterward sold at Cairo to a Jew, who made a present of him to Ibrahim, the aspiring chief already mentioned. In the house of his patron he received the customary education of a page, which consists in horsemanship, in the ready use of the carbine, pistol, and sabre, in throwing the lance, and sometimes in a little reading and writing. In these exercises he displayed an activity and fire which obtained for him the surname of Djendali, or Madcap. But the solicitude of ambition soon moderated this excessive warmth. At the age of eighteen he received the gift of manumission from his indulgent master, who soon afterward appointed him to a government, and procured for him a place among the twenty-four beys, at once the tyrants and protectors of the unhappy natives.

The death of Ibrahim, we have remarked, was a signal to his dependants for rapacity and intrigue. Ali Bey was neither the least active nor the least successful. He precipitated Rodoan from his guilty elevation, and was preparing to realize a plan for thinning still farther the ranks of his opponents, when he was compelled to leave the city and take refuge in a temporary exile. At the end of two years, which he had spent in making the necessary arrangements, he appeared suddenly in Cairo; slew four beys who were his enemies; banished four others; and became from that moment the chief of the prevailing party. He no longer thought it necessary to conceal his ulterior views; but expelling the pasha, and refusing the tribute annually remitted to Constantinople, he assumed the supreme power, and even proceeded so far as to coin money in his own name.

The Porte did not behold without indignation such an attack upon its authority; but being occupied with the affairs of Poland and the pretensions of Russia, could not bestow a sufficient degree of attention on the revolted province. The usual methods of poison and the bowstring were repeatedly attempted; but Ali, whose vigilance was ever awake, turned these deadly instruments against the lives of those who bore them. To consolidate his power, he equipped a fleet in the Red Sea, and took possession of Mecca and of Djidda; at the latter of which places he meant to establish the emporium of Indian commerce, and thereby to supersede the tedious voyage by the Cape of Good Hope. His chief undertaking, however, was directed against the Turkish arms in Syria. Sheik Daher, already in rebellion, was a powerful and faithful ally; while the extortions of the pasha of Damascus, by driving the people to revolt, afforded the most favourable opportunity for invading his government.

In the year 1771 a force, amounting to about sixty thousand men, crossed the frontier under the command of Mohammed Bey, the friend of Ali. Daher sent four or five thousand irregular cavalry to strengthen the expedition, led by his son, a youth of great military promise. On the other hand, the pashas of Sidon, Tripoli, and Aleppo mustered their several contingents, and advanced to join Osman the governor of Damascus, whose territory was menaced with invasion. On the 6th of June an action took place, when the Mamlouks and their allies rushed with so much fury on the Turks, that the latter, terrified at the carnage, had immediate recourse to flight. The troops of Ali instantly became masters of the whole country, and took possession of the capital without opposition, there being neither soldiers nor walls to defend it. The castle alone made a show of resistance; for the garrison, being already conquered by their fears, hastened to capitulate in order to prevent the horrors of an assault.

But the morning on which the place was to be surrendered witnessed an extraordinary scene. At dawn of day the Egyptian army was beheld in full retreat towards the Nile. In vain did Daher fly to demand the cause of so strange a measure; Mohammed made no other answer to the anxious interrogatories of the Syrian rebel than that it was his pleasure to retire, and that no one was entitled to question the prudence of his conduct. Nor was it merely a retreat conducted on military principles; it was a positive flight, the Mamlouks rushing from before the walls as if hotly pursued by a victorious enemy, while the road from Damascus to Cairo was covered with men on foot, and with the stores and baggage which they had abandoned. This singular occurrence was attributed at the time to a pretended report of the death of Ali Bey; but the real cause, soon afterward discovered, was no other than a conference with Osman, held in the tent of the Egyptian commander, when the pasha gained him and the beys under his orders to the interests of the Sublime Porte. Convinced by the arguments addressed to their avarice not less than to their fears, they swore by the sabre and the Koran to return home without delay; and so suddenly did they execute their determination that the news of their coming preceded their actual arrival at Cairo only by six hours. Ali would at once have punished this treason by the death of his general; but finding him supported by many powerful individuals in the army, he suppressed his rage, thinking it more politic to reserve the moment of revenge till he could gratify it without danger.

To effect the ruin of Mohammed, whose conduct even after the affair of Damascus continued to excite suspicion, he gave orders, on one occasion, that no Mamlouk should be suffered to pass the gates of Cairo in the evening or at night; and, at the same moment, commanded his rival into exile. He had hoped, it was supposed, that the object of his displeasure, as he must necessarily leave the city before morning, would be detained by the guards for attempting to violate the regulation just mentioned, and be thereby placed entirely in his power. But the soldiers, imagining that their general was charged with private instructions from Ali, allowed him to pass without interruption, although accompanied with a formidable retinue; nor was the mistake discovered until it was too late to pursue him. Mohammed retired into the Saïd, where he drew around him all the discontented Mamlouks, and waited with impatience an opportunity for avenging their common cause.

In a little time the force of this disaffected chief was so greatly augmented that he thought himself sufficiently strong to make an attempt upon Cairo. A battle ensued in a plain adjoining to the city, which terminated so decidedly to the advantage of the insurgents, that Ali found some difficulty to escape at the head of eight hundred Mamlouks, who accompanied his flight into Syria. There he joined his old ally Daher, who still held out against the government of Constantinople; and, having strengthened the camp with so seasonable a reinforcement of well-disciplined cavalry, he took share in an expedition at that instant meditated by the revolted pasha, the object of which was to raise the siege of Sidon.

The Turks, unwilling to be attacked in their trenches, drew out their tumultuary bands to a little distance from the town, and prepared for a general action. Fortune once more smiled on Ali and his confederates, who soon saw the army of the enemy, three times more numerous than their own, entirely defeated, and scattered over the face of the country.

Flushed with this success, the exiled ruler longed to return to his capital, where, as he was insidiously informed by the agents of Mohammed, the majority of the inhabitants were anxious to behold him restored to his former power. He was also deceived by his superstition, which taught him to believe that the hour of his ascendant was come, and that the stars pointed out the path to a renewed and permanent glory. Had he listened to the voice of prudence, he would have waited for the assistance promised by the Russians, who did not disdain to consider him a useful ally in their war with the Porte,—and for the troops detached by Daher, to secure a victorious return, whatever might be the intentions or military resources of the hostile beys. But yielding to an inconsiderate impatience, with the remains of his Mamlouks and fifteen hundred Sifadians he entered the desert, where he was met by Mourad at the head of a superior force; wounded by the hand of this young officer; taken prisoner; and forthwith conducted into the presence of Mohammed. On the third day after this event, his death was announced to the soldiers, who were desired to ascribe it to the severe hurts which he had received in the fight; but who, notwithstanding, were generally disposed to trace it to the operation of poison, or to the less tedious application of the dagger.

Thus terminated the career of this celebrated person, who for some time engaged the attention of Europe, and afforded to many politicians the hopes of a beneficial revolution. That he was an extraordinary character cannot be denied; but it is exaggeration to place him in the class of great men. The accounts given of him by those who knew him best prove, that though he possessed the seeds of great qualities, the want of culture prevented them from coming to maturity. But in Ali Bey we must admire one property which distinguished him from the multitude of tyrants who have governed Egypt, and which is never the portion of vulgar minds; he was actuated by the desire of attaining glory, although a vicious education prevented him from discovering its true elements as well as the path which leads to it. To be a great statesman as well as a warrior he wanted nothing but the lessons of civilized life, or the aid of enlightened counsellors; and of those who are born to command, how few are there who merit even this restricted eulogium!*

The death of Ali Bey did not produce any change favourable to Egypt; on the contrary, Mohammed, into whose hands the supreme power fell undivided, displayed, during the two years of his government, no qualities higher than the ferocity of a robber and the baseness of a traitor. He began, indeed, by renewing the customary tribute to the sultan, and even paid the arrears due by his predecessor; but his conduct soon proved, that instead of acting on the principles of an enlightened patriotism, he intended no more than to purchase the means of gratifying political revenge, and of depressing a formidable neighbour. He sought permission to wage war with Daher, and to reduce the whole of Syria to the obedience of the Porte; thereby covering the deep feeling of private resentment under the cloak of public duty.

After due preparation, he undertook the siege of Jaffa, which, owing to the ignorance of the assailants rather than the courage of the garrison, was protracted to the end of six weeks. At length conditions were agreed on, and the treaty might be considered as concluded, when, in the midst of the security occasioned by that belief, the Mamlouks rushed into the town, and subjected it to all the horrors of an assault, putting women and children, old and young, to death; while Mohammed, equally mean and barbarous, caused a pyramid formed of the heads of these unfortunate sufferers to be raised as a monument of his victory. He advanced next to Acre, where the Shiek Daher had established his government, and demanded that all the riches accumulated within the city should be delivered up to him, under the pain of a universal massacre of the inhabitants, not excepting the European merchants. But before the day arrived on which he intended to realize his savage

* Volney's Travels through Egypt and Syria, vol i. p. 130; Edinburgh Encyclopædia, article Egypt.

threatening, he was carried off by a malignant fever in the very prime of life.

This event took place in the summer of 1776; upon which the army, as on a former occasion, dispersed in the greatest disorder, and accomplished a tumultuous march into Egypt. Mohammed had left at Cairo one of his freedmen, Ibrahim Bey, as governor of the city, taking with him into Syria the more warlike Mourad, to whom he confided the management of the campaign. These two chiefs were now prepared to dispute the succession, and every appearance at first threatened open hostilities; but when they had time to consider the power and resources of each other, they determined to avoid the issue of a combat, and to share the authority which neither was content to relinquish.

Their joint administration, however, was soon disturbed by the jealousies of the other beys, who thought themselves unjustly deprived of the influence which belonged to their rank,—a feeling which made the deepest impression on certain individuals who had belonged to the house of Ali, the great patron of their order. Two of that number, Hassan and Ishmael, collected their adherents and took the field. Mourad pursued them into the Saïd, where the greater part either dispersed or capitulated without coming to action.

Dissension at length divided the interests of the sovereign colleagues, and even drove them to arms. Each in his turn fled from Cairo, and formed an encampment in Upper Egypt; but no sooner did their troops appear in sight of one another than the chiefs induced them to settle their differences on the basis of a new treaty. Matters continued in this precarious situation till 1786, when, peace being established between the Russians and the Turks, the sultan resolved to reduce Egypt once more to a state of obedience. With this view he despatched the celebrated Hassan Pasha at the head of 25,000 men, who, landing at Alexandria in the month of July, made instant preparations for advancing towards the capital. Mourad and his Mamlouks met him at Mentorbes, where a desperate battle ensued. The ground being still very soft from the effects of the inundation, the Turkish infantry gained a decided advantage over horsemen whose movements were constantly impeded, and who, sinking in the mud, were equally incapable of attack or defence.

Cairo opened its gates to Hassan, who, after appointing a governor, continued his march in pursuit of the rebellious beys into Upper Egypt. The difficulties of this undertaking, however, induced him in the course of the following year to accede to a treaty, by which they were left in full possession of the country from Barbieh to the frontiers of Nubia, on condition of relinquishing all claims to the territory below the limits now specified.

The wisdom and moderation of the Turkish pasha procured the inestimable blessing of a settled government to the inhabitants of Lower Egypt. He lightened their burdens, redressed their numerous grievances, and fortified the city so as to protect it from a sudden inroad on the part of the disaffected beys.. But in 1790 the plague appeared in its most virulent form, and after committing frightful devastation among the lower classes, put an end to the life of Ishmael. Only a short interval elapsed, during which an attempt was made to perpetuate the authority of the Porte, when Mourad and Ibrahim returned from their exile, and assumed once more the sovereign power in defiance of the sultan and his divan.

But the domestic struggles of party were now about to be superseded by an event which threatened the existence of Egypt as a province of the Turkish empire. In 1798 a French army under General Buonaparte effected a landing near Alexandria, with the avowed object of restoring the legitimate influence of the grand signior, but with the real intention of adding that important country to the dominions of the new republic. The Mamlouks resolved to dispute his passage towards the capital, and accordingly awaited his approach at Imbaba, a village about seven miles distant from the Great Pyramids. As might have been expected, the discipline of the French triumphed over the wild courage of their opponents, gained a complete victory, and opened the way for the possession of Grand Cairo. Ibrahim fled into the eastern parts of the Delta, while Mourad with the remnant of his brave horsemen retreated into the desert beyond Sakhara.

The possession of Egypt had long been viewed by the politicians of France as an object of great importance. It is therefore an error to suppose that the scheme of conquering that country originated with Napoleon Buonaparte; for he, in adopting this bold measure, did no more than follow up the ideas of several writers who had great influence on the public mind of Europe. Sanuto the Venetian, for example, mentions the subjugation of Egypt by some nation whose territory bordered on the Mediterranean, as the most effectual blow that could be struck against the power of the Crescent, as well as the most likely means for recovering the East India trade. Count Daru, who in his history of Venice repeats the arguments of Sanuto, reminds his readers that the communication between India and the southern parts of Europe, by the channel of the Red Sea, was the shortest, the surest, and the most economical; that it would not be difficult to establish a communication between the Red Sea and the Nile; that, independently of the commerce of India, there was on the eastern coast of that sea a country abounding in aromatics and perfumes; that Africa itself, by its gold and ivory, offered rich materials for trade; and, in short, that the possession of Egypt by one of the maritime powers of the Mediterranean was preferable to the possession of all the provinces of Hindostan.

Leibnitz, too, addressed to Louis the Fourteenth a memorial on the same subject, advising that monarch to lay hold of Egypt for the purpose of destroying the maritime and commercial ascendency of the Dutch, which he alleges depended mainly on the success of their Indian trade. Hence it is manifest that Buonaparte only revived an old theory, and attempted to launch against Britain the weapon which the German philosopher had forged for the destruction of the merchants and shipmasters of Holland.[*]

The government of the sultan, who could not mistake the motives of Buonaparte, declared war in the following year against the French republic. Throwing off the mask, political and religious, which did not deceive even the Arabs and Fellahs of Egypt, the invader led his army into Syria, and laid siege to the principal towns on the coast. El Arish and Jaffa were quickly reduced; upon which he opened his

---

[*] Histoire de Venice, tom. iii. p. 75, 76; Webster's Travels through the Crimea, Turkey, and Egypt. The Venetians solicited the authority of the pope to trade with infidels; but in the mean time, says the historian, they made no scruple to conform to the errors of the Mussulmans, by enacting treaties "in the name of the Lord and of Mahomet"—*au nom du Seigneur et de Mahomet.*

trenches before Acre. The result of this memorable enterprise is too well known to require any details. Buonaparte,
after sacrificing his heavy artillery, commenced a retreat
towards Egypt under the most unfavourable circumstances;
his track through the desert being marked by the dead bodies
of French soldiers who had sunk under fatigue, or were
sabred by the light cavalry of the enemy.

Dessaix, who had been left to prosecute the war against
the Mamlouks, found himself unable to bring them to a
general action. Mourad retired before him as far as Syené,
occupying such positions as rendered an attack impossible;
and no sooner did the French turn their backs, than he as-
sailed their rear or cut off their supplies. Meanwhile a
Turkish fleet appeared on the coast with eight thousand
men on board. Hardly had they landed when they were
met by Buonaparte, who, after an obstinate and sanguinary
conflict, overwhelmed them with a complete destruction; the
most of those who escaped his bayonets being drowned in
attempting to regain their ships.

Although we profess not to be the historian of the military proceedings which determined the fate of Egypt at the
beginning of this century, we cannot pass without remark
the exaggeration of Denon, who says that at Aboukir the
French destroyed twenty thousand Turks, six thousand
being killed, two thousand taken, and the remainder driven
into the sea. Such statements were written to gratify the
pride or amuse the anxiety of the Parisians, who could not
conceal from themselves that their country had sacrificed a
fleet and an army to the romantic ambition of a popular
general; and it is no longer denied by the biographers of
Buonaparte, that he was in the practice of dictating falsehoods, to be given to the world in the form of public despatches, in order to withdraw attention from the amount
of his disasters.

The victory of Nelson, and the repulses sustained in
Syria, indicated to this chief that the star of his fortune was
not to reach its ascendant in Egypt. Intrusting the command to Kleber, he departed in a secret manner from head-
quarters, and sailed for France, where he hastened to forget
the companions of his toil in the deep game of politics which
soon afterward placed him on a throne. Buonaparte is
understood to have instructed his successor to enter into

negotiation with the government of the Porte, for the purpose of evacuating the country, on condition that certain commercial advantages should be conceded to the French republic. Failing in this, it is related that Kleber consented to withdraw his army on the simple terms of being allowed to retain private property, and of having the safety of his men guarantied against the Mamlouks on shore and the British at sea. But the treaty does not appear to have been signed; each party imagining that their circumstances might be improved by another appeal to arms. The French general, indeed, was soon after assassinated at Cairo; but Menou, who succeeded to the chief authority, being encouraged by the expectation of receiving fresh supplies from Europe, resolved to keep possession of the country at all hazards, and to defend his positions against the combined forces of the Turks and English.[*]

The debarkation of the army under Sir Ralph Abercrombie, the gallant actions which succeeded, and the defeat of the French near Alexandria, on the 21st March, 1800, are matters of general history familiarly known to every reader. Egypt at this moment became the scene of European wars; the policy of two great nations was brought into collision on the banks of the Nile; and the fate of India, or at least the temporary security of the British possessions in that vast country, appeared to depend on the success or failure of this unwonted expedition into an African province. Each party

---

[*] Sir Robert Wilson (History of Expedition, p. 65, quarto edition) assigns a reason for the renewal of the war highly creditable to the British character. Admiral Keith refused to give his consent to the conditions agreed upon at El Arish, communicating to the Turks his conviction of the greater expediency of driving the French out of the country altogether. Kleber was at Cairo, and making preparations to evacuate the capital, when a notice arrived from Sir Sidney Smith, that hostilities were to be continued, and that he was not expected to fulfil the terms of a convention which was not to be observed by the other party. The Turks, it is said, meant to take advantage of Kleber's ignorance, and to attack him while reposing on his arms. It is added, that they never forgave Sir Sidney for his generous honesty, considering him as little better than a traitor to their cause.

Others insinuate that Kleber had no intention of acceding to the treaty, and that he negotiated with the allies only to gain time until the arrival of reinforcements from Europe should enable him to act with greater certainty of success. See Wilson; Dr. Clarke, vol. iii.; Life of Buonaparte in Family Library; Bourrienne's Memoirs; and the Modern Traveller.

professed to support the legitimate power of the grand signior; but even the simplest of the Arab tribes could not fail to perceive that their land was desolated by the ambition of the Franks, who, they suspected, were accustomed to avow one motive and to act upon another.

The siege of Alexandria was rendered remarkable by an expedient which necessity appeared to sanction, though doubts have since been entertained both of its wisdom and humanity. It is worthy of notice, at the same time, that it was suggested by the French; for in the pocket of General Roiz, who was killed in the action of the 21st, there was found a letter written by Menou, expressing an apprehension that the British would cut the embankment which forms the canal of Alexandria, and thereby admit the waters of the sea into Lake Mareotis. "From that moment," says Sir Robert Wilson, "it had become the favourite object of the army; as, by securing the left and part of its front, the duty would be diminished, the French cut off from the interior, and a new scene of operations opened." But there were very serious objections to the measure. The mischief it might do was incalculable. The Arabs could give no information where such a sea would be checked: the ruin of Alexandria might probably be the consequence; and, while it covered the British left, it would also secure the front of the French position, except from a new landing. But the urgency of the present service, says the historian, at length superseded all remoter considerations. General Hutchinson reluctantly consented, and the army was in raptures. Never did a working party labour with more zeal; every man would have volunteered with cheerfulness to assist. Four cuts were made of six yards in breadth, and about ten distant from each other; but only two could be opened the first night. At seven o'clock the last fascine was removed, and the joy was universal. The water rushed in with a fall of six feet; and the pride and peculiar care of Egypt, the consolidation of ages, was in a few hours destroyed by the devastating hand of man. Two more cuts were finished next day, and three more marked out; but the force of the water was such as soon to break one into the other; and now an immense body of water rushed in, which continued flowing for a month with considerable violence.

U

After a variety of skirmishes, which usually terminated to the advantage of the British and their allies, General Hutchinson resolved to lay siege to Cairo, where the main strength of the French army was now assembled. Beliard, who commanded in that city, proposed terms of capitulation; being at length perfectly satisfied, that without reinforcements from Europe the war could not be carried on with any rational prospect of success. On the 27th June articles were signed, by which the garrison consented to evacuate the capital on condition of being sent to France.

Meantime the blockade of Alexandria was prosecuted with vigour under the direction of General Coote; Menou having expressed his determination to bury himself in its ruins rather than pull down the flag of the victorious republic. But no sooner had a regular bombardment commenced from the ships in the harbour and the batteries on land, than his resolution failed, and he expressed his readiness to listen to terms. On the 2d of September the garrison laid down their arms, on the usual condition of being sent to their own country without any impeachment on their honour as soldiers; and thus Egypt, after having been more than two years the theatre of a destructive war, found itself once more under the government of the Turks, and acknowledging the authority of the Sublime Porte.

The British general exerted himself to the utmost to procure favourable terms in behalf of the Mamlouk beys, who, it was well known, had resolutely opposed the French, and suffered no small loss both in men and property, in the earlier period of the invasion. Mourad had already fallen a victim to the plague, and Ibrahim, now well advanced in age, was at the head of their affairs, assisted by Osman Tambourji, an active and very gallant officer. On the surrender of Cairo, General Hutchinson insisted that the Mamlouks should have restored to them all their rights and dignities, on condition of paying their annual tribute to the sultan, and of permitting the pasha to exercise the authority belonging to a viceroy at the head of a competent body of troops.

The grand vizier, who was still in Egypt, ostensibly concurred in this arrangement, and reinstated Ibrahim in his former office of Sheik el Belled, or governor of Cairo; but it was, nevertheless, the intention of the court to depress the beys to such a degree that they should no longer have it in their power to disturb the tranquillity of the province. With this view the capitan pasha invited their leader with his principal officers to his camp at Aboukir. These rough soldiers, dreading no treachery, repaired into the admiral's presence, and were received with every demonstration of esteem. Pleasure and amusements were freely lavished on them; but as this complaisance had no apparent object, the guests became tired of it, expressed their suspicions to the British general, and even threatened to leave the camp without permission. That officer assured them of the friendly intentions of the pasha and of their own safety; not suspecting the frightful atrocity which the barbarian chief was actually meditating.

A short time afterward, when Lord Hutchinson was about to leave the country, Hassan again invited the beys to a sumptuous entertainment; when, at his importunate request, they consented to go on board some pleasure-boats which he had provided for the purpose. When they had proceeded to a little distance at sea, they were followed by a fast-sailing skiff, sent, as it were, with intelligence to the pasha; which he no sooner perceived than he mentioned the necessity of conversing with the messenger, apprehending that he might be the bearer of important despatches from Constantinople. The cutter came alongside, and what appeared to be ample despatches were handed to the Turk, who, on pretence of reading them more at his leisure, stepped into the small vessel, which immediately fell back. The Mamlouks, still unsuspecting the snare which was laid for them, proceeded on their course; but no sooner did they enter Aboukir Bay than they saw some large ships, filled with soldiers, and ready for action. They now perceived their danger, and their worst fears were about to be realized; for discharges of musketry and artillery hurled destruction among the boats, and killed nearly all who were on board. Those who escaped death were taken prisoners, and forced to swear on the Koran that they would not reclaim the protection of the English. Our countrymen, however, indignant at this abominable instance of Mussulman treachery, and sensible that their own faith had been pledged for the safety of the beys, addressed to the pasha a very severe remonstrance: they insisted that the prisoners should be liberated, and that the bodies of the murdered chiefs should be buried with military honours.

On the departure of Hassan, Mohammed Kusrouf, his favourite slave, was appointed pasha of Grand Cairo. A Georgian by birth, this minion of fortune showed himself equally weak and tyrannical, and seemed to confine all the energies of his government to the extermination of the hated Mamlouks. He invited them to fix their residence in the capital; and upon meeting a direct refusal, he sent a strong force against them into Upper Egypt, under the command of Taher, and the celebrated Mohammed Ali, then beginning to rise into power. All attempts at negotiation having failed, Kusrouf sent a larger army, which he intrusted to Yousef Bey, with orders to prosecute the war with the utmost vigour. A battle ensued in the neighbourhood of Damanhour, in which the Turks were miserably defeated, with the loss of five thousand men killed and wounded. The Mamlouks, being very little weakened, might have pushed their success to the gates of Cairo; but, from ignorance and dissension, they threw away the fruits of their victory, and allowed the viceroy time to rally the fugitives, and place the city in a posture of defence.

Yousef attributed his want of success to the disaffection or the cowardice of Mohammed Ali, who appears to have been second in command,—a charge which was eagerly listened to by the pasha, who had already seen reason to apprehend the ambitious projects of this remarkable person, whose character has since made so deep an impression on the history of modern Egypt. The attempt which was made to bring him to trial occasioned a revolution in the government, the effects of which have been perpetuated to the present day; but in order that the connexion of events may be more clearly traced, we must indulge in a brief retrospect of his earlier progress towards the distinction which he still occupies.

The present viceroy of Egypt is a native of Cavalla, a small town in Roumelia, a district of Albania. Losing his father in early life, he was protected by the governor of the place, who bestowed upon him that species of training which qualifies a man to rise under a despotic government, where vigilance, intrepidity, and a ready use of arms are held the most valuable accomplishments. His activity recommended him to an appointment as a subordinate collector of taxes; and in the performance of his duty it was observed that he set a higher value on the money which he was ordered to exact, than on the blood or even the lives of the unhappy peasantry over whom his jurisdiction extended. On one occasion the inhabitants of a village refused payment, resisted, threatened, and rose in rebellion. The governor was alarmed at this unusual firmness, and applied to Mohammed. The young functionary undertook to reduce them to obedience; and for this purpose he proceeded to the refractory hamlet at the head of a few men hastily equipped, announcing that he was charged with a secret mission. He entered a mosque, and sent for several of the principal inhabitants, who, not suspecting any violence, instantly obeyed his summons. No sooner were they within the walls, than he ordered them to be bound hand and foot, and immediately set off for Cavalla, regardless of the pursuing multitude, whom he overawed by threatening to put his captives to death.

This resolute step procured for him the rank of Boulouk-bashi and a rich wife, a relation of his patron, the governor. As it is not uncommon among the Turks to unite the duties of a soldier with the pursuits of a merchant, Mohammed became a dealer in tobacco,—a business which he appears to have followed with considerable success till the invasion of Egypt by the French called him to fulfil a higher destiny in a scene of active warfare. The contingent of three hundred men, raised by the township of Cavalla, was placed under the command of Ali, who was now decorated with the higher title of Bimbashi, and recognised as a captain of regular troops.

His conduct in the field of battle soon attracted the notice of the pasha, who recommended him to Kusrouf, the governor of Cairo. After the massacre of the Mamlouks at Aboukir, the young Albanian obtained the command of a division in the army of Yousef Bey, and joined the expedition against the insurgent chiefs, which terminated so fatally to the lives as well as to the reputation of the Turks. Yousef, it has been already mentioned, accused Mohammed of misconduct or disaffection so extremely palpable as to have been the main cause of their miserable defeat. Whether there was any real ground for this charge

at is impossible to determine; but at all events it was
believed by Kusrouf, who resolved forthwith to expel the
Cavalliot from the country, as a person in whom he could
no longer place confidence.

But the pasha was not aware of the character with whom
he had come into collision. The pay of the troops was considerably in arrear; and this Mohammed demanded in a
resolute tone, as the sole condition on which he would yield
obedience. The governor sent orders that he should appear
before him in the night; but the Roumelian leader, not un-
acquainted with the object of such private interviews, returned for answer that he would show himself in broad daylight in the midst of his soldiers. Perceiving the danger
with which he was threatened, Kusrouf admitted into Cairo
the Albanian guards under Taher Pasha, hoping that the
intrigues of the one chief would counteract those of the
other. But in this expectation he was grievously disappointed; for the mountaineers, in whatever points they
might differ, were unanimous in demanding their pay, and
in all the measures which were suggested for compelling
him to advance it. They attacked the palace, reduced the
citadel, drove Kusrouf and his household from the city,
and finally deposited the viceregal power in the hands of the
Pasha Taher.

The tyrannical measures of this new ruler brought his
reign to a close at the end of twenty-two days, and the actual government of the country reverted to the hands of the
Mamlouks, under the aged Ibrahim, Osman Bardissy, and
Mohammed Ali. The Porte, indeed, sent a pasha of high
rank to assume the direction of affairs at Cairo; but the
beys, having once more the upperhand, and mindful of the
cruel treachery inflicted upon them by Hassan, seized the
viceroy at Alexandria, and put him to death.

The undisputed ascendency of the Mamlouks might in the
end have proved fatal to Mohammed Ali, who did not belong
to their body. For this reason he contrived to embroil Bardissy, who has been called the Hotspur of the beys, with
some of his associates; and, finally, attacking him with his
own hand, drove him from the capital, and reinstated the
exiled pasha, whom he intended to use merely as a tool for
effecting his own purposes. The grand signior, suspecting
his ambitious views, issued orders, in the year 1804, that

the Albanians should return into their own country; intending, it may be presumed, to garrison the Egyptian fortresses with troops less disposed to insubordination. Mohammed, whose plans were gradually advancing towards completion, disregarded the mandate; intimating that his services were still necessary to repress the daring designs of the Mamlouks, who continued to occupy the greater part of the kingdom, while they breathed avowed hostility against the government of the Porte. The following year a firman arrived, conferring upon him the enviable appointment of pasha of Djidda, and of the port of Mecca on the eastern shore of the Red Sea. On this occasion he acceded so far as to assume the mantle and cap peculiar to his new office; but the army, prepared for the scene which ensued, flocked around him, uttering the most seditious language, and threatening immediate violence if their arrears were not discharged. Mohammed alone could rule the disturbed elements in this furious tempest. He was entreated to take upon him the duties of viceroy,—to save Egypt from rebellion and bloodshed,—and to preserve an important province to the Turkish empire. The wily Albanian seemed to be amazed at this proposal, and refused; but in so faint a tone, that the petitioners were induced to repeat and urge still more strongly their request. He yielded at length to entreaties which he himself had suggested, accepted the insignia of office, and was proclaimed by the shouts of his numerous adherents the new representative of the grand signior.*

Kourschid Pasha, who was now in the capital, endeavoured, by inviting the dangerous aid of the Mamlouks, to oppose this nomination. But while he was making preparations to take the field against the usurper, the capitan pasha unexpectedly cast anchor before Alexandria; who forthwith sent orders to him to place the citadel in the hands of Mohammed, and also to repair in person, without delay, to his head-quarters on the seacoast. Kourschid obeyed, and, after a short period of service in other quarters of the Turkish empire, lost his life.

The Mamlouks, who had been summoned to the standard of the governor, were unwilling to lay down their arms

* Webster's Travels, vol. ii. p. 56.

until they should have once more tried the fortune of war
against their old enemy the Albanian pasha. The latter,
who was contriving a snare for these turbulent horsemen,
wished nothing more ardently than that they should attack
him in Cairo; nay, he suggested to the sheiks, on whom
he had the greatest reliance, to encourage the beys in their
meditated assault, and even to promise them assistance
should they resolve to enter the city. The Mamlouks,
reposing implicit faith in these pretended friends, seized
the first opportunity of bursting in at one of the gates,
which had been opened for the purpose of admitting some
countrymen with their camels. Dividing their numbers
into two parties, they advanced along the streets sounding
their martial instruments, and anticipating a complete
triumph. But they soon discovered their mistake; for,
being attacked by the inhabitants on all sides, driven from
post to post, and slaughtered without mercy, they sustained
so severe a loss as from that moment to cease to be formidable. All the prisoners met the same fate; and eighty-three
heads were sent to Constantinople to grace the walls of the
imperial seraglio.

But the Sublime Porte, unwilling that any one interest
should obtain the ascendency in Egypt, determined now to
support the beys; and accordingly a capitan pasha was
despatched to Alexandria with instructions to assist Elfy,
well known by his residence in England, in his endeavours
to assume the viceregal mantle, and thereby to depress the
rising power of Mohammed. This envoy, upon his arrival,
sent a capidji bashi to Cairo, summoning Ali to appear immediately at that port, where his master was ready to bestow
upon him the government of Salonica. The Albanian
chief had too much knowledge of the policy usually pursued
in the divan to accept of such promotion. He asked those
around him whether he should not show himself a fool and
a craven if, after having won the supreme station with only
five hundred men at his disposal, he were to abandon his
post to his enemies, now that he counted at his side fifteen
hundred resolute countrymen and companions in arms.
' Cairo is to be publicly sold!" he exclaimed;—" whoever
will give most blows of the sabre will win it, and remain
master!"

His demeanour towards the pasha was, at the same time

submissive and dutiful; he regretted that the mutinous state of the army would not permit him to obey the summons of his highness, and to have the pleasure of showing how ready he was on all occasions to bow the knee before a representative of his imperial lord. At this very moment he was plotting with the beys, and sending large sums of money to Constantinople, to secure friends on both sides of the Mediterranean. At length the sultan, finding that Ali could not be deposed, and perceiving himself on the eve of a war with Russia, forwarded secret orders to the capitan. to make the best terms he could with the usurper, and to leave him in possession of the viceroyalty. A short time after this occurrence, the regular diploma confirming him in his office was transmitted by the Porte; and as Elfy Bey and Bardissy, the most powerful of his enemies, died about the same period, Mohammed found himself the master of Egypt, invested with a legal title, and opposed by no one whom he had any reason to fear. To complete his conquest, indeed, he advanced into Upper Egypt to attack the Mamlouks. There he defeated a large body of their troops, and was preparing to follow them, in the hope of effecting their utter annihilation as a political body, when he received despatches from Turkey announcing the commencement of hostilities between Great Britain and the Ottoman empire.[*]

It was in the year 1807 that the English ministry sent a second expedition into Egypt, with the view of preventing that country from falling again into the hands of the French, whose ambassador at Constantinople was understood to direct the politics of the grand signior. The number of troops under the British general did not exceed five thousand; and it was entirely owing to the ignorance of our government in regard to the amount of the Turkish forces at Alexandria, and the strength as well as the disposition of the Mamlouks, that they exposed such a handful of men, to certain destruction. The beys availed themselves of this opportunity to make their peace with Mohammed Ali, and consented to follow his standard against the invaders, who had established a footing on their coast. The melancholy result is well known. Alexandria yielded to General Fraser

[*] Webster's Travels, vol. ii. p. 67.

after a smart encounter; but, failing in his successive attempts on Rosetta and El Hamet, the flower of our little army was cut off, wounded, or taken prisoners. Four hundred and fifty of their heads were publicly exposed at Cairo, while the unfortunate captives were treated with every species of contempt and cruelty.

The departure of the British allowed the pasha to return to the internal affairs of his turbulent province. As he relied chiefly upon the army, he had increased its numbers till the expense of maintenance emptied his coffers, and compelled him, in order to replenish them, to resort to measures of extreme severity. He felt that his popularity was endangered; and being convinced that the Mamlouks would embrace the first opportunity of attempting to precipitate him from the viceregal throne, he resolved upon their final destruction at whatever expense of candour or humanity. This horrible determination, it has been conjectured, was confirmed by the necessity imposed upon him of conducting the war against the Wahabees in Arabia,—an undertaking in which he could not engage without employing in that country his best troops and commanders. The Porte had urged him to prepare for this expedition, so important to the purity of the faith and to the integrity of the empire; rewarding him, beforehand, by conferring upon his favourite son, Toussoun, the dignity of a pasha of the second order.

The same youth had been appointed by his father general of the army which was destined to serve in Arabia. The 1st day of March, 1811, was named for the investiture of the new chief,—a ceremony which was to take place in the citadel. The Mamlouks were invited to share in the parade and festivities of the occasion; and accordingly, under the command of Chahyn Bey, and arrayed in their most splendid uniform, they appeared at the hall of audience, and offered to the pasha their hearty congratulations. Mohammed received them with the greatest affability. They were presented with coffee, and he conversed with them individually with apparent openness of heart and serenity of countenance.

The procession was ordered to move from the citadel along a passage cut out in the rock; the pasha's troops marching first, followed by the Mamlouk corps mounted as usual. As soon, however, as they had passed the gate, it was shut behind them, while the opposite end of the defile, being also closed, they were caught, as it were, in a trap. Mohammed's soldiers had been ordered to the top of the rocks, where they were perfectly secure from the aim of the Mamlouks, while they poured down volleys of shot upon their defenceless victims, who were butchered almost to the last man. Some of them, indeed, succeeded in taking refuge in the pasha's harem, and in the house of Toussoun; but they were all dragged forth, conducted before the kiaya bey, and beheaded on the spot. The lifeless body of the brave Châhya was exposed to every infamy. A rope was passed round the neck, and the bloody carcass dragged through various parts of the city. Mengin, who was in Cairo at the time, assures his readers that the streets during two whole days bore the appearance of a place taken by assault. Every kind and degree of violence was committed under pretence of searching for the devoted Mamlouks; and it was not until five hundred houses were sacked, much valuable property destroyed, and many lives lost, that Ali and his son ventured out of the citadel to repress the popular fury.[*]

Mohammed noted among the slain four hundred and seventy mounted Mamlouks, besides their attendants who usually served on foot. The number of victims in the end did not fall short of a thousand; for orders were given to pursue this devoted race into the remotest parts of the country, and, if possible, to exterminate them throughout the whole pashalic. The heads of the principal officers were embalmed, and sent as an acceptable present to the sultan at Constantinople. Only one of the beys, whose name was Amim, is understood to have escaped the massacre in Cairo. Being detained by business, he was too late to occupy his proper place in the procession, and he only arrived at the citadel at the moment when the troops were passing the gate. He waited till they had entered the fatal passage, intending to join his own body; but, seeing the gate shut suddenly, and hearing, almost immediately after, the discharge of firearms, he put spurs to his horse and

---

[*] Histoire de l'Egypte sous le Gouvernement de Mohammed Ali, par M. Felix Mengin, &c. tom. 1. p 363-365.

galloped out of the city. He afterward retired with a small suite into Syria.

'It is impossible to refrain from condemning the cruel and faithless conduct of Mohammed on this memorable occasion. He may have received orders from Constantinople to annihilate those ambitious and turbulent soldiers who acknowledged no master but their own chief, and no laws except such as suited their licentious habits. But it is difficult, notwithstanding, to find an apology for the deliberate cold-hearted treachery which disgraced the execution of the imperial mandate. So little compunction, too, did he feel when reflecting on the occurrence, that we are told by Mengin, on being informed that he was reproached by all travellers in their narratives for this inhuman massacre, he replied, that he would have a picture of it painted together with one of the murder of the Duc d'Enghien, and leave to posterity what judgment it might pass on the two events. This *argumentum ad hominem* might silence a Frenchman who had followed the standard of Buonaparte, but it goes only a very little way to remove the impression of abhorrence which must be retained by every heart not altogether insensible to those eternal distinctions on which all moral judgments must be founded.*

* For a striking account of the massacre of the Mamlouks, see " Life and Adventures of Giovanni Finati," vol. i. p. 101, &c. He varies in a few particulars from the narrative of Mengin, although in the essential points there is no material difference. The beys, he tells us, were not assembled to grace the reception of the Pelisse by the young pasha, but to consult with the viceroy about the approaching war with the Arabian schismatics; and Mengin himself related that Toussoun was not invested with the ensigns of his office till more than a mouth afterward. The chief, too, called Chahyn by the latter author, is by Finati denominated Salm,—an example of the discrepancy which arises from the practice adopted by travellers in Egypt of spelling according to the pronunciation of their respective countries.

It is remarkable that the Frenchman should have omitted an anecdote of Amin Bey, which made a great noise at the time, and was repeated to Mr. W. Banks by that officer himself when he met him at a subsequent period in Syria. "This chief, who was brother to the celebrated Elfy, urged the noble animal which he rode to an act of greater desperation, for he spurred him till he made him clamber upon the rampart, and preferring rather to be dashed to pieces than to be slaughtered in cold blood, drove him to leap down the precipice, a height that has been estimated at from thirty to forty feet, or even more; yet fortune so favoured him, that, though the horse was killed, the rider escaped."—Finati, 110.

Sir F. Henniker says of him, "His horse leaped over the parapet, like leaping out of a four pair of stairs window. The horse was killed.

Mohammed Ali was now at liberty to devote his attention to the state of things in Arabia, whither his son Toussoun Pasha, had been sent to command the army. His campaign had already been crowned with several successes against the Wahabees; he had taken the city of Medina, the keys of which his father had sent to the Porte, with large presents of money, jewels, coffee, and other valuable articles. The viceroy himself now thought it time to pay his devotions at the shrine of Mecca, and accordingly made a voyage across the Red Sea. At Djidda he was received with all kindness and hospitality by the Shereef Ghaleb; in return for which, to gratify either his avarice or his political suspicion, he gave secret orders to Toussoun to seize and convey him to Cairo. Meanwhile he plundered the palace of immense treasures, part of which he applied to the support of the army, and part he shared with his master, the sultan; but the latter, on understanding the manner in which they had been obtained, had honesty enough to return them to their owner through Mohammed.

The various occurrences of the Arabian war are not of sufficient interest to the general reader to warrant a minute detail. Suffice it to observe, that under the direction of Toussoun the Egyptian army suffered considerable reverses, and was not a little reduced both in number and in spirit when Mohammed Ali himself assumed the command. His presence in the camp immediately restored discipline and confidence to such a degree that the troops longed for an opportunity to revenge their losses in the field, and, if possible, to bring the contest to the issue of a general action. Their wishes in this respect were soon gratified; for the enemy, who had begun to despise the invaders, and even to pour upon them the most insolent and opprobrious language, were easily induced to relinquish their position where they could not have been attacked, and to meet the viceroy on equal ground, where he could hardly fail to secure a decisive victory. The battle of Basille terminated the campaign of 1815, and opened up to the conqueror a flattering view of ultimate success. But disease found its way into his ranks; the Albanians were fatigued and disgusted with a war of posts

The bey intrusted himself to some Arabs (Albanians according to Finati), who, notwithstanding the offer of a large reward, would not deliver him up." P. 64.

X

against barbarians still more savage than themselves; and they did not conceal from the pasha that they expected to be relieved, and allowed to seek for health on the banks of the Nile. This chief knew his countrymen too well to resist their inclinations in a matter so closely connected with their feelings, he acknowledged the justice of their claim; assured them that he also meant to return to Cairo; and proceeded instantly to make arrangements for carrying his plan into execution.

The military experience which Mohammed had acquired when opposed to European armies convinced him of the necessity of improving the tactics of his Turks and Arabs. For this purpose he employed several French soldiers, who deserted during the expedition under Buonaparte, to introduce the new system; and immediately a regular course of drilling was begun, and enforced, too, with a strictness and severity that only tended to exasperate the feelings, and to ripen projects of resistance and revenge. From the very first the native troops regarded this discipline with the utmost jealousy and aversion, as a direct invasion of the rights and liberties of their profession. Their resentment soon found vent against the subaltern officers, whom they assassinated in the streets, and even on parade. This, however, far from deterring the government, only led to higher degrees of constraint and compulsion, till at length the odium which had ceased to attach itself to the mere instruments of the experiment, extended to the highest authorities, and even to the ruler himself. If we *must* have the French discipline, said the discontented, let us carry the French system a little farther, and let us have our revolution too. Accordingly, upon a day previously fixed,—the 4th August, 1815,—all the troops in the neighbourhood of Cairo broke out into open mutiny and revolt, with the professed purpose of plundering the city, and putting Mohammed Ali to death. After falling upon such of the officers as had escaped the violence directed against them individually, they marched towards the citadel in a formidable body; and, had not the pillage of the bazaars attracted their attention in the first instance, the chiefs of the government, who were quite unprepared for the attack, could hardly have found safety.

The pasha fortunately was not in the citadel, but in one

of his palaces which stands in a large open square, near
the European division of the capital. More mindful of the
Franks than of his own welfare, he sent to them, upon the
breaking out of the disturbance, five hundred muskets, with
ammunition sufficient to serve the purpose of their defence.
Meanwhile, it being taken for granted that he was in the
fortress, no search was made for him elsewhere; though he
had to endure many bitter hours of suspense, galled as he
must have been by the ingratitude of his army, and liable
every moment to be dragged forth to destruction. He was
at length extricated from his perilous situation by the fidelity
and courage of Abdim Bey, an Albanian, brother to Hassan Pasha, whom he had left in the command of the Arabian
army. This officer had a particular attachment to his
person; and having drawn together about three hundred oɪ
his own nation who had continued loyal, went to the palace
where he was concealed, placed him under this faithful
escort, and forced a passage to the citadel, where he was
lodged in perfect security.

This took place late in the evening of that day of confusion and terror; and when it was discovered that the pasha
had been so long within their reach, disappointment exas-
perated the soldiers to fresh excesses, and a renewal of the
pillage. Before morning Mohammed had proclaimed a
general amnesty, on condition that the troops would return
to their duty, pledging himself, at the same time, that the
obnoxious system should be discontinued, and promising to
the merchants and inhabitants who had been pillaged a full
indemnity for their losses. This declaration produced the
desired effect, and Cairo was immediately restored to a
state of tranquillity and peace; while the great number of
individuals who were implicated in the guilt of disaffection,
rendered it prudent in his highness to adhere strictly to the
terms of the pardon which he had announced.

It could hardly be doubted that in a rising of this nature,
where there was evidently so much of concert and of
secrecy, there must have been some prime mover, possessing weight and influence among the soldiers; and hence no
pains were spared by the government in order to obtain information. Giovanni Finati, who was himself an actor in
the scene which he describes, asserts that no clew was ever
obtained which could lead to a discovery of the principal

insurgents. But Belzoni, who was in Egypt at the same period, remarks that there was reason to think the pasha knew who the chief instigators were, for it was found that several persons shortly after "died of sudden deaths; and indeed many of the chiefs and beys disappeared."*

No attempt appears to have been made for some time after the failure now described to introduce the European discipline. In the year 1821, when Sir F. Henniker was at Grand Cairo, the old system prevailed, and is amusingly exposed in the following description :—" Saw the infantry (Albanians) mustered. An attempt to drill these lawless ragamuffins occasioned the last insurrection,—no marching and countermarching,—no playing at soldiers. They, however, suffer themselves to be drawn up in line to listen to the music,—if such it may be called when produced by drums and squeaking Moorish fifes in the hands of Turks; a number of voices frequently chimed in, and destroyed the monotony; during this the soldiers were quiet. It is nearly impossible to distinguish officers from privates; every man provides himself with clothes and arms according to his means; there is only this family likeness among them,—that pistols, swords, and a shirt, outwardly exhibited, are necessary. An Albanian is not improved since the time of Alexander; he is still a soldier and a robber. Ibrahim Pasha having, as he says, conquered the Waha-bees, made his triumphal entry this morning; first came the cavalry,—horses of all sizes, ages, colours, and quali-ties; an Arab Fellah attendant upon each soldier carried a musket; every soldier carried—a pipe; occasionally the prelude of a kettle-drum, hammered monotonously with a short leathern strap, announced a person of consequence: the consequence consisted in eight or nine dirty Arabs, carrying long sticks, and screaming tumultuously; then came the infantry, a long straggling line of Albanians; then a flag; then a long pole, surmounted by a gilt ball,— from this suspended a flowing tail of horsehair; then a second flag, a second tail, a third flag, and the pasha's third tail; the victor covered with a *white satin* gown, and a high conical cap of the same military material; this Cæsar

* Life and Adventures of Giovanni Finati, vol. ii. p. 71; Belzoni's Narrative, vol. ii. p. 9.

looked like a sick girl coming from the bath. The mobility closed this Hudibrastic triumph. Having traversed the town, they vented their exultation in gunpowder. The Turkish soldiers, whether in fun or earnest, always fire with ball; and on a day of rejoicing it commonly happens that several are killed; these *accidents* fall in general on the Franks."*

In relating the triumph of Ibrahim, we have somewhat anticipated the course of events. His brother Toussoun had some time before fallen the victim of poison or disease, whence arose the necessity of appointing a new commander of equal rank to carry on that war, already waged so long and with so little success against the heretics of Derayeh. More than a century had passed since Abdul Wahab, the Socinus of the Mohammedans, disturbed the belief of the faithful by certain innovations in their doctrine respecting the character and offices of the prophet. The austerity of his life drew around him a great number of followers, and at length, finding himself sufficiently strong to brave the power of the provincial governors, he attacked without any reserve the rank idolatry of the wonted pilgrimages to the tomb of Mohammed, and the absurdity of putting any trust in relics, ablutions, or any outward ceremonies. He inculcated the principles of pure deism, and reduced the whole duty of man, as a religious being, to prayer and good works.

Had he confined the objects of his mission to articles of faith or new modes of piety, it is not probable that the Ottoman Porte would have disturbed him in the exercise of his vocation. But as he found the use of arms necessary to convince hardened skeptics, as well as to destroy the monuments of their idolatry, he permitted the zeal of his followers to display itself in military ardour, and in the formation of disciplined bands. On one occasion his success advanced into Persia at the head of 20,000 men, resolving to capture the city of Kirbeleh, and to lay waste the tomb of Hassan, the son of Ali and grandson of the prophet. The spirit of persecution breathed in all his actions; the inhabitants were put to the sword; and the

* Notes during a Visit, &c. By Sir Frederick Henniker, p. 66.
X 2

sepulchre—a favourite place of pilgrimage among the Persians,—was plundered and desecrated.

In short, a dynasty of these fanatical warriors had established itself on the throne of Derayeh. In the beginning of the present century Abdelazeoz, the son of Abdul, was murdered by a native of Kirbeleh, to revenge the indignities committed upon the holy tomb,—an event which was followed by a renewal of hostility and the shedding of much blood. His successor, Sehood, began his career of retaliation by directing the power of his arms against Bassora and Irak. The Shereef of Mecca, who took the field in order to check his progress, was defeated in every battle and compelled to sue for peace. But no sooner were terms concluded than the Wahabite, at the head of 40,000 men, marched to Medina, which was obliged to open its gates; when, following up his success, he proceeded to Mecca, where he met with as little opposition. Here he ordered the tomb of the prophet to be opened, whence he abstracted the numerous jewels, consisting of diamonds, pearls, rubies, and emeralds, which had been long venerated by the pious disciples of the Koran. He melted the golden vessels, the chandeliers, and vases; and having exposed the whole to public sale, he distributed the money among his soldiers. This act of daring sacrilege excited against Sehood the indignation of every Mussulman who had not thrown off all reverence for the founder of his religion; while his military resources, employed with so much vigour, did not fail to alarm the government at Constantinople, who immediately sent orders to Mohammed Ali to chastise the presumptuous heretic and deliver the holy city from his arms.

But the success which finally attended the expedition of the Egyptian pasha was owing to the death of Sehood rather than to the bravery or skill of the Turkish generals. The Wahabite chief was succeeded by his son Abdallah, who possessed neither talent nor courage equal to the arduous duties which he was called upon to discharge. After a vain attempt at negotiation he allowed himself to be besieged in his capital, which, after a feeble defence during three months, he was obliged to surrender together with his own personal liberty. He was sent to Constanti-

nople, where he was first exposed to the execration and
contempt of the populace, and then deprived of his head
like a common malefactor. Ibrahim is remembered as the
scourge of Arabia and the curse of Derayeh. His father,
in a moment of passion against the Wahabees, had threatened to destroy their city so that one stone of it should not
be left upon another,—a menace which was executed to the
fullest extent. The inhabitants who escaped the sword
were chased into the desert, where many of them must have
perished; meantime the pasha returned in triumph to
Cairo in the manner described by Sir F. Henniker.

But the severity of Ibrahim did not put an end to the
Wahabite reformation, nor to the spirit of resistance by
which its abetters were animated. On the contrary, the
war was renewed in 1824 with as much ferocity as ever,
and apparently with increased means on the part of the insurgents of bringing it to a successful issue. It was protracted during the three following years with alternate
advantage; having been, during the latter portion of that
interval, allowed to slumber, owing to the struggle made by
the Greeks in the Morea to recover their liberty. The particulars of the several campaigns are given with considerable minuteness by Planat, who held an office under the
viceroy of Egypt, and who took upon himself to write the
history of the "Regeneration" which that remarkable personage has effected in the kingdom of the Pharaohs.
Suffice it to observe that it was in a succession of battles
with the Wahabees that Mohammed Ali first derived
advantage from his improved system of tactics. His infantry, disciplined by French officers and instructed in the
European method of moving large masses in the field,
proved decidedly superior in every conflict where the nature
of the ground permitted a military evolution.[*]

It may be inferred from the statement just made that the
viceroy was not deterred by the tumult at Cairo from
resuming at a proper time the plan he had already matured
for introducing into his army the drill of modern Europe.
Aware of the obstinacy which characterizes the Albanians,

* Histoire de la Régénération de l'Egypte, &c. Par Jules Planat,
ancien Officier de l'Artillerie de la Garde Imperiale, et chef d'Etat-major
au service du Pacha d'Egypte. Genève, 1830, p. 239.

he left them to be shamed out of their awkward and inef-
ficient system by witnessing the improvement of the other
troops; resolving to put his experiment to the test on the
Fellahs of Egypt, and on the still more unsophisticated
natives of Sennaar and Kordofan.   With this view, as well
as to reduce the remoter provinces of the upper country to
his obedience, he fitted out, in 1820, an expedition which
he placed under the command of his son Ishmael, whom he
charged with instructions for accomplishing the double purpose now stated.   The success of the young general fulfilled
the expectations of Mohammed Ali.   Thousands of captives
were sent from the conquered districts to the neighbourhood
of Es Souan, where they were formed into battalions, and
subjected to all the restraint and fatigue of European discipline.

We are told that these unhappy beings were in the first
place vaccinated; and that, as soon as they recovered from
this factitious distemper, they were put into the hands of
French officers to be instructed in the manual exercise and
other military arts, according to the latest institutions of the
Buonapartean school.   The hopes of the pasha were at first
greatly disappointed in these black troops.   They were indeed strong and able-bodied, and not averse from being
taught; but when attacked by disease, which soon broke
out in the camp, they died like sheep infected with the rot.
The medical men ascribed the mortality to moral rather
than to physical causes.   It appeared in numerous instances, that having been snatched away from their houses
and families, they were even anxious to get rid of life; and
so numerous were the deaths which ensued, that out of
20,000 of these unfortunate persons, three thousand did
not remain alive at the end of two years.

But nothing could shake the determination of the viceroy.
He placed five hundred faithful Mamlouks under the charge
of Colonel Sève, formerly aid-de-camp to Marshal Ney,
who were trained to fulfil the duties of officers.   As the
blacks, for the reasons already mentioned, were found unfit
for this laborious service, he impressed, according to the
rules of a national conscription, about thirty thousand
Arabs and peasants, whom he sent under a military guard
to Upper Egypt.   Planat informs us, that in 1827 twelve
regiments were organized, tolerably well clothed in a plain

uniform, and armed after the manner of European soldiers ; and as it is intended that every regiment shall consist of five battalions of eight hundred men, the military establishment, in infantry alone, will amount to about fifty thousand. There are, besides, several corps of cavalry, artillery, and even marines ; which last are stationed at Alexandria, to serve on board the ships of war whenever it may be necessary to meet an enemy at sea.

The colonels of regiments are extremely well paid, having allowances which amount to not less than 1500l. a-year. Their dress, too, is very rich, consisting of red cloth, covered with gold lace, and a cluster of diamonds, in the form of a half-moon, on each breast.. Over this they wear, on state occasions, a scarlet pelisse, which fastens over the body with two large clasps of gold set with emeralds. Their upper dress is closed with a sash ; and the Turkish full trousers have given way to a more convenient habiliment, which is tied under the knee, and fitted to the legs like gaiters. The pay of the non-commissioned officers is likewise ample ; and that of the men eighteen piasters a month, with full rations of good provisions, and their clothing. They are now content, and even attached to the service ; while a considerable spirit of emulation prevails among them, excited in a great measure by the impartial manner in which promotion from the ranks is bestowed, according to the merit of the candidates. It is worthy of notice, too, that the men are no longer liable to arbitrary punishment. Every one committing a fault must be tried before he can be bastinadoed, and generally some other penalty is inflicted, such as confinement, degradation, or hard labour. The officers, again, when they forget their duty or their character, are placed under arrest ; and even the viceroy himself does not pretend to decide as to their guilt, but leaves the result to the award of justice, regulated by martial law.

The superiority of troops prepared for the field according to the European method was, as we have already stated, most distinctly manifested in the several campaigns which they served against the Wahabees,—a circumstance which afforded to the viceroy a degree of delight almost beyond expression. This first step in the improvement of an art, valuable above all others to a governor placed in the circumstances which he occupied, was due almost entirely to Colonel Sève, whose name has been already mentioned. This able officer encountered much opposition from the barbarians whom he was appointed to superintend; but, with the tact which belongs to a man who has inspected society in all its forms, he subdued the ferocity of the savage by assuming a tone more commanding than that of mere animal courage. The Mamlouks were occasionally so discontented as to threaten his life; but he never lost his firmness; and, by offering to meet single-handed those who conspired against his authority, he gained the respect which is always lavished by untutored minds upon fearless hardihood, and at length became a favourite among all classes of the military. Planat tells us, that on one occasion, when a volley was fired, a ball whizzed past the ear of Sève. Without the slightest emotion, he commanded the party to reload their pieces. "You are very bad marksmen," he exclaimed;—"Make ready,—fire!" They fired, but no ball was heard; the self-possession of the Frenchman disarmed their resentment; they thought him worthy of admiration; and at length were ready to acknowledge that in point of acquirement and professional experience he was decidedly a better man than themselves.[*] He afterward fell while serving in Greece.

Great merit was unquestionably due to this officer for the reformation which he had effected in the viceroy's army; but beyond this we cannot speak of him without the strongest expressions of contempt and detestation, it being universally known that he had adopted the religion of Mohammed,—soothing and cloaking his degradation with the name of Suliman Bey, and under the title of Mir allai, or commander of four thousand. He received his pelisse and his advancement on the morning of Christmasday,—as if he had expressly intended to insult the faith which he had just renounced,—a sacrifice on his part which, however trifling it might appear, would not exalt him in the eyes of his new sovereign, who has never required any of his Christian servants to change their creed.

The invasion of the upper provinces by the army under the command of Ishmael, belongs to the history of Nubia

[*] Histoire de la Régénération, p. 58.

rather than to that of Egypt ; for which reason we shall not enter into its details at present farther than to state, that owing to an insult inflicted upon one of the native chiefs, this favourite son of Mohammed Ali was cut off ·by a most miserable death. The cottage in which he and his personal attendants had taken up . their quarters was surrounded with · a mass of combustible materials, and burnt to the ground ; no one escaping through the flames except the physician, who was reserved for more protracted suffering. Ibrahim, the conqueror of Derayeh, avenged in some degree the murder of. his brother, and even extended the ·dominion of the Egyptian arms into districts which neither the Persians nor the Romans ·had .ventured to penetrate. But the affairs of Greece, which began to occupy the full attention of the Porte, supplied a new theatre for the military talent of .his lieutenant, who, at the command of his father, withdrew, his troops from the deserts of Dongola and Kordofan to transport them to the more sanguinary fields of the Morea. .

As it belongs not to this narrative to record even incidentally the events of the war to which we have just referred, we shall conclude this chapter with a brief outline of the character of that remarkable person who at present fills the viceregal throne of Egypt, and whose genius seems destined to accomplish a greater change on the condition. of that country than has been effected by conquest or revolution since the days of Alexander the Great.

Perhaps the actions of this ruler are the best expression of his views and feelings, and might alone be appealed to as a proof of ·an elevated and aspiring mind, still clouded indeed with some of the darkest shades of his original barbarism, and not unfrequently impelled by the force of passions which are never allowed to disturb the tranquillity of civilized life. He is now about sixty years of age, rather short in stature, with a high forehead and aquiline nose, and altogether possessing an expression of ·countenance which shows him to be no ordinary man. His dress is usually very plain ; the only expense which he allows himself in matters connected with his person being lavished upon his arms, some of which are studded with diamonds. Like Buonaparte, his outward appearance seems to have changed considerably with the progress of his years ; for although, when between thirty and forty, he was described by a British traveller as "of a slender make, sallow complexion, and under the middle size," he is reported by the latest visiters to have become "thick-set," and somewhat full in the figure.

" On our arrival being announced," says an author whom we have already quoted, " we were immediately ushered into his presence, and found him sitting on the corner of the divan, surrounded by his officers and men, who were standing at a respectful distance. He received us sitting, but in the most gracious manner, and placed the Earl of Belmore and Mr. Salt upon his left-hand, and his lordship's two sons and myself at the top of the room on his right. The interpreter stood, as well as the officers and soldiers, who remained in the room during the whole time of the visit. He began the conversation by welcoming us to Cairo, and prayed that God might preserve us, and grant us prosperity. He then inquired of the noble traveller how long he had been from England, and what was the object of his journey to Egypt; to all which he received satisfactory answers. His highness next adverted to the prospect before him, the Nile, the grain-covered fields, the Pyramids of Djizeh, the bright sun, and the cloudless sky, and remarked, with a certain triumphant humour on his lip, that England offered no such prospect to the eye of the spectator."

He was told that the scenery of England was very fine. " How can that be, he shortly rejoined, seeing you are steeped in rain and fog three quarters of the year.—He next turned the conversation to Mr. Leslie's elegant experiment of freezing water in the vacuum of an air-pump; which he had never seen but admired prodigiously in description, and seemed to anticipate with great satisfaction a glass of lemonade and iced water for himself and friends, as the happiest result of the discovery. Talking of his lordship's intended voyage up the Nile, he politely offered to render every possible facility; cautioning him at the same time to keep a sharp lookout among the Arabs, who, he believed, would not take any thing from him or his party by violence, but would certainly steal if they found an opportunity of doing it without the risk of detection. He then related a number of anecdotes, touching the petty larcenies of that most thievish race some of which were by no means without contrivance or dexterity. But the one which seemed to amuse both himself and his friends the most was that of a traveller, who, when eating his dinner, laid down his spoon to reach for a piece of bread, and by the time he brought back his hand the spoon was away; the knife and fork soon shared the same fate; and the unfortunate stranger was at length reduced to the sad necessity of tearing his meat, and lifting it with his fingers and thumb, like the Arabs themselves. Many persons were near, but no one saw the theft committed; and all search for the recovery of the property was in vain.—We now took leave of the viceroy, leaving him in the greatest good-humour; he said we might go every where, and see every thing we wished, and that he hoped to have the pleasure of seeing us again."*

In reference to the freezing experiment, we may mention that Mohammed Ali, very soon after the visit now described, obtained from England, through Mr. Salt, the requisite apparatus. The machine on its arrival was conveyed to his palace, and some Nile water was procured for the purpose. He hung over the whole operation with intense curiosity; and when, after several disappointments, a piece of real ice was produced, he took it eagerly in his hand, and danced round the room for joy like a child, and then ran into the harem to show it to his wives.†

No one has attempted to conceal that there is in the temper of Mohammed Ali, intermingled with many good qualities, a deep tincture of barbarism and fierceness. Impatient of opposition, and even of delay, he occasionally gives himself up to the most violent bursts of passion; and in such moments there is hardly any cruelty which he will not perpetrate or command. For instance, some time ago he had ordered that the dollar should pass for a fixed number of piastres, and it was mentioned in his presence that the rate was not strictly followed. His Highness expressed some doubt of the fact, when the head interpreter carelessly observed that a Jew broker, whom he named, had a few days before exchanged dollars for him at the rate asserted.—" Let him be hanged immediately," exclaimed the pasha! The

* Richardson's Travels, vol. i. p. 101.
† Carne's Letters from the East, vol. i. p. 88.

Y

interpreter, an old and favourite servant, threw himself at his sovereign's feet, deprecating his own folly, and imploring pardon for the wretched culprit. But all intercession was in vain; the viceroy said his orders must not be disregarded, and the unfortunate Jew was instantly led to his death.[*]

We find proofs of a similar sally at Djidda, where he appears to have used his own hands to inflict a punishment which he thought inexpedient to remit. Hoseyn Aga, the agent for the East India Company, resident in that town, was, says a recent traveller, a remarkably fine-looking man, displaying an air of dignity mixed with hauteur; handsomely clad, too, though the heavy folds of his muslin turban were studiously drawn over his right eye to conceal the loss of it,—for Mohammed Ali one day in a fit of rage pulled it out! Yet these men are friends,—great friends just at present, and will remain so as long as it may be convenient and agreeable to both parties to consider each other in that light.[†]

But the master of Egypt is not at all times so ferocious. For example, when Mrs. Lushington was at Alexandria, intelligence was brought to him that a small fort at the entrance of the harbour had been taken possession of by certain Franks, and that the Turks belonging to it had been made prisoners. Some consternation prevailed among his people; but instead of being angry he laughed heartily, and swearing by his two eyes,—his favourite oath,—that they must be English sailors, he directed his interpreter to write to their captain, to order his men on board ship again. Upon inquiry it proved as the pasha had anticipated; the men had landed, got drunk, and crowned their liberty by seizing on the fort, and confining the unfortunate Turks, who, indolently smoking their pipes, never could have anticipated such an attack in time of profound peace. He evinced equal self-command, and still more magnanimity, when he first heard of the event which destroyed his infant navy and humbled his power. We allude to the battle of Navarino. He had not finished the perusal of the unwel come despatches, when he desired a European consul to assure his countrymen and all the other Franks that they

* Narrative of a Journey from Calcutta to Europe, p 179.
† Journey Overland, vol. i. p. 306.

should not be molested, and that they might pursue their wonted occupations in perfect security.

Among the ships lying in the harbour was the wreck of one of the pasha's own vessels. The captain had committed some crime which was represented by his crew to the viceroy, who ordered him immediately on shore to answer his accusers. Knowing his guilt he pretended sickness, till a second message from the same quarter left him no alternative; and unable longer to evade his fate, he sent all his crew ashore, and calling to an old and faithful servant, the only person on board, he bade him jump out of the port into the sea; at the same time, having loaded two pistols, he fired into the magazine, and blew up the ship and himself together. When the story was related to the pasha, he said, "These are Frank customs; this is dying like an Englishman!"*

There is something characteristic in the following notice by Sir F. Henniker, who remarks, that the pasha appeared to him to have a vulgar, low-born face, but a commanding, intelligent eye. "He received us in the court-yard, seated on a sofa, and wielding a pipe, dressed like a private individual, as Turks of real consequence generally are, excepting on gala days. The vice-consul and myself sat down on the sofa with him. Pipes are not offered except to equals; coffee served up,—no sugar, even though the pasha himself has a manufactory of that article,—the attendants ordered to withdraw; no pride, no affectation, even though the pasha is an upstart. Remained nearly an hour discoursing on English horses, military force, the emerald mines at Cosseir, his son's victory over the Wahabees, and his expected triumphal entry."†

It is generally stated, that since Mohammed Ali has felt himself secure in the pashalic he has ceased to be cruel. Seldom now does he take away life, and never with torture; and if his subordinate officers were as well disposed as himself, the people, notwithstanding the oppressive taxes, would feel their property more secure. One instance of his prompt justice excited much astonishment; although a slower and more regular method would not, it is probable, in a nation so completely disorganized, have produced an equal effect. A cachief who had not been long accustomed to the government of the viceroy punished one of his own servants with death. He was called before Mohammed, who asked him by what authority he had committed this outrage. He thought it enough to urge in his defence that the man was his own servant. True, retorted the pasha, but he was my subject; and, in the same breath, passed sentence that the culprit should be immediately beheaded,—an effectual warning to the rest of the grandees present. This act of severity has saved the lives of many of the Arabs, who, in former times, were sacrificed by their Turkish masters on the most trifling pretences.

In short, Mohammed is well spoken of by most European travellers, though in general they estimate his character by too high a standard,—the principles and habits of their own countries. There is only one author whose impression was rather unfavourable :—"I sat in the divan," says he, "with my eyes fixed on him; I wanted to examine the countenance of a man who had realized in our day one of those scenes in history which, when we have perused it, always compels us to lay down the book and recover ourselves. There he sat,—a quick eye, features common, nose bad, a grizzled beard, looking much more than fifty, and having the worn complexion of that period of life. They tell you he is not sanguinary; men grow tired of shedding blood as well as of other pleasures; but if the cutting off a head would drop gold into his coffers, he would not be slow to give the signal. His laugh has nothing in it of nature; how can it have? I hear it now,—a hard, sharp laugh, such as that with which strong heartless men would divide booty torn from the feeble. I leave him to his admirers."*

"In the usages of the table," says Mr. Carne, "he is still an Osmanli; knives, forks, and other useful appendages never make their appearance at his meals. About five years ago some English travellers were graciously received by him, and pressingly invited to dine. But not even in compliance with the taste of his guests would he depart from his own habits; for, wishing to show a noble lady particular attention, he took a large piece of meat in

* Scenes and Impressions, p. 176.

his hand, and politely placed it before her. Perfectly dismayed at the compliment, and the sight of the savoury morsel which rested on her plate, she turned to her companion, who was more used to oriental manners, and earnestly asked what she was to do. 'Eat it to be sure, was the reply. She looked at the pasha; his fine dark eye seemed to rest on her with a most kind and complacent expression; and there was no help for it but to follow the excellent advice given her by her more experienced friend."*

That Mohammed Ali is a despot, and even in some respects a barbarian, cannot be denied; but there is, notwithstanding, in all his institutions so much of wisdom and patriotism that he unquestionably deserves to occupy a high place among those adventurers who have so well profited by revolutions as to place themselves on a throne. His ambition, though dishonoured by the means which he has occasionally found it necessary to adopt, is, upon the whole, of the right kind, and has all along been directed to the promotion of the national welfare rather than to his own personal aggrandizement. If he has died his hands in blood, it has been in that of the worst enemies of Egypt; and if he has in numerous cases had recourse to arbitrary government, his object, it must be acknowledged, has ever been the security and improvement of the distracted country over which it has been his lot to preside.

* Recollections of the East, p. 268.

Y 3

CHAPTER VIII.

The Actual State of Egypt under the Government of Mohammed Ali.

Nature of Innovations—Members of Government—Household—Tenure
o Land—Resumption of it by the Pasha—Condition of the People—
Army—Military Schools—European Arts—Canal of Mahmoudieh—
Introduction of Cotton Manufactures—Exportation of the raw Material
to England—Fear of Plague—Silk, Flax, Sugar—Monopoly of Vice-
roy—Disadvantages of it—Caravans—Imports and Exports—Revenue
and Expenditure—Population—Copts, Arabs, Turks, Greeks, Jews, and
Syrians—Characteristics—Cairo—Houses—Citadel—Joseph's Well,
Joseph's Hall—Necropolis—Tombs—Mosques—Palace at Shoubra—
Splendid Pavilion—Comparison of Egypt before and under the
Government of Mohammed Ali—Future Prospects under his Suc-
cessor.

In a country where the administration of law depends
almost entirely upon the character of an individual, and
where at the same time the nomination to the supreme
authority is usually determined by intrigue or in the field
of battle, the mere form of government cannot be of very
much consequence. But the sagacity of the present ruler
of Egypt, who is aware of the influence exerted on the
minds of men by custom and the use of certain modes of
speech, has dictated to him the expediency of innovating
less in the outward structure of the constitution than in
those internal parts whence all real power is derived, and
by means of which it is diffused to the remotest extremity
of the vast province of which he has assumed the command.
Although virtually independent, he has hitherto continued
a formal acknowledgment of that superiority which belongs
to the head of the Ottoman empire; and while he wields
the sceptre with as little restriction as the most arbitrary
of oriental despots, he carefully preserves the appearance
of only sharing with others the portion of a delegated
authority.

The administration is in the hands of the following officers:—1st, The Kiaya Bey, who may be called the prime

minister; 2d, The Aga of the Janizaries, or chief of the war department; 3d, The Ouali, or head of the military police; 4th, The Mohtesib, or superintendent of the markets; and, 5th, The Bash-aga, or master of the civil police. In every district there is also a headsman, who is authorized to determine differences by arbitration, and watch over the peace and good order of his neighbourhood. All fees have been abolished, and competent salaries are appointed; and so effectually are these duties performed that the streets of Cairo are as safe as those of London, except on occasions, now almost never known, when the military break loose for want of pay, or to revenge themselves for some professional grievance. All criminal prosecutions are settled by a cadi or judge, who is sent annually from Constantinople, and assisted by a number of sheiks, or others learned in the law. A civil process is stated to cost four per cent. of the value in dispute; of which the cadi takes four-fifths to himself, and gives one-fifth to the lawyers who have aided him in the decision.

Besides the public officers now mentioned, there are others attached to the household of the viceroy, such as the treasurer, the sword-bearer, the inspector of provisions, the commandant of the citadel, and the superintendent of customs and excise, who in Egypt act under the immediate direction of the head of the government. There is also a body-guard, consisting of four hundred Mamlouks, to which may be added six hundred gentlemen of the privy chamber, as they are called, or yeomen of the palace. Including all the subordinate functionaries in the civil and military departments, the domestic establishment of the pasha comprehends not fewer than fifteen hundred individuals.

So numerous and rapid are the changes to which Egypt has been subjected under a succession of dynasties, and even of foreign conquerors, that it is extremely difficult to ascertain on what tenure the land was held, in the early ages of the monarchy, by the persons who devoted their labour and capital to its cultivation. We know that the Pharaoh who reigned in the days of Joseph transferred to the crown a large portion of it, by supplying to the famished peasantry a quantity of corn in return for their fields; and hence we may infer, that, prior to the date at which this transaction took place, a distinct property in the soil was recognised by the Egyptian sovereigns. But during the long interval which has elapsed since the Macedonian conquest, it is probable that the territorial domain was occupied upon conditions similar to those which were implied in the ancient system of fiefs at one time universal throughout Europe,—a certain portion of the annual produce being made payable to him whose sword, or whose influence with the monarch, had procured to him the feudal superiority.

Before the accession of Mohammed Ali, the representative of the sultan was satisfied with a *miri*, or land-tax, according to the quality and other advantages of the soil, and had even acknowledged in some of the occupants a right almost equivalent to that of a permanent owner. The present viceroy, however, has taken into his own hands the greater part of the territorial possessions; granting, in name of compensation, a yearly pension for life to the several moultezims, or proprietors, whom he has thus deprived, but leaving to them nothing which they can bequeath to their children or heirs. The lands which Mohammed has seized in the way now described belonged, generally speaking, to the Mamlouks, whom except in their capacity of soldiers he wishes to extirpate; 2dly, To certain establishments for feeding the poor, or for supporting mosques, fountains, public schools, and other national charities; and, finally, to the ancient class of feuars in whose management or principles he could not be induced to repose a sufficient degree of confidence. But it is added, that even the owners of those lands which have not yet been seized are not masters of their crops; they cannot dispose of any part of them until the agents of government have taken what portion they may think proper at their own price; and, in place of the established *miri*, all the families attached to the court are served with agricultural produce at half its value, while the pasha regulates the price of all that can be spared for exportation. Such a system will fully explain the observation of M. Mengin, that "the traveller sees with astonishment the richness of the harvests contrasted with the wretched state of the villages;" and that, "if it be true that there is no country more abundant in its territorial preductions, there is none perhaps whose inhabitants upon the whole are more miserable."*

As to the agricultural labourers, or Fellahs, the innovations of the pasha have probably left them in nearly the same state in which, as far as history goes, they appear always to have been, with the additional disadvantage, if such it must be esteemed, of submitting to the military conscription. But perhaps, although in appearance the most tyrannical measure that Mohammed has enforced in the progress of his regeneration, the establishment of a regular army is not an evil of an unmixed nature. Heretofore the sword has been exclusively in the hands of foreigners, originally slaves of the most degraded caste, and afterward the most haughty and insatiable of masters; while at present the natives are taught the use of arms; are permitted to rise in the service according to a scale of merit; and are, in short, put in possession of means whereby they may protect their own rights against the avarice of the Turks and the insolence of the Mamlouks.

We have already stated, on the authority of the latest work which has been published on Egypt, that the pasha has formed twelve regiments of infantry, consisting each of five battalions, and including, when on the war establishment, forty-eight thousand men.† We presume that he has hitherto satisfied himself with little more than half that number of foot-soldiers,—a large proportion of whom are drawn from the Arab population, and even from the conquered districts of Sennaar and Kordofan. Planat, who held a high office in the viceroy's staff, speaks highly of the negroes in point of bodily strength, faithfulness, and sobriety, while he ascribes all the difficulties which were encountered by the Europeans appointed to introduce the new discipline to the apathy, the self-conceit, and religious prejudices of the higher order of Turks. But so far as we consider the condition of the people at large, who are thus

* Histoire de l'Egypte sous le Gouvernement de Mohammed Ali, &c &c. Par M. Felix Mengin.
† In 1826, Planat informs us that six regiments were fully equipped, amounting in all to 24,000. L'armée se forma alors par régimens, de cinq bataillons chacun, à 800 hommes par bataillon, ce qui donnait un effectif de 24,000 hommes. Les six régimens regurent leurs numeros et leurs drapeaux. Régénération de l'Egypte, p. 30.

rendered liable to be called from their mud hovels to the camp, the improvement in food and clothing seems no inadequate compensation for the precarious liberty of which they are temporally deprived.

To complete his arrangements, the pasha has founded several military schools, in which young persons of all classes, especially from among the Arabs, are instructed in mathematics, fortification, gunnery, foreign languages, and in the principles of European tactics. An extensive arsenal is established in Cairo, where cannon are cast, muskets fabricated, and gunpowder manufactured in great abundance. The latest inventions are imported from France and England; the most expensive apparatus and instruments are purchased; the mysteries of gas, and steam, and lithography are subjects of familiar study in the Egyptian capital, encouraged by the viceroy, and patronised by his court.

Mrs. Lushington visited the military college in Cairo, where she found masters in all the different branches of art and science which are deemed subservient to the profession of a soldier. "Besides these professors there were other instructers, chiefly Italians, who, in addition to their own language, taught Arabic, Turkish, and French, as also botany and arithmetic. Of the pupils three hundred were military conscripts, one hundred and fifty Greek slaves, and the rest Turkish boys from Roumelia, and many Egyptians, who were either Mamlouks or slaves of the pasha. These were divided into classes of sixty or a-hundred each, every class under an instructer and subordinate monitors. Besides the mathematical students, twenty were learning Persian, a great many French and Italian, and the whole were taught to read and write Turkish and Arabic. Of the fourteen hundred boys of which the college consists, five hundred are boarders, and the rest are day-scholars; all appeared healthy, clean, and well clothed.

" The munificence of the pasha allots above six thousand dollars a month to the maintenance of this seminary; which, though a small sum when compared with what would be the expenses of a similar establishment in England, is adequate to its purpose in a country where the necessaries of life are both cheap and abundant. The lithographic and printing presses next engaged our attention. They were apparently well conducted, under the management of a Druse, a native of Mount Lebanon, a young man of polite manners, lively and intelligent, and one of the many who had been sent by the pasha to Europe for education. I saw printing in all its branches, from the formation of the letters to the completion of a book. The works already printed were, a 'Turkish History' by an officer of the grand vizier; 'Correspondence between the Pasha and the Porte;' a translation in Turkish of some French authors on military and naval gunnery; the Persian poem called Goolistan; and some grammars. The presses were made under the superintendence of this Druse, but the paper was of European manufacture."*

Having experienced much difficulty, and several disappointments, as long as he was obliged to employ foreigners in his different undertakings, the pasha perseveres in the scheme, which he adopted some years ago, of sending young men of talent to Italy, France, and England, to study the respective arts of these enlightened countries. Several of his pupils have visited London and other parts of Great Britain, where they endeavoured to make themselves acquainted with every mechanical pursuit or ingenious invention that was likely to give pleasure to their sovereign, and to benefit their native land. At the present time, besides some small colonies stationed at Genoa and Leghorn, there are about forty individuals in Paris, under the direction of Messrs. Jomard and Agoub, learning various branches of science, the liberal arts, and even the outlines of European literature.

It is sometimes a misfortune for a man to live in advance of his age, and we accordingly find that the pasha is not only far from being popular, but that he is disliked by the more influential classes of his subjects on account of his

* Narrative of a Journey, p. 171. This college, we believe, is at Boulak, the port of Cairo, and not within the walls of the city. We were struck with a remark made by the pasha when visiting one of his military schools. Addressing the young officers, whom he exhorted to redouble their zeal and perseverance as the first difficulties were already overcome, he said, "If I had any influence in heaven, I should work miracles in your behalf; but I am nothing more than a man, and can only give you salaries." "Si j'avais du credit dans le ciel, je ferais pour vous des miracles; mais je ne suis qu'un homme, je ne puis vous offrir que des salaires." Planat, p. 181.

most meritorious exertions. The indulgence, for example, which he grants to religious sects of every denomination; the use of the vaccine discovery as well as of other surgical practices borrowed from Europe; and, above all, the school of anatomy recently founded, which creates a necessity for human subjects even in addition to the waxen models which he has procured from Italy, are innovations highly disagreeable to the bigoted Mussulmans. In fact, they perceive that he is a Turk only to his own countrymen, with whom he is rigidly strict; while to all others he displays a degree of liberality to which they are disposed to give the name of dishonesty or indifference.

His labours are somewhat better appreciated when they are directed to the embellishment of mosques, the decoration of fountains and reservoirs, or to the erection of a colonnade of white marble in honour of a patron saint. But whatever may be thought of his conduct at home, he has every where else obtained great praise for his indefatigable exertions in opening the ancient canals, which had been closed up for centuries, and in digging new ones, in order to promote the safety as well as the extension of commerce. Among these is particularly deserving of notice the cut which connects the harbour of Alexandria with the Nile, near Fouah,—a magnificent work, forty-eight miles in length, ninety feet broad, and about eighteen in depth, and supplying the means for bringing the whole produce of the country, without danger or interruption, to the port of shipment. In the winter of 1817, we are told, when a scarcity of grain prevailed all over Europe, vessels flocked to Egypt, where there was abundance; but owing to the bar at the mouth of the Nile near Rosetta, and the tempestuous weather along the coast, none of it could be conveyed in time to Alexandria. Hence, of the ships which had assembled, above three hundred in number, some at length went away in ballast, and others with half cargoes,— a circumstance which occasioned not only a very heavy loss to the owners, but endless disputes among the agents and merchants. It was then that the advantages of a navigable canal were urged upon the pasha, who resolved to engage immediately in the arduous undertaking.

In pursuance of this object, all the labouring classes of Lower Egypt were put in requisition, and a month's pay advanced to them to provide necessaries. To each village and district was allotted, as to the Roman legions of old, the extent of work which they were expected to perform. The Arabs were marched down in multitudes, under their respective chiefs, along the line of the intended canal; and it has been confidently stated, on good authority, that the number employed at one time amounted to upwards of two hundred and fifty thousand men. In little more than six weeks the whole excavation was completed, and the mass of the people returned home to their respective habitations; but, in the autumn, a few thousands were called upon to face parts of the bank with masonry, and to make the whole navigable for vessels of considerable burden. The canal, named Nahmoudieh, was opened with great pomp on the 7th December, 1819, and promises to confer a great benefit on the natives themselves as well as on the foreign merchant who sends ships to their port.

It has been stated by more than one of the late writers on Egypt, that twenty thousand labourers fell a sacrifice to the urgency of the pasha on this occasion, and that, as the Franks are accused of having suggested the improvement, they share with his highness the odium which attaches to the remembrance of so oppressive a servitude. But, making allowance for the exaggeration usual in such cases, it is probable that the loss of life was not so great as it has been represented; and, besides, it is more likely to have fallen upon the women and children, who, as in the patriarchal times, follow the migration of the males, than upon the workmen who were actually employed in the excavation. We are inclined to adopt this view of the matter from a fact stated by Planat in regard to the military conscription about five years ago. The number of recruits wanted for the army was 12,000, but the multitude who appeared at the camp, including all ages and both sexes, was found to exceed 70,000, and who, before they could return to their dwellings, must have been subjected to much suffering, and to almost every species of privation.

The zeal and energy of the viceroy have been rewarded by a great increase of trade, and a corresponding rise in the value of raw produce; but accident has conferred upon him a greater boon than could have been derived from the wisest arrangements. M. Jumel discovered, one day, in

Z

the garden of a Turk, called Mako, a plant of the cotton tree, which he afterward propagated with so much skill and success as to have changed, says Planat, the commerce and statistics of Egypt. This important vegetable bears the name of the Frenchman who first made the government acquainted with its manifold uses as an article of domestic manufacture and of foreign trade. Jumel erected at Boulak, near Cairo, a superb establishment, equal in its structure to the finest European manufactory, for spinning, weaving, dying, and printing of cotton goods. The latest improvements in machinery were borrowed from Rouen or Manchester; steam is the principal moving power; and gas is employed for the purposes of artificial light.

At Siout Mr. Webster found a cotton manufactory in full operation. "It was established," says he, "some six years ago, and gives employment to eight hundred men and boys, who earn ten, fifteen, twenty, or thirty paras, and sometimes three piasters. Little boys of seven or eight were seen in all parts of the process. The Arab boys are singularly active and intelligent-looking. They work with an air of sharpness which is quite remarkable,—a sort of style and flourish which shows a full comprehension and mastery of what they are about. They appear much quicker than English boys of the same age. Young girls were once tried in the factory-work, but were found to be of no service. The manager and sub-manager accompanied us round with great pleasure. Cotton factories are by no means uncommon in Egypt."*

M. Mengin made a remark, which we have seen confirmed by other authors, namely, that during the prevalence of the desert winds, machinery is very liable to be disordered by the impalpable dust which then fills the air, and is so extremely penetrating, that, as the natives assert, it will enter into an egg through the pores of the shell. This powder finds its way into the wheel-work and finer parts of a piece of mechanism, disturbing and sometimes stopping the movements; while the wood, in similar circumstances, warps or splits, and the threads, owing to the excessive dryness of the climate, are very apt to break and snap asunder. But notwithstanding all these disadvantages, which peo-

* Travels, vol. ii. p. 133.

haps find a full compensation in the cheap labour of a country whose inhabitants have few wants, the pasha is able to compete with the European manufacturers in every market to which he is admitted, and even to undersell the merchants of India in their own ports.*

It has happened, fortunately for the pasha, that this cotton-wool is not the usual coarse kind hitherto grown in Egypt, but of a very superior quality, equal to the best American. In the year 1822, the crop yielded about 5,600,000 lbs.,—a portion of which, being sent to Liverpool on trial, was sold at the rate of a shilling a pound. In 1823, the produce was so abundant, that after supplying the countries on the borders of the Mediterranean, it was calculated that at least 50,000 bags might be exported to England. The pasha is still extending the culture of this useful plant on tracts of ground long neglected, by clearing out the old canals, and digging others for the purpose of irrigation; so that it is very probable the quantity of cotton which may be raised in Egypt will at no distant period equal the whole importation from 'America; because, as the crop is not exposed, on the banks of the Nile, to the frosts and heavy rains which frequently injure it in the less temperate climate of the United States, it is much less precarious. Besides, this new source of supply acquires additional importance from the consideration that it will be brought to England in British shipping, and will, therefore, almost necessarily lead to an increase of our export trade to Egypt.

It was at one time apprehended that fear of the plague in this country might prove an obstacle to the extension of the cotton-trade with the dominions of the pasha. An alarm, which no one at first thought could pronounce altogether groundless, seized the magistrates of Liverpool, who forthwith consulted the physicians, both as to the risk of infec-

* While we write, the following notice appears in a Calcutta paper, dated towards the end of last year:—"An Arab ship has arrived from the Red Sea, and brought 250 bales of cotton-yarn, the manufacture of the pasha at his spinning-mills near Cairo. It is reported that he has sent 500 bales to Surat, 1000 to Calcutta, and that he intends next season to send long-cloths, maddapollans, &c., having established power-looms! These goods are at present admitted at 60 per cent. invoice cost, besides 4½ per cent. customs. What will the mercantile community say to this new competitor?"

tion, and the proper means for preventing so formidable an evil. But the experience of more than a century proves, that with suitable precautions the disease in question can be effectually guarded against, even in climates which might be imagined to predispose the human constitution to its influence. The Mediterranean States, for example, have found that the establishment of quarantine protects the health of their inhabitants; while many intelligent medical men hold the opinion that the atmosphere of Great Britain, combined with the improved police of our larger towns, is itself a sufficient antidote to the malady, which occasionally carries death through the crowded, filthy, and ill-ventilated lanes of the modern Alexandria. The pasha himself has undertaken to extirpate the plague from Egypt; and we have no doubt, that by the use of the means which he has been advised to adopt he will ultimately succeed. The rules enforced by the English Board of Health in that country in 1801 had the effect, in the first instance, of causing its gradual disappearance, and, finally, of bringing it to a total cessation; and the whole of Egypt remained perfectly free from it during the ten succeeding years. At all events, a trade with Turkey has been carried on with perfect impunity from a very remote period; comprehending cotton-wool, cotton-yarn, mohair-yarn, and carpets, articles not less to be suspected as vehicles of contagion than the commodities produced by Mohammed Ali.[*]

Besides cotton, this enterprising monarch has bestowed a similar attention on silk, flax, and the sugar-cane. To these may be added indigo, safflower, and henneh, which are of great use in the various processes of dying and calico-printing. In the valley of Tumulaut, the ancient Land of Goshen, he has established a colony of five hundred Syrians, for the purpose of cultivating the mulberry and rearing silkworms; while in the beautiful province of Fayoum the vine and the olive are again approaching that perfection which they once enjoyed, and for which the genial climate of Egypt appears so well calculated. Tobacco is likewise cultivated to a great extent; but, being weaker than the American, is not so much liked in Europe, and is, therefore, chiefly confined to domestic consumption,

[*] See Quarterly Review, vol. xxx. p. 500. Planat and Volney:

In a word, it is impossible to set limits to the productive powers of that fine country, stimulated by heat and moisture to an extent which in some degree may be regulated by the wants of the agriculturist, and of which the soil is constantly repaired by the annual depositions of the river. Nothing seems wanting but a more enlightened experience, and the enjoyment of greater freedom on the part of the cultivator to render the dominions of Mohammed Ali the richest country on the face of the earth, the abode of plenty, civilization, and knowledge.

But it must not be concealed, that at present the pasha is too much disposed to interfere with the private industry of his subjects. His views of political economy are narrow in the extreme. Having created the commerce and manufactories of Egypt, he regards the whole as his own property, or at least so much under his control that no one is permitted to think for himself, to fix his price, or to choose his market. His excise officers rival in activity the agents of the oldest European nation; and hence we are assured, that if a peasant sows a little cotton, and his wife spins it into a garment, it is liable to seizure, unless it be stamped with the viceroy's mark as a proof of its having paid duty. We are further told, that he furnishes the shoemaker with leather, who cuts it and makes it into shoes, and when they are finished carries them to the agent of the pasha, who pays him so much a day for his labour. The shoes are then deposited in a general store, out of which they are sold to the public. The same thing is done in regard to the cloth manufactures. He provides the weaver with the yarn, who, when he has completed his web takes it to the viceroy's overseer, who remunerates him at a certain rate for his work; the stuff is then lodged in the government warehouse, where it is either sold for domestic use, or exported by foreign merchants, at a considerable profit to the vigilant pasha.

The same principle applies to the largest establishments. Every landholder and manufacturer is obliged to convey the produce of his labour to some central depot, where it is purchased by the agents of government at fixed prices; and all articles must be marked, otherwise they cannot be legally sold. Even in the speculations of foreign trade the pasha claims the right of taking a share with the merchants. so far at least as to advance funds and enjoy a portion of the profit. But should the adventure turn out unfavourably, he does not think himself bound to bear any part of the loss; confining his generosity on such occasions to an ample allowance of time for reimbursing the stock which he may have contributed.

Hence, it has been alleged that his countenance has in many cases proved a positive disadvantage; because he has induced mercantile houses into speculations in which they would not have voluntarily engaged, and involved them in difficulties from which some who possessed but a small capital have never recovered. It is in the Indian trade chiefly that these disasters have occurred; sufficient atten- tion not having been paid to the length of the voyage, the slowness of the returns, and, above all, the frequent gluts to which those distant markets are liable. But so desirous is Mohammed of establishing an intercourse with the East, that there are no expedients within the range of human means which he will not employ in order to realize his pur- pose. The recovery of the trade which was withdrawn from Egypt by the barbarism of its government, as well as by the improvements in navigation which crowned the efforts of the European powers in the beginning of the six- teenth century, is a favourite object with the politicians of Cairo, and engages deeply the attention of their chief. He can already supply the states on the shores of the Mediter- ranean with wax, hides, coffee, myrrh, frankincense, coccu- lus indicus, asafœtida, ivory, rhinoceros-horn, tortoise-shell, sal ammoniac, senna, tamarinds, ostrich-feathers, incense, balsam of Mecca, gum-arabic, gum-copal, benzoïn, Soco- trine aloes, coloquintida, gum-ammoniac, galbanum, sagape- num, opoponax, spikenard, sulphur, musk, and gold-dust.

The intercourse by land with the countries towards the south and west is carried on by caravans. Those from Sennaar and Darfûr arrive in September or October, and depart when they have sold their goods and completed their purchases. The sacred convoy of pilgrims bound to Mecca reaches Egypt about the Ramadan, or general fast, and sets off immediately after Beïram, the great Mohammedan feast, that it may enter the holy city before the month of the fes- tival has expired. Caravans from Mount Sinai appear in the spring, bringing dates and charcoal; similar commodities are sent from the oases on the backs of camels; the same mode of conveyance being still used to transport the cargoes of Arabia, Persia, and Hindostan from the Red Sea to the capital.

The caravans from Abyssinia travel northward through the desert, on the east side of the Nile, as far as Esneh. They bring ivory and ostrich-feathers; but their principal trade consists in gum and in slaves of both sexes, Cairo being the ultimate destination of the latter, the place where the sales are made. They carry home Venetian glass manufactures, woollen dresses, cotton and linen stuffs, blue shawls, and some other articles which they purchase at Siout and Kenneh. The Ababdé and Bicharis tribes also come to Esneh for metals, utensils, and such grain as they require. They sell slaves, camels, and gum, which they gather in their deserts, as well as the charcoal which they make from the acacia trees. But the most valuable commodity that they bring is senna, which they collect in the mountains between the Nile and the Red Sea, where it grows without culture.

The trade to Cossier, on the shores of that gulf, is only a feeble remnant of that by which Egypt was once enriched. The exports are wheat, barley, beans, lentils, sugar, carthamon flowers, oil of lettuce, and butter. The importations are coffee, cotton cloth, Indian muslins, English silks, spices, incense, and Cashmere shawls. This branch of commerce is conducted by persons going on their pilgrimage to Mecca.

The principal imports from the nations of Europe may be reckoned as follows :—The French cloths called mahouts and londrins, silks, scarlet caps, gold-lace, blotting-paper, glass, earthenware, hardware, watches, and many inferior objects from Marseilles; every variety of cotton goods, superfine broadcloths, lead, tin, iron, steel, vitriol, gun-barrels, firearms, and watches, from England; similar articles from Germany and Italy, especially the scarlet bonnets or scull-caps which are indispensable to the Turks. Such goods brought directly from the place of manufacture pay an impost duty of three per cent.; while Turkish commodities are charged five per cent. at Alexandria, and four per cent. at Boulak. For goods brought by land from the interior nine per cent. is exacted at one payment. The export duty is three per cent. to Europe, and five per cent. to Turkey on either side of the Hellespont. Cargoes sent by the Red Sea pay ten per cent. each way, with certain exceptions too minute to be specified on the present occasion. The fullest details, with ample lists of exports and imports, are given by M. Mengin, in the work already so often referred to, where the mercantile reader will find much to gratify his curiosity in regard to the commercial system pursued by Mohammed Ali.

The revenue of Egypt has been estimated at 2,249,879l., —arising from the *miri*, or land-tax; the customs; the resumed lands, amounting to nearly all the cultivable soil; the conquered territories, Darfûr, Sennaar, Nubia, and a large part of Arabia; the monopoly of nearly all the Egyptian commerce; and, finally, an excise on manufactures, raw produce, and provisions. The annual expenditure is calculated at 1,757,840l., of which more than one-half is required for the army, including the erection of barracks and the supply of arms. About 90,000l. is remitted to Constantinople in name of tribute; 14,000l. is devoted to the support of the church and the law; an equal sum is expended on the pilgrimage to Mecca; and nearly 200,000l. on the pasha's household, his guards, and his yeomen of the palace.

In former times the revenue passed through the hands of the beys, who, after charging it with the expenses of government, were understood to remit the surplus to Constantinople. But the different agents and collectors managed so adroitly that the grand signior very seldom touched any portion of the taxes; on the contrary, he was often called upon to pay for the repairs of buildings and canals which were never executed. It is generally believed that the Mamlouks drew from Egypt, in the shape of public and private income, about a million and a half sterling. When the French were in possession of the country the imports varied from year to year according to the state of the war. General Reynier valued their average amount at about nine hundred thousand pounds sterling, or from twenty to twenty-five millions of francs.*

It has not been found an easy task to ascertain the popula-

* Malte Brun, vol. iv. p. 100.

tion of modern Egypt. M. Sylvestre de Sacy, Mengin, and others, have supplied certain facts, from which we may infer that it amounts to about two millions and a half; but it remains doubtful whether we ought to include in that number the Arabs who occupy the deserts between the Nile and the Red Sea, or to restrict it to the inhabitants of towns, and to such of the peasantry as are made subjects of taxation. The last of the authors just named, who professes to have paid great attention to this article of Egyptian statistics, reckons in Cairo eight persons to a house, while in the provinces he assigns only four individuals to every family. The amount is as follows:—

	Houses.	Inhabitants.
In Cairo	25,000	200,000
In the provincial towns of Alexandria, Rosetta, Damietta, Old Cairo, and Boulak	14,532	58,128
In fourteen provinces, containing 3475 villages	564,168	2,256,272
	603,700	2,514,400

Compared with the pompous narratives of the ancient historians, the present population of the great valley of the Nile sinks into insignificance. Before the Persian conquest the inhabitants, including all classes who acknowledged the authority of the Pharaohs, were estimated at seven millions, —a number which, if we consider the extreme productiveness of the country, yielding in many parts two crops every year, will not be pronounced altogether improbable. Besides, we are satisfied that the Libyan Desert now covers a great breadth of soil which was at one time under crop, and which, even in our own days, is not quite beyond the reach of irrigation by means of canals drawn from the higher sections of the Nile,—an expedient not unlikely to suggest itself to that energetic governor, who has already made an extensive cut near Elephantiné in order to avoid the disadvantages of the Cataracts.

The people of Egypt may be divided into Copts, Arabs, Turks, Greeks, Jews, and Syrians. The first are the most ancient, and bear, as Malte Brun observes, the same relation to the Arabs that the Gauls did to the Franks under the first race of the French kings. But the victors and the vanquished have not, as in the latter case, been amalgamated into one national body. The followers of Mohammed, in their fierce intolerance, reduced the unhappy Greeks and Egyptians to a state of painful degradation; forcing them to live apart from their proud masters, and to earn a livelihood by constant labour. They did not, however, peremptorily insist on the alternative of conversion or utter extermination, as the Romish Christians did with the Arabian Mussulmans in Spain; while the talent possessed by the Copts for writing and keeping accounts recommended them to their conquerors, and at the same time supplied the means of perpetuating their own race. The Arab, who knew no art but that of war, saw that he had an interest in preserving them; and hence we find, that after all the contumely and oppression they have undergone, their number amounts to about two hundred thousand. They are seen in all parts of the country from Alexandria to the Cataracts; but their principal residence is in the Saïd, where they occasionally constitute almost the exclusive inhabitants of whole villages.

Egypt has been so frequently invaded, overrun, and colonized, that there no longer exists a pure race among its inhabitants. The Copts are usually regarded as the de-
Egyptians, the subjects of Amenophis

their descent from the people who were
he Arabs,—that is, from that mixture of
of Greeks, who under

more probable, if we consider the distinguishing features of this race of people : we shall find them all characterized by a sort of yellowish dusky complexion, which is neither Grecian nor Arabian : they have all a puffed visage, swollen eyes, flat noses, and thick lips ;—in short, the exact countenance of a mulatto. I was at first tempted to attribute this to the climate ; but when I visited the Sphinx, I could not help thinking the figure of that monster furnished the true solution of the enigma, observing its features to be precisely those of a negro."[*]

Those writers who have gone in search of the etymological

* Travels, vol. 1. p. 79.

neither in their features nor in their complexion have the Copts the smallest resemblance to the figures of the ancient Egyptians represented in the tombs at Thebes, or in any other part of the country; and he accordingly supposes that they are a mixed race, bearing in their physiognomy the marks of an alliance to the great Circassian family, and obviously distinguished from the children of Mizraim, the aboriginal Egyptians. The Nubians, on the contrary, resident at Elephantiné, are described by him as perfectly black, but without possessing the least of the negro feature; the lips small, the nose aquiline; the expression of the countenance sweet and animated, and bearing a strong resemblance to that which is generally found portrayed in the temples and tombs of the ancient Egyptians. He also noticed several families of a *third* race, differing both in complexion and feature from the inhabitants of Es Souan and of Nubia. Their hue was more of a bronze or reddish brown, resembling mahogany; approaching nearer, both in feature and in complexion, to that which is called the head of the young Memnon, and to the figures in the tomb at Beban el Melouk, than any of the human race that ever fell under his observation. They are as different, he subjoins, from the Copt in Egypt, both in hue and feature, as a Hindoo is from a Frenchman.*

Hence it has been concluded, with considerable probability, that the ancient Egyptians were, as regards colour, blacks, although essentially distinguished in their physiognomy from the negro. The inhabitants of modern Egypt have by other authors been rated as follows:—

Copts	160,000
Arab Fellahs	2,250,000
Bedouin Arabs	150,000
Arabian Greeks	25,000
Jews	20,000
Syrians	20,000
Armenians	10,000
Turks and Albanians	20,000
Franks or Levantines	4000
Mamlouks	500
Ethiopians, &c.	7,5000†

The Arabs may be divided into three classes; first, the

* Travels, vol. i. p. 90. 261. † Modern Traveller.

A s

wild independent Bedouins who occupy the desert; then
the pastoral tribes who feed their flocks on the borders of
Egypt and occasionally enter the cultivated districts; and,
lastly, the peasants or Fellahs, who devote themselves to
agriculture and the arts, and are the principal inhabitants
of the villages both in Upper and Lower Egypt. This
people are distinguished by a lively and expressive physiog
nomy, small sparkling eyes, short pointed beards, and a
general angularity of form : their lips, being usually open,
show their teeth; their arms are extremely muscular; the
whole body, in short, is more remarkable for agility than
for beauty, and more nervous than handsome. The tented
Arab, hovering with his flocks along the borders of the
fertile valley of the Nile, is the same in character, manners,
and customs as he has been since the days of the patri-
archs; regarding with disdain and proud independence all
other classes of mankind, but more particularly those of his
own nation who in his eyes have degraded themselves by
taking up their abodes in fixed habitations, and whom he
calls, in contempt, the Arab of the Walls.

The Turks have graver features and sleeker forms, fine
eyes, but overshaded so much as to have little expression;
large noses, handsome mouths, good lips, long tufted beards,
lighter complexions, short necks, a grave and indolent
habit of body; and in every thing an air of weight which
they associate with the idea of nobleness.

The Greeks, who must now be classed as foreigners,
present the regular features, the delicacy and the versatility
of their ancestors; they are charged with a certain degree
of sharpness and roguery in their mercantile transactions,
qualities for which they are indebted, perhaps, to the oppressive domination of their Moslem conquerors. We
are told that there are about five thousand descendants of
the ancient Greek colonists, who form quite a distinct race
from the modern Greeks. They have lost their original
tongue, and speak a kind of Arabic; most of them are mariners, but in general they pursue the inferior and handi-
craft trades.

The Jews have the same physiognomy as in Europe,
and are here, as well as every where else, devoted to the
pursuits of commerce. Despised and buffeted, without
being actually expelled, they compete with the Copts in

the large towns for situations in the customs, and for the management of property belonging to the rich. M. Mengin reckons that there are about four thousand of this singular people resident in the dominions of Mohammed Ali, three thousand of whom inhabit a part of Cairo which bears the distinction of their name. The streets are so narrow as to be almost impassable; the houses are dark, crowded together, filthy, and so infectious, that when the plague breaks out, the first inquiry is, if it has appeared in the Jews' Quarter.*

There are about two thousand Arabians who reside principally in the capital, where they exercise every kind of trade, and are much concerned in money transactions with the government. The Greek Christians of Syria may be estimated at three thousand in Cairo, and one thousand in the other cities of Egypt. They were formerly the wholesale merchants who supplied the land proprietors and others with various kinds of articles, and were in general wealthy; but the monopoly of the viceroy has very considerably lessened their business and diminished their funds.

The spirit of improvement which distinguishes the reign of Mohammed has produced less change on the external appearance of Cairo than on the temper and views of its inhabitants. We have elsewhere stated that this celebrated city was founded in the tenth century by the first caliph of the Fatimite dynasty, and that the famous Saladin, about two hundred years afterward, built the ramparts with which it is surrounded, extending more than eighteen thousand yards in length. In ascending the Nile the traveller arrives first at Boulak, the port of the capital, where the vessels are moored that come from the coast. Farther south is Old Cairo, at which there is a harbour for the reception of the traders that descend from Upper Egypt. Between these two ancient towns is Cairo, properly so called, removed from the river about a mile and a half, and stretching towards the mountains of Mokattam on the east,—a distance of not less than three miles. It is encircled with a stone wall, surmounted by fine battlements, and fortified with lofty towers at every hundred paces. There are three or four

* Mengin, Histoire de l'Egypte; Malte Brun vol. iv; Malus, Mémoire sur l'Egypte; Denon, tom. i. p. 88; Hasselquist, Voyage, p. 68.

beautiful gates built by the Mamlouks, and uniting a simple style of architecture with an air of grandeur and magnificence.

But in this vast metropolis we find only one street, narrow and unpaved. The houses, like all others in Egypt, are badly built of earth or indifferent bricks, and are only distinguished by being two or three stories high. Lighted by windows looking into back-courts or quadrangles, they appear from the streets like so many prisons, though the general aspect is a little relieved by a number of large squares and many fine mosques. That of Sultan Hassan, built at the bottom of the mountain on which the citadel is placed, is in the form of a parallelogram, and of great extent; a deep frieze goes all the way round the top of the wall, adorned with sculptures which we call Gothic, but which were introduced into Europe by the Arabians who invaded Spain.

Cairo is traversed by a canal which issues from the Nile a little below the old town, and having passed through immense and innumerable heaps of rubbish, enters the modern capital on the south side, goes out at the north, and winding round the wall makes a second entrance on the west, and terminates in the Birket-el-Esbequier. The outline of the city is nearly that of a quadrant, being square towards the north and east and circular towards the south and west. This artificial river is of the greatest consequence to the inhabitants; for, besides furnishing them while the inundation continues with an abundant supply of water for all the purposes of domestic life, it affords the means of replenishing a variety of small lakes, both inside and outside the walls, on which they ply their pleasure-boats, and enjoy a variety of other recreations suited to their indolent luxury or to the softness of their delicious climate. On the borders of these, especially within the town, may be seen in an evening fireworks pouring their light into the air, dancing-dogs, dancing-monkeys, dancing-girls, and all the people making merry and rejoicing, as in the days of old when the Nile had attained its due elevation, and promised to bless their fields with an ample increase. In one of these sheets of water is observed the lotus,—that mysterious plant so highly esteemed by the ancient Egyptians, the flower of which contrasts so beautifully with the liquid ground on which it reposes, as well as with the arid waste by which it is surrounded.

The citadel, which occupies part of the ridge of Mokattam, is a place of considerable strength, but, like most other ancient buildings in Egypt, greatly encumbered with ruins. The palace of the pasha is not worthy of notice on any other account than as being the residence of so distinguished a person when he chooses to live in his capital. It is a small house, plain, and without any exterior decoration, except that it has more glass-windows in front than Turkish dwellings usually exhibit. The Well of Joseph, in the middle of the fortress, calls us back to the twelfth century, the era of the renowned Saladin, by whom it was excavated, and whose name, Yousef, it continues to bear. It is about 45 feet in circumference at the top, and is dug through the soft calcareous rock to the depth of about 270 feet, where it meets a spring of brackish water on a level with the Nile, from which indeed it is derived,—owing its saline impregnation to the nature of the soil through which it has filtered. The water is raised in buckets by two wheels drawn by oxen,—the one being on the surface of the ground, the other at the depth of 150 feet. The main use of this celebrated cistern, besides partly supplying the garrison, is to irrigate the adjoining gardens, and keep alive the little verdure which adorns the interior of the fortress; but it is preserved in tolerable repair from the consideration, that were the place ever subjected to a siege, the stream of Joseph's Well would become the sole reliance of the troops as well as of the numerous inhabitants.

The memory of Saladin is farther associated with the citadel by means of a ruin called Joseph's Hall, and which is understood to have formed part of the palace of that warlike prince. The columns, it is manifest, have been taken from some more ancient building at Memphis, being generally monolithic, or consisting of a single stone, tall and massy, and adorned with highly-wrought capitals. In the days of Saracenic magnificence, this must have been a truly splendid edifice, meriting in some degree the praises bestowed upon the royal residences of that aspiring and ingenious people. But it is now in a very dilapidated condition, part being converted into a magazine, and part used as a granary; while the whole has such a waste and mournful

appearance, as to be, in truth, more desolate and less interesting than if it were a complete ruin.*

But, in describing Joseph's Hall, we apprehend that we
have spoken of an architectural relic which no longer
exists.   In the year 1824 the citadel was much shaken by
the explosion of a magazine; whence arose the necessity
of a thorough repair in several of the remaining buildings
of the fortress.   Among the ruins pointed out for demolition were the surviving walls of Saladin's palace; on the
site of which was about to be erected a square, meant probably for the better accommodation of the troops.   The roof
of this edifice, which might long have withstood the ravages
of time, was very much admired.   It was formed of a succession of little domes made of wood, into which were
introduced concave circles containing octagons of blue and
gold.   The corners and arches of the buildings were carved
in the best Saracenic manner, and in many places the
colours and gilding continued perfectly bright.

Cairo, although it cannot boast of an origin so ancient
as that of Thebes, nor of a mythology which connected the
present life so closely with the next, has nevertheless a city
of tombs, a Necropolis on which has been lavished much
treasure combined with a certain portion of architectural
taste.   The desert towards the east is studded with sepulchres and mausoleums, some of which produce a very striking
effect.   As every Turk throughout the empire, from the
grand signior to the meanest peasant, is compelled to be of
some profession; and as every calling has its peculiar headdress, which is represented on a pole at the grave of the
deceased,—a burial-place in a Moslem country has necessarily a singular appearance.   The celebrated tombs of the
Mamlouks are going fast to decay, their boasted magnificence being now limited to a gilt inscription; but, in order
that the reader may be enabled to form a judgment as to
their grandeur in former days, we insert a drawing taken
from the splendid work on Egypt published by the imperial
government of France.

The cemetery of the pasha is the most sumptuous of
modern structures in the Necropolis of Cairo.   It is a
vaulted stone building, consisting of five domes, under

* Richardson, vol. i. p. 48.

which, in splendid chambers composed of marble, are laid the bodies of his two sons Toussoun and Ishmael, and of his favourite wife the mother of these youths. Having mentioned this lady, it may not be out of place to add that she possessed an astonishing degree of influence over her impetuous husband, who always regarded her as the foundation of his good fortune. She was much esteemed, too, and beloved by the people; for her power was uniformly exerted on the side of justice and mercy. Much of her time was occupied in receiving petitions; but it was seldom she had to refer them to the pasha, as her ascendency was too well known by the ministers to require this last appeal. If, however, in consequence of any demur on their part, she had to apply to him, he answered their remonstrance by saying,—" 'Tis enough. By my two eyes! if she requires it the thing must be done, be it through fire, water, or stone."

Mohammed Ali generally resides at Shoubra, where he has built a splendid palace, and planted a garden after the European fashion. The ceilings, executed by a Grecian artist, are lofty and vaulted, ornamented with gold, and with representations of landscapes, or of palaces and colonnades, the whole being painted in light and pleasing colours. The sultana's private sitting-room is still more sumptuous. During the heats of summer his highness occupies an apartment below, particularly adapted for coolness, having a marble fountain in the centre amply supplied with a constant stream of water. On one of the walls is inscribed, in large Arabic characters, a verse from the Koran, signifying "an hour of justice is worth seventy days of prayer."

But the chief embellishment of the place is a magnificent pavilion, about 250 feet long by 200 broad. On its sides run four galleries or colonnades, composed of elegant pillars of the finest white marble, surrounding a sunken court six feet deep, paved throughout with the same beautiful material. At each corner of the colonnade is a terrace, over which water passes into the court below in a murmuring cascade, having on its ledges figures of fish, sculptured so true to nature that they appear to move in the flowing stream. The whole supply of water rises again through a fountain in the centre, and reappears in a beautiful jet-d'eau, lofty, sparkling, and abundant. In fine weather the pasha occasionally resorts to this splendid fountain with the ladies of his harem, who row about in the flooded court for the amusement of his highness, while he is seated in the colonnade. Great is the commotion when the ladies descend into the garden. A signal is given, and the gardeners vanish in a moment. Mrs. Lushington was struck with the ruddy cheeks and healthy appearance of these men. They are principally Greeks; and the gay colours of their fanciful costume,—each with a nosegay or bunch of fruit in his hand,—combined with the luxuriant scenery around, gave them more the semblance of actors in a ballet representing a fête in Arcadia than the real labourers of a Turkish despot.[*]

This chapter would be incomplete were we not to compare what Egypt is at present with what it was at the beginning of the century.

When Mohammed assumed the command anarchy reigned in every department. The country was distracted by the conflicting pretensions of the Mamlouks, aided by the Bedouin Arabs, the Albanians, and the Turks, with many rival chieftains. The soldiers were mutinous; the finances were exhausted; property was insecure; agriculture was neglected; and commerce languished. But now every thing is improved; the wild Arabs are submissive; the military are controlled, lodged in barracks or tents, and regularly paid; the finances prodigiously increased; new articles of produce raised; and trade carried on to an extent formerly unknown. The whole country from Alexandria to Syené is perfectly tranquil, and travellers pass unmolested with as much freedom and safety as on the continent of Europe. It is not pretended that the viceroy has not his failings; he has many: but to estimate his character he should be judged by the standard of other Mohammedan princes,—of the pashas of Syria or Turkey, for example;—and which of all these can be compared to him? It is hardly fair to try him by our notions of excellence, when every thing—custom, religion, government—are so different. His defects are those of education and example; his improvements are the fruit of his own genius and patriotism.[†]

---

[*] Narrative of a Journey, p. 128.
[†] Quarterly Review, vol. xxx. p. 508. Mr. Carne remarks that the firm and decisive character of Mohammed is in nothing more visible than

A report has reached Europe that this remarkable person has conceded to his people the benefits of a representative government and a voice in the administration of public affairs. But the information is much too vague to be entitled to a place in the records of history.

The future prosperity of Egypt depends in a great degree upon the successor of the present viceroy. Ibrahim, the son of his wife, and the Defturder, who is his son-in-law by marriage, will probably divide the choice of Mohammed. The former is more likely to obtain the recommendation of the pasha and the sanction of the Sublime Porte, because he is more friendly than the other to the regeneration which has been effected throughout the country with results so favourable even to the supreme government Should the election fall on the husband of Ali's daughter, the consequences will be deplorable; for he is not only a decided enemy to the Franks and to the late innovations, but regards them both with the eye of a bigoted Mussulman.

in the perfect security and quietness that reign throughout his dominions. The traveller there dreams no more of violence than he would do in any town throughout Scotland or Wales; from the capital to the Cataracts every man's hand is at peace with him, and he may ramble along the banks of the Nile with as entire an ease and *abandon* as on those of his native rivers or in his own garden at home.—*Recollections of the East* p. 384

CHAPTER IX.

The Oases, Ancient Berenice, and Desert of the Thebaid.

THE territory of Egypt includes certain fertile spots in the Libyan desert, which, from the peculiarity of their situation, amid an ocean of sand, have been denominated islands. The term oasis, in the ancient language of the country, signifies an inhabited place, a distinction sufficiently intelligible when contrasted with the vast wilderness around, in which even the most savage tribes have not ventured to take up their abode. It has been observed, at the same time, that as this descriptive epithet is applied to a cluster of oases as well as to a single spot of verdant ground, the use of it has become somewhat ambiguous. In this respect, indeed, they bear a striking resemblance to islands in the great sea, where one of larger size is usually surrounded by others of smaller dimensions; all taking their name from some circumstance, geographical or physical, which is common to the whole.

Like Egypt itself, these isolated dependencies have been described in very opposite colours by different writers. The Greeks called them the islands of the blessed; and without doubt they appear delightful in the eyes of the traveller who has during many painful weeks suffered the privations and fatigue of the desert. But it is well known that they were generally regarded in a less favourable aspect by the Greeks and Romans, who not unfrequently assigned them as places of banishment. The state malefactor and the ministers of the Christian church, who were sometimes comprehended in the same class, were, in the second and third centuries, condemned to waste their days as exiles in the remote solitude of the Libyan Oasis. They were usually reckoned three in number; the Great Oasis, of which the principal town is El Kargeh; the Little Oasis, or that of El Kassar; and the Northern Oasis, more frequently called Siwah. To these is now added the Western Oasis, which does not appear to have been mentioned by any ancient geographer except Olympiodorus, and which was never seen by any European until Sir Archibald Edmonstone visited it about ten years ago.

The Great Oasis, the most southern of the whole, consists of a number of insulated spots, which extend in a line parallel to the course of the Nile, separated from one another by considerable intervals of sandy waste, and stretching not less than a hundred miles in latitude. M. Poncet, who examined it in 1698, says that it contains many gardens watered with rivulets, and that its palm-groves exhibit a perpetual verdure. It is the first stage of the Darfûr caravan, which assembles at Siout, being about four days' journey from that town, and nearly the same distance from Farshout. The exertions of Browne, Caillaud, Edmonstone, and Henniker have supplied to the European reader the most ample details relative to this interesting locality, which, there can be no doubt, must have been the scene of civilized life, and perhaps of political institutions, at a very remote era.

An interesting account of the architectural ruins of the Great Oasis is to be found in the pages of Sir A. Edmonstone, who tells, that about a mile and a half towards the north of El Kargeh, he observed on an eminence a building which proved to be a small quadrangular temple 31 feet long by 21 broad, of which three sides are still remaining. The walls on the inside are covered with figures and hieroglyphics, greatly defaced, but of distinguished elegance. There was the usual enclosure of unburnt brick,—a defence necessary in a country so much exposed to hostile incursions as this has always been. From hence he discovered a larger temple at a short distance to the north-west, and on a high ground still farther in the same direction several buildings like the ruins of an Arab town. On approaching the temple he was struck with the beauty of the situation, in the midst of a rich wood, consisting of palm, acacia, and other trees, with a stream of water in front.

In point of magnitude it far exceeded any thing he had hitherto seen. The entry is through a *dromos*, of which the enclosures are so broken that it is difficult to discern the shape. He could distinguish, however, that it had been formed by a parapet wall surmounted with a cornice, connecting ten columns, with spaces on each side to admit an easy approach. The temple stands east and west, and a rich cornice runs all round the top. The front is completely covered with colossal figures and hieroglyphics, which, as they extend but half-way to the north and south sides, give the whole exterior rather an unfinished appearance. The great doorway is much ornamented, and leads to a magnificent apartment, 60 feet by 54, with twelve columns, 13 feet in circumference. The second chamber, 54 feet by 18, is divided from the first by a sort of screen, formed by a wall lower than that of the temple, intersected by four columns, which, together with four others in the centre of the apartment, now fallen, are of the same size with those above mentioned. The chamber is traced all over with figures and hieroglyphics on stucco, retaining marks of paint, particularly blue and red; whereas, the first is quite plain, except on the west side. The third apartment 31 feet by 29, is ornamented likewise, and contains eight columns, but of much smaller dimensions than the others. Last comes the *adytum*, or shrine, 20 feet by 8, richly carved, though blackened with smoke. On each side are two compartments detached, but so choked up that it was impossible to ascertain their shape. The roof of the rest of the building is fallen in, except some slabs occasionally supported by pillars; but that of the adytum, which is lower, is entire. One of the stones used for covering this latter apartment is 36 feet by 19 feet 4 inches, and 2 feet 3 inches thick.

To the east of the temple are three detached doorways, at different intervals, and of different proportions. As they do not resemble the propyla which are usual in other parts of Egypt, Sir Archibald is of opinion that this edifice was originally surrounded with a triple wall, in the manner described by Diodorus as applicable to the fane of Jupiter Ammon. The first is a solid building, with figures all round it; among others, on the inside, is a colossal representation of Osiris at a banquet. The same is again found on the west front. On the roof are four spread eagles or vultures, painted red and blue. The second doorway, which is at some distance in the same direction, but not in the same line, is considerably higher than even the temple itself. Only one-half is standing, having a few figures inside carved in relief, and some remains of brickwork strongly piled on the top. As it is too high for any pur poses of defence, a conjecture has been advanced, that it may have been the residence of one of the Stelite hermits, of whose superstitious practices many traces still remain. The last of the three propyla is low and imperfect; but it is remarkable for an inscription in Greek letters, with which the east end is completely covered, containing a rescript, published in the second year of the emperor Galba, relating to a reform in the administration of Egypt.

In regard to what appeared at first as the ruins of an Arab town, we are informed, that, upon a closer examination, it proved to be a necropolis or cemetery, consisting of a great variety of buildings, not fewer than two or three hundred, each the receptacle of a number of mummies. The greater part are square, and surmounted with a dome similar to the small mosques erected over the tombs of sheiks; having generally a corridor running round, which produces an ornamental effect very striking at a distance, and gives them a nearer resemblance to Roman than to any existing specimen of Greek or Egyptian architecture. Some few are larger than the rest. One, in particular, is divided into aisles like our churches; and that it has been used as such by the early Christians is clearly evinced by the traces of saints painted on the walls. In all there is a Greek cross, and the celebrated Egyptian hieroglyphic, the *crux ansata*, or cross with a handle, which, originally signifying life, would appear to have been adopted as a Christian emblem, either from its similarity to the shape of the cross, or from its being considered the symbol of a future existence.

But the great peculiarity is a large square hole in the centre of each, evidently for the purpose of containing a mummy, and which, from the fragments and wrappings which lay scattered about, had probably been ransacked for the sake of plunder.   Sir Archibald imagines these sepulchres to be of Roman construction at an early period, since it is generally believed that the practice of embalming was gradually discontinued in Egypt after the extension of Christianity; but he adds, "among the various receptacles for the remains of the dead, from the stupendous pyramid to the rudest cavern, I know of none, existing or recorded, at all corresponding to them in shape and appearance."[*]

There are several other ruins in the neighbourhood of El Kargeh, which appear to combine the relics of Egyptian paganism with the symbols of Christian worship, and thereby lead us to conclude that the edifices may have been repaired in the early ages of our faith after being relinquished by the more ancient occupants.   For a more minute account of these remains we take leave to refer the curious reader to the work already indicated.

Sir F. Henniker speaks rather contemptuously of the ecclesiastical architecture which happened to fall under his notice in that oasis.   There is a temple which he describes as a small building composed of petty blocks of stone, the pillars of which are only two feet six inches in diameter, and, "even these, instead of being formed of one solid block, are constructed of millstones."   He adds, that the surface of the earth in the vicinity of the temple is very remarkable; it is covered with a lamina of salt and sand mixed, and has the same appearance as if a ploughed field had been flooded over, then frozen, and the water drawn off from under the ice.[†]

This remark suggests a question relative to the origin of these grassy islands in the desert. Major Rennel thinks that they may be attributed to the vegetation which would necessarily be occasioned by springs of water; the decay of the plants producing soil until it gradually increased to the extent of several leagues.   They are universally surrounded by higher ground,—a circumstance which accounts for the abundance of moisture.   Fezzan, in particular, is

* Edmonstone's Journey to two of the Oases of Upper Egypt, p. 62, &c.
† Notes, p. 188.

nearly encircled with mountains; and the descent from the
western barrier of Egypt into the middle level of the Greater
Oasis is distinctly marked by Mr. Browne.' Their fertility
has always been deservedly celebrated. Strabo mentions
the superiority of their wine; Abulfeda and Edrisi the
luxuriance of the palm-trees; and our poet Thomson extols

——"the tufted isles
That verdant rise amid the Libyan wild."
Summer, v. 912.

The climate, however, is extremely variable, especially in
winter. Sometimes the rains in the Western Oasis are
very abundant, and fall in torrents, as appears from the
furrows in the rocks; but the season Sir A. Edmonstone
made his visit there was none at all, and the total want of
dew in the hot months sufficiently proves the general dryness of the atmosphere. The springs are all strongly impregnated with iron and sulphur, and hot at their sources;
but, as they continue the same throughout the whole year,
they supply to the inhabitants one of the principal means
of life. The water, notwithstanding, cannot be used until
it has been cooled in an earthen jar.

It was in the year 1819 that the author just cited, in
company with two friends, Messrs. Hoghton and Master,
joined a caravan of Bedouins at Beni Ali, and entered the
Libyan desert, proceeding towards the south-west. At the
end of six days, having travelled about one hundred and
eighty miles, they reached the first village of the Western
Oasis, which is called Bellata. Having explained to the
inhabitants that their object was "old buildings," they were
informed that there were some in the neighbourhood.
"Accordingly," says Sir Archibald, "in the evening we
rode to see them, and in our way passed through a beautiful
wood of acacias, the foliage of which, at a little distance,
recalled English scenery to our recollection. The trees far
exceeded in size any I had ever seen of the kind, and upon
measuring the trunk of one it proved to be 17 feet 3 inches
in circumference."*

El Cazar, however, appears to be the principal town of
the oasis. The situation of the place, we are told, is per-

* Journey to Two of the Oases, p. 44.

fectly lovely, being on an eminence at the foot of a line of rock which rises abruptly behind it, and encircled by extensive gardens filled with palm, acacia, citron, and various other kinds of trees, some of which are rarely seen even in those regions. The principal edifice is an old temple or convent called Daer el Hadjur, about fifty feet long by twenty-five wide, but presenting nothing either very magnificent or curious. The first chamber is 24 feet by 20, supported by four pillars five feet in diameter at the shaft, the walls, as far as they are visible, being traced with figures and hieroglyphics. The winged globe, encompassed by the serpent, the emblem of eternity, is carved over one of the doors.

This oasis is composed of twelve villages, of which ten are within five or six miles of each other; the remaining two being much farther off at the entrance of the plain, and searcely looked upon as belonging to this division. The sheik expressed his belief that there was inhabited land to the westward,—adding that some Arabs, who had lately attempted to explore the country in that direction, met at the end of three days such a terrible whirlwind as compelled them to return.

The prevailing soil is a very light red earth, fertilized entirely by irrigation. The people are Bedouins, who acknowledge the sovereignty of the pasha, and pay an annual tribute. The only manufacture worthy of notice is that of indigo, the method of producing which is very simple: the plant, when dried, is put into an earthen jar with hot water, and agitated by means of a palm branch, resembling the handle of a churn, until the colour is pressed out. The liquid is then strained through the bark of a tree into another jar, where it is left for eight or nine days, during which time part of the water escapes by trickling through a small aperture half-way down the side of it, leaving the sediment at the bottom. It is afterward put into a broad but very shallow hole formed in the sand, which absorbs the remaining liquid, and leaves the indigo in solid cakes on the surface. This commodity is the property of the richer inhabitants, and is one of the very few articles which the pasha has not monopolized, probably from ignorance of its existence in that remote district.*

* Journey, p. 56.

The latitude of the Western Oasis is nearly the same as that of Thebes and the Great Oasis, or about 26° north. The longitude eastward from Greenwich may be a little more or less than twenty-eight degrees, El Kargeh being estimated at thirty degrees ten minutes, and the distance between it and Bellata amounting to a journey with camels of thirty-five hours, or one hundred and five miles. We may add, that it was on his return from the remoter oasis to the Nile that Sir Archibald visited the cluster of islands of which El Kargeh is the chief, and where he found the remains of the magnificent temple already described.

The Little Oasis, or that of El Kassar, has been less visited than either of the two others which have been longest known to European travellers. We owe the latest and most distinct account to Belzoni, who, proceeding in search of it westward from the valley of Fayoum, arrived at the close of the fourth day on the brink of what he calls the Elloah,—that is, the El Wah, or El Ouah, from which the Greeks formed the more common term oasis. He describes it as a valley surrounded with high rocks, forming a spacious plain of twelve or fourteen miles in length, and about six in breadth. There is only a small portion cultivated at present, but there are many proofs remaining that it must at one time have been all under crop, and that with proper management it might again be easily rendered fertile. The first village he entered was called Zaboo, where he met with a kind reception upon the whole, although the simple inhabitants could not comprehend why a man should encounter the toils and perils of the desert merely to gratify his curiosity in regard to old buildings. They endeavoured to persuade him that the Devil had taken possession of all the vaults which he wished to examine; and when he came out they expected to find him loaded with treasure,—the only intelligible object for which, in their estimation, he could brave so formidable an enemy.

From Zaboo he went to El Kassar, the chief village in that group of oases. There he saw the remains of a Greek temple, consisting of a high wall with two lateral wings, and an arch in the centre. It is so situated that it must have been built on the ruins of another of greater dimensions. Its breadth is about sixty feet, and its length, it is presumed, must have been in proportion. There were several tombs excavated in the rock somewhat like those of Egypt, in which Mr. Belzoni found several sarcophagi of baked clay with the mummies inside,—their folding not so rich nor so fine, the linen of a coarse sort, and the corpses, being without asphaltum, not so well preserved. His attention was also attracted by the account which he had received of a well sixty feet deep, whose water varies in its temperature twice every day. When he first put his hand into it, being a little after sunset, he felt it warm; but at midnight it was apparently much warmer; and before sunrise it was again somewhat cooler, though less so than in the evening. " For instance," says he, " if we were to suppose the water to have been 60° in the evening, it might be 100° at midnight, and in the morning about 80°; but when I returned at noon it appeared quite cold, and might be calculated in proportion to the other at 40°." Whatever may be the causes of this apparent change of temperature, it was of importance to prove the existence of the fountain itself, according to the description found in Herodotus, who says that there is a well near the temple of Jupiter Ammon, whose water is cold at noon and midnight, and warm in the morning and evening.*

It is now known that such fountains are not peculiar to any one of the oases, having been discovered in various parts of the Libyan Desert; and hence the argument of Belzoni, in regard to the situation of the temple of Ammon, entirely loses its force. All the waters in that division of Africa are strongly impregnated with saline and mineral substances,—an example of which, in the form of a rivulet, he records as having presented itself to his observation in the neighbourhood of Zaboo. " It is," says he, " curious water; for if white woollen-cloth be put into it, after twenty-four hours it is taken out as black as any dier could make it." The change of temperature is obviously effected by the chymical qualities of the strata through which the spring makes its way under ground, modified in a certain degree by evaporation and the presence of light during the heat of the day.

As to the natives, we are told that their mode of living is very simple : rice, of which they have great abundance, is their chief food; but it is of so inferior a sort that they have little traffic in it, and what they do enjoy is only among the Bedouins who go thither yearly to purchase dates. They have a few camels and donkeys, several cows, buffaloes, goats, and sheep, and could be happy in this Elysium, as it is separated from the rest of mankind; but, subjoins Mr. Belzoni, "they are mortal, and they must have their evils!" Their greatest enemies are their own neighbours at another village, which they described as being on the opposite side of a high rock, removed from them three days' journey. They are continually in dispute, and often attack one another for the most trifling causes.*

The traveller was very desirous to cross the desert north-wards to the Oasis of Siwah, but he could not, either by promises or entreaties, prevail upon any one to become his guide in so perilous an adventure. He then resolved to pro-ceed in a south-west direction, in search of a similar district known at El Kassar by the name of El Haix, and situated at the distance of thirty hours' journey. Upon his arrival, he found it a tract of land forming a crescent of more than twenty miles in extent, and presenting some spots of fertile ground and various springs of excellent water. He traced the remains of an ancient town, the baths of which are still in a state of good preservation. A Christian church of Grecian architecture and the ruins of a convent were like-wise clearly distinguished; but as the guide selected by Belzoni was recognised at El Haix as the sheik of one of the predatory hordes of Bedouins, who from time to time carry terror over the face of the whole desert, a regard to his personal safety induced him to shorten his visit.

Soon after his return to El Kassar he set out in a south-easterly direction for a place called El Moele, where he once more found the ruins of a small village, and the re-mains of a very large Christian church and convent. Some of the paintings on the wall are finely preserved, particularly the figures of the twelve apostles on the top of a niche over an altar; the gold is still to be seen in several parts, and the features are perfectly distinct. El Moele is situated at the extremity of a long tract of land which had been culti-vated in former times, but is now abandoned for want of

* Researches, vol. ii. p. 198.

water. It extends more than ten miles from west to east; whence it required a long day's journey to bring him again to the banks of the Nile.

We have still to mention the Oasis of Siwah, in some respects the most interesting of the whole, and more especially as connected with the traditions of Jupiter Ammon, whose temple it is generally understood to contain. It is situated in lat. 29° 12' N., and in long. 26° 6' E.; being about six miles long, and between four and five in width, the nearest distance from the river of Egypt not exceeding one hundred and twenty miles. A large proportion of the land is occupied by date-trees; but the palm, the pomegranate, the fig, the olive, the vine, the apricot, the plum, and even the apple are said to flourish in the gardens. No soil can be more fertile. Tepid springs, too, holding salts in solution, are numerous throughout the district; and it is imagined that the frequency of earthquakes is connected with the geological structure of the surrounding country.

"The external appearance of the town of Siwah is striking and singular, as well as its internal arrangements. It is built on a steep conical rock of testaceous limestone, and both in its form and its crowded population bears a resemblance to a beehive. The streets, narrow and crooked, are like staircases, and so dark from the overhanging stories, that the inhabitants use a lamp at noonday. In the centre of the town the streets are generally five feet broad and about eleven feet high; but some are so low that you must stoop to pass through them. Each house has several floors, the upper communicating with the lower by galleries and chambers which cover the streets. The number of stories visible is three or four, but there are in fact five or six. On every marriage the father builds a lodgment for his son above his own, so that the town is continually rising higher. The houses and walls are for the most part built of natron or mineral soda, and rock salt mixed with sand, coated with a gypseous earth which preserves the salt from melting. The town is divided into two quarters: the upper is inhabited only by married people, women, and children; the lower by widowers and youths, who, though allowed to go into the other quarter by day, must retire at dusk under the penalty of a fine. The total population of the town is between,

2000 and 2500; that of the oasis at large is supposed to amount to 8000 souls."[*]

But a description of the temple of Ammon must prove more interesting to the reader than any details respecting the mode of life pursued by barbarians. A league and a half, then, from the town of Siwah, towards the east, are the ruins of an edifice built in the Egyptian style, to which the natives give the name of Omn Beydeh. The vestiges of a triple enclosure, enormous stones lying on the ground, and masses still standing prove it to have been a monument of the first order. The portion still remaining and in tolerable preservation is thirty-three feet in length, and consists of part of a gateway and two great walls, which are covered with three immense stones measuring thirty-four feet by twenty-seven. The only apartment that could be distinctly made out was 112 feet in length; the whole area of ruins being a rectangular space about 360 feet by 300.

The decorations are observed to bear the closest resemblance to those of the Egyptian monuments; the figures, scenes, and arrangements being entirely the same. Here is the god with the ram's head, such as is seen at Thebes and Latopolis, who also receives the homage of the priests. The ram is the animal that most frequently occurs among the ornaments. The interior and the ceiling of the apartment still standing are richly adorned with hieroglyphic sculptures in relief and coloured. The figures of the gods and priests form long processions, occupying three rows, surmounted with a multitude of hieroglyphic tablets painted blue or green. The same style and the same cast of countenance are remarked here as in the monuments of the Thebaid,—the same costumes and sacrifices. The roof is occupied by two rows of gigantic vultures with extended wings, with tablets of hieroglyphics, and stars painted red on a blue ground. Under the ruins of the entrance-gate, and on two of the faces of a rectangular block, is sculptured in full relief the figure of Typhon or the evil genius, about five feet high. A similar block has been used in the basis of the mosque of Siwah; being without doubt the pedestals

[*] Modern Traveller, Egypt, vol. ii. p. 200; Cabinet of Foreign Voyages, vol. i.

of columns erected after the manner of the Typhonium of Edfou, to which these ruins bear a resemblance, though on a larger scale.[*]

This description, which does much credit to the penetrating eyes and vivid fancy of a French traveller, the zealous M. Drovetti, may be contrasted with the sober delineation of an Englishman, who saw no more than was actually to be seen in the mouldering walls of the famous El Birbe, which adorn the Oasis of Siwah.[†]

Nearly a mile from these ruins, in a pleasant grove of date-palms, is still discovered the celebrated Fountain of the Sun, dedicated of old to the Ammonian deity. It is a small marsh rather than a well, extending about ninety feet in length and sixty in width, but is at the same time perfectly transparent, though a constant disengagement of air reveals the chymical action which gives a peculiar character to its waters. At present, not less perceptibly than in the days of Herodotus, the temperature is subject to a diurnal change. In the night it is apparently warmer than in the day; and in the morning, as was observed by the ancients, a steam rises from it, denoting the refrigeration of the atmosphere. Close by this spring, in the shade of the palm-grove, are the traces of a small temple, supposed to be the relics of the sanctuary mentioned by Diodorus Siculus as being near the Fountain of the Sun.

The character of the ruins now described carries back their date beyond the era of Christianity,—an inference which is confirmed by the appearance of a mountain in the neighbourhood, a great part of which has been converted into catacombs. Some of these sepulchral chambers are on a magnificent scale, and bear a considerable degree of resemblance to the celebrated tombs of Thebes, having the same variety of apartments, and even of decoration, sculpture, and painting. But, unfortunately, none of them have escaped violation, and in the greater number nothing remains except relics of ancient mummies, crumbling bones, and torn linen. About ten years ago a part of the excavations was possessed by a tribe of Arabs, who turned them into a subterraneous village.

[*] Cabinet of Voyages, vol. l. p. 205.
[†] See Travels in Africa, Egypt, and Syria, by W. G. Browne. Second edition, p. 14, &c.

The interest of the traveller is still excited by a succession of lakes and temples which stretch into the desert far towards the west; all rendered sacred by religious associations and by the traditionary legends of the native tribes. Tombs, catacombs, churches, and convents are scattered over the waste, which awaken the recollections of the Christian to the early history of his belief, and which at the same time recall to the Pagan and the Mohammedan events more interesting than are to be found in the vulgar annals of the human race, or can touch the heart of any but those who are connected with a remote lineage by means of a family history. At a short distance from the sacred lake there is a temple of Roman or Greek construction, which in modern times bears the name of Kasr Roum. The portion still standing is divided into three apartments, the longest of which is fifty feet by twenty-two, and the height eighteen feet. The roof, composed of large stones, is still remaining in a part of the building; but, generally speaking, both the covering and the walls have fallen down. Perhaps the only remarkable feature attending this building is the fact that the architecture is of the Doric order, the sculptures, cornices, and friezes being executed with much care and precision,—a circumstance which cannot fail to excite surprise in a country surrounded by the immense deserts of Libya, and at the distance of not less than four hundred miles from the ancient limits of civilization.

In the consecrated territory of that mysterious land is the salt lake of Arashieh, distant two days and a half from Siwah, in a valley enclosed by two mountains, and extending from six to seven leagues in circumference. So holy is it esteemed, that M. Cailliaud could not obtain permission to visit its banks. Even the pasha's firman failed to alter the determination of the sheiks on this essential point. They declared that they would sooner perish than suffer a stranger to approach that sacred island, which, according to their belief, contained treasures and talismans of mysterious power. It is said to possess a temple, in which are the seal and sword of the prophet, the palladium of their independence, and not to be seen by any profane eye. A reasonable doubt may indeed be entertained as to these assertions; for M. Drovetti, who accompanied a detachment of troops under Hassan Bey, walked round the borders of the lake, and observed nothing in its bosom but naked rocks. Mr. Browne, too, remarks, that he found "misshapen rocks in abundance," but nothing that he could positively decide to be ruins,—it being very unlikely, he adds, that any should be there, the spot being entirely destitute of trees and fresh water.

Major Rennell has employed much learning to prove that the Oasis of Siwah is the site of the famous temple of Jupiter Ammon. He remarks, that the variations, between all the authorities ancient and modern, amount to little more than a space equal to thrice the length of the oasis in question, which is at the utmost only six miles long. "And it is pretty clearly proved that no other oasis exists in that quarter within two or more days' journey; but, on the contrary, that Siwah is surrounded by a wide desert: so that it cannot be doubted that this oasis is the same with that of Ammon; and the edifice found there the *remains* of the celebrated temple from whence the oracles of Jupiter Ammon were delivered."*

At different distances in the desert, towards the west, are, other oases, the exact position and extent of which are almost entirely unknown to the European geographer. The ancients, who we are satisfied had more certain intelligence in regard to that quarter of the globe than is yet possessed by the moderns, were wont to compare the surface of Africa to a leopard's skin; the little islands of fertile soil being as numerous as the spots on that animal. It is probable that these interesting retreats will soon be better known; for the authority of Mohammed Ali being recognised as far as his name is known, the traveller will find the usual facilities and protection which are so readily granted to the Franks whom an enlightened curiosity leads into his dominions.

The desert which bounds the eastern side of the Egyptian valley, and stretches to the shores of the Red Sea, presents likewise to the philosopher several points worthy of consideration. Mr. Irwin, who travelled from Kenneh to Cairo by a road which passes obliquely through the northern part of this wilderness, found some delightful ravines in the hilly barrier by which it is guarded, ornamented with beautiful

* The Geographical System of Herodotus Examined and Explained, &c., vol. ii. p. 230. Second edition.

shrubs, and affording a safe retreat to the timid antelope. Some tufts of wild wheat, a date-tree, a well, and a grotto call to mind the old anchorets who chose in these solitudes to relinquish all intercourse with the sinful world. Two verdant spots, of a similar character, near the Arabian Gulf, between Suez and Cosseir, contain the monasteries of St. Anthony and St. Paul, surrounded with thriving orchards of dates, olives, and apricots.

But the most interesting object on the shores of the inlet just mentioned are the remains of Berenice, a town which connects the history of ancient Egypt with that of the Macedonian and Roman power in Africa, and at the same time indicates one of the channels through which commerce was carried on between the remoter parts of Asia and the nations of Europe. According to Pliny, it was through Berenice that the principal trade of the Romans with India was conducted, by means of caravans, which reached the Nile at Coptos, not far from the point at which the present shorter road by Cosseir meets the river. By this medium it is said that a sum not less than 400,000*l.* was annually remitted by them to their correspondents in the East, in payment of merchandise which ultimately sold for a hundred times as much.

An exaggerated account of an ancient city, said to have been discovered in that neighbourhood, was published some years ago in a French work, purporting to convey intelligence recently received from M. Caillaud, a young traveller in Africa. The situation was described as being a few leagues from the Red Sea, and currently known among the Arabs by the name of Sekellé. The ruins consisted of many temples, palaces, and private houses still standing, so that they might in some respects be compared to the relics of Pompeii; the architecture was Grecian, with some Egyptian ornaments; several inscriptions seemed to prove that the town must have been built by the Ptolemies, while one of the temples was evidently dedicated to Berenice. The hope of examining so many splendid monuments of ancient taste induced Belzoni and Mr. Beechey to undertake a painful journey across the desert, from Esneh to the Red Sea; in the course of which, after having inspected the surrounding country with the greatest minuteness, and that, too, under the direction of the same guide who had attended

M. Caillaud, they had the mortification to discover that the ardent Frenchman, beguiled either by the mirage or by his own heated fancy, had seen towers, palaces, and temples, which to more ordinary observers were entirely invisible. The strictures of Belzoni, whose mind was entirely devoted to matters of fact, are more amusing than complaisant. "All that we saw was the summits of other lower mountains, and at last we began to be persuaded that no such town existed, and that Monsieur Caliud (so he spells the name) had seen the great city only in his own imagination. It was rather provoking to have undertaken such a journey in consequence of such a fabricated description; and I hope this circumstance will serve as a warning to travellers to take care to what reports they listen, and from whom they receive their information. From the accounts of persons who are so given to exaggeration, one cannot venture on a journey without running the risk of being led astray and disappointed, as we were in our search after the said town with its eight hundred houses,—and very like Pompeii!"

But his labour was at length rewarded by discovering the site of the real Berenice on the margin of the sea, and at no great distance from the position in which it is laid down by M. D'Anville. The ruins have assumed the appearance of little mounds, but the lines of the principal streets, nevertheless, can still be distinctly traced, and even the forms of the houses, though these last are for the most part filled with sand. The materials used by the architects of Habesh were somewhat singular, for Belzoni assures us that he could see nothing but coral, roots, madrepore, and several petrifactions of seaweed. The temple, he adds, is built of a kind of soft calcareous and sandy stone, but decayed much by the air of the sea.

It is well known that Berenice was built by Ptolemy Philadelphus, a little after the establishment of Myos Hormus. Situated in a lower part of the gulf, it facilitated navigation by enabling mariners to take advantage of the regular winds. The inland route between Coptos and Berenice was opened with an army by the same prince, who established stations along it for the protection of travellers. This relation, which is given by Strabo, agrees with the Adulitic inscription preserved in Cosmas, which records the Ethiopian conquests of Ptolemy Euergetes, who seems to have adopted the commercial plans of his father, and to have endeavoured to extend them. The Romans, when they conquered Egypt, immediately perceived the importance of these arrangements; Berenice became the centre of their Eastern trade, and Myos Hormus sunk to a subordinate station. The only Greek author who gives an account of this emporium, is the geographer just named. All the details, indeed, concerning the inland route from Coptos to Berenice are Roman. It occupied twelve days, and is estimated at 258 miles by Pliny and the compiler of the Peutingerian Tables. The port of Habesh, the name that the harbour corresponding to Berenice now obtains, is derived from the appellation which the African shore in the parallel of Syené often receives.*

The situation of this interesting town must have been delightful. The sea opens before it on the east; and, from the southern coast to the point of the cape, there is an amphitheatre of mountains, with a single break on the north-west, forming the communication which connects it with Egypt. Right opposite there is a fine harbour entirely made by nature, guarded on the east by a projecting rock, on the south by the land, and on the west by the town. The extent covered by the ruins was ascertained to be 2000 feet by 1600, which was calculated to contain 4000 houses; but, that he might "not be mistaken for another Caliud," Mr. Belzoni reduces the number to 2000, which at the rate of five to a family gives a population of about 10,000 persons, old and young. The temple, which measured 102 feet in length by 43 in width, proved to be Egyptian both in its plan and its architecture, having figures sculptured in basso relievo, executed with considerable skill, together with many hieroglyphics. The plain that surrounds the town is very extensive; the nearest point in the mountains which form the crescent being not less than five miles distant. The soil is so completely moistened by the vapour from the sea as to be quite suitable for vegetation, and would produce, if properly cultivated, abundant pasture for camels, sheep, and other domestic animals. At present it abounds with acacias and a small tree called suvaro, which last grows so close to the shore as to be under water every

* Murray's Historical Account, vol. ii. p. 187.

high tide.   Unfortunately, there are no wells nor springs in the neighbourhood, and hence a difficulty in accounting for the supply of an article altogether indispensable to a town so considerable as Berenice must have been during the government of the Ptolemies.   It is presumed that the contiguous hills would afford the means of answering this claim, though at present no traces of an aqueduct can be discovered.

From this narrative it should seem that the city which bears the name of Ptolemy's mother is situated near the 24th degree of latitude, or in the same parallel with Syené. The seashore in that vicinity is formed almost entirely of calcareous matter, in the shape of madrepores, corals, and shells, all aggregated into a solid mass like a rock, and stretching from the bank of sand which constitutes the boundary of the tide to a great distance into the water.   A similar phenomenon occurs in Ceylon, where the lime held in solution at the mouths of the rivers combines with the siliceous and argillaceous ingredients of the beach, and gives rise to a continued extension of the coast as well as to those coral reefs which prove so dangerous to the mariner.   "All the shore," says the traveller, "as far as we could see, was composed of a mass of petrifactions of various kinds."   In some places there are beds of sand, but there is not a spot for a boat to approach the beach without the risk of being staved against the rock.

At the distance of twenty-five miles, in a straight line from the Red Sea, are the famous Emerald Mountains, the highest of which, from a reference to its subterranean treasure, is called Zubara.   These mines were formerly visited by Bruce, whose account of them is amply confirmed by the latest travellers, who in verifying his statements do no more than justice to his memory, so long and so ungenerously reviled.   The present pasha of Egypt made an attempt in the year 1818 to renew the process, which had been long relinquished, for finding those precious stones so much prized by the former conquerors of the land.   About fifty men were employed when Mr. Belzoni passed the establishment; but, although they had toiled six months, nothing was found to satisfy the avarice of their powerful employer, whom they execrated in their hearts.   The mines or excavations made by the ancients were all choked up with the rubbish of the roof that had fallen in, and the labour to remove it was great; for the holes were very small, scarcely capable of containing the body of a man crawling like a chameleon. These unfortunate wretches received their supply of provisions from the Nile; but occasionally it did not arrive in due time, and great famine of course prevailed among them. The nearest well was distant about half a day's journey; whence it is not surprising that, deprived of the necessaries of life, and feeling that they were doomed to be sacrificed in the desert, they should have repeatedly risen against their leaders and put them to death.[*]

The great wilderness of Eastern Egypt is occupied by various tribes of Arabs, who consider its different sections as their patrimonial inheritance. The Ababdeh rule over that portion of it which stretches from the latitude of Cosseir to a distant part of Nubia; the Beni Wassel join them on the north; and these again are succeeded by the Mahazeh, who claim an authority as far as the parallel of Beni Souef. The desert, which comprehends the Isthmus of Suez, is in the possession of a fourth family, who are known by the designation of Hooat-al, and sometimes by that of Atoonis or Antonis, derived, it is probable, from the name of the saint whose convent gives celebrity to the neighbourhood.

It has been observed that this sterile region exhibits the form of a triangle, the apex of which is placed at Suez, while the two sides rest upon the Red Sea and the Nile. In the parallel of Cairo the river is scarcely three days' journey distant from the sea; at Keft the distance is considerably increased; farther south it becomes nine days' journey; while at Syené it is computed to be about seventeen. This district, which from its eastern situation is denominated Sharkin,—a word latinized into Saracene,—is by the ancients frequently termed Arabia, from the similarity both of the country and the inhabitants. It has also been termed Asiatic Egypt. The chain of mountainous ridges which confine the eastern bank of the Nile is so steep and precipitous that it frequently exhibits the aspect of an artificial fortification, interrupted at intervals by deep and rugged ravines. But, as if this natural defence had not been sufficient, the remains of a real wall, about twenty-four feet thick, formed of huge stones, and running from north to south, is asserted to have been discovered in this desert. This the Arabs suppose to have been constructed by an ancient Egyptian king, and hence the name which it continues to bear,—*The Wall of the Old Man.* The greater part of this arid desert affords no traces of animal or vegetable life: "The birds," says Dr. Leyden, "shun its torrid atmosphere, the serpent and the lizard abandon the sands, and the red ant, which resembles in colour the soil on which it lives, is almost the only creature that seems to exist among the ruins of nature. But the monasteries of St. Anthony and St. Paul are still inhabited by Coptic monks, who, while they claim an absolute power over demons and wild beasts, are unable to protect themselves from the wandering Arabs,—more formidable than either to an unarmed ascetic."*

Towards Suez the shore is skirted by some small islands, which are as barren as the mainland. The principal of these are the Jaffatines, four in number, and arranged in the form of a semicircle. After passing Djibel-el-Zeil the harbour of Myos Hormus presents itself, anciently selected by Ptolemy Philadelphus in preference to Suez. For a considerable period this was the emporium of the Arabian trade, until, as we have already stated, in the time of the Romans it was supplanted by Berenice. Cosseir, the Leucos Portus of the geographer Ptolemy, has long given place to a more modern town of the same name, which stands in lat. 26° 7′ N., and long. 34° 4′ E., and is said to be built among hillocks of moving sand: The houses are formed of clay, and the inhabitants, in their manners and features, have a greater resemblance to the Arabians of the opposite shore than to the native Egyptians. It now derives its chief importance from being one of the stations at which the pilgrims assemble on their route to the holy cities of Mecca and Medina.†

* Murray's *Historical Account of Discoveries and Travels in Africa*, vol. ii. p. 182.
† Ibid. vol. ii. p. 185

CHAPTER X.

Manners and Customs of the Egyptians.

IN a country, the inhabitants of which acknowledge so
many different descents, the manners and customs must
partake of an equal variety. The habits of the Moslem, for
example, can have little resemblance to those of the Copt,
the Mamlouk, the Bedouin, or the Jew; for in points where
hereditary attachments do not interfere, the authority of
religion continues to perpetuate a distinction. Our best
guides as to modern Egypt are Mr. Browne and Dr. Hume,
both of whom were a considerable time resident in the
country, and well qualified by their knowledge of society to
supply an intelligible account of what fell under their observation. In regard to the more ancient periods, it is
obvious that we do not possess sufficient information of domestic life from which to furnish a narrative that might
prove agreeable to the general reader, who cannot be supposed to take much interest in the details of a superstitious
worship, or in the opinions of a mystical philosophy. We
shall therefore confine ourselves to a single extract from
Diodorus Siculus, relative to the funeral ceremonies which
were observed in the days of the Pharaonic dynasty. He
tells us that a talent of silver—450l.—was sometimes expended in performing the last offices to a distinguished
individual.

The relatives of the deceased, says he, announce to the judges and to all the connexions of the family the time appointed for the ceremony, which includes the passage of the defunct over the lake or canal of the Nome to which he belonged. Two-and-forty judges are then collected, and arranged on a semicircular bench, which is situated on the bank of the canal; the boat is prepared, and the pilot, who is called by the Egyptians *Charon*, is ready to perform his office; whence it is said that Orpheus borrowed the mythological character of this personage. But before the coffin is put into the boat, the law permits any one who chooses to bring forward his accusations against the dead person; and if it is proved that his life was criminal the funeral rites are prohibited; while, on the other hand, if the charges are not substantiated, the accuser is subjected to a severe punishment. If there are no insinuations against the deceased, or if they have been satisfactorily repelled, the relations cease to give any further expression to their grief, and proceed to pronounce suitable encomiums on his good principles and humane actions; asserting, that he is about to pass a happy eternity with the pious in the regions of Hades. The body is then-deposited in the catacomb prepared for it with becoming solemnity.*,

This narrative is confirmed by various pictorial representations still preserved, which exhibit the forty-two judges performing the duty here assigned to them, as well as by certain inscriptions which distinctly allude to the same remarkable custom. Hence is likewise established the opinion, conveyed by several of the Greek historians and philosophers, that the ancient Egyptians believed in a future state of reward and punishment.

In civil suits, according to the same author, the number of judges was only thirty; and it is worthy of special notice, as bearing some affinity to a usage well known in a neighbouring nation, that their president wore a breastplate adorned with jewels, which was called Truth. The eight books of the laws were spread open in court; the pleadings of the advocates were exclusively conducted in writing, in order that the feelings of the judges might not be improperly biassed by the too energetic eloquence of an impassioned

* Diodor. Sicul. Hist. lib. i. cap. 92

orator. The president delivered the sentence of his colleagues by touching the successful party with the mysterious symbol of truth and justice which adorned his person.[*]

Dr. Hume relates, that when at Rosetta he and a friend were invited by a Coptic merchant to witness the christening of a child. On entering they were received by the lady of the house with great civility. She poured a little perfumed rose-water into their hands from a bottle covered with silver filigree of very fine work; and as they passed into the room they were sprinkled over with rose-water. This was found to be a common custom in all Coptic and Levantine houses when a person makes a visit of ceremony. The apartment into which they were introduced was in the highest floor, where was a table covered with all kinds of sweetmeats and fruits. The mistress of the family and her sister, also a married lady, with her husband and other guests, soon made their appearance. The infant was completely swathed. The ceremony was performed by a Coptic priest, according to a service which he read from a manuscript ritual; which, if we may trust to the description given by Pococke, consists in plunging the child three times into water, after which it is confirmed, and receives the other sacrament,—that is, the minister dips his finger in consecrated wine and puts it to the infant's mouth.[†]

Having mentioned the Levantines, we may add that the people who go by this name are the descendants of Franks born in Egypt and Syria, and that they are thereby distinguished from the natives of European countries. The ladies of this class imitate the Arabs in dying their eyelashes, eyebrows, and hair with a dark colour, and dress in the costume of the higher order of that description of society.

The Moslem marriages are always regulated by the elder females, the bridegroom seldom seeing the bride until the day of their union. It is merely a civil contract between their mutual friends, and signed by the young man and his father. There is a procession consisting of many persons, male and female, who accompany the young lady to the house of her future husband, where she is received by her female friends. As soon as the ceremony is performed the

* Philosoph. Trans., 1819; Supplement to Ency. Brit., vol. iv. p. 52.
† Walpole's Memoirs, p. 400; Pococke's Travels, vol. i. p. 246

women raise a shout of congratulation, which is repeated
at intervals during the entertainment that follows. After
this burst of joy they make another procession through the
streets, the females all veiled; and a person mounted on a
horse richly caparisoned carries a red handkerchief fixed to
the end of a pole after the fashion of a military banner.
They then return to the house, where they pass the
remainder of the day and part of the night in feasting,
looking at dancing-girls, and listening to singing-men.

Mr. Browne, who witnessed the marriage of the daughter
of Ibrahim Bey, describes it in the following terms:—"A
splendid equipage was prepared in the European form of a
coach drawn by two horses and ornamented with wreaths
of artificial flowers, in which a beautiful slave from the
harem, personating the bride (whose features were very
plain), was carried through the principal streets of Cairo.
The blinds of the coach were drawn up, and the fair deputy
sat concealed. The procession was attended by some beys,
several officers, and Mamlouks, and ended at the house
of the bridegroom, who received her from the carriage in
his arms." In general at Cairo, the bride, who is completely veiled, walks under a canopy supported by two
women to the house of the bridegroom. He adds, that the
ladies of the capital are not tall but well formed. The
upper ranks are tolerably fair, in which and in fatness consist the chief praises of beauty in the Egyptian climate.
They marry at fourteen or fifteen, and at twenty are past
their prime. For what reason the natives of hot climates
ordinarily prefer women of large persons, he acknowledges
that he was not able to discover. Nevertheless the Coptic
ladies have interesting features, large black eyes, and a
genteel figure.*

Speaking of the original inhabitants of Egypt, this author
confirms the opinion given by recent travellers in opposition
to that supported by Malte Brun, and obviously borrowed
from Volney. He admits that there is a peculiarity of
feature common to all the Copts, but asserts that neither
in countenance nor personal form is there any resemblance
to the negro. Their hair and eyes are indeed of a dark hue,
and the former is often curled, though not in a greater

* Travels in Africa, Egypt, and Syria, p. 76.

degree than is usually seen among Europeans. The nose
is generally aquiline, and though the lips be sometimes
thick, they are by no means generally so; and, on the
whole, he concludes a strong resemblance may be traced
between the form of visage in the modern Copts and that
presented in the ancient mummies, paintings, and statues.

Dr. Hume was admitted into the harem of Hassan Bey,
and saw three of its inmates. They were seated in a small
room, on the sides of which was a divan or sofa covered
with crimson satin,—a Turkey carpet being spread on the
middle of the floor. The crimson satin was fancifully em-
broidered with silver flowers. The ladies wore white
turbans of muslin, and their faces were concealed with long
veils, which in fact were only large white handkerchiefs
thrown carelessly over them. When they go abroad they
wear veils like the Arab women. Their trousers were of
red and white striped satin, very wide but drawn together
at the ankle with a silk cord, and tied under their breasts
with a girdle of scarlet and silver. Something like a white
silk shirt with loose sleeves and open at the breast was
next the skin. Over all was thrown a pelisse; one of them
wore light blue satin, spangled with small silk leaves, while
the two others were decked in pink satin and gold.

"We were treated with coffee, and were fanned by the
ladies themselves with large fans, a perfume being at the
same time scattered through the room. This was composed of rose-water, a great quantity of which is made in
Fayoum. They were reserved at first, but after conversing
with the Mamlouk who attended me they were less careful
to conceal their faces. Their beauty did not equal what I
had anticipated from the fineness of their skins. They
were inclined to corpulence; their faces were round and
inexpressive, but the neck, bosom, arms, and hands were
of great fairness and delicacy. My dress seemed to amuse
them very much, and they examined every part of it, particularly my boots and spurs. When drinking coffee with
the Turkish officers I chanced to forget my handkerchief,
and as I seemed to express a desire to find it, one of the
ladies took off a handkerchief from her head and presented
it to me, having first perfumed it."*

* Walpole's Memoirs, p. 305.

After this visit, Dr. Hume, expressing to a Mamlouk some curiosity in respect to the female establishment of Hassan Bey, was informed that the whole amounted to more than twenty, several of whom were Circassians ; but he added that his master had in reality only one wife, who was not among the ladies to whom the stranger was introduced, and that 'all the others were simply her attendants This arrangement is more general than is commonly believed, for even the Arabs usually content themselves with one wife ; or, when they have two, the second is always subservient to her predecessor in the affairs of the house.

The Ethiopian women brought to Egypt for sale, though black, are exceedingly beautiful ; their features being perfectly regular, and their eyes full of fire. A great number of them had been purchased by the French during their stay in the country, who were anxious to dispose of them previously to their departure for Europe ; and it was the custom to bring them to the common market-place in the camp, sometimes in boys' clothes, at other times in the gaudiest female dress of the Parisian fashion. The price was generally from sixty to a hundred dollars, while Arab women could be purchased as low as ten. The Circassians at all times are exposed to sale in particular markets or khans, and occasionally bring large sums of money to their owners. Their beauty, however, is not very highly prized by Europeans, who are at a loss to account for those lofty descriptions which fill the pages of oriental romance, and ascribe all the attractions of female form to the natives of one favoured portion of Asia.

In the house of a Turk the apartments for the women are furnished with the finest and most expensive articles ; but those of the men are only remarkable for a plain style of neatness. They breakfast before sunrise, make their second meal at ten, and their third at five in the afternoon ; using at all times an abundance of animal food. A large dish of pilau appears in the middle of the table, surrounded with small dishes of meat, fish, and fowl. Their drink is confined to water, but coffee is served immediately after the meal. At the tables of the great sherbet is introduced ; for as the manufacture of wine is not encouraged in Egypt the quantity that is used by the Greeks and Franks must be procured from abroad. The Egyptians still prepare a fermented liquor of maize, millet, barley, or rice, but it has very little resemblance to our ale. It is sufficiently pleasant to the taste, and of a clear light colour; but being very weak and pregnant with saccharine matter, it does not keep fresh above a day. The native Christians distil for themselves a liquor known by the general name of araki. It is made of dates, currants, or the small grapes which are imported from the Seven Islands. But the example of Mohammed Ali, who does not disdain to drink wine, has introduced some degree of laxity into the manners of the metropolis, where there are many who hold the opinion that the great wisdom of their pasha is entitled to equal respect with the injunctions of their prophet.

The style of living among Europeans is considerably different, but not uniform; every consulate setting an example to the people under its protection, and varying according to the seasons of the year. "One cannot find," says Mr. Carne, "the comforts of an English breakfast at Cairo; a cup of coffee and a piece of bread are ready at an early hour for whoever chooses; at midday comes a luxurious dinner of foreign cookery, with the wines of Europe and fruits of the East; and seven in the evening introduces supper,—another substantial meal, though rather less profuse than the dinner; and by ten o'clock most of the family retire. This is not the way of living best adapted to the climate, which seems to require only a slight refreshment during the sultry hours, and the solid meal to be reserved till the cool of the day. A singular luxury in this city, as well as in every other in the East, is the caimac, or clouted cream, exactly the same as that made in Devonshire and Cornwall, and manufactured in the same manner. It is cried about the streets fresh every morning, and is sold on small plates; and, in a place where butter is never seen, it is a rich and welcome substitute."* It may be remarked in passing, that except for the purposes of cookery fire is never used in the houses of Cairo, it being found more convenient to compensate the diminished temperature of the cold season by an addition to their clothing than by grates or stoves.

There are in the same capital more than three hundred

* Carne's Letters from the East, vol. 1. p. 96.

mosques, four or five of which are very splendid, more especially the one dedicated to Jama el Azhar, which is ornamented with pillars of marble and Persian carpets. A sheik, being at the same time an ecclesiastic of a high order, presides over the establishment, to which an immense property was formerly attached, and which still supports a number of persons who have the reputation of being distinguished for profound skill in theology ahd accurate knowledge of the Arabic language. It is furnished also with an extensive collection of manuscripts; and lectures are read on all subjects which among Mohammedan churchmen continue to be regarded as scientific, although entirely unconnected with the improvements of modern times.

The character of the viceroy, who labours under the imputation of being a freethinker, has not failed to operate a certain effect on the sentiments of the higher class of persons in Cairo. It is said of him that he values no man's religious opinions a single straw; as long as they serve him well, they may be Guebres, or worshippers of the Grand Lama. The celebrated traveller Burckhardt, with whom he was very fond of conversing, presented himself one day before him. "Pasha," he said, "I want to go and see the Holy City, and pray at the Prophet's tomb; give me your leave and firman for the journey."—"You go to Mecca and our blessed Prophet's tomb!" said the prince, "that's impossible, Ibrahim! you are not qualified; you know what I mean; nor do I think you are a true believer."—"But I am, pasha," was the reply: "you are mistaken, I assure you; I am qualified, too, in every respect; and as to belief, have no fears about that; tell me any part of the Koran that I will not believe!"—"Go to the Holy City, go, Ibrahim," said the pasha, laughing heartily; "I was not aware you were so holy a man. Do you think I'll vex myself with questions from the Koran? Go and see the Prophet's tomb, and may it enlighten your eyes and comfort your heart!"*

We are rather surprised to find both Mr. Browne and Dr. Hume maintaining that the Coptic language is entirely extinct, and no longer used in any part of Egypt. The former relates that in the Christian monasteries the prayers are read in Arabic, and the epistle and gospel in Coptic;

* Carne's Recollections of Travels in the East, p. 248.

observing, however, in regard to this last, that the priest is a mere parrot repeating a dead letter. Manuscripts in that language are, nevertheless, still found in some of the convents, leave to copy which might easily be obtained from the patriarch; and by these means a valuable addition would be made to the collections of M. Quatremère, to whom the scholars of Europe have been so much indebted.[*]

We have already stated that the Coptic creed is heretical in regard to the point on which Eutychius was accused of an erring faith. The moderns, notwithstanding, have adopted transubstantiation, thereby approximating more closely to the Roman belief than their orthodox neighbours of the Greek communion. They have, at the same time, adopted from the Mohammedans the custom of frequent prostrations during divine service; of individual prayer in public; and various other ceremonies suggested by the peculiarity of their climate.

The festival of opening the Calige, or cutting the bank of the Nile, is still annually observed at Cairo, and is one of the few ancient customs which continue to identify the inhabitants of the modern capital with their remotest ancestors. The year in which Mr. Carne visited Egypt, the 16th of August was the day appointed for this solemnity, the inundation having reached nearly its greatest height. Accompanied by some friends, he repaired about eight in the evening to the place, which was a few miles distant from the city, amid the roaring of cannon, illuminations, and fireworks. The shores of the Nile, a long way down from Boulak, were covered with groups of people,—some seated beneath the large spreading sycamores smoking, others gathered around parties of Arabs, who were dancing with infinite gayety and pleasure, and uttering loud exclamations of joy, affording an amusing contrast to the passionless demeanour and tranquil features of their Moslem oppressors. Perpetually moving over the scene, which was illumined by the most brilliant moonlight, were seen Albanian soldiers in their national costume, Nubians from the burning clime of farther Egypt, with Mamlouks, Arabs, and Turks.

[*] Maillet remarked, " Aujourd'hui la langue Copte n'y est plus entendue par les Coptes mêmes : le dernier qui l'entendait est mort en ce siècle " P. 24.

At last day broke, and soon after the report of a cannon announced that the event so ardently wished for was at hand. In a short time the kiaya bey, the chief minister of the pasha, arrived with his guard, and took his seat on the summit of the opposite bank. A number of Arabs now began to dig down the dike which confined the Nile, the bosom of which was covered with a number of pleasure-boats full of people, waiting to sail along the canal through the city. Before the mound was completely demolished, the increasing dampness and shaking of the earth induced the workmen to leave off. Several of them then plunged into the stream, and exerting all their strength to push down the remaining part, small openings were soon made, and the river broke through with irresistible violence; for some time it was like the rushing of a cataract.

According to custom, the kiaya bey distributed a good sum of money,—throwing it into the bed of the canal below, where a great many men and boys scrambled for it. It was an amusing scene, as the water gathered fast round them, to see them struggling and groping amid the waves for the coin; but the violence of the torrent soon bore them away There were some, indeed, who had lingered to the last, and now sought to save themselves by swimming,—still buffeting the waves, and grasping at the money showered down, and diving after it as it disappeared. Unfortunately, this sport costs a few lives every year, and the author informs us, there was one young man drowned on the present occasion.

The different vessels, long ere the fall had subsided, rushed into the canal, and entered the city, their decks crowded with all ranks, uttering loud exclamations of joy. The overflowing of the Nile is the richest blessing of Heaven to the Egyptians; and as it finds its way gradually into various parts of Cairo, the inhabitants flock to drink of it, to wash in it, and to rejoice in its progress. The vast square called the Birket, which a few hours before presented the appearance of a dusty neglected field, was now turned into a beautiful scene, being covered with an expanse of water, out of the bosom of which arose the finest sycamore trees. The sounds of joy and festivity, of music and songs, were now heard all over the city with cries of "Allah.

Allah!" and thanks to the Divine bounty for so inestimable a benefaction.*

It is admitted on all hands that, long before its arrival, Cairo stands greatly in need of this annual ablution. Dr. Clarke, at whose presence all the plagues of Egypt were revived in more than their original horrors, consents to acknowledge, that when the canal was filled with its muddy water, the prodigious number of gardens gave to the capital so pleasing an appearance, and the trees growing in those gardens were so new to the eye of a European, that for a moment he forgot the innumerable abominations of the dirtiest city in the whole earth. But he adds, that the boasted lakes, or rather mudpools, into which the waters of the river are received, particularly the famous Esbequier Birket, would certainly be considered nuisances in any part of the civilized world.†

A tradition prevails, that in ancient times a virgin was annually sacrificed to the Nile, in order to propitiate the deity who presided over its waters, and who, it was imagined with the view of obtaining the wonted victim, occasionally postponed or diminished the periodical flood. The only memorial now existing of this obsolete practice appears in the form of a pile or statue of mud, called Anis or the Bride, which is raised every year between the dike of the canal and the river, and is afterward carried away by the current when the embankment is broken down. Moreri, Murtadi, and other writers, allude to the same custom; and assign the motive already suggested for its introduction among the Egyptian idolaters. "They imagined," says the former, "that their god Serapis was the author of the marvellous inundation of the Nile, and accordingly, when it was delayed, they sacrificed to him a young girl. This barbarous devotion was abolished, if we may believe the Arabian historians, by the Caliph Omar."‡

It has become usual to resolve this statement into a mythological legend or astronomical emblem; but the prevalence of a similar custom in other parts of the world, and more especially in India, compels us to adhere to the literal import of the narrative, however abhorrent it may be to all

* Carne's Letters, vol. i. p. 99. † Travels, vol. v. p. 108.
‡ Diction., vol. vii. p. 1041.

the sentiments of modern times. For example, Bishop Heber relates that the images of a man and a woman, used in a Hindoo festival, were thrown into the Ganges ; and he describes it " as the relic of a hideous custom which still prevails in Assam, and was anciently practised in Egypt, of flinging a youth and maiden, richly dressed, annually into their sacred river. That such a custom formerly existed in India is, I believe, a matter of pretty uniform tradition."*

Some indistinct recollection of a similar fact appears to have reached the time of Ovid, who relates, that after nine years' drought, it was suggested that this grievous calamity might be averted by the sacrifice of a human being, a stranger in the land,—a corrupted allusion, perhaps, to the events which happened in the days of the patriarch Joseph.

> Dicitur Ægyptios caruisse juvantibus arva
> Imbribus, atque annos sicca fuisse novem.
> Cum Thraseas Busirin adiit, monstratque piari
> Hospitis effuso sanguine posse Jovem.

The practice of hiring women to lament for the dead is still observed at Cairo, to the great annoyance of the Frank population, whose ears reject the monotonous accents in which this nightly dirge is performed. Upon inquiry it was found that the wealthier the family the more numerous were the hired mourners, and of course the louder the lamentation ; that these singers exhibited the most frightful distortions, having their hair dishevelled, their clothes torn, and their countenances disfigured with paint and dirt,—that they were relieved at intervals by other women similarly employed,—and that the ceremony might thus be continued to any length. A principal part of their art consists in mingling with their howling such affecting expressions of praise or pity as may excite the tears of the relations who are collected around the corpse.†

* Journal, vol. ii. p. 391.

† Clarke's Travels, vol. v. p. 105. It is evident, as Dr. Clarke observes, that this custom, like the *caoineadh* of the Irish and the funeral-cry of other nations, are remains of ceremonies practised in honour of the dead in almost every country of the earth. They are the same that Homer describes at the death of Hector, and they are frequently alluded to in the sacred Scriptures. " Call for the mourning women, that they may come ; and send for cunning women, that they may come : and let them make haste, and take up a wailing for us, that our eyes may run down with tears, and our eyelids gush out with waters "—*Jer.* ix. 17, 18.

The females of Cairo are often seen in the public streets riding upon asses and mules: they sit in the masculine attitude, like the women of Naples and other parts of Italy. Their dress consists of a hood and cloak extending to the feet with a stripe of white calico in front, concealing the face and breast, but having two small holes for the eyes In this disguise, if a man were to meet his own wife or sister, he would not be able to recognise her unless she spoke to him; and this is seldom done, because the sus picious Moslems, observing such an intercourse, might sup pose an intrigue to be going on, in which case they wou. put one if not both of them to death. Sir F. Henniker com pares a lady mounted in the way just described, and wrapped up in a black mantle from head to foot, to a coffin placed perpendicularly on a horse, and covered with a pall.

The inhabitants of Cairo, fond of shows, like the populace of all great cities, amuse themselves chiefly with feats of bodily exercise, such as leaping, rope-dancing, and wrestling matches; also singing and dancing. They have buffoons, whose rude pleasantries and stale jests excite the ready laugh among an ignorant and corrupt people. The almehs, or female improvisatores, who amuse the rich with the exercise of their talent, differ from such as exhibit to the multitude. They come to relieve the solitude of the harem, where they teach the women new tunes, and repeat poems which excite interest from the representations which they give of national manners. They initiate the Egyptian ladies in the mysteries of their art, and teach them to practise dances of rather an unbecoming character. Some of these females have cultivated minds and an agreeable conversation, speaking their native language with purity. Their poetical habits make them familiar with the softest and best-sounding expressions, and their recitations are made with considerable grace. They are called in on al. festive occasions. During meals they are seated in a sort of desk, where they sing. Then they come into the draw ing-room to perform their dances, or pantomimic evolutions of which love is generally the groundwork. They now lay aside the veil, and with it the modesty of their sex.*

We shall take no farther notice of the disgraceful scene.

*Malte Brun, iv. p. 72.

which too often accompany the exhibitions of these dancing-women, nor shall we draw aside the veil which conceals from the common eye the sensualities of the Egyptian capital. It would be almost equally disagreeable to copy the descriptions given by several British travellers of the sufferings inflicted upon the senses and imagination of a European by the reptiles, flies, fleas, and other more nauseous vermin. Dr. Clarke informs us that a singular species of lizard made its appearance in every chamber, having circular membranes at the extremity of its feet, which gave it such tenacity that it walked upon window-panes of glass, or upon the surfaces of pendent mirrors. This revolting sight was common in every apartment, whether in the houses of the rich or of the poor. At the same time such a plague of flies covered all things with their swarms, that it was impossible to eat without having persons to stand by every table with feathers or flappers to drive them away. Liquors could not be poured into a glass; the mode of drinking was, to keep the mouth of every bottle closed till the moment it was applied to the lips, and instantly to cover it with the palm of the hand when removing it to any one else.

The utmost attention to cleanliness, by a frequent change of every article of wearing apparel, could not prevent the attacks of vermin, which seemed to infest even the air of the place. A gentleman made his appearance, to receive a company whom he had invited to dinner, with lice swarming upon his clothes; and the only explanation he could give as to the cause was, that he had sat for a short time in one of the boats upon the canal. Nay, it is ascertained that certain winds cover even the sands of the wilderness with this abominable insect. Sir Sidney Smith, on one occasion, apprehending the effects of sleeping a night in the village of Etko, preferred a bed on the bare surface of the adjoining desert; but, so far from escaping the evil he had dreaded, he found himself in the morning entirely covered with that mysterious plague over which the magicians of Pharaoh had no power. In regard to frogs, of which the Nile at one period of its annual increase seems to be almost exclusively composed; the "boils breaking out with blains;" and other peculiarities which continue to afflict the land of Ham, we must restrict ourselves to a simple reference to

such writers as Drs. Clarke, Shaw, and Pococke, who
groan over the long catalogue of human sufferings; or to
Sir F. Henniker, and other facetious tourists, who convert
these short afflictions into a subject of merriment.[*]

The French were less difficult to please, and much more
open to favourable impressions. Denon, for example,
speaks of the pleasurable sensations daily excited by the
delicious temperature of Cairo, causing Europeans, who
arrive with the intention of spending a few months in the
place, to remain during the rest of their lives without ever
persuading themselves to leave it. Few persons, however,
with whom our countrymen associate, are disposed to ac-
quiesce in this opinion. Those, indeed, who are desirous
of uninterrupted repose, or who are able to endure the in-
variable dulness which prevails in every society to which
strangers are admitted, may perhaps tolerate without murmuring a short residence in the midst of what Dr. Clarke
calls a "dull and dirty city." The effect, it is admitted,
whether it be of climate, of education, or of government,
is the same among all the settlers in Egypt except, the
Arabs,—a disposition to exist without exertion of any kind,
—to pass whole days upon beds and cushions,—smoking
and counting beads. This is what Maillet termed the true
Egyptian taste; and that it may be acquired by residing
among the native inhabitants of Cairo is evident, from the
appearance exhibited by Europeans who have passed some
years in that city.[†]

The lower orders of Egyptian Arabs are described as a
quiet, inoffensive people, with many good qualities; and
they are upon the whole more active in agricultural employ-
ments than we should be led to imagine from the habits of
the better class of them in towns, who pass their time in
listless indolence. Their dress consists simply of a pair
of loose drawers, blue or white, with a long blue tunic,
which serves to cover them from the neck to the ankle, and
a small red woollen scull-cap, round which they occasion-

---

[*] "The dust of the earth became lice upon man and upon beast
throughout all the land of Egypt. This application of the words of
sacred Scripture," says Dr. Clarke, "affords a literal statement of
existing evils; such a one as the statistics of the country do now
warrant."

[†] La Vraie Génie Egyptienne.

ally wind a long white stripe of the same material. The articles of furniture in their houses are extremely few. "The rooms of all people of decent rank," says Dr. Hume, "have a low sofa, called a divan, extending completely round three sides, and sometimes to every part of them except the doorway; but it is most commonly confined to the upper end of the chamber. On this divan the hours not devoted to exercise or business are invariably passed. It is about nine inches from the floor, and covered with mattresses; the back is formed by large cushions placed all along the wall so close as to touch each other, and more or less ornamented according to the wealth or taste of the owner. The beds are generally laid on wickerwork strongly framed, made of the branches of the date-tree, or consist of mattresses placed on a platform at the end of the room. For their meals they have a very low table, round which they squat on the mats covering the floor; and in houses of repute I have sometimes seen this table made of copper thinly tinned over. The mats used in Egypt are made of straw, or of the flags attached to the branches of the date-tree, and are very neatly worked in figures, such as squares, ovals, and other forms, with fanciful borders. They are very durable, but harbour numbers of fleas, with which all the houses swarm, particularly in hot weather."*

The poorer sort of these Arabs seldom can afford to eat animal food, but subsist chiefly on rice made into a pilau, and moistened with the rancid butter of the country. Sometimes they make a hearty meal on boiled horse-beans steeped in oil. The date supplies them with sustenance a part of the year; and in summer the vast quantities of gourds and melons which are then produced, place within their reach an agreeable variety. Their drink is the milk of buffaloes, or the water of the Nile purified and preserved in cisterns. None but the higher orders or those of dissolute lives ever taste wine; and hence, although grapes grow abundantly in several parts of Egypt, only a very small portion is manufactured into that exhilarating beverage which is forbidden to every true believer in the Prophet.

Some particular traits distinguish the Egyptian Arabs from other orientals. A country frequently laid under

* Walpole's Memoirs, p. 386.

water makes the art of swimming a valuable acquisition. The children learn it at play ; even the girls become fond of it, and are seen swimming in flocks from village to village with all the dexterity of the fabled nymphs. At the festival of the opening of the canals, several professional swimmers perform a mock fight in the water, and land to attack an enemy in presence of the pasha. Their evolutions are executed with surprising vigour. They sometimes float down the river on their backs, with a cup of coffee in one hand and a pipe in the other, while the feet are tied together with a rope.*

In many parts the barbers are still the only practitioners in physic ; and in a country where every man's head is shaved, the professors of the healing art cannot fail to be numerous. Their knowledge is of course extremely confined. They perform a few surgical operations, and are acquainted with the virtues of mercury and some standard medicines. The general remedy in cases of fever and other kinds of illness is a saphie from a priest, which consists of some sentence from the Koran written on a small piece of paper and tied round the patient's neck. This, if the sick man recovers, he carefully preserves by keeping it constantly between his scull-caps, of which he generally wears two or three. Saphies are very commonly used by the Mohammedans, being considered to possess much efficacy for the body as well as the soul, and occupy the same place in the estimation of the superstitious as did the frontlets of the Jews and the phylacteries of the early Christians. In every bazaar, however, some shops are found in which are sold some of the most common drugs, such as opium, rhubarb, and senna.†

The Egyptian Arabs are punctual in the performance of their religious duties at the stated hours appointed by their Prophet. They are often seen, after a hard day's work, kneeling with great devotion, offering up their prayers with their foreheads at times touching the ground. The respect in which idiots are held by the Mohammedans is well known ; it being imagined that these unfortunate persons are possessed by a benign spirit, and under the special pro-

* Malte Brun, iv. p. 108.
† Dr. Hume in Walpole's Memoirs, p. 389.

tection of Heaven. It is to be regretted that these notions
of sanctity sometimes lead to customs not to be reconciled
to European ideas of decorum; the use of clothes being
thought inconsistent with the purity of mind and the holy
functions which the superstition of an ignorant people has
attributed to the natural fool. .

Until the present viceroy introduced the European press,
a printed book was a rare sight in Egypt either among
Turks or Arabs. A class of men, similar to the copyists
and caligraphers of the middle ages, earned a livelihood by
forming manuscripts of the Koran and other works in high
reputation, some of which were most beautifully executed
in inks of various colours. The notes were generally done
in red or light blue. Dr. Clarke, who made considerable
purchases, informs us that writings of celebrity bear very
great prices, especially treatises on history, geography, and
astronomy. The Mamlouks are fonder of reading than the
Turks; and some of their libraries in Cairo contained
volumes valued at immense sums. This traveller obtained
a transcript of the "Arabian Nights," which was brought
to him in four quarto cases, containing one hundred and
seventy-two tales, separated into one thousand and one
portions for recital during the same number of nights. This
valuable acquisition was unfortunately lost,—an event
which is the more to be regretted, because many of the
tales related to Syrian and Egyptian customs and traditions,
which have not been found in any other copy of the same
work.*

A custom still prevails in Egypt, which may be traced to
the remotest times, as being alluded to by Herodotus, and
distinctly mentioned by Pliny,—the practice of taming serpents, of sporting with the bites of the most poisonous
vipers, and even of eating these animals alive. "A tumultuous throng," says Dr. Clarke, "passing beneath the windows of our house, attracted our attention towards the
quay; here we saw a concourse of people following men
apparently frantic, who with every appearance of convul-
sive agony were brandishing live serpents, and then tearing
them with their teeth; snatching them from each other's
mouths with loud cries and distorted features, and afterward

* Travels, vol. v. p. 111.
E •

falling into the arms of the spectators as if swooning; the women all the while rending the air with their lamentations."

This singular power over so dangerous an animal is claimed only by one tribe, who, on account of some signal act of piety performed by their ancestors, are understood to be protected by the Prophet from any injury that might befall them. These persons, however, do not always escape; for the author of the book of Ecclesiasticus asks, Who will pity a charmer that is bitten by a serpent? Forskal says, that the leaves of the *aristolochia sempervirens* was used during forty days by those who wished to be rendered invulnerable; and we observe in the examination which an Abyssinian ecclesiastic underwent at the instance of some British travellers who wanted to ascertain the accuracy of Bruce, it is stated that the plant must be used at the moment the charm is performed.

' At Pella, too, if we may believe Lucian, the serpents were rendered so tame and familiar that they were fed by the women, and slept with the children. Dr. Hume relates, that when he lived at Alexandria a nest of snakes was discovered in his house. Following the advice of his interpreter he sent for one of the gifted family, who was an old man, and by trade a carpenter. He prayed fervently at the door a quarter of an hour, and at length, pale and trembling, he ventured into the room; while an English sailor, who was employed as a servant, cleared away the rubbish in which they were concealed, and killed them with a shovel.

We conclude this chapter with a remark truly characteristic of the manners of modern Egypt, and of the feelings which were ingrafted upon the minds of the higher class by the long-continued sway of the Mamlouks. Before the reign of the present viceroy, it was customary, even among a people rigidly attached to the distinctions of hereditary rank, to reserve their highest respect for the purchased slave whose relations were unknown, and whose bravery or other personal qualities had raised him to the first honours in the country. General Reynier mentions that he has heard even Turkish officers say of persons who occupied great posts, " He is a man of the best connexions,—he was bought."[*]

---

[*] Reynier, L'Egypte, p. 66, quoted by M. Malte Brun, vol. iv. p. 165.

CHAPTER XI.

The Natural History of Egypt.

GEOLOGY—Valley of the Nile—Alluvial Formation—Primitive Rocks—Serpentine—Of Upper Egypt—Limestone Strata—Sandstone and Trap—Puddingstone—Verde Antico—Natron Rocks—Minerals—Precious Stones—Ores—ZOOLOGY—Camelus Dromedarius—Giraffe—Civet Cat—Ichneumon—Sorex, or Shrew—Jerboa—Hippopotamus—Crocodile; cherished by Ancients—Monitor of the Nile—Hyena—Capra Aigrus—Ovis Tragelaphus — Locust — BIRDS—Chenclopex— Ostrich—Ibis Ardea; Ibis Religiosa—Vulture; Mistake of Bruce—Oriental Dotterell—Charadrius Himantopus—Corvus Ægyptiacus—Aicedo Ægyptiacus—Anas Nilotica—Sterna Nilotica—The Pelican—The Quail, or Tetrao Coturnix—FISHES—Echeneis Neucrates—Sparus Niloticus—Labrus Niloticus—The Perch—Silurus Clarias—Salmo Niloticus—Tetraodon—Mugil Cephalus and Clupea Alosa—PLANTS—Papyrus; Uses—Persea—Lotus—Rose-lily—Rhamnus Lotus—Phœnix Dactylifera— Ficus Sycomorus — Plantain-tree —Cucumis Chate—Cucurbita Lagenaria—Colocasium—Carthamus Tinctorius—Acacia: Gum; Frankincense—Henna—The Aloe—ZOOPHYTES—Corallines—Red Coral—Sponges—Polypes—Madrepores, Millepores, Gorgonia or Sea-fan.

SECTION I.—GEOLOGY.

THE valley of the Nile, which taken by itself is strictly an alluvial formation, presents, nevertheless, a variety of features highly deserving the notice of the geologist. It is bounded by two chains of hills, which, after gradually passing from the primitive order of rocks into the secondary and floetz-trap, terminate in deposites belonging to the most recent description of stratified minerals.

The district between Philoe and Es Souan, on the left bank of the river, is occupied by the northern extremity of that granitic range which stretches into Nubia; containing a particular species of stone to which, from the mixture of a small portion of hornblende, the name of syenite is usually given. It is in this neighbourhood that those quarries are still seen from which the ancients hewed the stupendous masses required for their colossal statues and obelisks. The granite is occasionally diversified by alternations of gneiss, porphyry, clay-slate, quartz, and serpentine, which contain, as imbedded minerals, a great variety of carnelions and jaspers. Serpentine likewise occurs on the Arabian side, along with beds of clay-slate and compact felspar, and has been erroneously described by some authors as a green-coloured marble. There has also been observed in Upper Egypt a true marble, or granular foliated limestone, exhibiting the various hues of white, gray, yellow, blue, and red ; and which, when combined with serpentine, forms the well-known rock called verde antico.

This section of the geological domain is succeeded towards the north by an argillaceous sandstone alternating with the carbonate of lime ; while the corresponding chain on the Arabian side continues to display serpentine and granite. At Esneh the rocks become more decidedly calcareous, retaining the same character till they sink into the plain which bounds the lower division of Egypt. The steep perpendicular cliffs which characterize this limestone formation give a monotonous and rather dreary aspect to the country, contrasting unfavourably with the bolder and more picturesque mountains of the south, which offer new views in rapid succession, and confer upon the landscape an agreeable variety of beauty and magnificence.

This limestone has a splintery or conchoidal fracture ; its colour is gray or variegated ; and it contains numerous petrifactions of shells, corals, and fishes. It extends from Syené to the Mediterranean ; and, in Lower Egypt, reaches from Alexandria to the Red Sea in the vicinity of Suez. A similar rock is discovered in the mountain-district which leads to Cosseir, and in the same country there are hills of limestone associated with gypsum or sulphate of lime. In the valleys which intersect that elevated ground, the sand is partly calcareous and partly quartose, indicating the quality of the strata from the waste of which it is formed. It is said that the ridge in question consists of three kinds of rock ; the first of which is a small-grained granite ; the second is a breccia, or puddingstone of a particular sort, known by the name of breccia de verde ; and to this succeeds, for a space of thirty miles, a schistose deposite, which seems to be of a contemporaneous formation with the breccias, since they are connected by gradual transitions, and contain rounded masses of the same substance.

At the wells of El-Aoosh-Lambazeh there occurs a singular chain of slaty mountains, presenting, in their composition, rock-crystal and steatitic rocks; but at the distance of eight miles from Cosseir they suddenly change their character, the greater part of them appearing in the form of limestone or alabaster, in strata lying nearly north and south. Here are found the remains of the astrea diluviana; and among the hills, considered by geologists as of later formation, are observed specimens of a schistose structure, together with porphyries not distinctly characterized. The bottom of the valley, covered with immense rocky fragments, presents a numberless variety of minerals,—clay-slate, gneiss, porphyry, granite, and certain compound rocks, —in which are actynolite, and a particular kind of steatite containing nodules of schistose spar. There is besides a new and peculiar substance, found also in several spots of the Desert of Sinai, and resembling the green shorl of Dauphiné. It has not been discovered in a separate state, but forms part of the granites, the porphyries, and other rocks.[*]

Greenstone, or the very common rock which is composed of hornblende and felspar, occurs in beds in Upper Egypt. It is sometimes porphyritic, forming a green-coloured basis, in which pale green crystals of felspar are imbedded, and constituting a beautiful stone, recognised among mineralogists as green porphyry. It is not unfrequently mistaken for the verde antico, which, as we have already described, is a compound of serpentine and granular limestone without either hornblende or felspar.

But the most remarkable geological formation in Egypt is that composed of the carbonate of soda, which skirts the valley of the Natron Lakes. The hills which divide the basin, now named from that of the Waterless River, consist in a great measure of this chymical compound mixed with a muriate of the same substance. In the valley of the Wilderness the latter salt is found in thin compact layers supported by strata of gypsum; and also in the other deserts it occurs very frequently in a state of crystallization, sometimes under the sand, but more frequently on the surface.

It is to be regretted that our travellers, generally speaking, have not bestowed that degree of attention upon the geological structure of Eastern Africa which it unquestion-

[*] Mém. sur l'Egypte, vol. iii. p. 255; Malte Brun, vol. iv. p. 29

ably deserves. Hitherto no extensive series of observations
have been made in regard to the general direction and dip
of the mountains in that part of the world, and hence the
relative positions of the great rock-formations remain very
imperfectly known. We can perceive in their narratives
some traces of the usual distinctions of mineral bodies into
primitive, secondary, floetz, and alluvial, and are thereby led
to conclude that there are in Egypt the same successions
and affinities which mark the geological relations of these
substances in all other portions of the globe that have been
minutely examined. But there is still a complete want of
systematic views in all the descriptions and details with
which we have been hitherto supplied; and thus are we
compelled to rest satisfied with conjecture when we are
most desirous to attain the means of establishing a philosophical principle.*

Of the more precious minerals found in Egypt the following are the best known, and the most interesting to the
common reader.

The topaz may still be seen in an island of the Red Sea,
called Zemorget, or the Island of Topazes, and is said to
have been collected by some of the ancient kings.

The emerald, it has been already mentioned, was understood to be procured in the ridge of mountains situated on
the western shores of the Arabian Gulf, and to have been
made an article of considerable commerce by the Romans.
Bruce speaks of an island in the same sea called the Island
of Emeralds, but which, upon being minutely examined,
was found to produce nothing more valuable than green-
coloured fluor spar.

Chrysoberyl is likewise enumerated among the mineral
productions of Upper Egypt. The rarest varieties of quartz,
too, met with in any part of Africa are the Egyptian avan-
turine and the rock crystal of the northern shores. Cal-
cedony also, as well as carnelion, have been picked up on
either bank of the Nile, both in the Upper and Lower provinces. Agate belongs to the rocks which diversify the
desert eastward of Cairo; while jasper occurs in veins of considerable thickness in the clay-slate which bounds the
western valley between Esneh and Siout.

There is a finer jasper, however, for which Egypt is cele-

* Murray's Discoveries in Africa, vol.

brated, and which occurs abundantly in the sandy waste between the capital and Suez. It has likewise been found in other parts below Beni Souef, imbedded in a species of conglomerate. Actynolite, epidote, and hornblende are frequently detected in the valleys which extend from the Upper Nile towards the Red Sea; to which may be added heavy spar or sulphate of barytes.

The mountains contiguous to Egypt have been so imperfectly explored that we are still ignorant as to the amount of their metallic treasures. We may, however, conclude, from the early advancement of the arts among the inhabitants of the Nile, that iron was not unknown to them; and thence proceed to the inference that this ore was found in the vicinity of the great works in which it was employed. Their quarries, their obelisks, their pyramids, and statues indicate, in a manner not to be misunderstood, that instruments of the best-tempered metal must have been placed in the hands of their artists.

Africa affords a considerable quantity of gold, which is always obtained in the form of dust and rolled masses, and is found in the sand of rivers, or the alluvial soil of valleys near a mountain-range. The position of Egypt deprives it of this source of wealth; but in the countries above the Cataracts, especially in Kordofan, there are several tracts remarkable for the quantity of this precious metal which they afford. Hence the opinion prevalent among the ancients that Ethiopia was rich in gold; which, in former times as well as at present, was brought to market in quills of the ostrich and vulture. But the main supply received in these days at Cairo and Alexandria is brought from the alpine region whence issue the Gambia, the Senegal, and the Niger,—as also from Bambouk, a district situated to the north-west of that lofty range, and verging towards the shore of the Atlantic. Of silver, copper, lead, and antimony we find no traces till we ascend as high as Abyssinia, or even to the borders of Mozambique and the central mountains which form the skeleton of the Libyan continent.[*]

SECTION II.—ZOOLOGY.

At the head of the animals which meet the eye of the traveller in Egypt we are naturally led to mention the

[*] Murray's Historical Account of Discoveries and Travels in Africa. Article on Natural History by Professor Jameson.

camel, or *Camelus dromedarius*, which, although a native of a more eastern climate, has long been domesticated in that country. It is the principal beast of burden, and has been emphatically named the "ship of the desert." But for this quadruped, so patient of thirst and fatigue, and capable of traversing with rapidity immense deserts covered with a deep and burning sand, vast tracts both of Asia and of Africa would necessarily be uninhabited.*

The giraffe or camelopard has been occasionally seen on the southern borders of Egypt. This animal, it is well known, is distinguished by an uncommon length of neck, and by a head which very much resembles that of a sheep, while it is provided with two undivided horns tipped with brushes of hair. It has been found fully eighteen feet high,—a form which qualifies it for gathering its food, the leaves of trees. It is at the same time a remarkably gentle creature. Hasselquist adds, that it is most elegant and docile,—that in his days it had been seen by very few natural historians,—and that none had given a perfect description or good figure of it. "I have only seen the skin of the animal," says he, " and have not had an opportunity of beholding it alive."†

The civet cat (*Viverra sivetta*) was not unknown to the ancient Egyptians ; but the chief object of their regard was the *Viverra ichneumon*, which was almost venerated with a species of worship.

This quadruped (*Herpestes Pharaonis*) is one of the most celebrated of the Egyptian animals. It possesses a strong instinct of destruction, and in searching for its prey exterminates the young of many noxious reptiles. The eggs of crocodiles form its favourite food ; and this portion of its history being mingled in early times with the fanciful notion of its being able to encounter and overcome that gigantic creature in the adult state, divine honours were awarded to it by the ancient Egyptians, and it became, and continued for ages. an object of superstitious reverence to a people prone to this symbolical worship of the powers of nature.

Ichneumons are still domesticated in Egypt, where they rid the houses of the smaller animals, and perform the office

* Murray's Historical Account of Discoveries and Travels in Africa,

Voyages, &c., p. 189

of our domestic cats. Like the latter, they are said to become strongly attached to their accustomed dwellings, from whence they seldom wander. They recognise the persons and the voices of their masters; and the chief remnant of their unsubdued or instinctive nature is perceptible during meal-time, when they retire with their food to some quiet and accustomed corner, and manifest by an angry growling their jealous dislike to interruption. The sense of smell is very acute in this animal. It dwells by the sides of rivers, and in addition to its favourite repast of crocodiles' eggs, it eagerly sucks the blood of every creature which it is able to overcome. Its body is about a foot and a half in length, and its tail is of nearly equal dimensions. Its general colour is a grayish brown; but when closely inspected each hair is found annulated with a paler and a darker hue.

The sorex, or shrew, also occurs in that country. The Cape shrew inhabits caverns, and is seen in the southern parts of Africa; while two other species (the *S. Olivieri* of Desmarets and the *S. religiosa* of Is. Geoffroy) are natives of Egypt, where they were formerly held sacred as objects of worship, and where their embalmed remains are still occasionally found in the catacombs of Sakhara. The last-named variety appeared to be extinct; but it has been lately ascertained to hold its place among the animals of India.

Of the marmot tribe, Egypt presents a particular genus called the *Dipus*, or jerboa. According to Sonnini, the sandy ruins which surround the city of Alexandria are much frequented by this creature. They live in society, and in burrows which they dig with their teeth and nails. It is even said that they make their way through a soft stone which lies beneath the stratum of sand. They are easily alarmed, and betake themselves precipitately to their holes on the slightest noise, and consequently can only be killed by surprise. The Arabs, however, force them out by stopping up all the avenues to their retreats but one. "In Egypt," says Sonnini, "I kept six of these animals for some time in a large iron cage. The very first night they entirely gnawed through the upright and cross pieces of wood, and I was obliged to have the inside lined with tin. They ate rice, walnuts, and all kinds of fruit. They delighted in being in the sun, and when taken into the shade huddled together, and seemed to suffer from the privation of heat."

The hippopotamus, or river-horse, appeared in Egypt in former times; but at present, either from an increase of his natural enemies or from a deficiency in the supply of his food, he is seldom seen below the Cataracts. Malte Brun asserts that the voracity of this animal, by annihilating the means of his support, has greatly reduced the number of his race. Abdollatiph, with some justice, denominates the hippopotamus an enormous water-pig. In the days of Hasselquist it was believed that the river-horse did much damage to the Egyptians. "He goes on shore," says that traveller, "and in a short space of time destroys an entire field of corn or clover, not leaving the least verdure as he passes; for he is voracious, and requiring much to fill his great belly."[*] This animal is well known to have cloven hoofs, the mane and tail of a horse, a thick and very heavy hide, and in size to be equal to a large ox. It was sacred in that district of Egypt where the crocodile was held as an abomination; and occasionally appears in the more ancient sculptures, associated with the figures of other less noble quadrupeds.

The crocodile (*Lacerta crocodilis*) is closely connected at once with the superstition and the natural history of Egypt. The form of this amphibious creature is familiar to the youngest reader. In the mouth are two rows of sharply-pointed teeth, thirty or more on each side; the upper part of the snout and forehead consists of one fixed bone, reaching to the ears, which are broad, surrounded with a small border, and growing near the joint of the upper jaw. The armour with which the body is covered may be considered as one of the most elaborate pieces of natural mechanism. In the full-grown animal it is so strong as easily to repel a musket-ball, appearing as if covered with the most regular and curiously carved work. The colour of an adult is blackish-brown above, and yellowish-white beneath; the upper parts of the legs and sides are varied with deep yellow, and in some parts tinged with green.

The female is said to be extremely cautious in depositing her eggs in the sand unobserved. The general number is from eighty to a hundred, which are rather smaller than those of a goose, and are left to be hatched by the heat of the sun. The young, which as soon as they burst the shell run into the water, become the prey of a great variety of ene-

* Voyages and Travels, p. 188.

mies both in the river and on land. The vulture destroys millions of them, and, as we have already mentioned, the ichneumon acquired divine honours by his useful instinct in searching for the eggs and brood of so formidable an animal.

We are told by Herodotus, that those who live near Thebes and the Lake Mœris hold the crocodile in religious veneration. As a proof of this, they select one which they tame, suspending golden ornaments from its ears, and sometimes precious stones of great value ; the forefeet, however, being secured by a chain. They feed it with the flesh of the sacred victims and with other suitable food. As long as it lives they treat it with unceasing attention ; and when it dies it is embalmed, and afterward deposited in a consecrated chest.

According to Labat, a negro armed only with a knife in his right hand, and having his left wrapped round with thick leather, will venture boldly to attack the crocodile in his own element. As soon as he observes his enemy near, the man puts out his left arm, which the beast immediately seizes with his teeth. He then gives it several stabs below the chin where the hide is very tender ; and the water coming in at the mouth, thus involuntarily laid open, the creature is soon destroyed.

The monitor of the Nile, known also by the name of ouran, the *Lacerta Nilotica* of Linnæus, is a species of lizard about three feet long, and was much venerated by the ancient Egyptians, because it also devours the eggs and the young of the crocodile. In Congo the same animal is of a much larger size, and is almost equally venerated by the inhabitants, to whom, as a destroyer of very noxious vermin, it proves extremely useful. The land monitor of Egypt, which is found in all the neighbouring deserts, is the *terrestrial crocodile* of Herodotus, and the true sincque of the ancients. The common chameleon, so remarkable for the power it possesses of changing its colour, is also a native of Egypt and of the countries which are contiguous to it on the west.

The hyena, which is so universally scattered over Africa, is well known in Egypt. It is a disgusting and troublesome animal, haunting the suburbs, and sometimes even penetrating into the streets after sunset, preying on offal and stealing the remains of dead carcasses.

There is no great variety of the goat or sheep tribes in

Egypt. The *Capra aigros*, or wild goat, is said to inhabit the north of Africa; while the mouflon occurs in the rocky deserts of Barbary, as well as in those which border on the Nile.

But the *Ovis tragelaphus* is a more interesting species It is about the size of a common ram; the throat is furnished with long pendulous hairs, and the knees are protected by a kind of ruffles, composed of straight hairs about five inches long, hanging quite around them. The specimen in the French Museum was shot in the vicinity of Cairo, though it is not supposed to occur habitually in that neighbourhood. This species appears to have been described by Dr. Caius so far back as the year 1561, from an individual brought into England from Barbary. The horns were above a foot in circumference at the base, and in front were only an inch asunder. The beard was formed by long hairs on the cheeks and under-jaw, and was divided into two lobes. A setaceous mane stood up along the neck, and particularly about the withers, where it was tufted, lengthened, erect, and of a darker colour than the rest of the body, which resembled in its hue the winter dress of the stag. This creature in the domestic state was gentle though petulant. It loved to ascend high places and the roofs of houses, and ran with great swiftness, sometimes making prodigious bounds.

We have omitted the dog, ape, buffalo, and other animals which figure in the Egyptian mythology, merely because they are not peculiar to that country, and do not present any thing remarkable either in their habits or conformation. In the *Lithostrotum Prænestinum* copied by Dr. Shaw, there is exhibited a great variety of zoological specimens, to which, for the reason just assigned, we pay no attention; for, although the creatures there represented were well known in Egypt, they were not unknown in other parts of the world.

Our limits do not permit us to insert a complete list of the reptiles and insects with which Egypt abounds at certain seasons of the year. We may, however, mention, that the *Cerastes*, which was probably the true Egyptian aspic, is still found in the neighbouring deserts. Dr. Shaw relates that he saw a couple of these vipers, which had been kept five years in a large crystal vessel without any visible food. They were usually coiled up in some fine sand, which was placed in the bottom of the jar; and at the time they were shown to him they had just cast their skins, and were as brisk and lively as if newly taken. The horns of this creature, from which it takes its name, are white and shining, and have some resemblance to a grain of barley.

The locust is a formidable enemy to the Egyptians, as well as to all the nations of Africa. When the *Gryllus migratorius*, or wandering locust, takes to flight, the air is darkened, and the surrounding countries are filled with terror. Mr. Barrow mentions, that in a part of the Libyan continent, where he happened to be travelling, the whole surface of the ground for nearly 2000 square miles might literally be described· as covered with them. They had devoured every blade of grass, and every green herb except the reeds.

For an account of the *Scarabæus*, the mystical beetle, the emblem of the sun and of the prolific powers of nature, we must refer to works on Egyptian mythology ; because, being received into the pantheon of ·oriental superstition, its imaginary qualities are completely removed beyond the precincts of natural history.

Connected in some degree with zoological investigation, we may simply allude to the fact mentioned by several travellers, that exotics, including even the human species, do not thrive in Egypt,—the apology usually urged for the constant purchase of white slaves to replace the loss of life which could not be supplied by propagation. To prove the absurdity of this statement, it will be sufficient to mention that the valley of the Nile has been successively in ·the hands of Copts, Persians, Greeks, Romans, Saracens, and Turks ; and that the progeny of all these races of men may be found in the mixed people who at present cultivate its fields or occupy its cities.

<hr>

SECTION III.—BIRDS.

It is admitted by the best naturalists that the birds of Egypt do not differ much from those of Europe. M. Geoffroy Saint Hilaire saw the Egyptian swan represented in many of the temples of that country, both in sculptures and in coloured paintings, and entertains no doubt that this bird was the chenelopex of Herodotus, to which the ancient inhabitants paid divine honours, and had even dedicated a town called *Chenoboscion*. It is not peculiar to

Egypt, but is found all over Africa, and over a great part of Europe.

The common ostrich, or *Struthio*, is one of the largest and most remarkable members of the feathered tribe, and has been celebrated from the most remote antiquity by many fabulous writers, who ascribed to it qualities more wonderful than even those which it possesses. It is not indeed found in the valley of the Nile, being a bird peculiar to the wilderness, but it occasionally occurs in the extensive desert which borders the western shore of the Red Sea,—a portion of territory which now acknowledges the government of Mohammed Ali. Its height is estimated at seven or eight feet, and in swiftness it surpasses every other animal. That it is gregarious no naturalist any longer doubts, being generally seen in large troops at a great distance from the habitations of man. The egg is about three pounds in weight, and in the warmer regions of Africa is usually hatched by the rays of the sun alone, though in less heated regions the bird is observed to sit upon them.

The ibis has been recognised under five or six different species, of which we shall notice only the *Ibis ardea* and the *Ibis religiosa*. The former of these is as large as a female raven, and is found in great numbers in Lower Egypt during the inundation of the Nile, feeding in those places which the water does not reach, and afterward on such spots as the water has deserted. Its food consists of insects and small frogs, which abound greatly while the river is at its height ; and hence the ibis is extremely useful to the inhabitants, who might otherwise experience every year one of the most disgusting plagues which afflicted their country in the days of Moses.

But the other, the *Ibis religiosa* of Cuvier, or Abbou Hannes of Bruce, is the most celebrated. It is a bird of very peculiar aspect, though undistinguished by much diversity in the colours of its plumage. It stands rather more than two feet high, and measures in length, from the tip of the bill to the extremity of the tail, about two feet six inches. The bill is long and arched, about seven inches long, and considerably thicker and broader towards the base than that of the scarlet ibis. The head and neck, for more than half a foot below the eyes, are entirely bare of feathers, and present nothing but a black cutaneous surface. A small portion of the lower part of the neck, the whole under parts of the body, likewise the back and scapulars, the greater and lesser wing-coverts, and the tail, are of a dingy or yellowish white. Long funereal-looking plumes, of a purplish-black colour, proceeding from beneath the tertary wing-feathers, hang not ungracefully on either side of the tail, and, when the wings are closed, conceal the points of the primary and secondary quills, both of which are white tipped with deep greenish black. The legs and feet are a deep lead colour, and the claws are black.

Among the ancient Egyptians, a people prone to award divine honours to the brute creation, the ibis was regarded as an object of superstitious worship, and hence its sculptured outline frequently occurs among the hieroglyphical images which adorn the walls of their temples. The conservation of its mystical body occupied the assiduous care of their holiest priests while living, and exercised the gloomy art of their most skilful embalmers when dead. To slay or insult it would have been deemed a crime of the darkest hue, and sufficient to call down upon the offender the immediate vengeance of Heaven.

The Egyptian vulture, or *Vultur percnopterus*, is described as a powerful but very disgusting bird. The face is naked and wrinkled, the eyes are large and black, the beak hooked, the talons long and extended for prey, and the whole body covered with filth. Notwithstanding, says Hasselquist, the inhabitants of Egypt cannot be too thankful to Providence for its services. All the places round Cairo, he tells us, were in his time filled with the dead bodies of asses and camels, and thousands of these birds fly about and devour the carcasses before they putrefy and fill the air with noxious exhalations. They assemble with the kites every morning and evening in the square called Rohneli, below the castle,—which is the place for executing capital offenders,—there to receive the alms of fresh meat left them by the legacies of wealthy great men. They are said even to follow the yearly caravan to Mecca, that they may devour the offal of the slaughtered beasts and the bodies of the camels which die by the way. The name of this bird among the Arabs is Rachama.*

* In the 7th volume of Bruce's Travels, p. 965, second edition, there is hazarded an unfortunate criticism suggested by the name of this bird It will not be improper," says the great traveller, " that I here take

The oriental dotterell, or *Charadrius Kervan,* a bird about the size of a crow, is frequently met with in Lower Egypt, in the acacia groves near the villages of Abousir and Sakhara, in the vicinity of sepulchres, and in the desert. It has a shrill voice resembling that of the black woodpecker,. and utters rather an agreeable note. Its principal food are the rats and mice with which, at certain seasons, the country abounds. It seldom drinks, being originally a native of the wilderness, and has been kept in a cage several months without water.

The *Charadrius himantopus,* on the contrary, comes to Egypt in the month of October, and is usually found in moist places and the neighbourhood of lakes; possessing nearly the same habits as the tringa Ægyptiaca, or plover, which appears at the ebb of the inundation.

The *Corvus Ægyptiacus,* or Egyptian crow, which is not larger than a lark, lives in trees, and feeds on insects. Hasselquist relates that he has found in its stomach the remains of scorpions and scolopendras.

The *Alcedo rudis,* and the *Alcedo Ægyptiacus,* or kingfisher, are observed in Egypt, chiefly on the banks of the Nile, where they live on small fish, frogs, and insects.

The bat, a member of the numerous family of the *Vespertiliones,* next invites our notice. The *Egyptian bat* is distinguished by its ash-coloured fur and its long and slender tail. It inhabits the subterranean galleries and other excavations of Egypt.

notice that the English translator, by his ignorance of language, has lost all the beauty, and even the sense of the Hebrew original. He makes God say (Exod. xix. 4), 'Ye have seen what I did unto the Egyptians, and how I bare you on eagles' wings, and brought you unto myself.' Now, if the expression had been really eagle, the word would have been nier, and would have signified nothing; but in place of eagle, God says vulture, the emblem of maternal affection; so that the passage will run thus: Say to the children of Israel, see how I have punished the Egyptians, while I bore you on the wings of the Rachama, that is, of parental tenderness and affection, and brought you home to myself. It is our part to be thankful that the truths of Holy Scripture are preserved to us entire, but still it is a rational regret that great part of the beauty of the original is lost by this kind of interpretation."

After all this minute criticism, the reader will find it hard to believe that the original word is not Rachama, as is here stated, but nisr,—or nisrim the plural form,—and consequently, according to Bruce's own argument, the authorized translation is right, and his correction founded in ignorance. He cannot have looked into the Hebrew Bible, where the language is עַל כַּנְפֵי נְשָׁרִים׃

The duck of the Nile, or *Anas Nilotica*, occurs wild in Upper Egypt, and, perhaps, on the shores of the Red Sea. The neck and superior part of the head are white with black spots, and a gray line runs lengthways behind the eyes; the under part of the body and the thighs are of the same colour. The Arabians call it bah; and in Lower Egypt it is often seen in a domesticated state among flocks of tame fowls.

The *Sterna Nilotica*, or Egyptian sea-swallow, is esteemed a beautiful bird. Its beak is black; its head and neck are grayish, with small black spots; the part round the eyes is black, spotted with white; the back, wings, and tail are gray; the belly and under part of the neck are white; the feet are red, and the toes black. The Arabs call it abunures. It is found on the Nile; but it seems to prefer the canals near Cairo when filled with the mud of the river.

The pelican, or *Pelecanus onocratalus*, is a migratory bird, which appears in Egypt about the middle of September. In their flight they form an acute angle, like the common wild-goose. Some of them remain at Damietta, or in the islands of the Delta, but the greater part go up as far as the capital.

The *Tetrao coturnix*, or quail, is likewise a bird of passage,—an amazing number of which migrate to Egypt in the month of March, the season at which the wheat ripens. They conceal themselves among the crops; but the peasants, aware of their arrival, spread nets over the corn, and surround the field, at the same time making a noise to rouse them from their feed. In this way vast multitudes are caught, which supply the natives with a very savoury dish. "If the food of the Israelites in the desert was a bird," says Mr. Hasselquist, "this is certainly it, being so common in the places through which they passed."

SECTION IV.—FISHES.

The only tenants of the water which can be considered as peculiar to Egypt are such as frequent the Nile; and to these narrow limits we shall confine our sketch of ichthyology.

The *Echeneis naucrates*, or sucking-fish, occurs at Alexandria, though very rarely, and is by the Arabs called chamet or feirhun.

The *Sparus Niloticus*, as its name imports, is found in the Nile; the vernacular appellation is giralle.

The *Labrus Niloticus*, called bulti by the Arabs, is esteemed the best fish in their waters.

The perch occurs under three different specific forms, —the *Ægyptiaca*, the *Nilotica*, and the *Damiettica*. They ascend the river considerably above Cairo, and are much sought after by the inhabitants of that city. The flesh is white, and has an exquisite flavour.

The *Silurus clarias*, a singular fish, called schielan by the Arabians, occurs sometimes in the Nile. It defends itself with its fins, the bones of which are understood to be poisonous. A similar character attaches to the *Silurus anguillaris*, and the *Silurus mystus*; neither of which, however, is so well known.

The *Salmo Niloticus*, or salmon of the Nile, is a very valuable fish, and ascends the stream as high as Cairo. It frequently weighs 100 lb.; but is, notwithstanding, very delicate eating; and is held to be one of the best dishes supplied by the river. The Arabs call it nefareh.

Very unlike the animal just described is the *Tetraodon*, which, according to the inhabitants, has recently taken possession of the Nile. The Arabs call it fahaka, and say that it grows to a prodigious size. When newly caught, the skin stings like a nettle, creating small pustules on the hands of the fishermen; and, if eaten, it causes almost instant death.

The *Mugil cephalus* and *Clupea Alosa*, the one the mullet and the other a herring, are well known to the Egyptians. The latter, to which the Arabs have given the name of sagboga, goes up from the sea in December and January towards the capital, where it exercises the ingenuity of the Arabian cooks, who are said to prepare it for the table in such a manner as to intoxicate the eaters.[*]

SECTION V.—PLANTS.

The *Papyrus*, or *Cyperus papyrus* of Linnæus, most naturally suggests itself whenever we turn our attention to the vegetable productions of Egypt. The stalk is of a vivid green, of a triangular form, and tapering towards the top. Pliny says that the root is as thick as a man's arm, and that

------

[*] Hasselquist's Voyages and Travels in the Levant, p. 223, &c

the plant occasionally exceeded fifteen feet in height. At present it is rarely found more than ten feet long,—about two feet or little more of the lower part of the stalk being covered with hollow sharp-pointed leaves, which overlap each other like scales, and fortify the most exposed part of the stem. These are usually of a yellow or dusky-brown colour. The head is composed of a number of small grassy filaments, each about a foot long. Near the middle each of these filaments parts into four, and in the point or partition are four branches of flowers, the termination of which is not unlike an ear of wheat in form, but is in fact a soft silky husk.

This singular vegetable was used for a variety of purposes, the principal of which was the structure of boats and the manufacture of paper. In regard to the first, we are told by Pliny, that a piece of the acacia-tree was put in the bottom to serve as a keel, to which the plants were joined, being first sewed together, then gathered up at stem and stern, and made fast by means of a ligature.

" Conseritur bibula Memphilis cymba papyro."

But it is as a substance for writing upon that the papyrus is best known and most interesting to the scholar. The process by which the plant was prepared for this purpose is briefly stated by the Roman naturalist. The thick part of the stalk being cut in two, the pellicle between the pith and the bark, or perhaps the two pellicles, were stripped off and divided by an iron instrument. This was squared at the sides so as to be like a riband, then laid upon a smooth table or dresser, after being cut into proper length. These stripes or ribands were lapped over each other by a very thin border, and then pieces of the same kind were laid transversely, the length of these last answering to the breadth of the first. This being done, a weight was laid upon them, while they were yet moist, after which they were dried in the sun. It was thought that the water of the Nile had a gummy quality sufficiently strong to glue these stripes together; but Mr. Bruce, who ascertained by experiment that this opinion is perfectly groundless, suggests that the effect was produced by means of the saccharine matter with which the papyrus is strongly impregnated.

The flower of this plant, it is well known, was used for religious purposes.*

The *Persea* is celebrated among the ancients as a beautiful fruit-tree, which adorned and enriched Egypt at an early period, although naturalists have failed to recognise it in that country in more recent times. It is supposed to be the Aguacate of St. Domingo, and has accordingly obtained from botanists the name of *Laurus Persea.* Others have attempted to prove the identity of it with the Sibesten, but the differences are too glaring to allow this hypothesis to be maintained. Perhaps its type may still be discovered in India, whence, it is more than probable, it was originally derived.

The *Lotus*, associated with so many fanciful ideas and religious rites, makes a greater figure than any other plant in the mythological history of the Egyptians. It is, properly speaking, a species of Nymphæa or water-lily, which on the disappearance of the inundation covers all the canals and pools with its broad round leaves; among which the flowers in the form of cups of bright white or azure blue, rest with inimitable grace on the surface of the water. There are two species of the lotus, the white and the blue, both known to the ancients, though the latter kind is seldom mentioned.

The rose-lily of the Nile, or the Egyptian bean, which is frequently found carved on the monuments, is not at present seen in that country; so that the plant would have been utterly unknown to naturalists, if they had not found it in India. It is the Nymphæa nelumbo of Linnæus, and is in truth the plant upon which the Egyptian lotophagi, or lotus-eaters, were accustomed to live.

But the fruits of the lotus, so much praised by Homer, and which so greatly delighted the companions of Ulysses, were those of the modern jujube or *Rhamnus lotus.* The same tree is described by Theophrastus under the name of the lotus, and is, perhaps, the dudaine of the Hebrew Scriptures. There is another species still, mentioned by Pliny as the *Faba Græca*, or *lotus*; but this has been ascertained to be different from the Egyptian, being no other than the *Diospyros lotus*,—a sort of *guayacana*, or ebony.†

* Plin. Hist. Nat. lib. xiii. cap. ii.; Bruce's Travels, vol. vii. p. 118.
† Malte Brun, iv. 42.

The *Phœnix dactylifera,* or date-tree, is of great value to the inhabitants of Egypt,—many families, particularly in the upper provinces, having hardly any other food a great part of the year; while the stones or kernels are ground for the use of the camels. The leaves are converted into baskets; the soft bark into ropes and rigging for their boats; and the timber, though soft, is used for rafters in the construction of houses.

The *Ficus sycomorus* is not less useful in a country destitute of all the harder description of forest trees. It grows to an immense size in Egypt, some specimens having been seen by travellers fully fifty feet in circumference. Of this tree the ancient inhabitants made coffins for their mummies; and no timber certainly could have been better suited for the purpose, as it resists the powers of decomposition during several thousand years. As it sends forth large leafy branches, it affords an excellent shade to the weary traveller; and the fruit, although rather insipid, is full of moisture, and on that account well adapted to the wants of the climate. It buds in the latter end of March, and the fruit ripens in the beginning of June.

The plantain-tree, or *Musa paradisaica,* flowers in October and November, or immediately after the inundation of the Nile, when the air is temperate and the earth still moist. The fruit is said to be sweet, somewhat hard, or between a pear and a date, a little viscid and mealy, melting in the mouth without being chewed. It is, however, highly valued, and brings a great price at Cairo, in the neighbourhood of which the tree does not thrive. The nitrous fields around Rosetta, and perhaps the breeze from the sea, constitute the soil and climate in which it prospers the most luxuriantly.

Egypt of course abounds in melons and cucumbers. There is one, however, the *Cucumis Chate,* which bears the name of the country, and is sometimes called the queen of cucumbers, which grows in the vicinity of Grand Cairo, and nowhere else. This fruit, says Hasselquist, is a little watery, the flesh is almost of the same substance as the melon, and tastes sweet and cool. The grandees and Europeans in the capital eat it as the most pleasant fruit they can find, and that from which they have the least to dread in point of health.

Allied to these are the gourds, one of which, called *Cu-*

curbita lagenaria, is much used by the poor people. It is boiled and seasoned with vinegar,—the shell, with the addition of rice and a little meal, being mashed into a kind of pudding. It grows in all parts of Egypt, and even in the deserts of Arabia, wherever there is found a little rich soil of the proper depth.

The *Colocasium,* or, as it is described by Hasselquist, the *Arum colocasia,* is still cultivated in Egypt for the sake of its large esculent roots, and continues to maintain the high character which it received from the ancients.

The *Carthamus tinctorius,* or safflower, is raised in large quantities throughout the country, and is a source of considerable profit to the natives. The leaves, which are used in dying, are gathered three times in the year; and after being carefully washed, pressed, and dried, are exported to all parts of Europe, where they supply the artisan with a beautiful yellow. At Cairo the young leaves are also esteemed an excellent sallad.

The *Acacia* of Upper Egypt, or the *Mimosa Lebbeck,* is cultivated in the gardens of Cairo, though it is very doubtful whether it be originally a native of the country. But the *Mimosa Nilotica,* or *Acacia vera,* is decidedly Egyptian in its origin, and is much valued on account of its producing the gum-arabic, or frankincense of Arabia. Alpinus confounded this with the *Mimosa Senegal,* and even described the celebrated gum as the produce of the latter; but the Egyptians know the one from the other extremely well, calling the true species charad, while the other, which is of no use or value, they denominate fetne. The genuine gum is gathered in great quantities in Arabia, and is itself of two kinds. The best is found along the northern bay of the Red Sea, near Thor or Thur, and hence the name *Thus* given to it by the Romans as well as by the dealers in Egypt. It is clearer or more pellucid than the inferior sort, which is collected in the desert between Cairo and the Isthmus of Suez.

The *Henna,* or *Lawsonia spinosa,* which is purely an article of female luxury, grows both in Upper and in Lower Egypt, and flowers from May till August. To obtain a deep yellow for their nails the ladies make a paste of the pulverized leaves, and bind it on their hands and feet all night. The die lasts for three or four weeks, after which it requires to be renewed. This custom is so ancient among the Egyptians, as well as other eastern nations, that mummies are occasionally discovered with a similar tincture on their nails. The Arabs call it chenna, or al-chenna.

Aloe perfoliata vera, the mitre-shaped aloe, is, among the Egyptian Moslem, a symbolic plant, and in some measure dedicated to religion. Whoever returns from Mecca hangs this plant over his street door, as a token of his having performed that holy journey. The superstitious natives believe that this shrub prevents evil spirits and apparitions from entering their houses; and in this feeling the Jews and Christians of Cairo participate, so far at least as to venerate the sacred aloe.

SECTION VI.—ZOOPHYTES.

These hold a rank between animals and vegetables, most of them taking root and growing up into stems and branches. Some are soft and naked, and others are covered with a hard shell.

The *Corallines* are composed of capillary tubes whose extremities pass through a calcareous crust, and open into pores on the surface. They are entirely submarine, and owing to their branches being finely divided and jointed resembling some species of lichen, they were till lately arranged by botanists with the cryptogamous plants. In appearance they certainly approach very nearly to some of the vegetables; but their calcareous covering is alone sufficient to prove that they are allied, in however humble a station, to a more elevated order of beings.

The *Red Coral,* or *Corallium rubrum,* is fished up in the Red Sea. It grows much slower than the madrepores, and never occurs in such masses. It is found at different depths, and it is remarked, says Professor Jameson, that light exerts a powerful influence on its growth as well as on its colour, the tint being darker in proportion to the deepness of the sea.

The *Sponges* consist of an entirely ramified mass of capillary tubes, and were at one time supposed by many to be the production of a species of worm which is often found straying about their cavities. Others have imagined them to be mere vegetables; but that they are possessed of a living principle seems evident from the fact of their alternately contracting and dilating their pores, and shrinking in some degree from the touch, whenever examined in their native waters. They are the most torpid of all the zoophytes. The officinal sponge is elastic and very full of holes ; it grows into irregular tubes of a woolly consistence, and generally adheres by a very broad base to the rocks. When it is first taken it has a strong fishy smell, and requires to be carefully washed in order to prevent its growing putrid.

The *Polypes* are gelatinous animals, consisting of a long tubular body, fixed at the base, and surrounded at the mouth by arms or tenacula ; but, as these are by no means peculiar to the oriental parts of Africa, we hold it sufficient to have mentioned their existence.

Madrepores are found on the east coast of Egypt, and along the shores of Africa, each species being peculiar to a certain latitude, and increasing in number according to the greater warmth of the climate. The Red Sea presents a considerable variety of millepores, sertularias, cellularias, alcyoniums, and sponges, and occasionally some fine specimens of the gorgonia or sea-fan.

It is well known that immense reefs and islands are produced by the minutest of zoophytic animals. These submarine formations, in some parts of the world, have been traced a thousand miles in length, fifty miles in breadth, and to depths almost unfathomable. There are found, too, at considerable elevations on the land, beds of rocks, and even entire hills, of very remote origin, containing a variety of corals ; thus affording a satisfactory proof that these animals must have existed in countless numbers in a former condition of our earth, and that then, as at present, they contributed greatly towards adding to the solid matter of the globe.

THE END.

Lightning Source UK Ltd.
Milton Keynes UK
UKHW012013221118
332793UK00010B/1734/P